WINTER HOMESCHOOLING JOURNAL

Name:_____

Date:_____

Age:_____

The Thinking Tree
PUBLISHING COMPANY

Sarah Janisse Brown

READ

DRAW

PLAY

JOY

PLAN

CREATE

LOVE

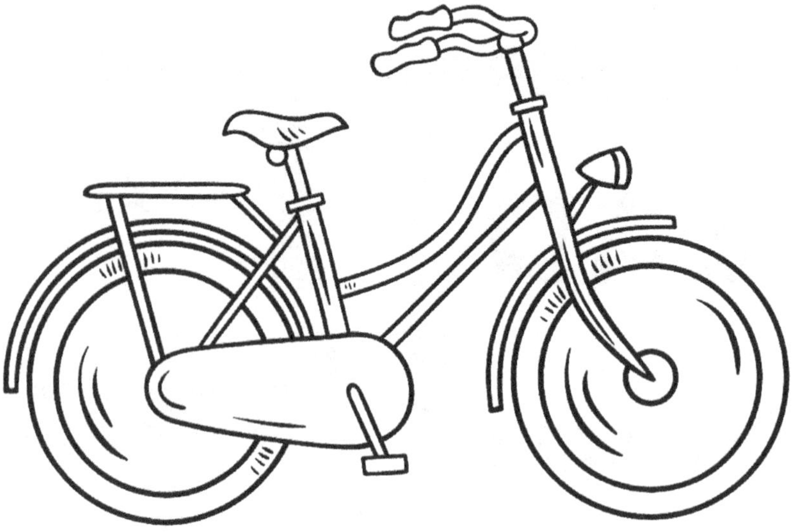

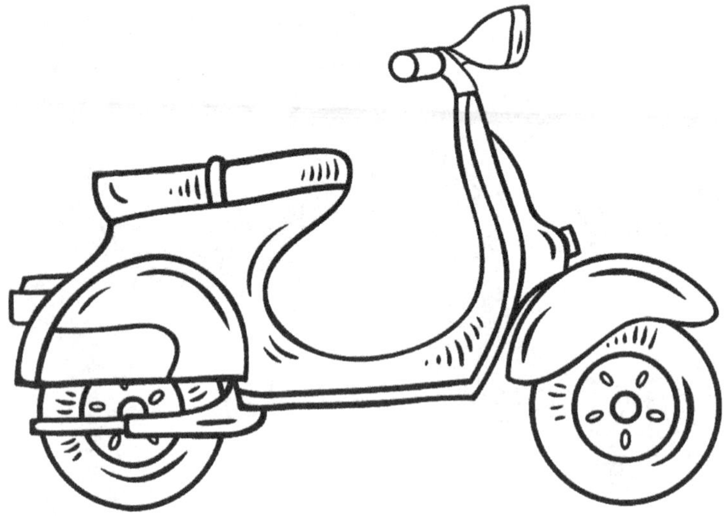

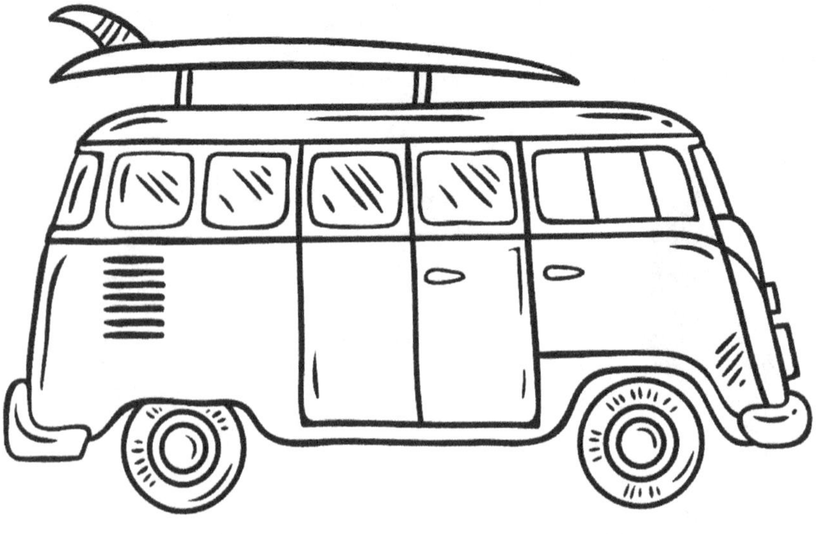

INSTRUCTIONS

LIST EIGHT THINGS - That you want to learn about:

1.
2.
3.
4.
5.
6.
7.
8.

Action Steps:

1. Go to the library or bookstore.
2. Bring home a stack of at least eight interesting books and movies about these topics. Choose some books that have diagrams, instructions and illustrations.

Supplies Needed:

You will need pencils, colored pencils, pens and markers. If learning from YouTube you need internet and a viewing device.

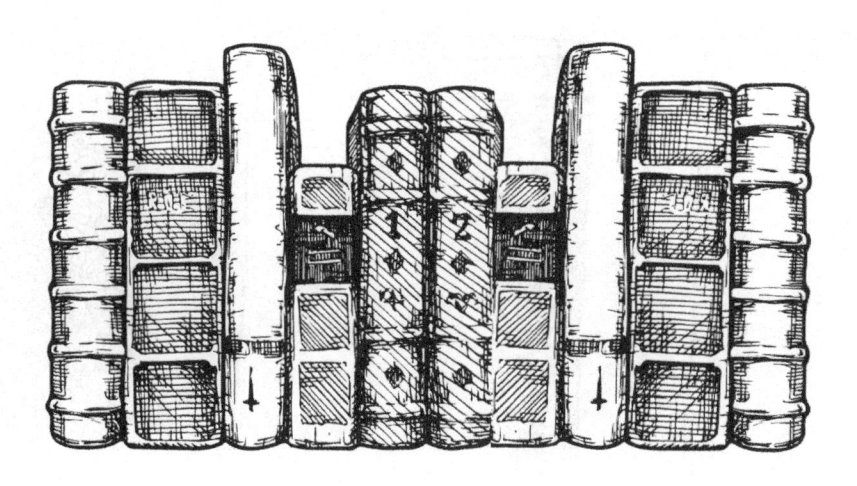

Choose EIGHT Books To Use As School Books!

1. Write down the titles on each cover below.
2. Keep your stack of books in a safe place.
3. Be ready to read a few pages from your books daily.
4. Complete 5 or 6 pages each day in this workbook.

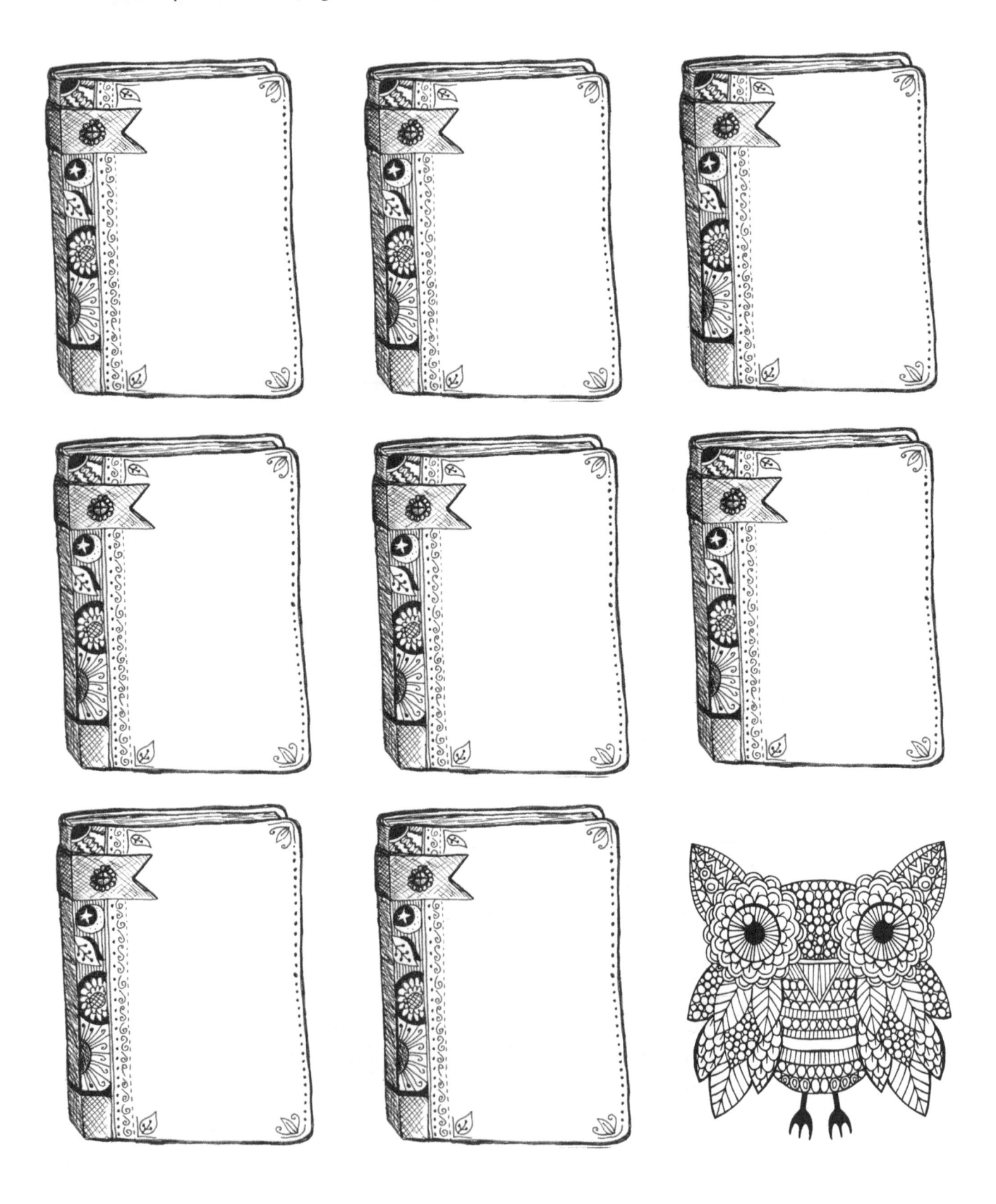

This page is for other books that you may use.

1. Write down the titles on each cover below.
2. Keep your stack of books in a safe place.
3. Be ready to read a few pages from your books daily.
4. Complete 5 or 6 pages each day in this workbook.

Circle Today's Date

January
February
March
April
May
June
July
August
September
October
November
December

1 2 3 4 5 6
7 8 9 10 11
12 13 14 15
16 17 18 19
20 21 22 23
24 25 26 27
28 29 30 31

MONDAY
TUESDAY
WEDNESDAY
THURSDAY
FRIDAY
SATURDAY
SUNDAY

2015
2016
2017
2018
2019
2020
2021
2022
2023
2024
2025
2026
2027
2028
2029

Write Today's Date: _____

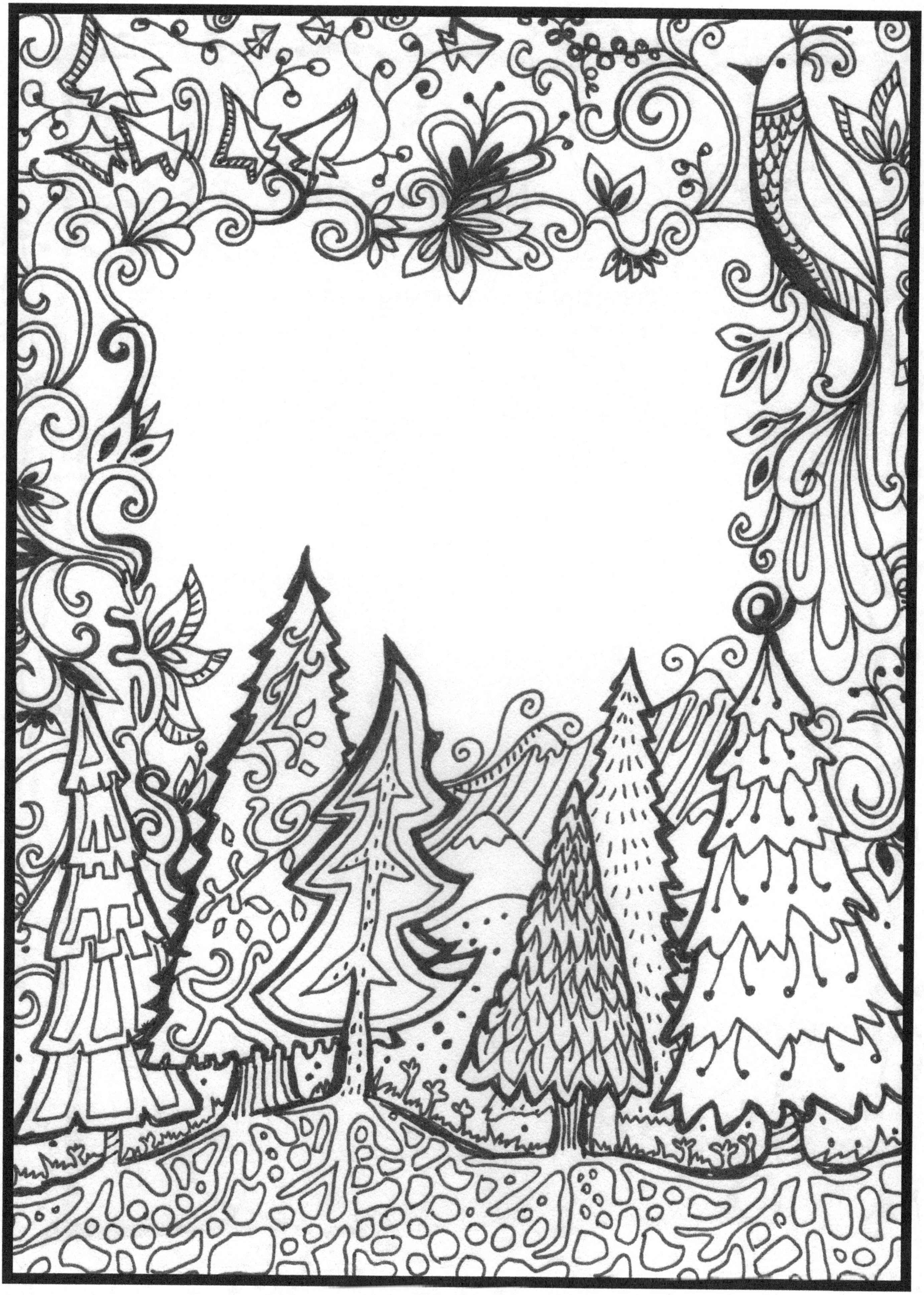

Nature Study

Go outside and make a realistic drawing of something you find in nature.

Draw a Meal PLAN

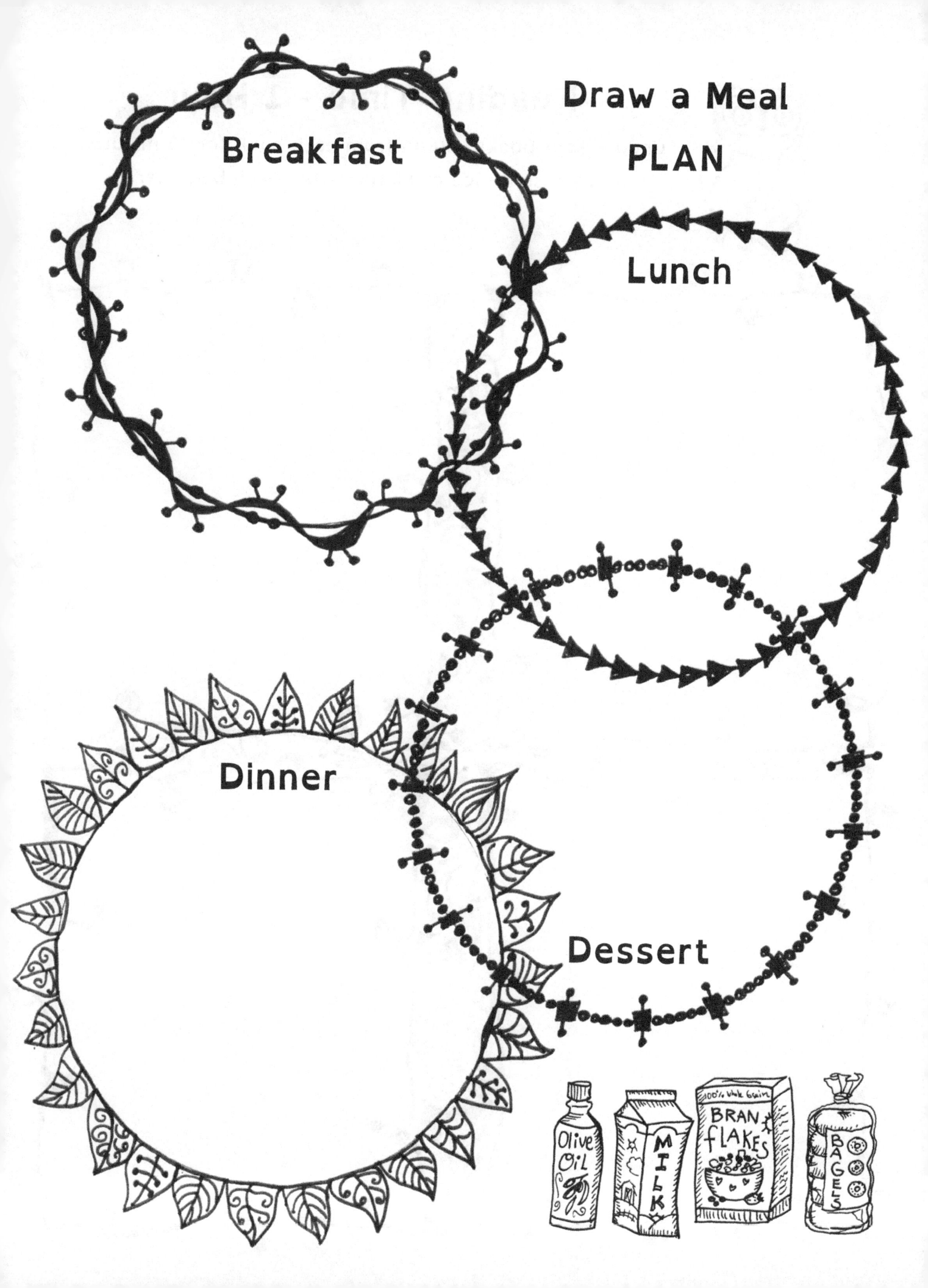

- Breakfast
- Lunch
- Dinner
- Dessert

Reading Time - 1 Hour

Choose Four Books - Read from each book for 15 minutes.
Copy a sentence or picture from each book here:

Learning a Skill

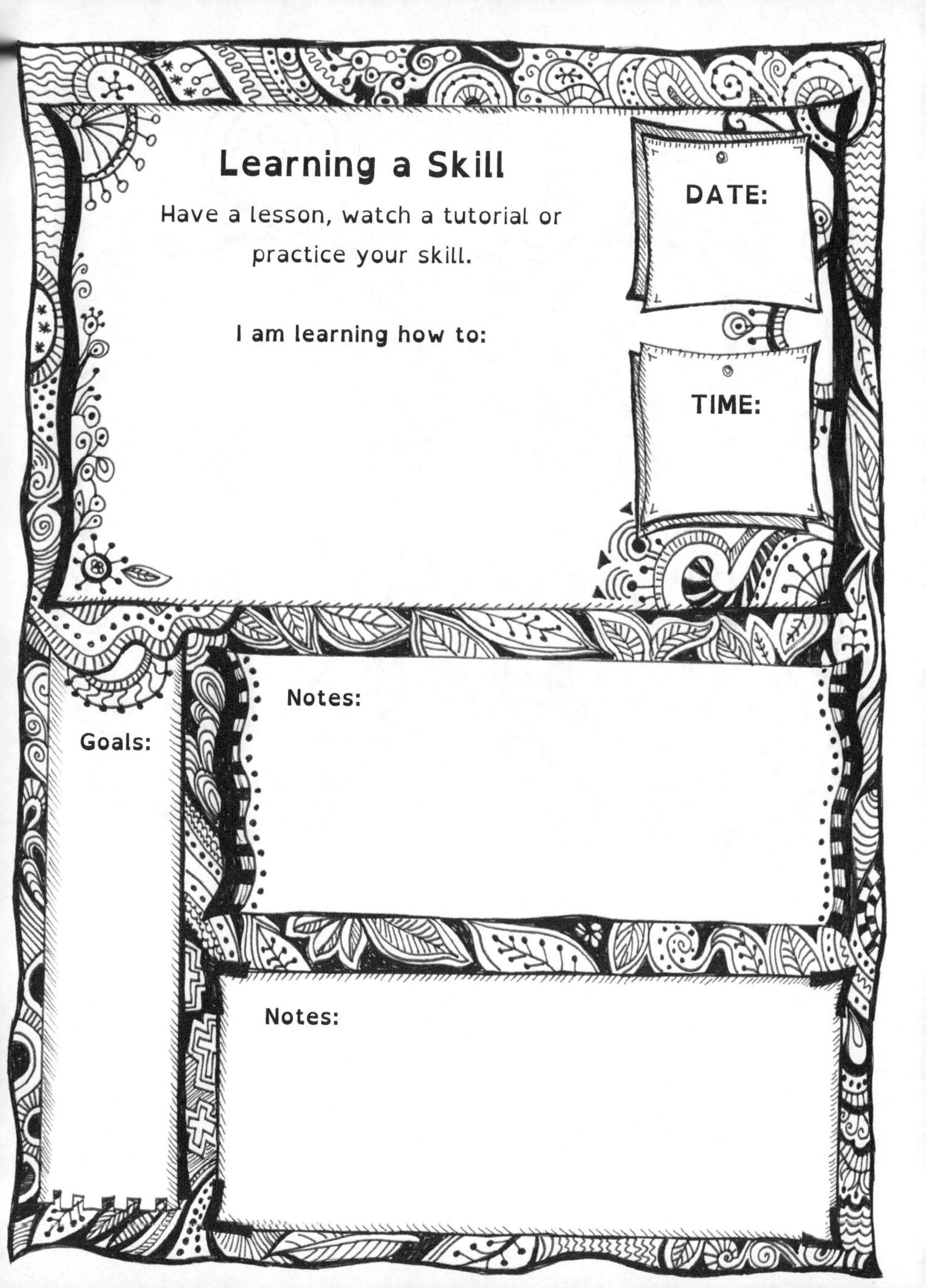

Have a lesson, watch a tutorial or practice your skill.

I am learning how to:

DATE:

TIME:

Goals:

Notes:

Notes:

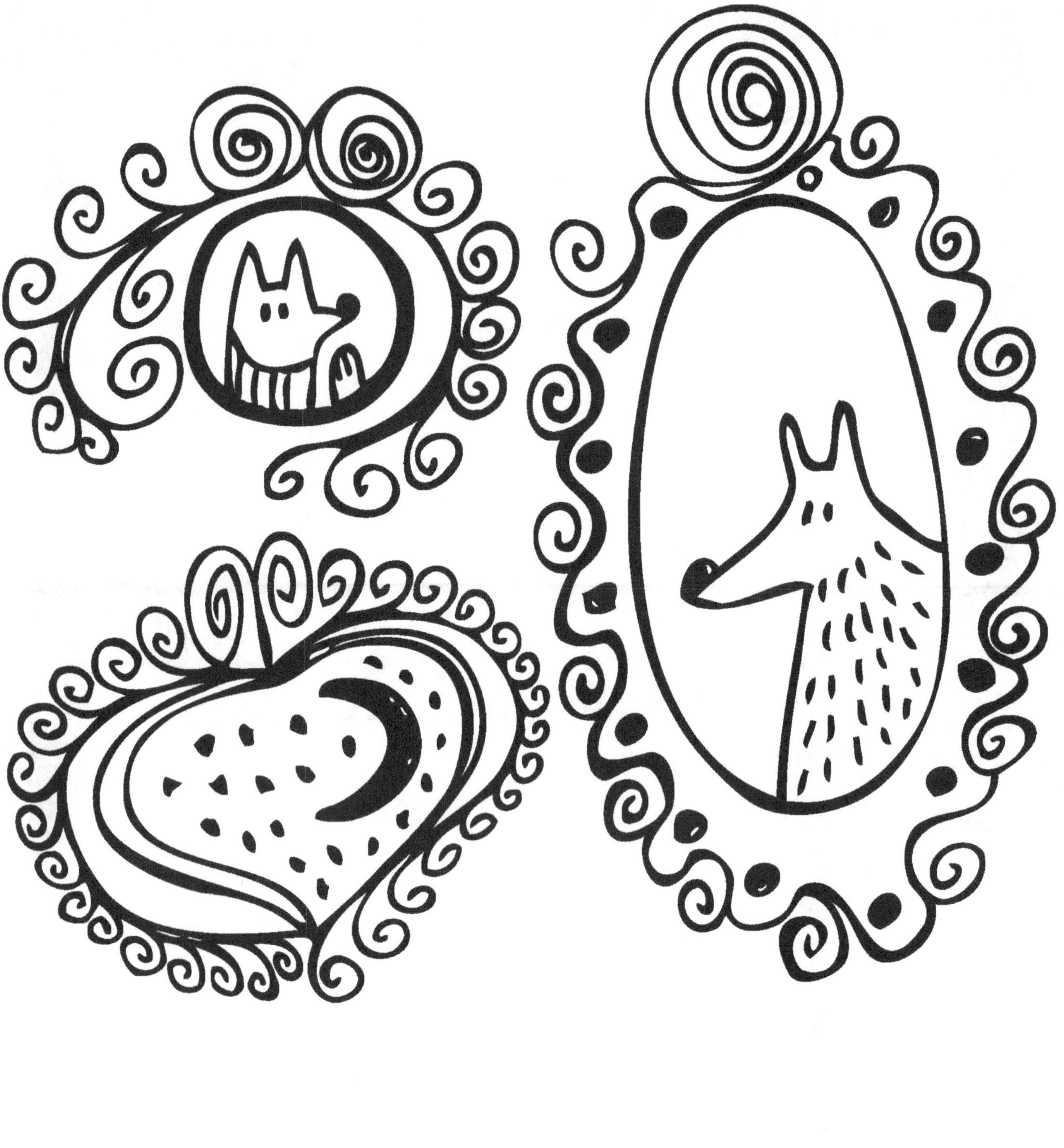

Circle Today's Date

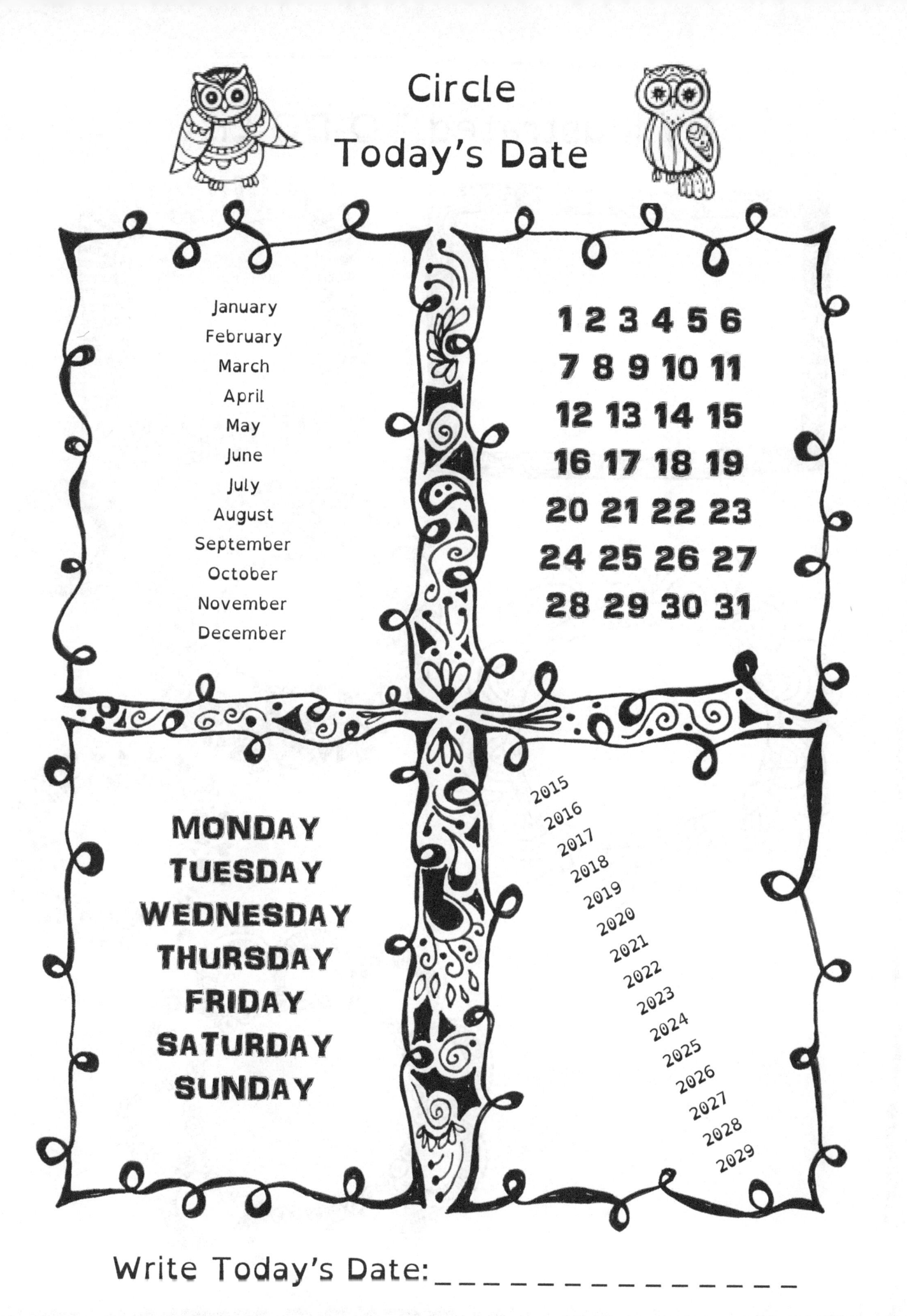

January
February
March
April
May
June
July
August
September
October
November
December

1 2 3 4 5 6
7 8 9 10 11
12 13 14 15
16 17 18 19
20 21 22 23
24 25 26 27
28 29 30 31

MONDAY
TUESDAY
WEDNESDAY
THURSDAY
FRIDAY
SATURDAY
SUNDAY

2015
2016
2017
2018
2019
2020
2021
2022
2023
2024
2025
2026
2027
2028
2029

Write Today's Date: _____

My Illustrated TO-DO List

Spelling Time

Find 20 Words with 7 letters each.
Look in your books for words.
Write the words here:

_____   _____
_____   _____
_____   _____
_____   _____
_____   _____
_____   _____
_____   _____
_____   _____
_____   _____
_____   _____

Film Study

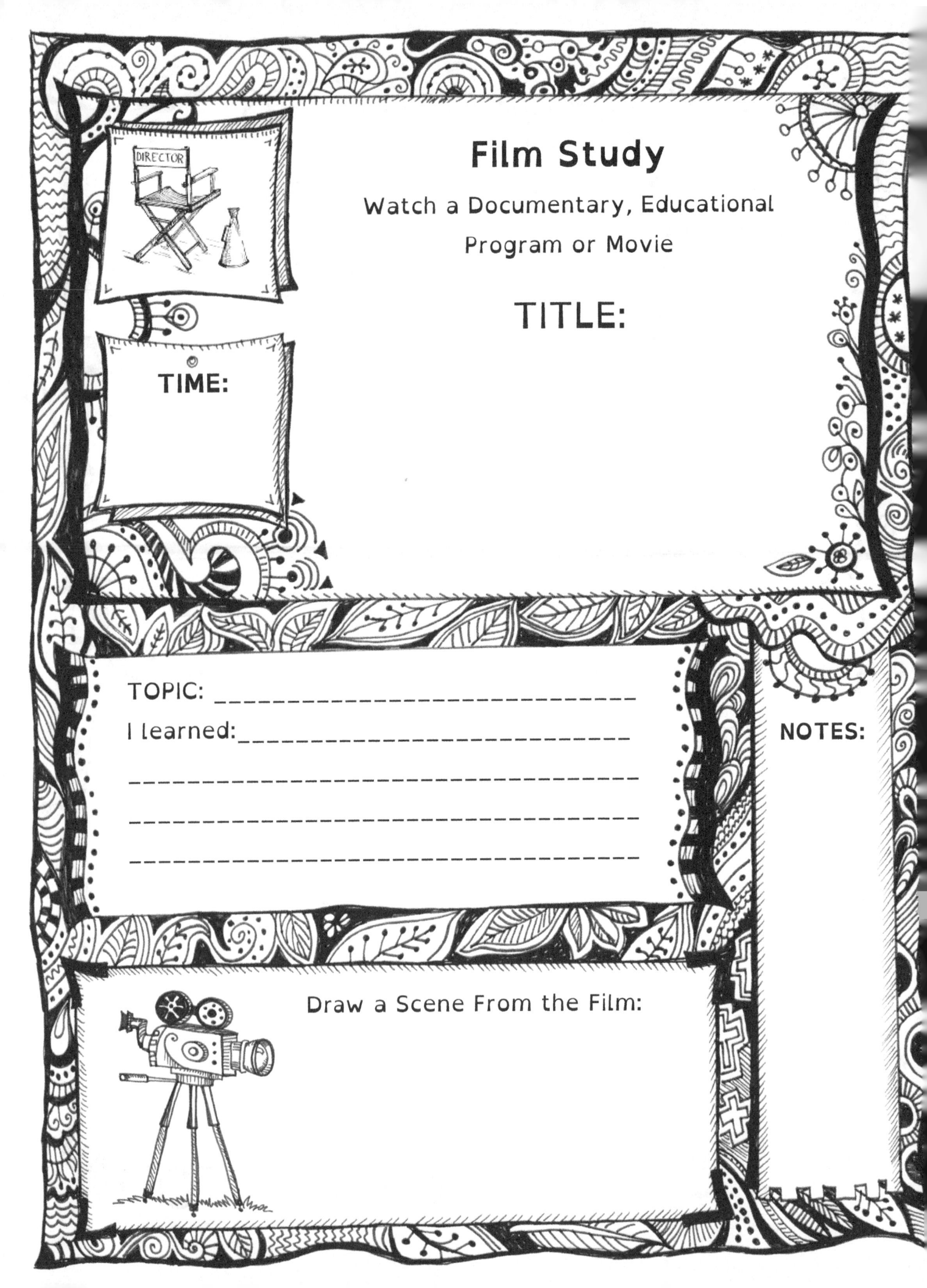

Watch a Documentary, Educational Program or Movie

TITLE:

TIME:

TOPIC: _____
I learned: _____
_____
_____
_____

NOTES:

Draw a Scene From the Film:

Copywork

Find an interesting paragraph in one of your books and copy it. Be diligent to make your writing look exactly like it does in the book.

TITLE:_____ Page Number:_____

Write & Draw
about something that really happened.

Circle Today's Date

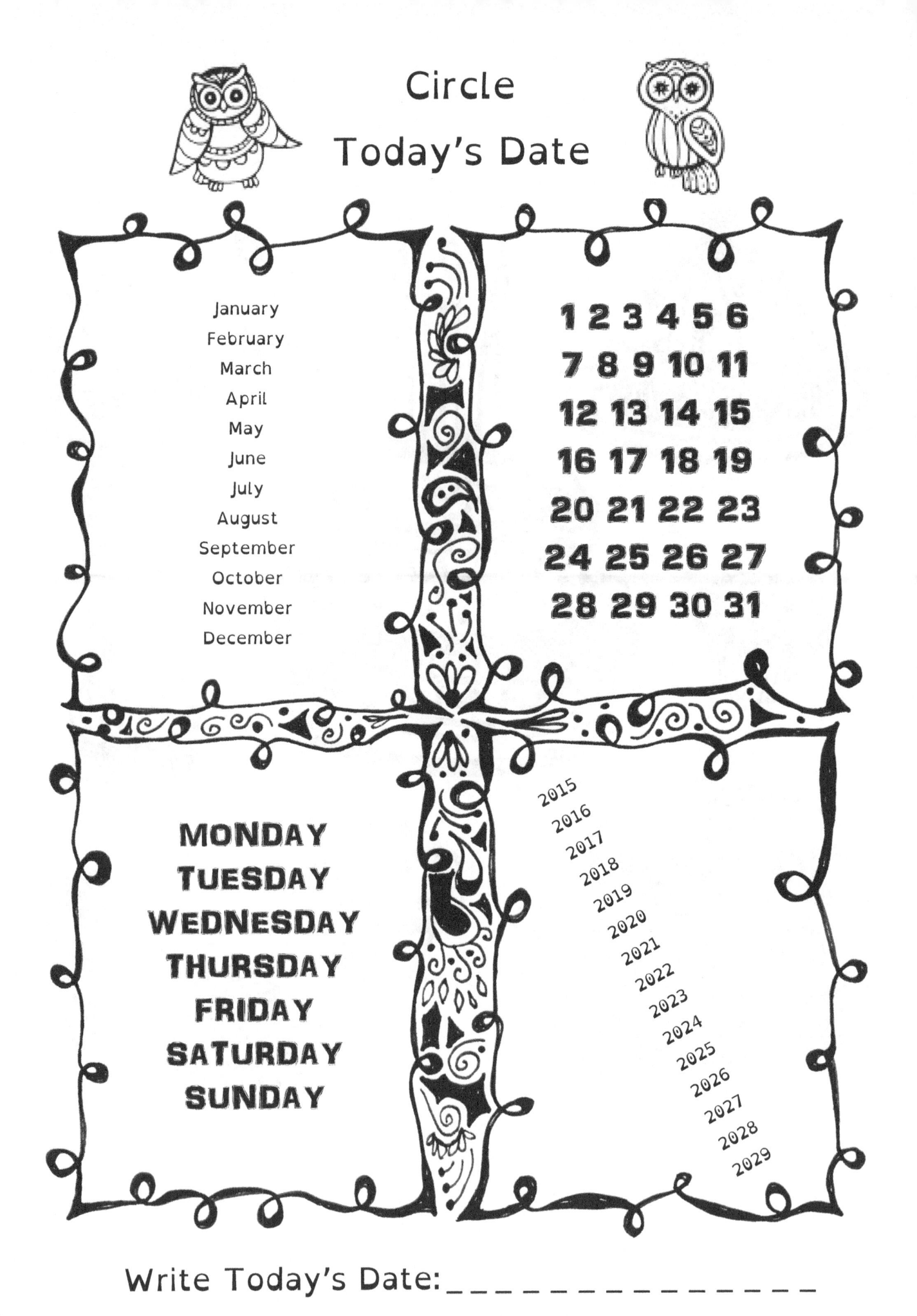

January
February
March
April
May
June
July
August
September
October
November
December

1 2 3 4 5 6
7 8 9 10 11
12 13 14 15
16 17 18 19
20 21 22 23
24 25 26 27
28 29 30 31

MONDAY
TUESDAY
WEDNESDAY
THURSDAY
FRIDAY
SATURDAY
SUNDAY

2015
2016
2017
2018
2019
2020
2021
2022
2023
2024
2025
2026
2027
2028
2029

Write Today's Date: _____

My Thinking Page

This is where you write down your ideas, goals, and plans - with a thankful heart!

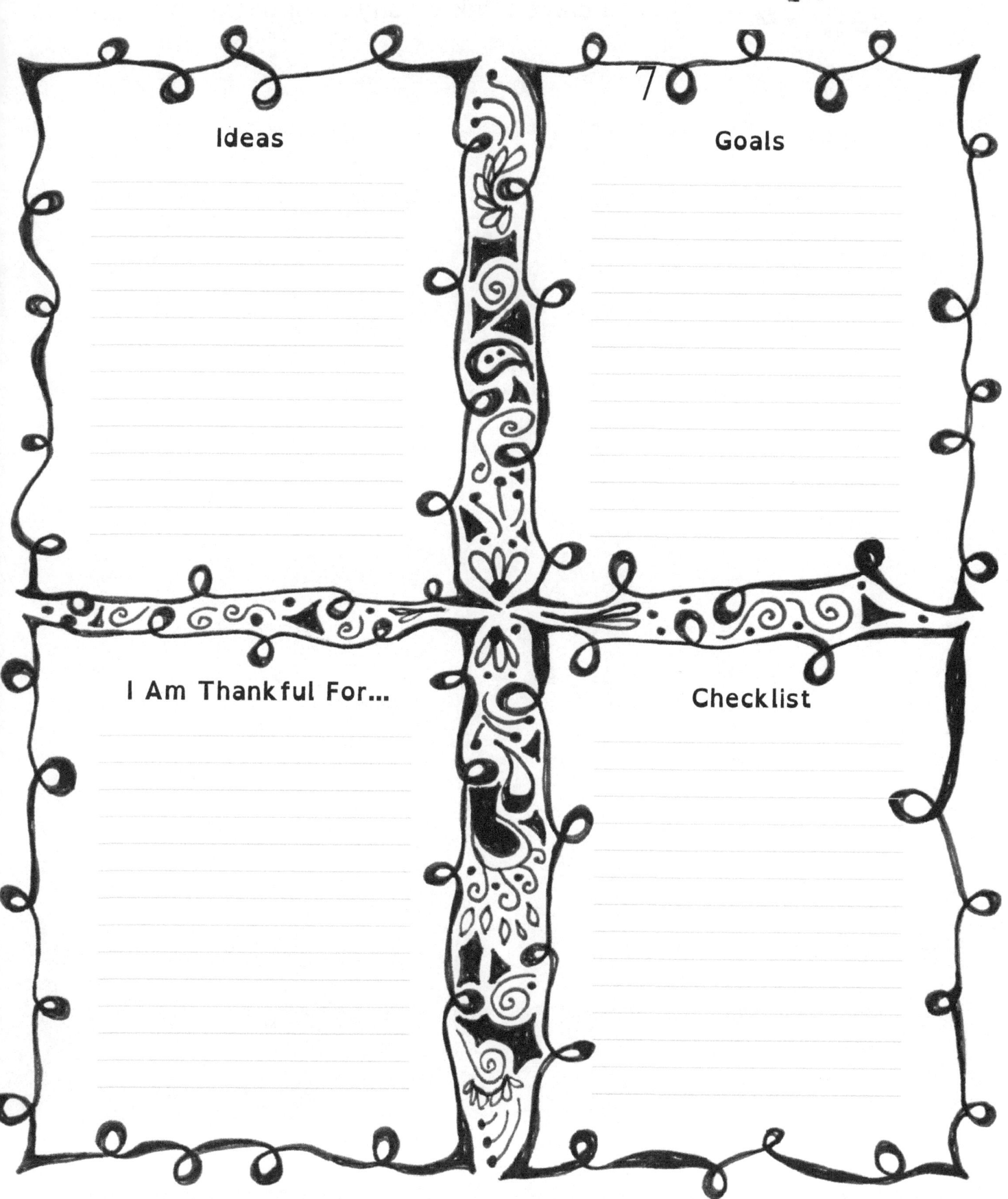

7

Ideas

Goals

I Am Thankful For...

Checklist

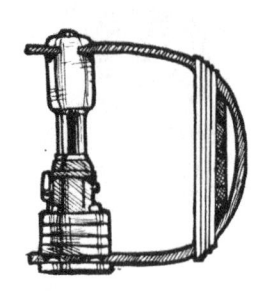

Design Something

Use this graph paper to design something.
If you can't think of anything design a house.

Film Study

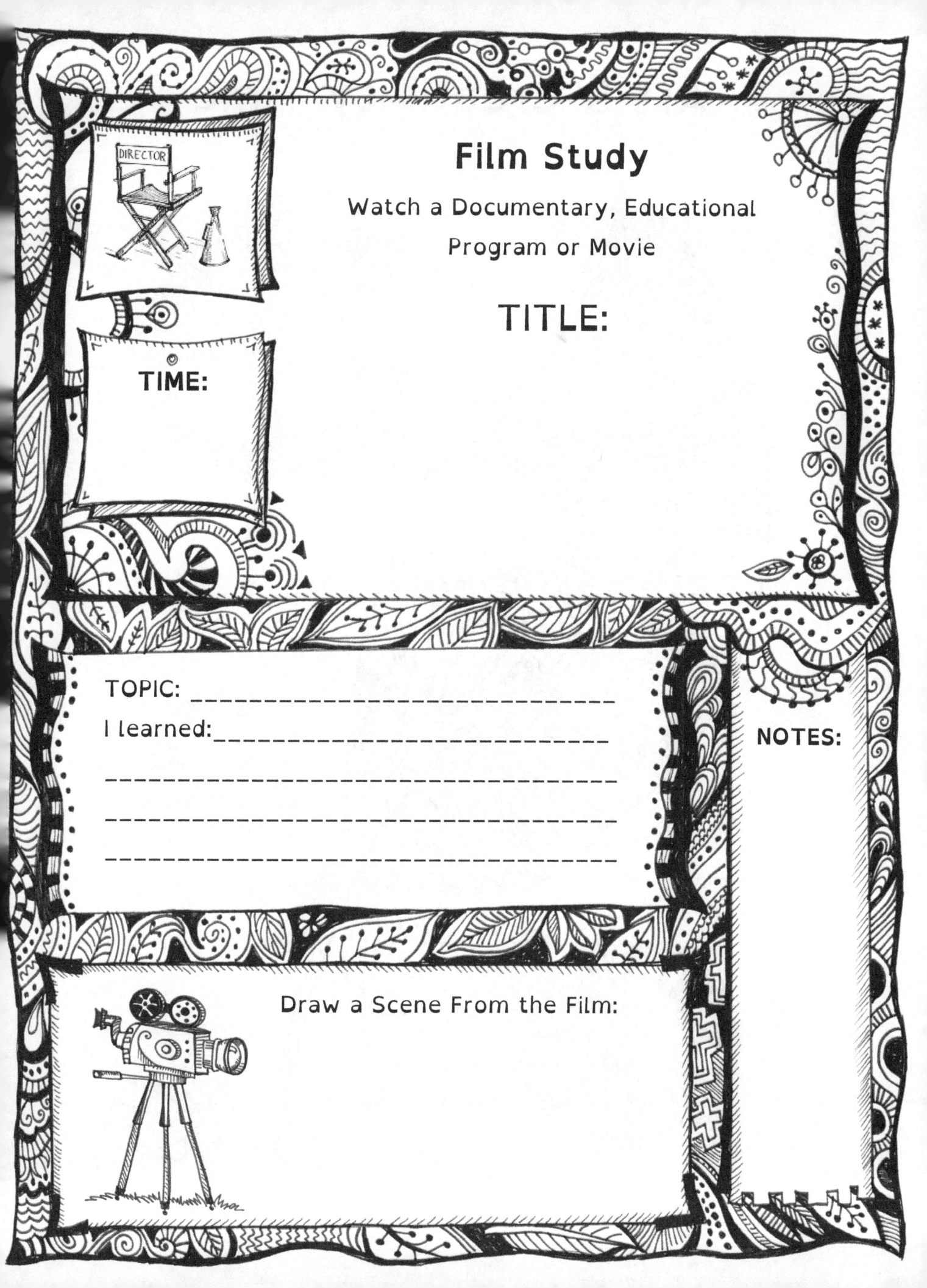

Watch a Documentary, Educational Program or Movie

TITLE:

TIME:

TOPIC: _____
I learned: _____
_____
_____
_____

NOTES:

Draw a Scene From the Film:

Art & Creativity Time

Reading Time - 1 Hour

Choose Four Books - Read from each book for 15 minutes.
Copy a sentence or picture from each book here:

Circle Today's Date

January
February
March
April
May
June
July
August
September
October
November
December

1 2 3 4 5 6
7 8 9 10 11
12 13 14 15
16 17 18 19
20 21 22 23
24 25 26 27
28 29 30 31

MONDAY
TUESDAY
WEDNESDAY
THURSDAY
FRIDAY
SATURDAY
SUNDAY

2015
2016
2017
2018
2019
2020
2021
2022
2023
2024
2025
2026
2027
2028
2029

Write Today's Date: _____

My Thinking Page

This is where you write down your ideas, goals, and plans - with a thankful heart!

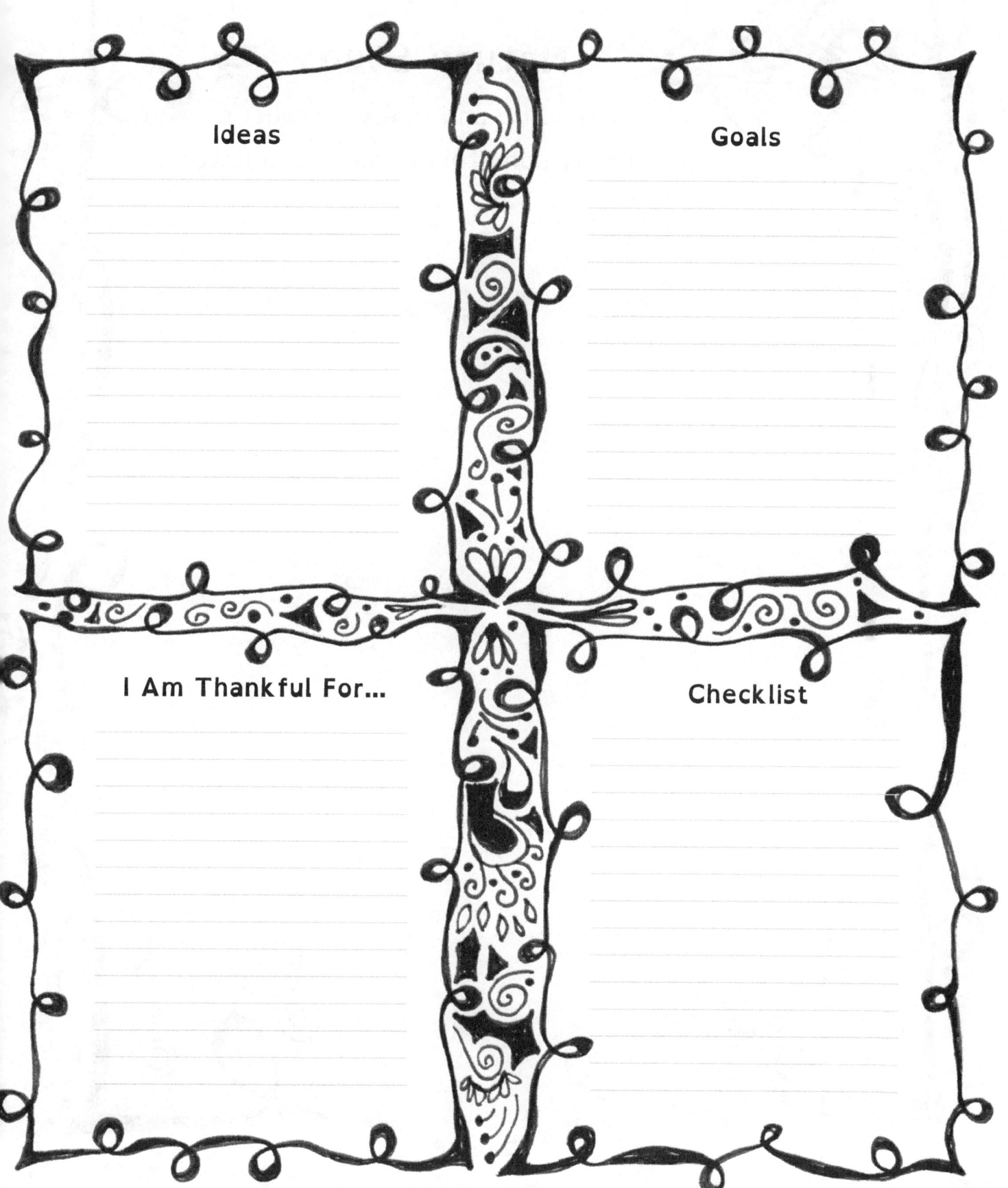

Ideas

Goals

I Am Thankful For...

Checklist

Nature Study

Go outside and make a realistic drawing of something you find in nature.

Draw a Meal PLAN

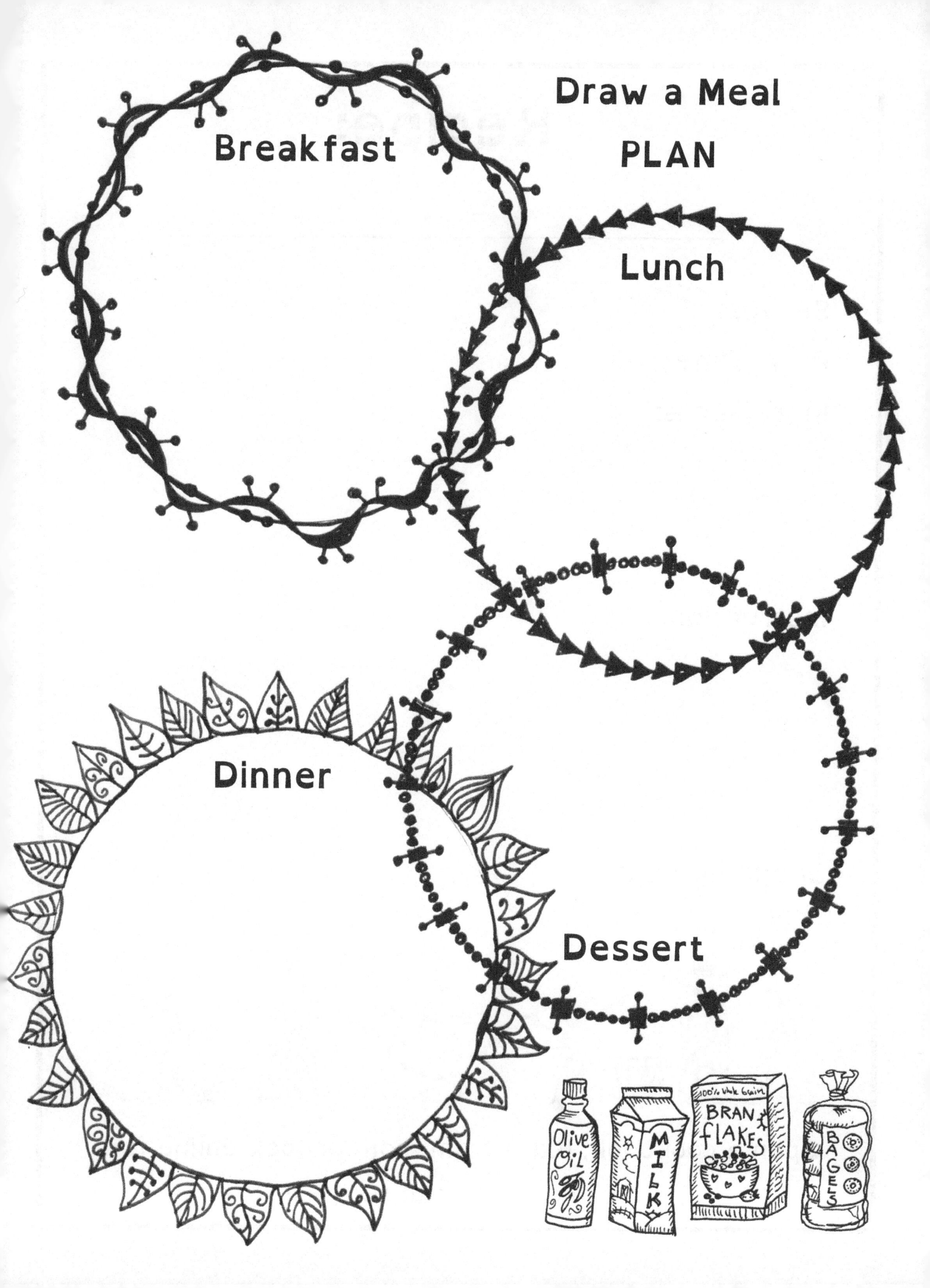

- Breakfast
- Lunch
- Dinner
- Dessert

Recipe:

_____

Serves:

Prep Time:

Ingredients:

Instructions:

Shopping List:

Open a cookbook, learn from mom or look online for some wonderful recipes!

Reading Time - 1 Hour

Choose Four Books - Read from each book for 15 minutes.
Copy a sentence or picture from each book here:

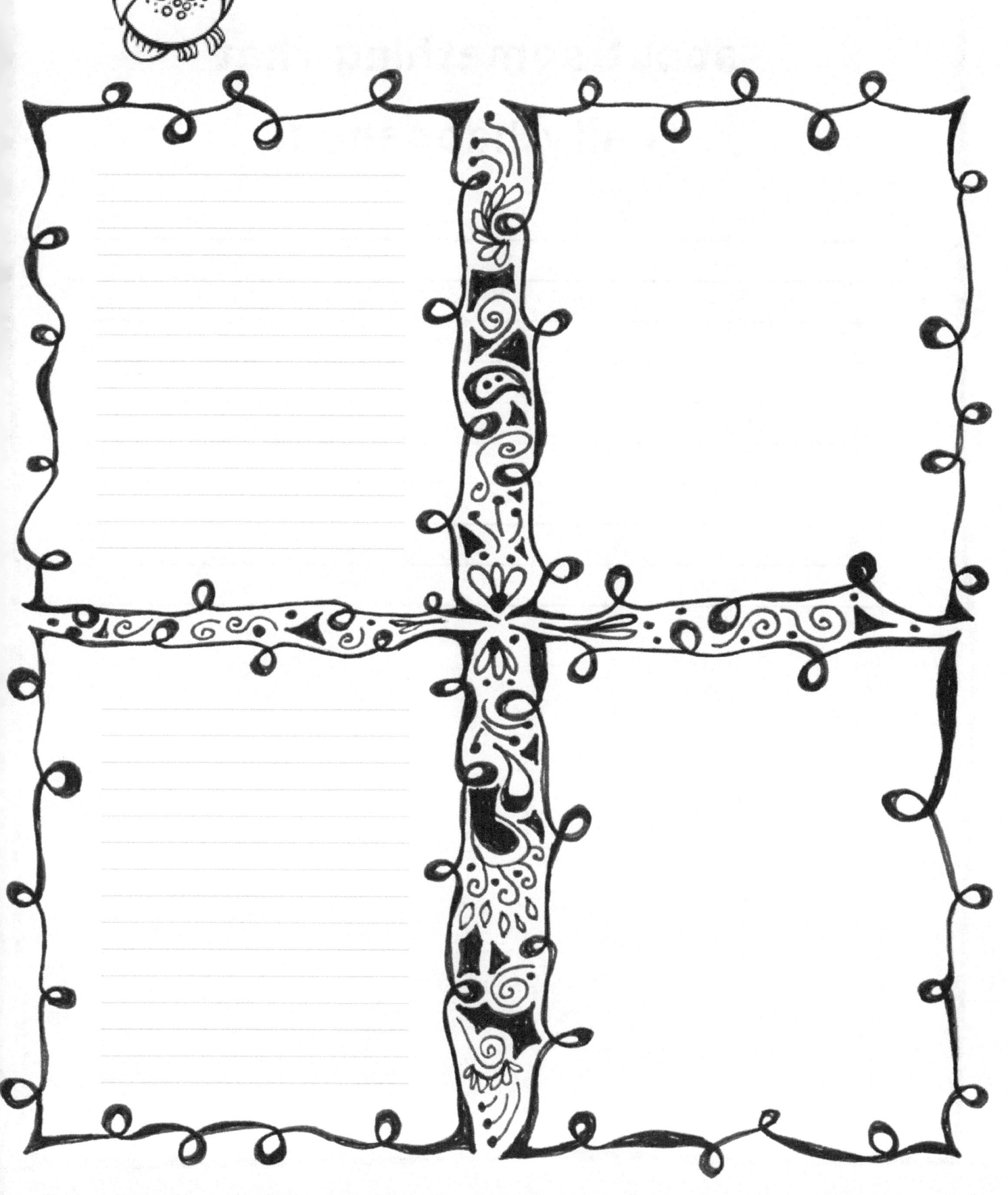

Write & Draw about something that really happened.

_____
_____
_____
_____
_____
_____
_____
_____
_____

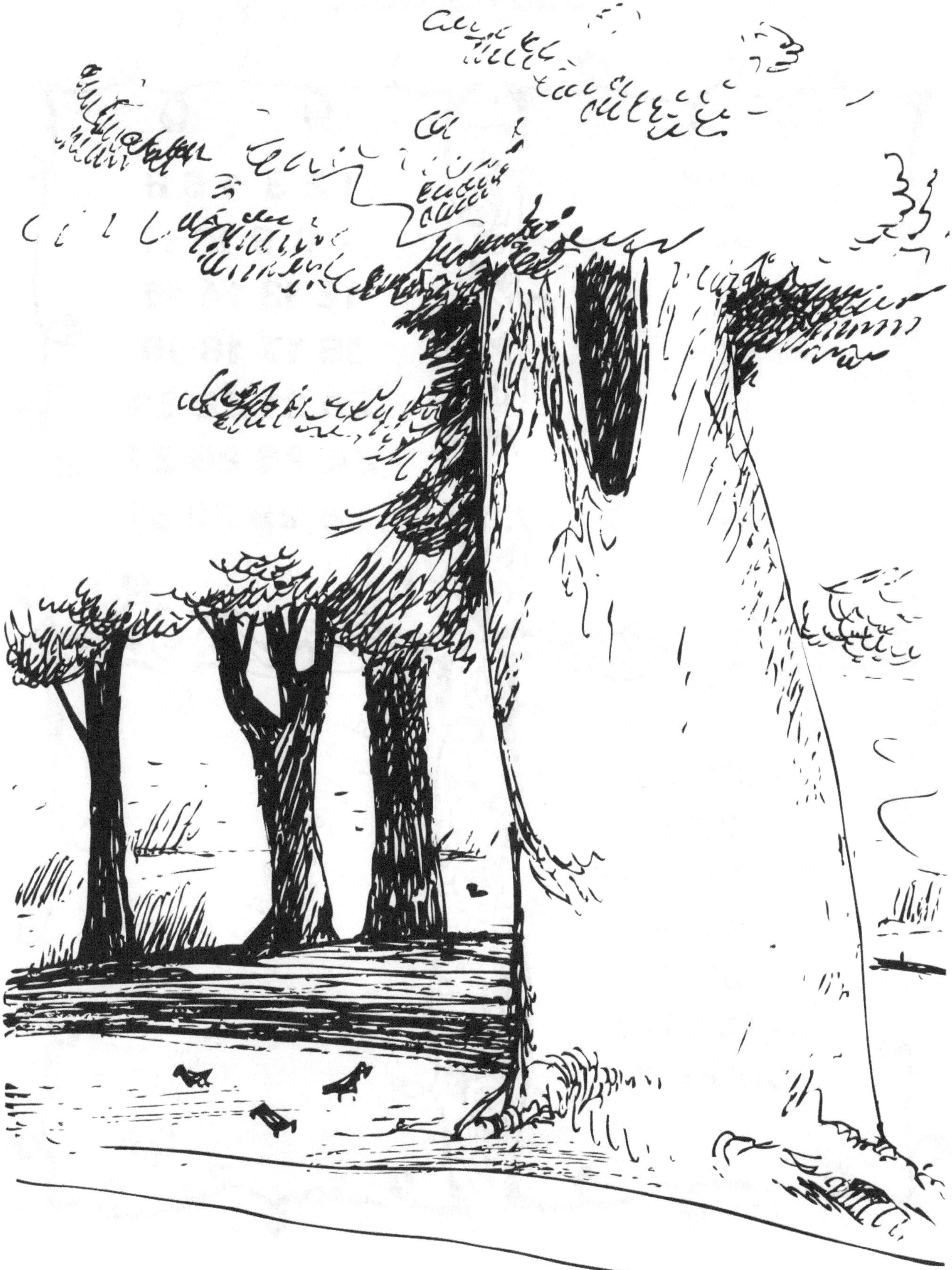

Circle Today's Date

January
February
March
April
May
June
July
August
September
October
November
December

1 2 3 4 5 6
7 8 9 10 11
12 13 14 15
16 17 18 19
20 21 22 23
24 25 26 27
28 29 30 31

MONDAY
TUESDAY
WEDNESDAY
THURSDAY
FRIDAY
SATURDAY
SUNDAY

2015
2016
2017
2018
2019
2020
2021
2022
2023
2024
2025
2026
2027
2028
2029

Write Today's Date: _____

My Illustrated TO-DO List

Spelling Time

Find 20 Words with 5 letters each.
Look in your books for words.
Write the words here:

Learning a Skill

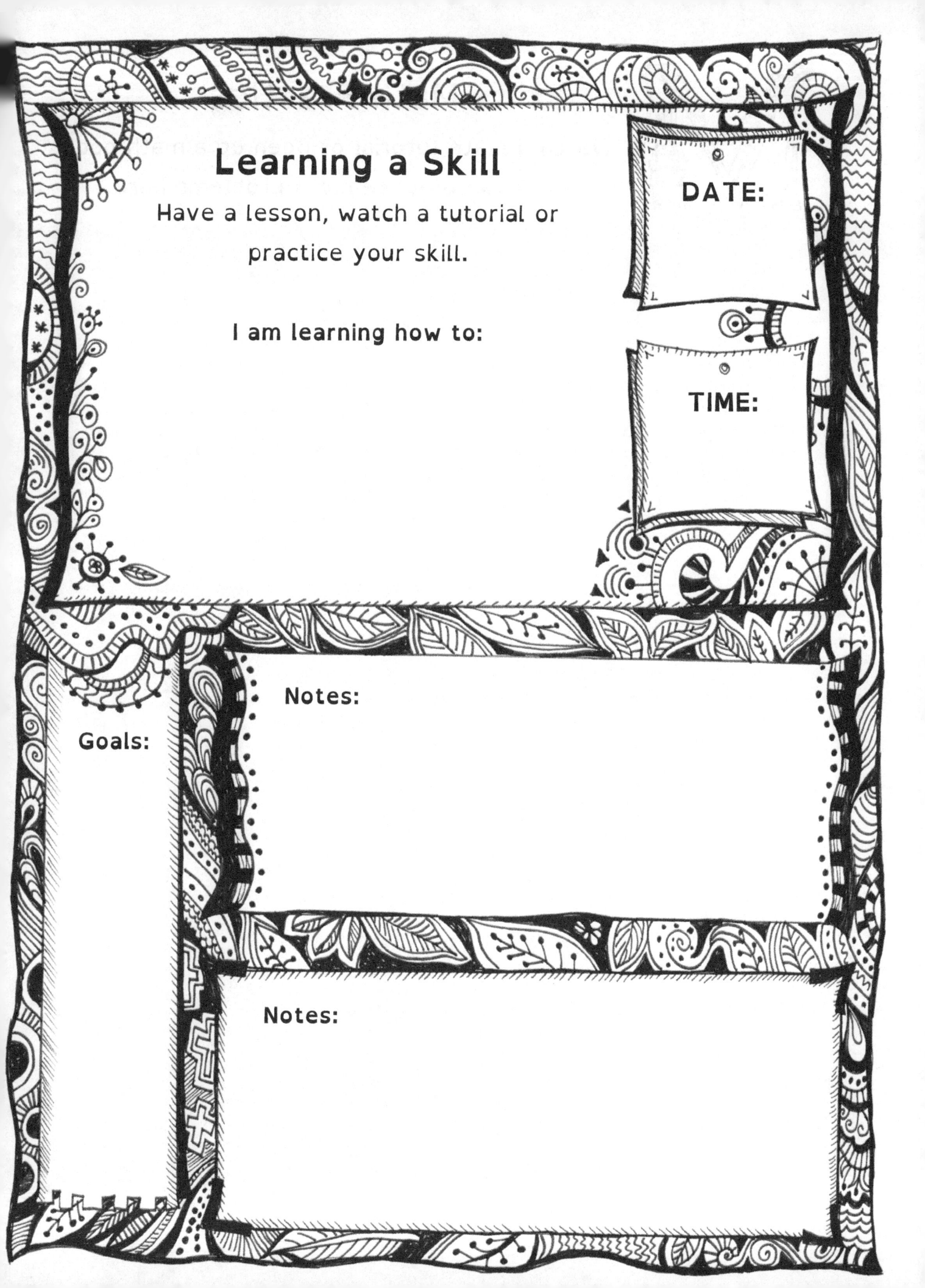

Have a lesson, watch a tutorial or practice your skill.

I am learning how to:

DATE:

TIME:

Goals:

Notes:

Notes:

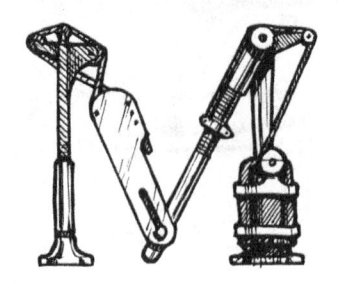

Math Practice

Watch a math tutorial or open up a math book.
You can practice math problems here.

Copywork

Find an interesting paragraph in one of your books and copy it. Be diligent to make your writing look exactly like it does in the book.

TITLE:_____   Page Number:_____

Sketch a Picture
Look through your library books and find something to draw.

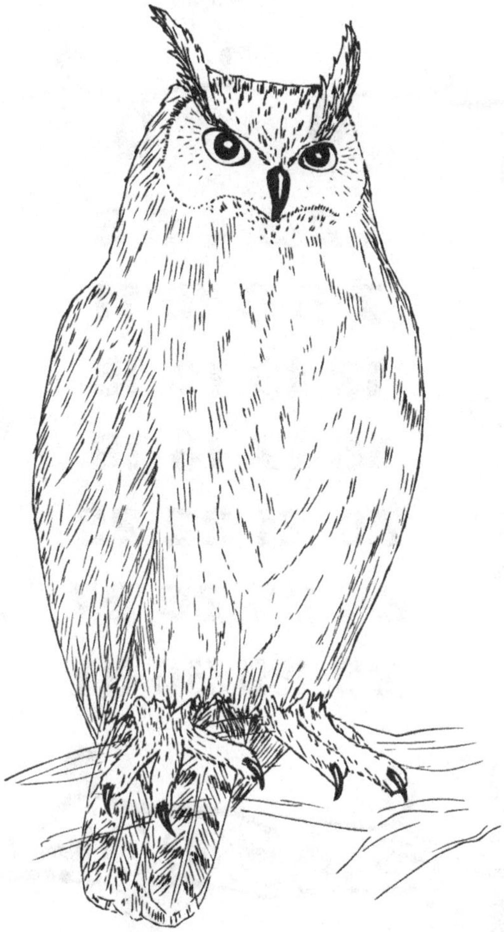
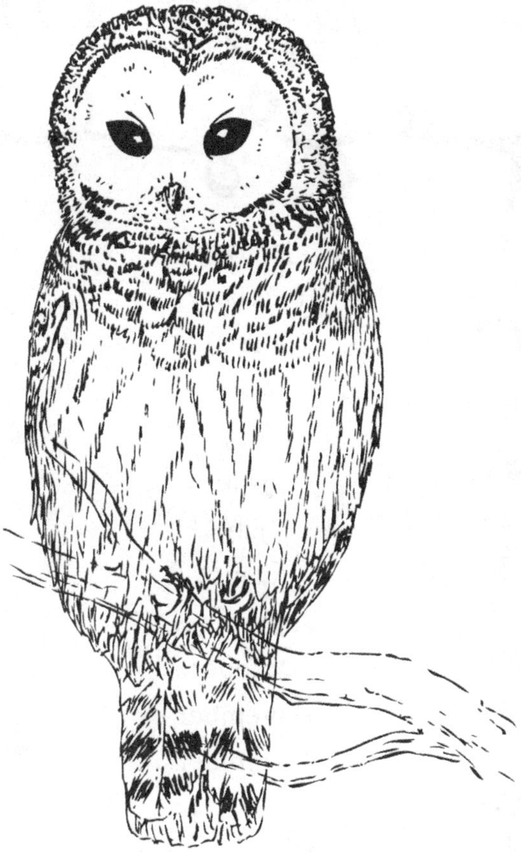
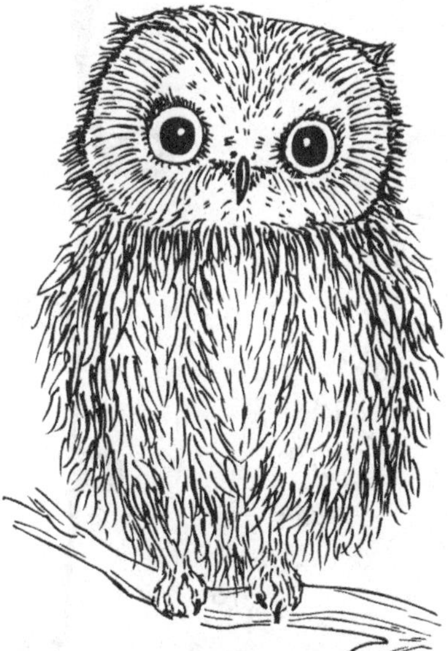
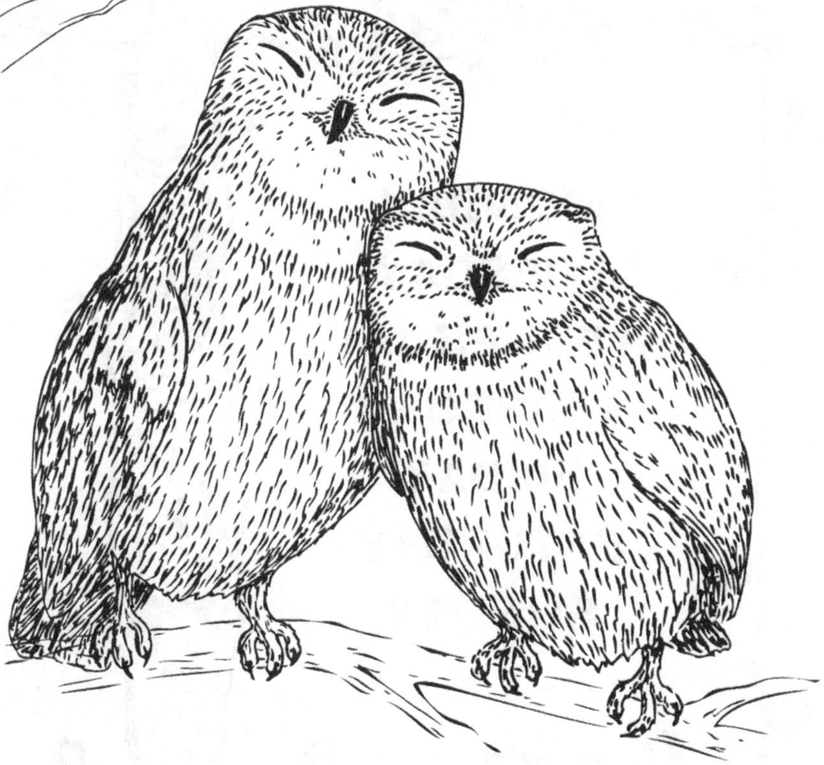

Circle Today's Date

January
February
March
April
May
June
July
August
September
October
November
December

1 2 3 4 5 6
7 8 9 10 11
12 13 14 15
16 17 18 19
20 21 22 23
24 25 26 27
28 29 30 31

MONDAY
TUESDAY
WEDNESDAY
THURSDAY
FRIDAY
SATURDAY
SUNDAY

2015
2016
2017
2018
2019
2020
2021
2022
2023
2024
2025
2026
2027
2028
2029

Write Today's Date:_____

Nature Study

Go outside and make a realistic drawing of something you find in nature.

My Thinking Page

This is where you write down your ideas, goals, and plans - with a thankful heart!

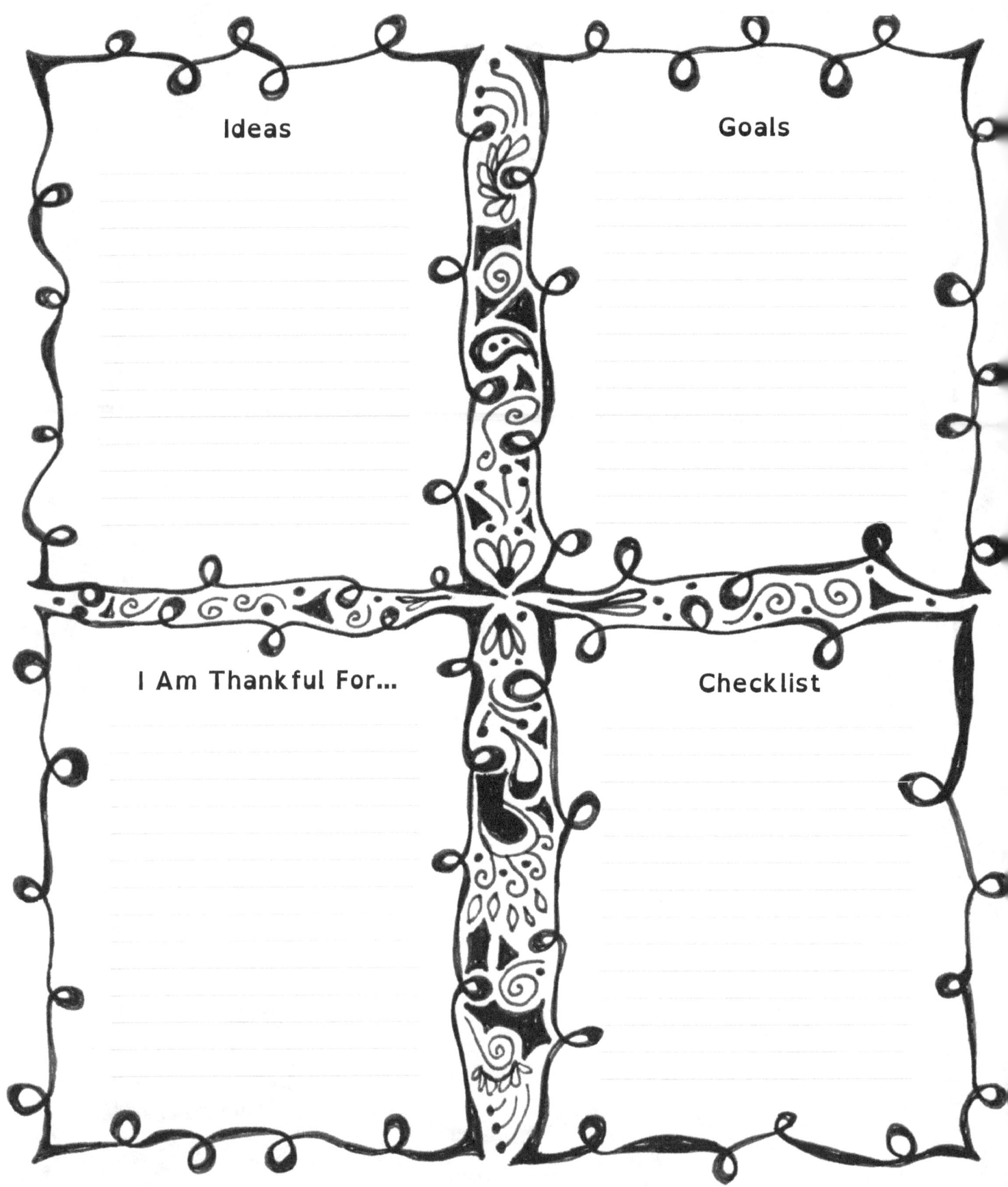

Ideas

Goals

I Am Thankful For...

Checklist

Draw a Meal PLAN

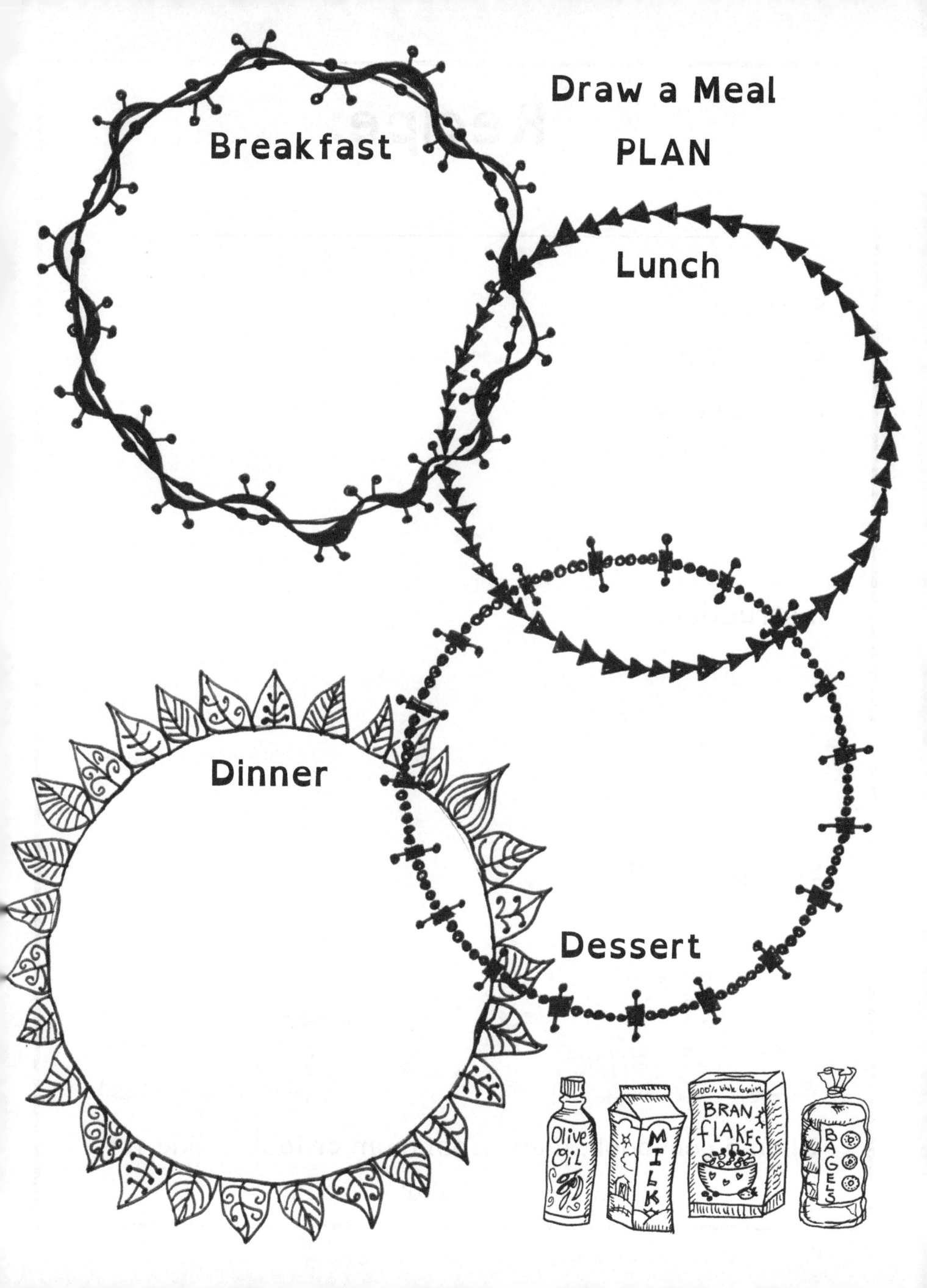

Breakfast

Lunch

Dinner

Dessert

Recipe:

_____

Serves:

Prep Time:

Ingredients:

Instructions:

Shopping List:

Open a cookbook, learn from mom or look online for some wonderful recipes!

Creative Writing

Draw a picture below.
Write a poem or short story about it.

TITLE: _____

_____
_____
_____
_____
_____
_____
_____
_____
_____
_____
_____
_____
_____
_____
_____

Reading Time - 1 Hour

Choose Four Books - Read from each book for 15 minutes.
Copy a sentence or picture from each book here:

Circle Today's Date

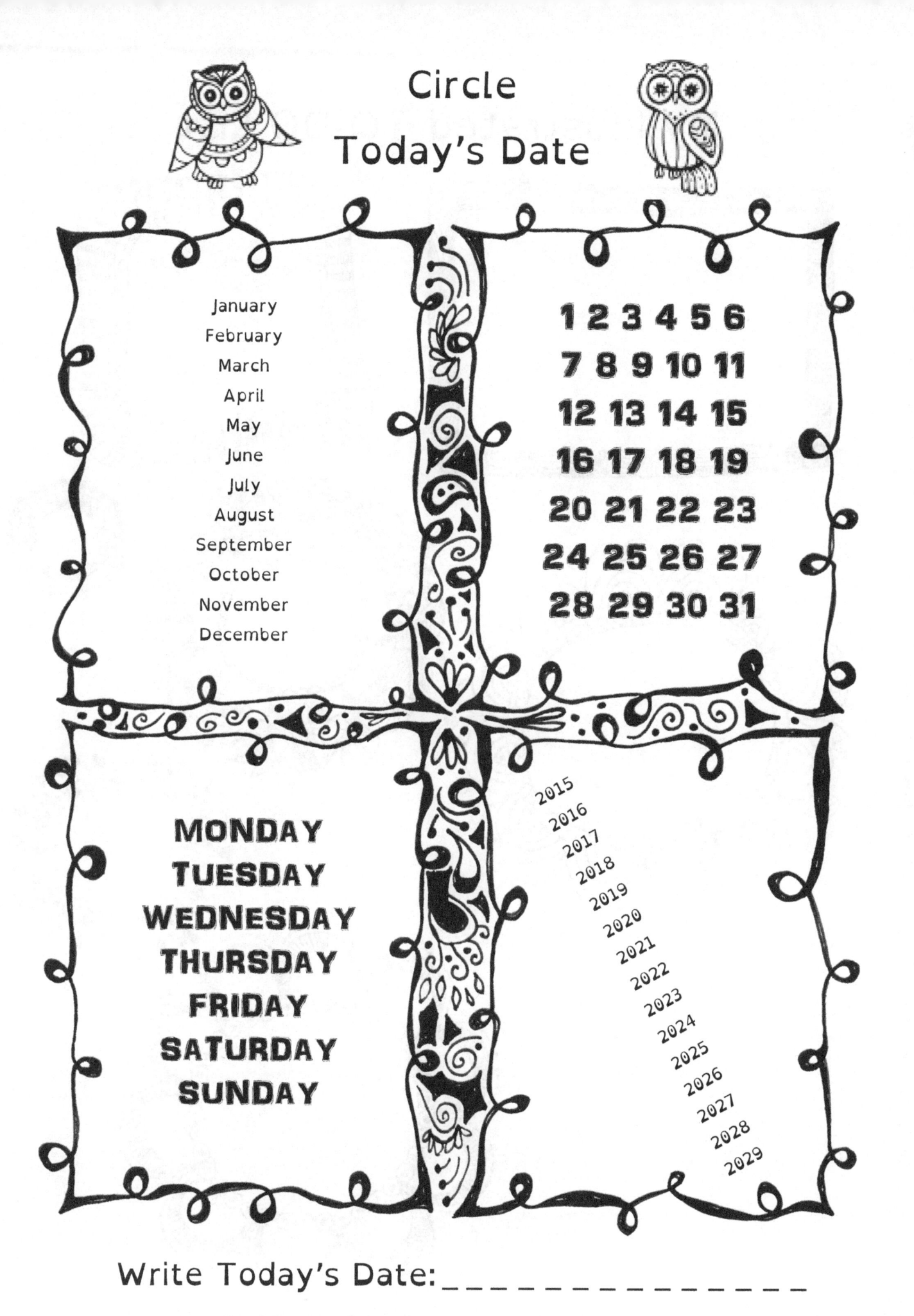

January
February
March
April
May
June
July
August
September
October
November
December

1 2 3 4 5 6
7 8 9 10 11
12 13 14 15
16 17 18 19
20 21 22 23
24 25 26 27
28 29 30 31

MONDAY
TUESDAY
WEDNESDAY
THURSDAY
FRIDAY
SATURDAY
SUNDAY

2015
2016
2017
2018
2019
2020
2021
2022
2023
2024
2025
2026
2027
2028
2029

Write Today's Date: _____

My Illustrated TO-DO List

Spelling Time

Find 20 Words with 6 letters each.
Look in your books for words.
Write the words here:

_____   _____

_____   _____

_____   _____

_____   _____

_____   _____

_____   _____

_____   _____

_____   _____

_____   _____

_____   _____

Film Study

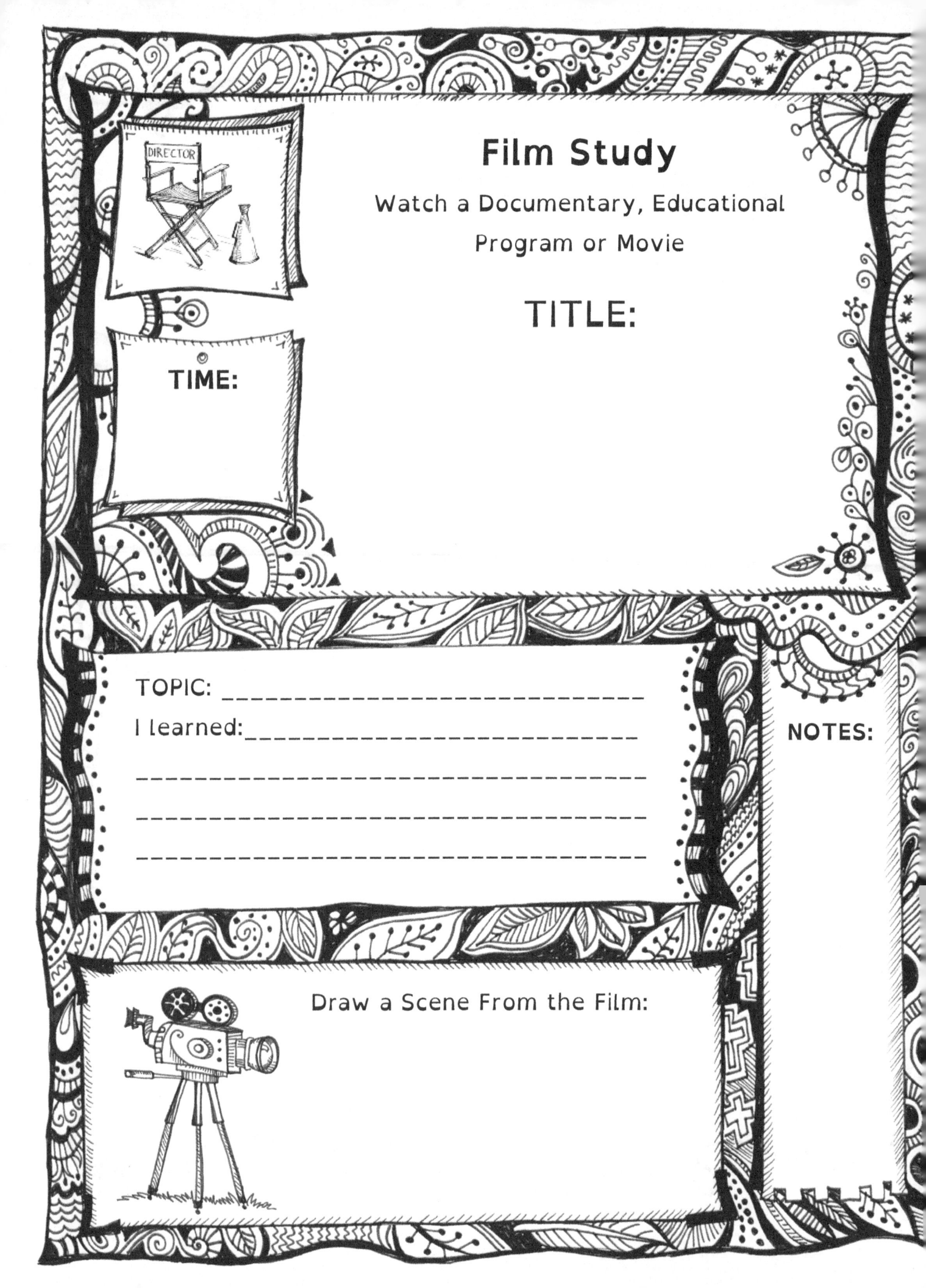

Watch a Documentary, Educational Program or Movie

TITLE:

TIME:

TOPIC: _____
I learned: _____
_____
_____
_____

NOTES:

Draw a Scene From the Film:

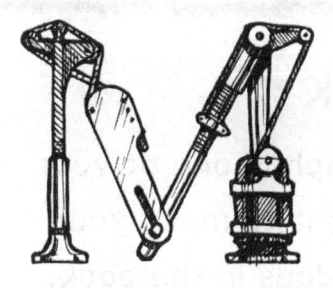

Math Practice

Watch a math tutorial or open up a math book.
You can practice math problems here.

Copywork

Find an interesting paragraph in one of your books and copy it. Be diligent to make your writing look exactly like it does in the book.

TITLE:_____ **Page Number:**_____

Sketch a Picture

Look through your library books and find something to draw.

Circle Today's Date

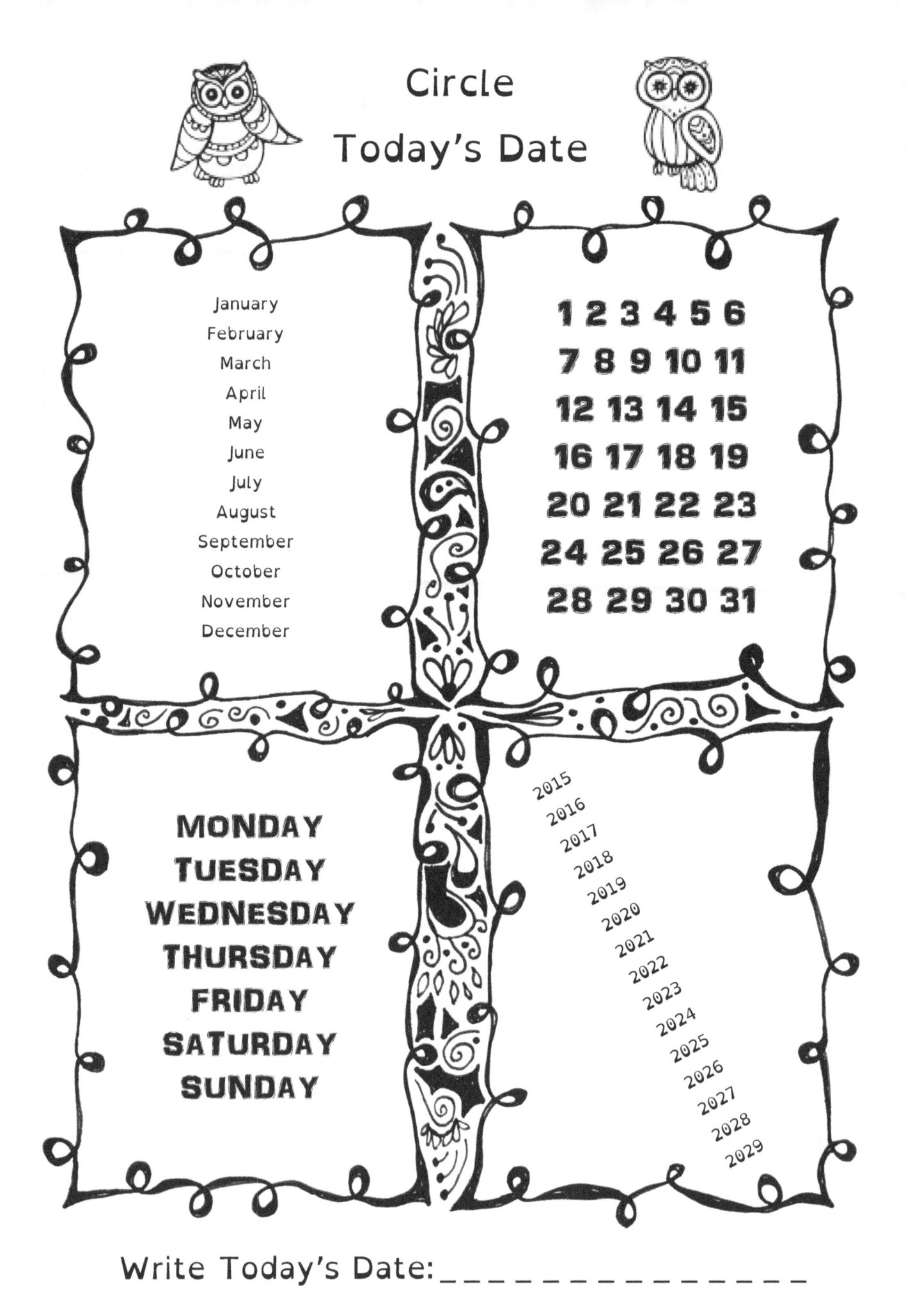

January
February
March
April
May
June
July
August
September
October
November
December

1 2 3 4 5 6
7 8 9 10 11
12 13 14 15
16 17 18 19
20 21 22 23
24 25 26 27
28 29 30 31

MONDAY
TUESDAY
WEDNESDAY
THURSDAY
FRIDAY
SATURDAY
SUNDAY

2015
2016
2017
2018
2019
2020
2021
2022
2023
2024
2025
2026
2027
2028
2029

Write Today's Date: _____

My Thinking Page

This is where you write down your ideas, goals, and plans - with a thankful heart!

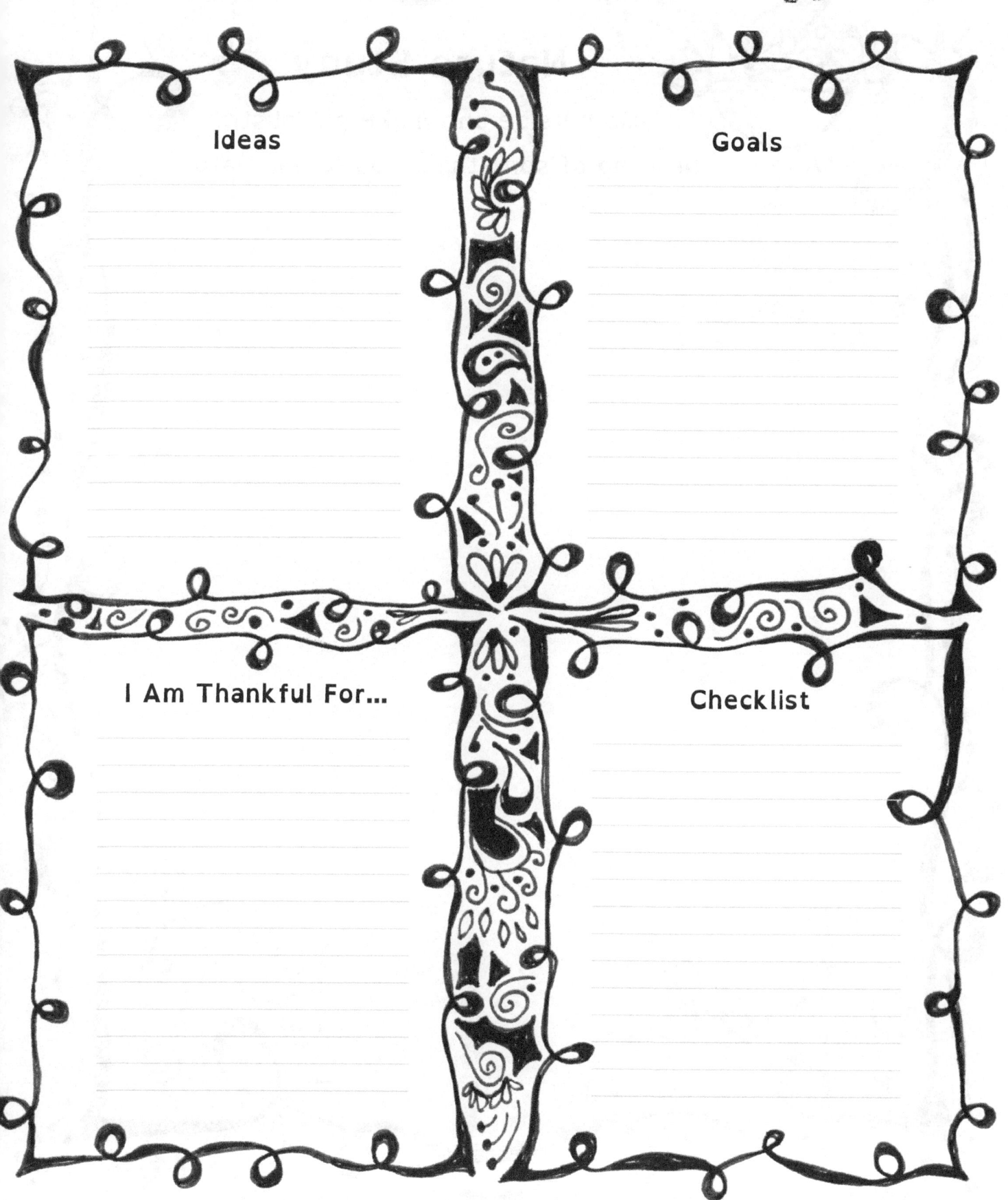

Ideas

Goals

I Am Thankful For...

Checklist

Nature Study

Go outside and make a realistic drawing of something you find in nature.

Creative Writing

Draw a picture below.
Write a poem or short story about it.

TITLE: _____

_____
_____
_____
_____
_____
_____
_____
_____
_____
_____
_____
_____
_____
_____

Listening Time

Listen to an audio book or classical music or ask someone to read a story to you while you color and draw on the next page.

What are you listening to?

_____

Reading Time - 1 Hour

Choose Four Books - Read from each book for 15 minutes.
Copy a sentence or picture from each book here:

Circle Today's Date

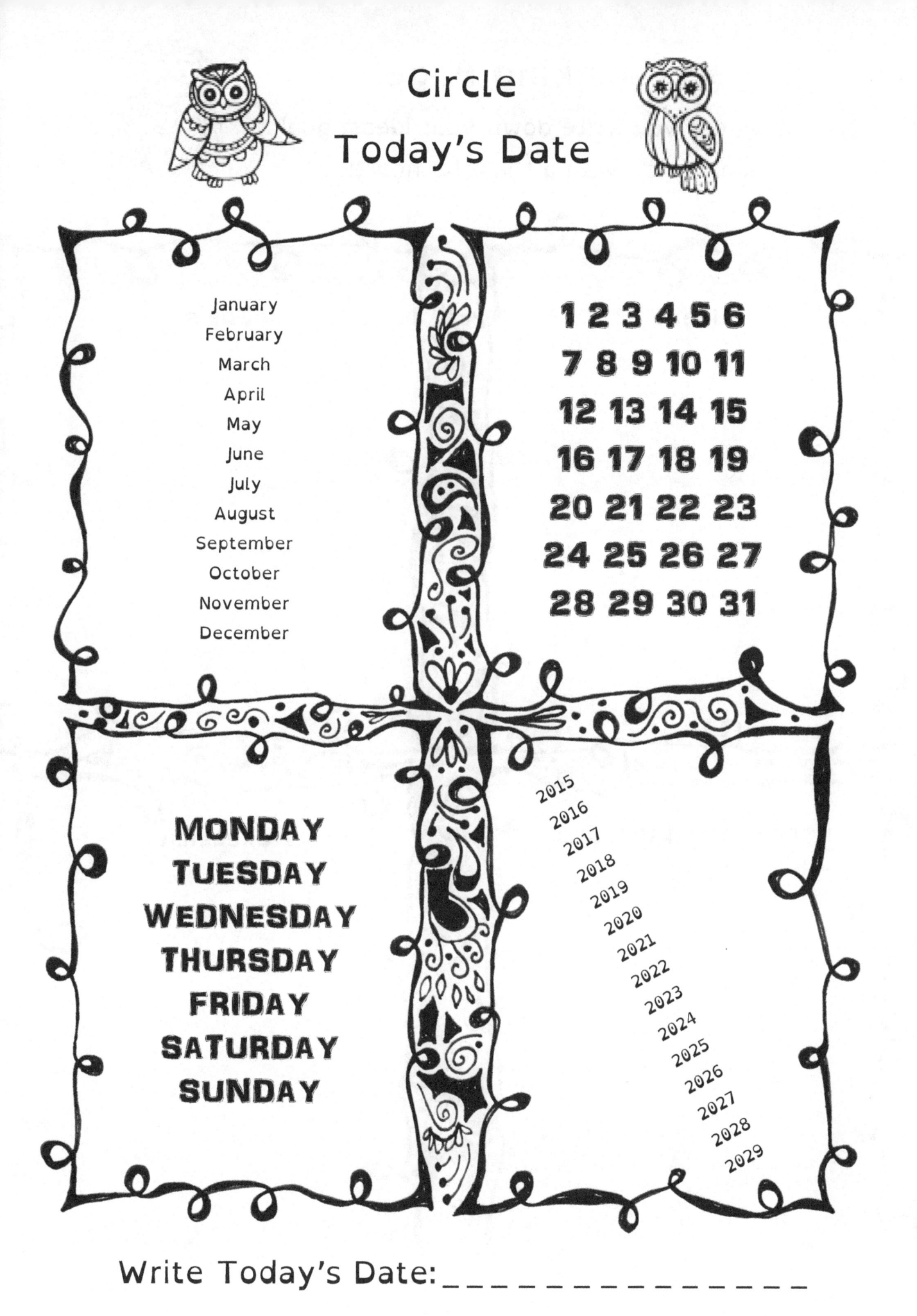

January
February
March
April
May
June
July
August
September
October
November
December

1 2 3 4 5 6
7 8 9 10 11
12 13 14 15
16 17 18 19
20 21 22 23
24 25 26 27
28 29 30 31

MONDAY
TUESDAY
WEDNESDAY
THURSDAY
FRIDAY
SATURDAY
SUNDAY

2015
2016
2017
2018
2019
2020
2021
2022
2023
2024
2025
2026
2027
2028
2029

Write Today's Date: _____

My Thinking Page

This is where you write down your ideas, goals, and plans - with a thankful heart!

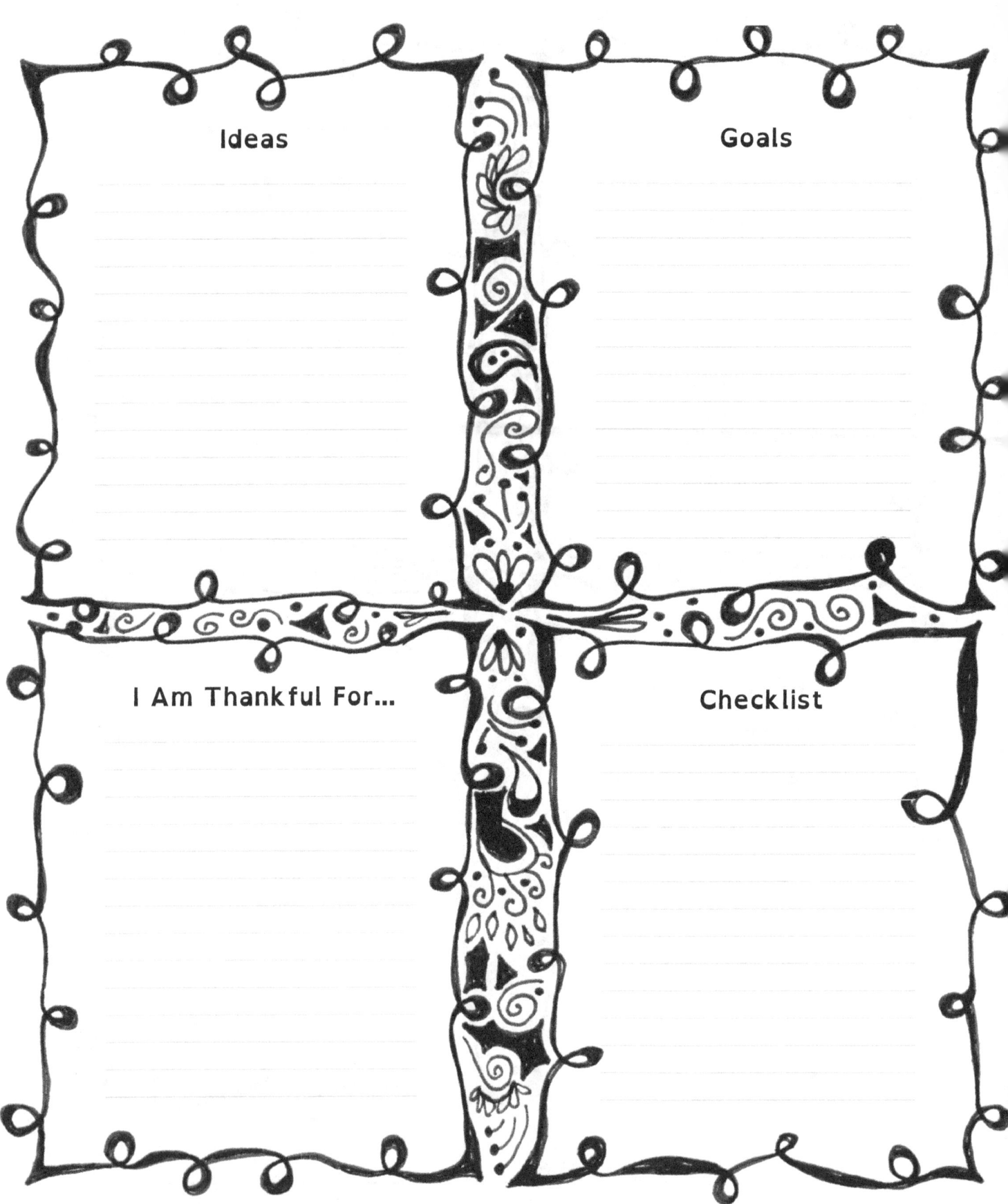

Ideas

Goals

I Am Thankful For...

Checklist

Art & Creativity Time

Spelling Time

Find 20 Words with 7 letters each.
Look in your books for words.
Write the words here:

Learning a Skill

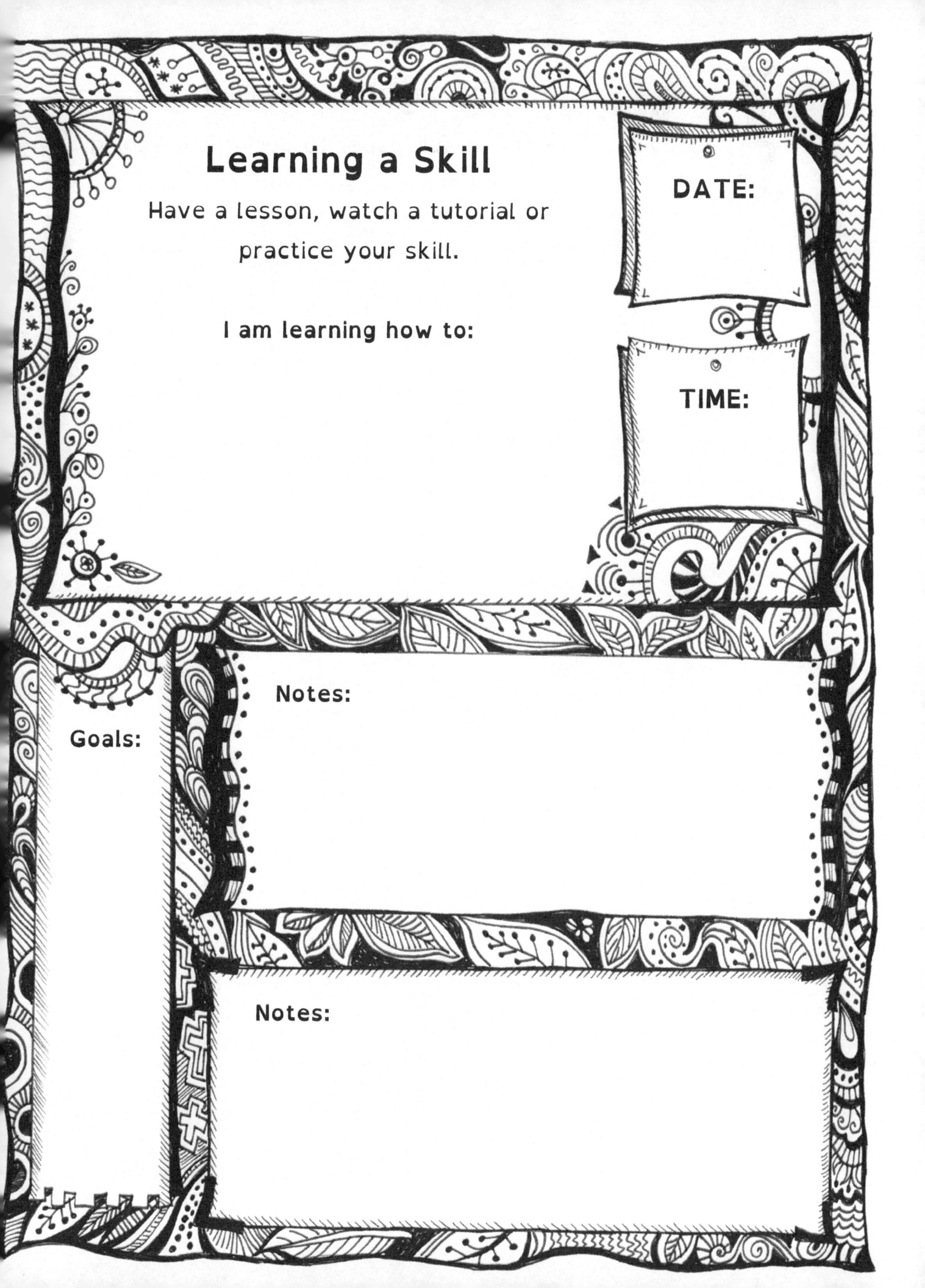

Have a lesson, watch a tutorial or practice your skill.

I am learning how to:

DATE:

TIME:

Goals:

Notes:

Notes:

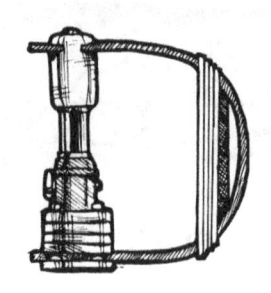

Design Something

Use this graph paper to design something. If you can't think of anything design a house.

Copywork

Find an interesting paragraph in one of your books and copy it. Be diligent to make your writing look exactly like it does in the book.

TITLE:_____ **Page Number:**_____

Sketch a Picture
Look through your library books and find something to draw.

Circle Today's Date

January
February
March
April
May
June
July
August
September
October
November
December

1 2 3 4 5 6
7 8 9 10 11
12 13 14 15
16 17 18 19
20 21 22 23
24 25 26 27
28 29 30 31

MONDAY
TUESDAY
WEDNESDAY
THURSDAY
FRIDAY
SATURDAY
SUNDAY

2015
2016
2017
2018
2019
2020
2021
2022
2023
2024
2025
2026
2027
2028
2029

Write Today's Date: _____

Nature Study

Go outside and make a realistic drawing of something you find in nature.

My Illustrated TO-DO List

Reading Time - 1 Hour

Choose Four Books - Read from each book for 15 minutes.
Copy a sentence or picture from each book here:

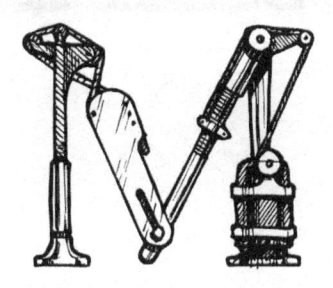

Math Practice

Watch a math tutorial or open up a math book.
You can practice math problems here.

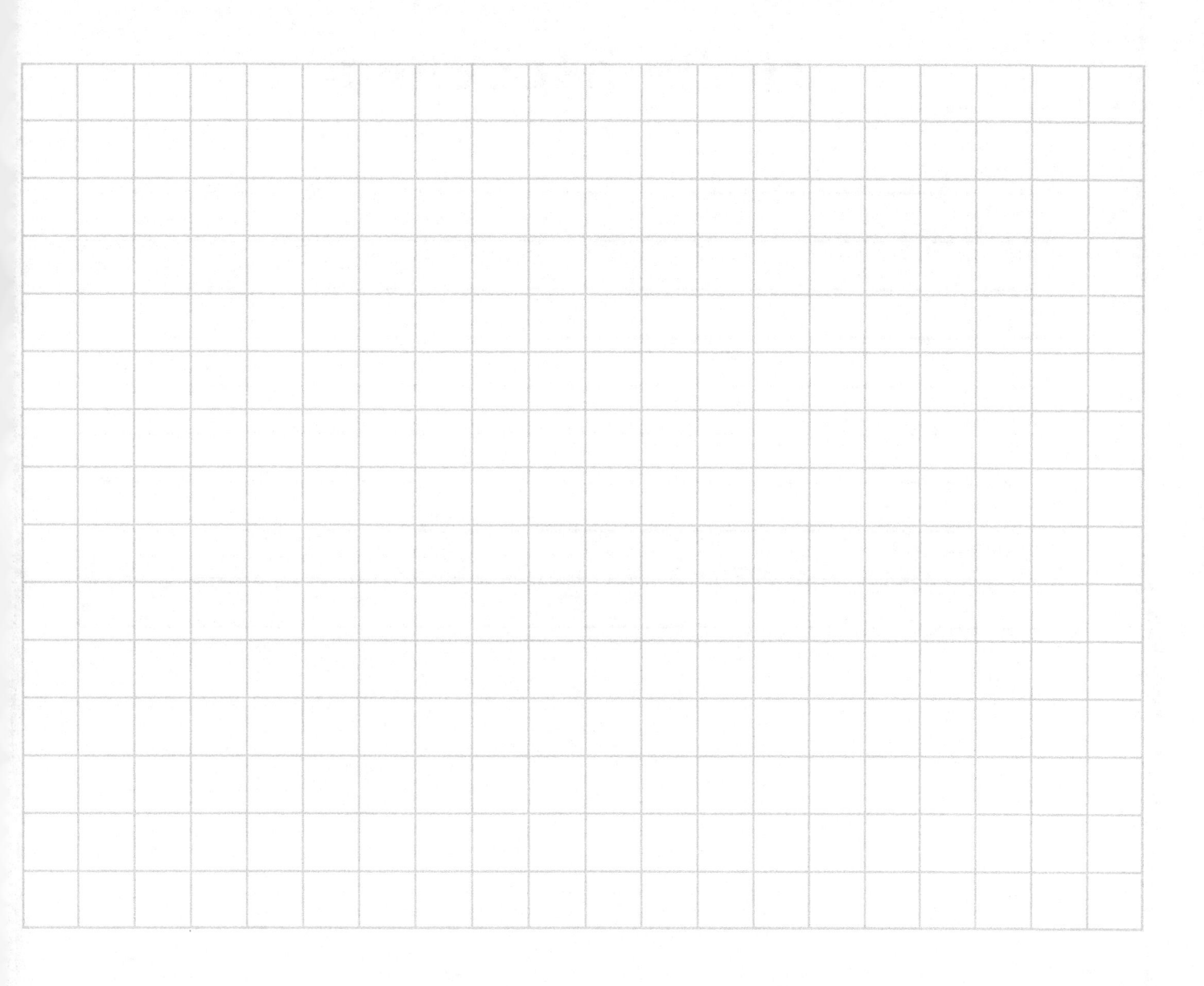

Write & Draw about something that really happened.

_____
_____
_____
_____
_____
_____
_____
_____

Circle Today's Date

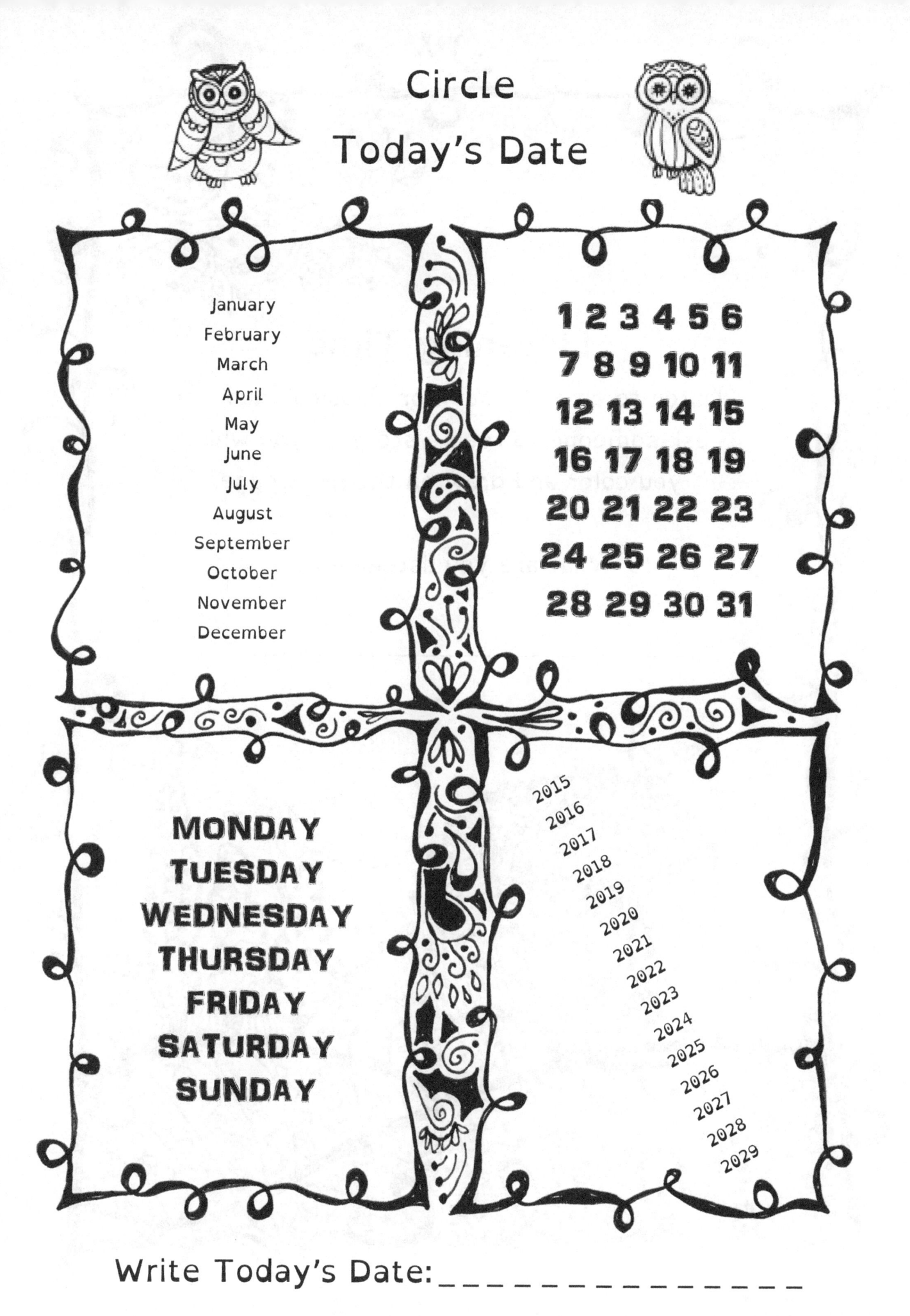

January
February
March
April
May
June
July
August
September
October
November
December

1 2 3 4 5 6
7 8 9 10 11
12 13 14 15
16 17 18 19
20 21 22 23
24 25 26 27
28 29 30 31

MONDAY
TUESDAY
WEDNESDAY
THURSDAY
FRIDAY
SATURDAY
SUNDAY

2015
2016
2017
2018
2019
2020
2021
2022
2023
2024
2025
2026
2027
2028
2029

Write Today's Date: _____

Listening Time

Listen to an audio book or classical music or ask someone to read a story to you while you color and draw on the next page.

What are you listening to?

_____

My Illustrated TO-DO List

Spelling Time

Find 20 Words with 8 letters each.
Look in your books for words.
Write the words here:

Film Study

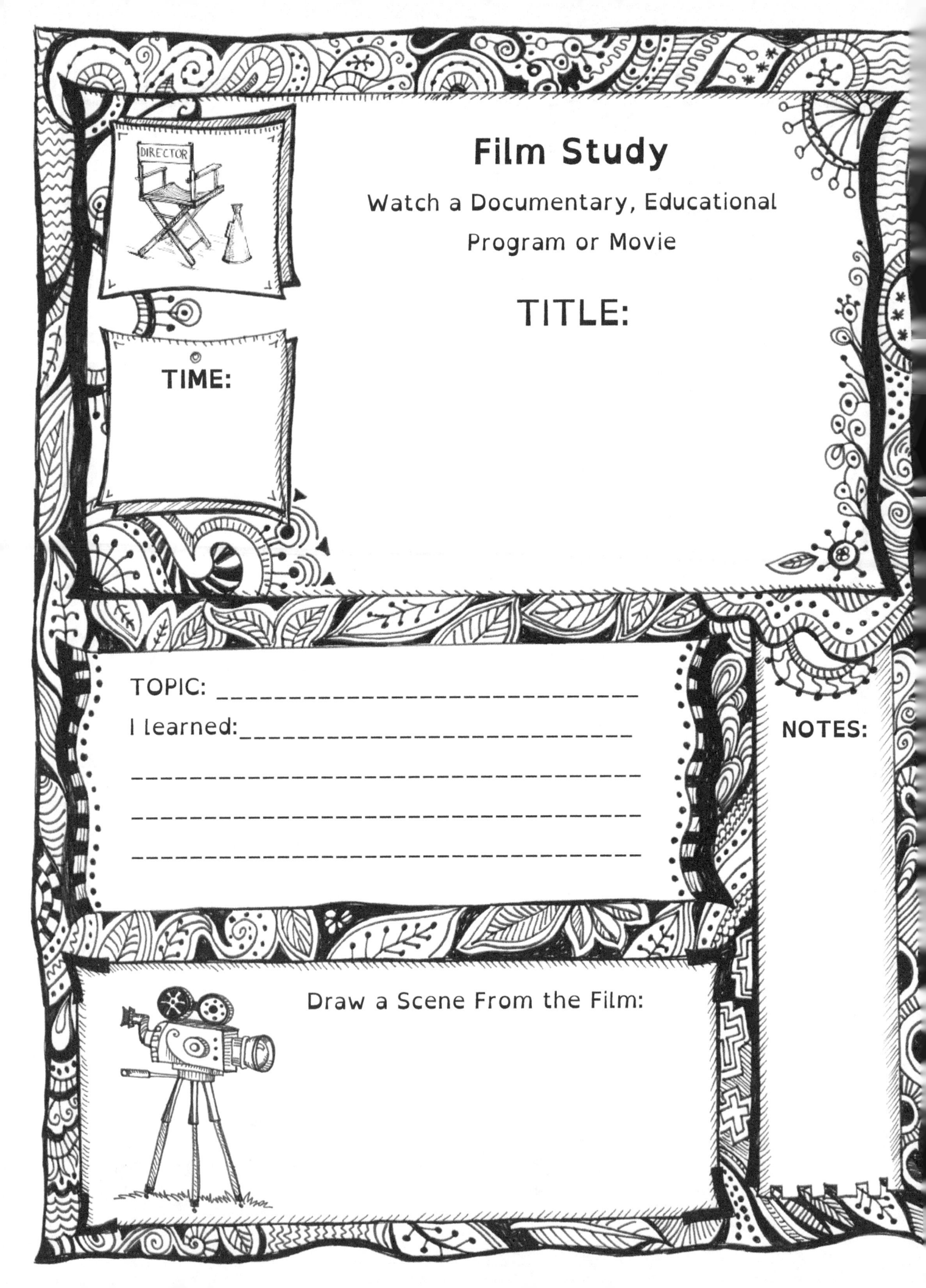

Watch a Documentary, Educational Program or Movie

TITLE:

TIME:

TOPIC: _____

I learned: _____

_____

_____

_____

NOTES:

Draw a Scene From the Film:

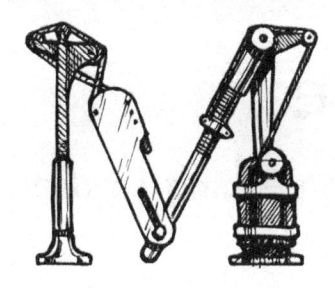

Math Practice

Watch a math tutorial or open up a math book.
You can practice math problems here.

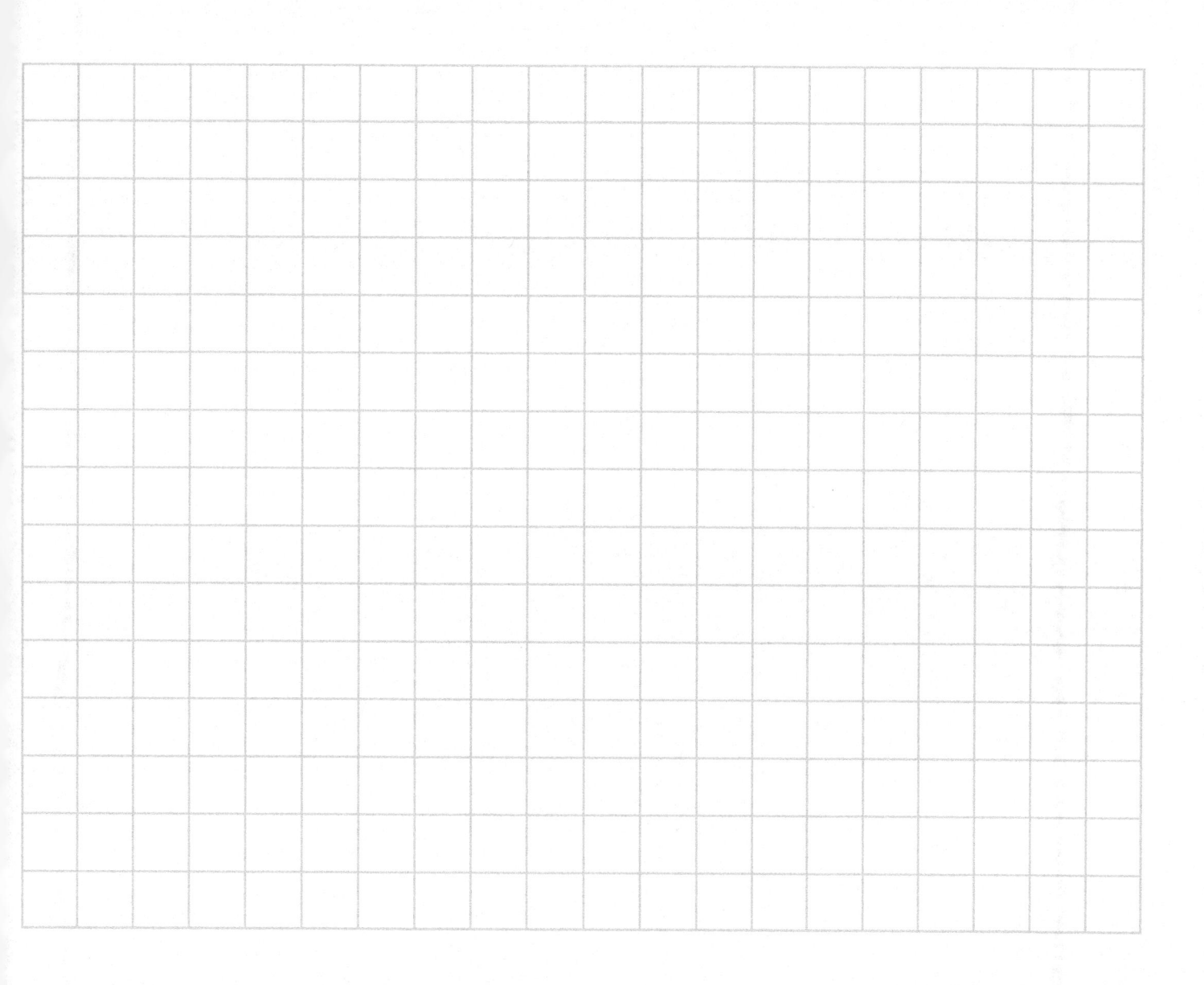

Sketch a Picture
Look through your library books and find something to draw.

Circle Today's Date

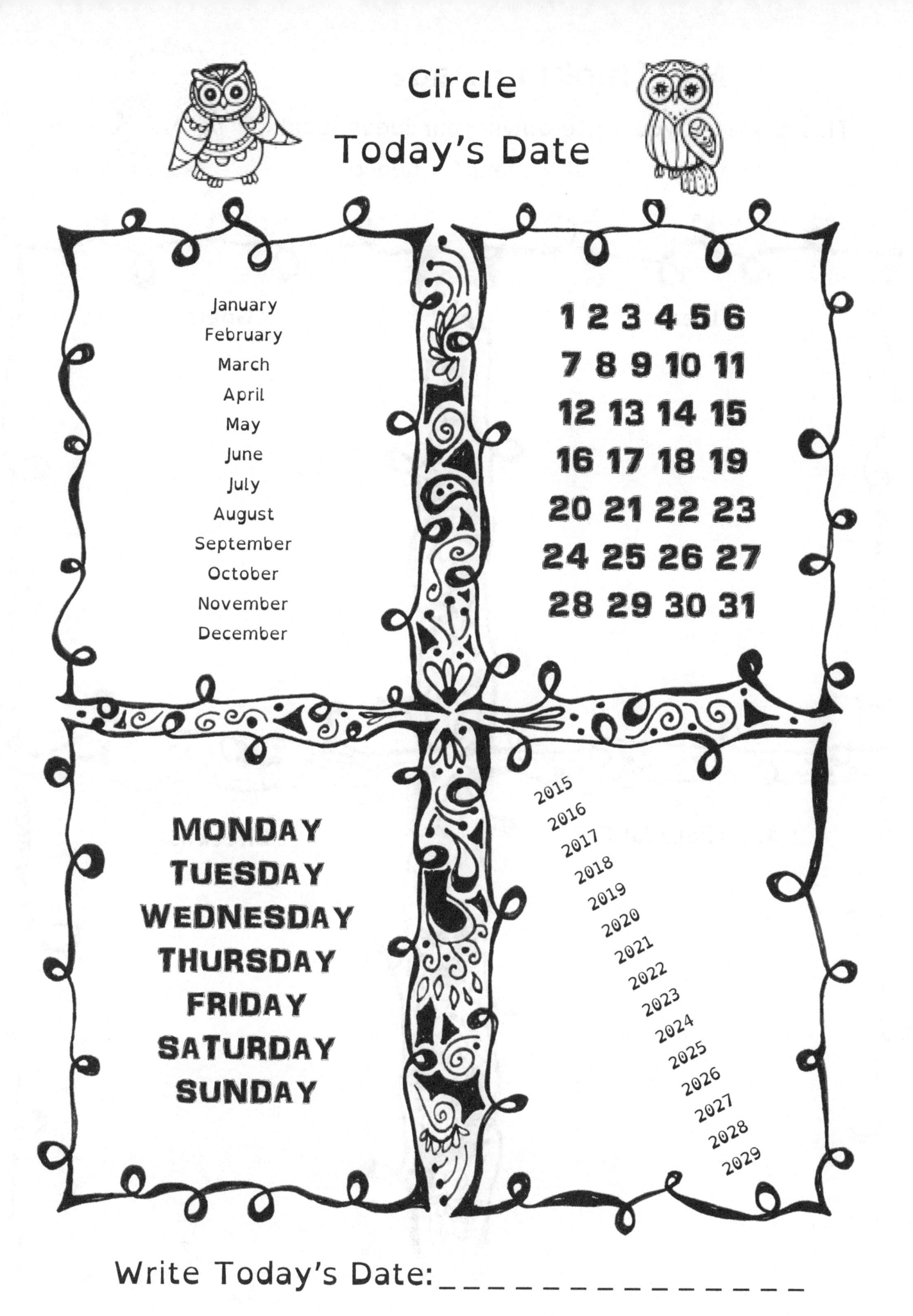

January
February
March
April
May
June
July
August
September
October
November
December

1 2 3 4 5 6
7 8 9 10 11
12 13 14 15
16 17 18 19
20 21 22 23
24 25 26 27
28 29 30 31

MONDAY
TUESDAY
WEDNESDAY
THURSDAY
FRIDAY
SATURDAY
SUNDAY

2015
2016
2017
2018
2019
2020
2021
2022
2023
2024
2025
2026
2027
2028
2029

Write Today's Date: _____

My Thinking Page

This is where you write down your ideas, goals, and plans - with a thankful heart!

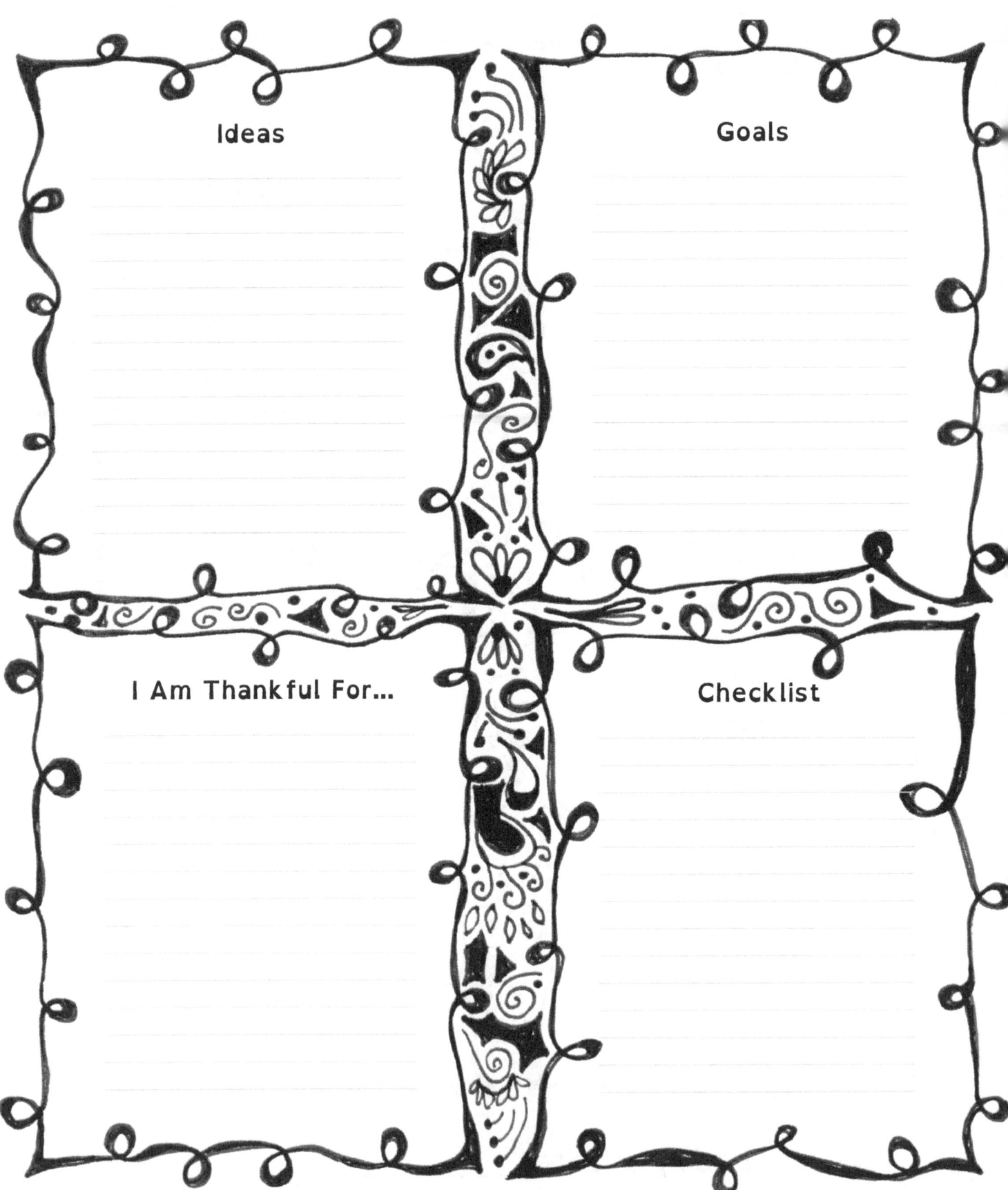

Ideas

Goals

I Am Thankful For...

Checklist

Nature Study

Go outside and make a realistic drawing of something you find in nature.

A B C D E F
G H I J
K L
M N

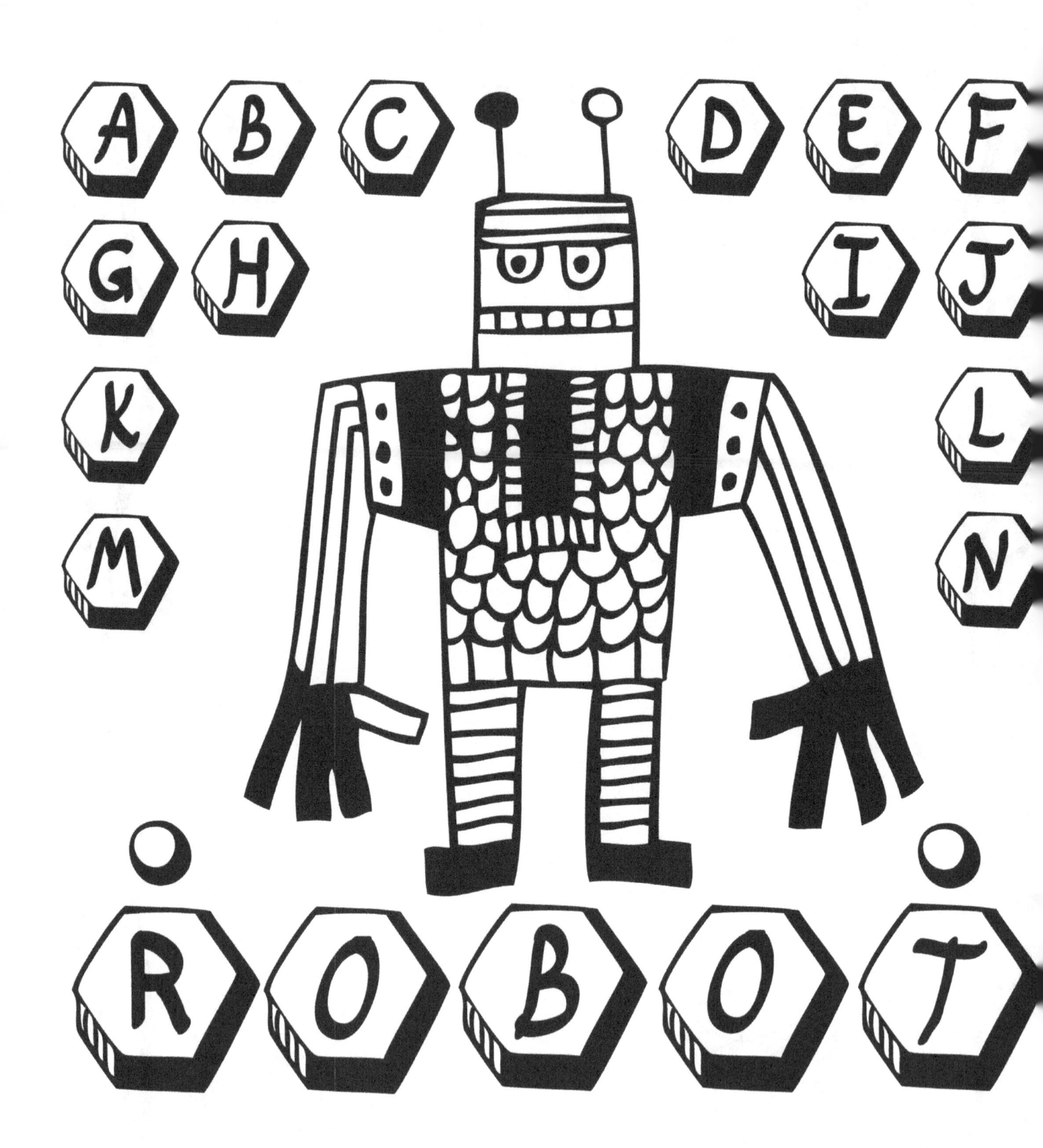

R O B O T

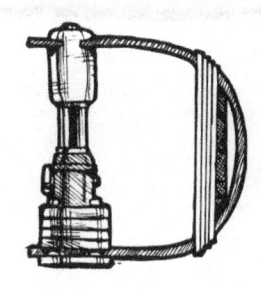

Design Something

Use this graph paper to design something.
If you can't think of anything design a house.

Write & Draw
about something that really happened.

_____
_____
_____
_____
_____
_____
_____
_____
_____

Reading Time - 1 Hour

Choose Four Books - Read from each book for 15 minutes.
Copy a sentence or picture from each book here:

Circle Today's Date

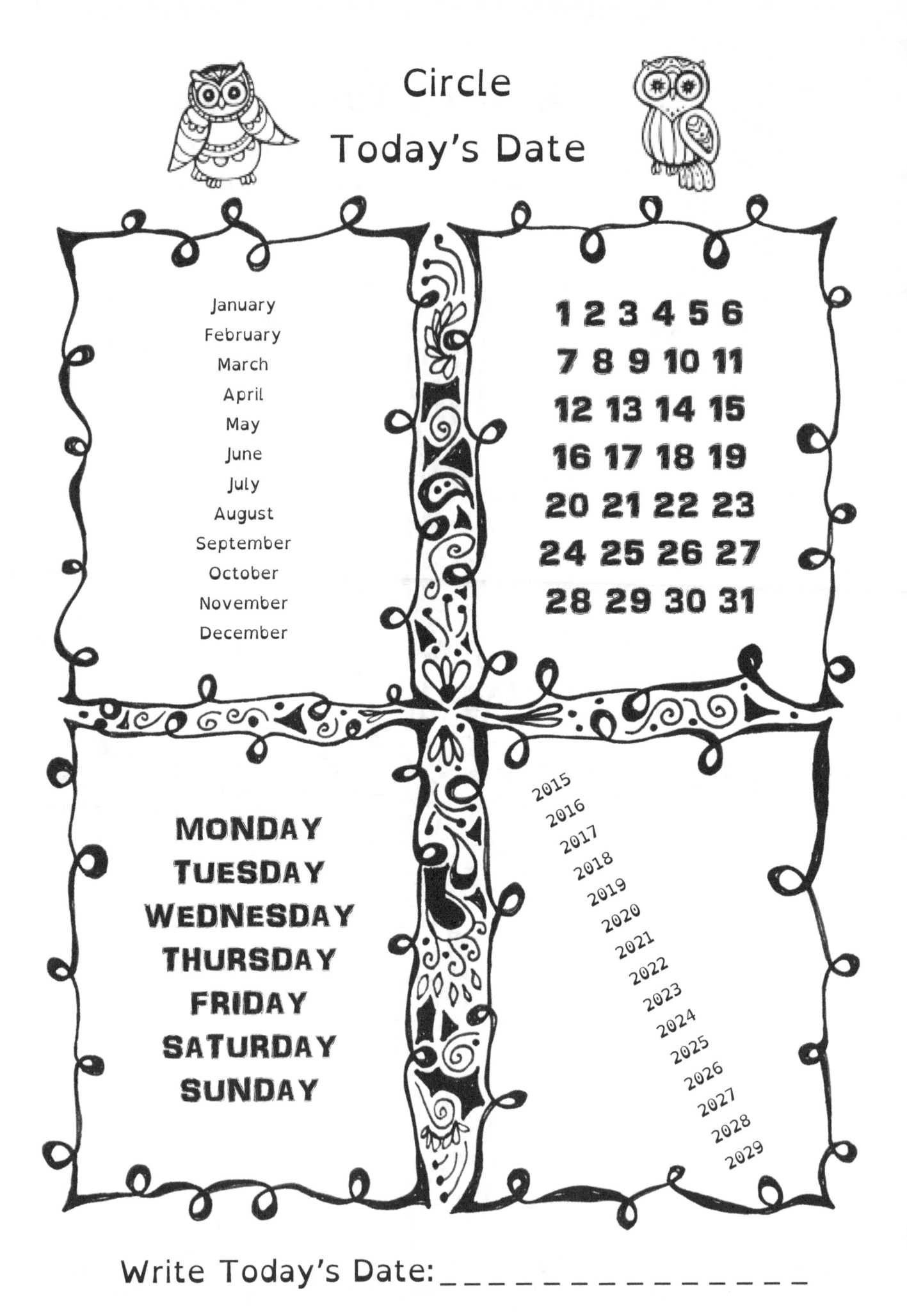

January
February
March
April
May
June
July
August
September
October
November
December

1 2 3 4 5 6
7 8 9 10 11
12 13 14 15
16 17 18 19
20 21 22 23
24 25 26 27
28 29 30 31

MONDAY
TUESDAY
WEDNESDAY
THURSDAY
FRIDAY
SATURDAY
SUNDAY

2015
2016
2017
2018
2019
2020
2021
2022
2023
2024
2025
2026
2027
2028
2029

Write Today's Date: _____

My Thinking Page

This is where you write down your ideas, goals, and plans - with a thankful heart!

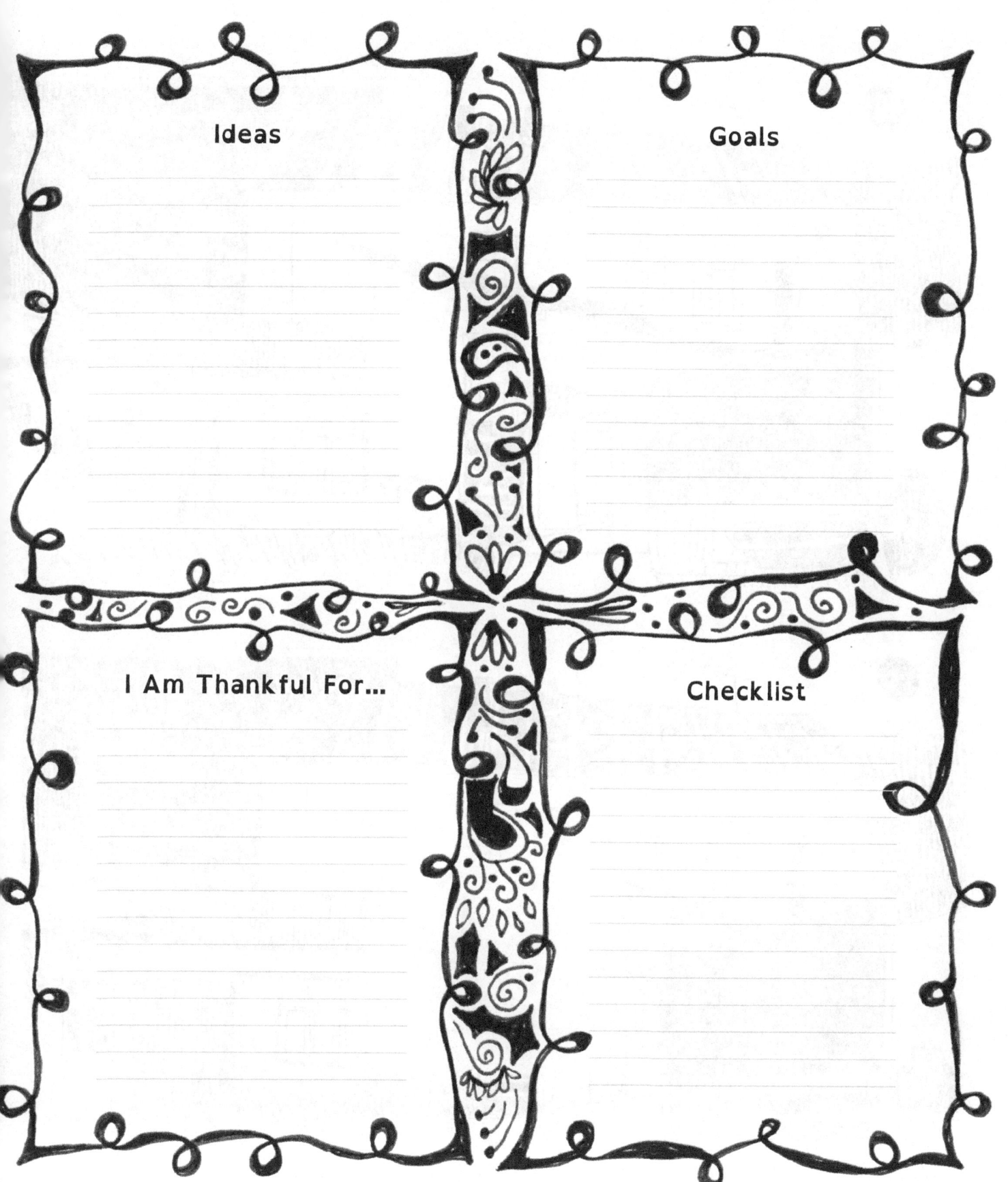

Ideas

Goals

I Am Thankful For...

Checklist

Art & Creativity Time

Learning a Skill

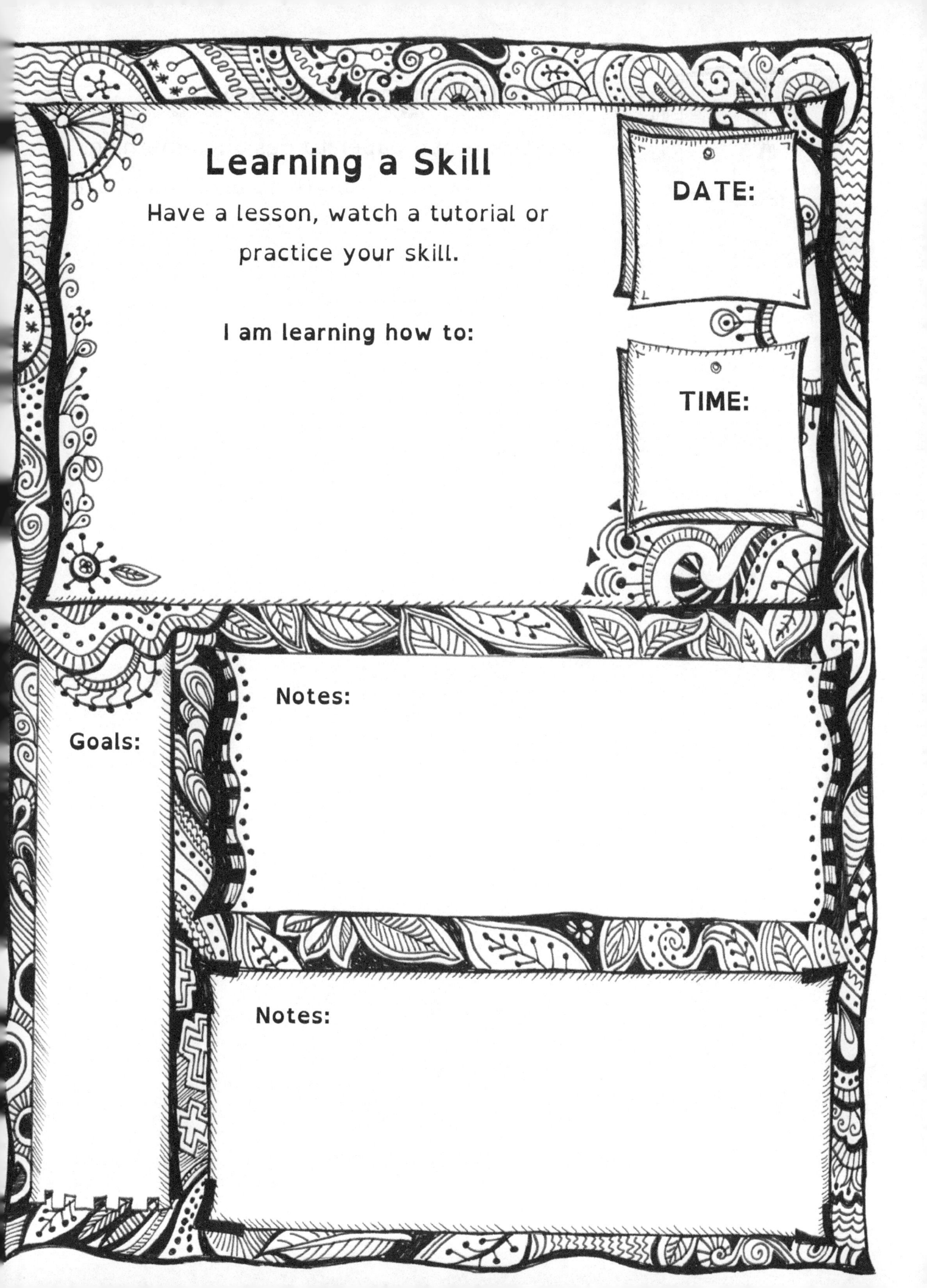

Have a lesson, watch a tutorial or practice your skill.

I am learning how to:

DATE:

TIME:

Goals:

Notes:

Notes:

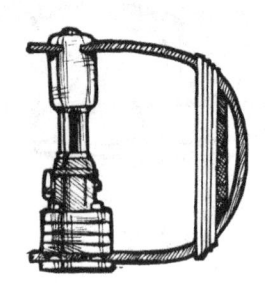

Design Something

Use this graph paper to design something.
If you can't think of anything design a house.

Copywork

Find an interesting paragraph in one of your books and copy it. Be diligent to make your writing look exactly like it does in the book.

TITLE:_____ **Page Number:**_____

_____
_____
_____
_____
_____
_____
_____
_____
_____
_____
_____
_____
_____
_____

Circle Today's Date

January
February
March
April
May
June
July
August
September
October
November
December

1 2 3 4 5 6
7 8 9 10 11
12 13 14 15
16 17 18 19
20 21 22 23
24 25 26 27
28 29 30 31

MONDAY
TUESDAY
WEDNESDAY
THURSDAY
FRIDAY
SATURDAY
SUNDAY

2015
2016
2017
2018
2019
2020
2021
2022
2023
2024
2025
2026
2027
2028
2029

Write Today's Date: _____

My Thinking Page

This is where you write down your ideas, goals, and plans - with a thankful heart!

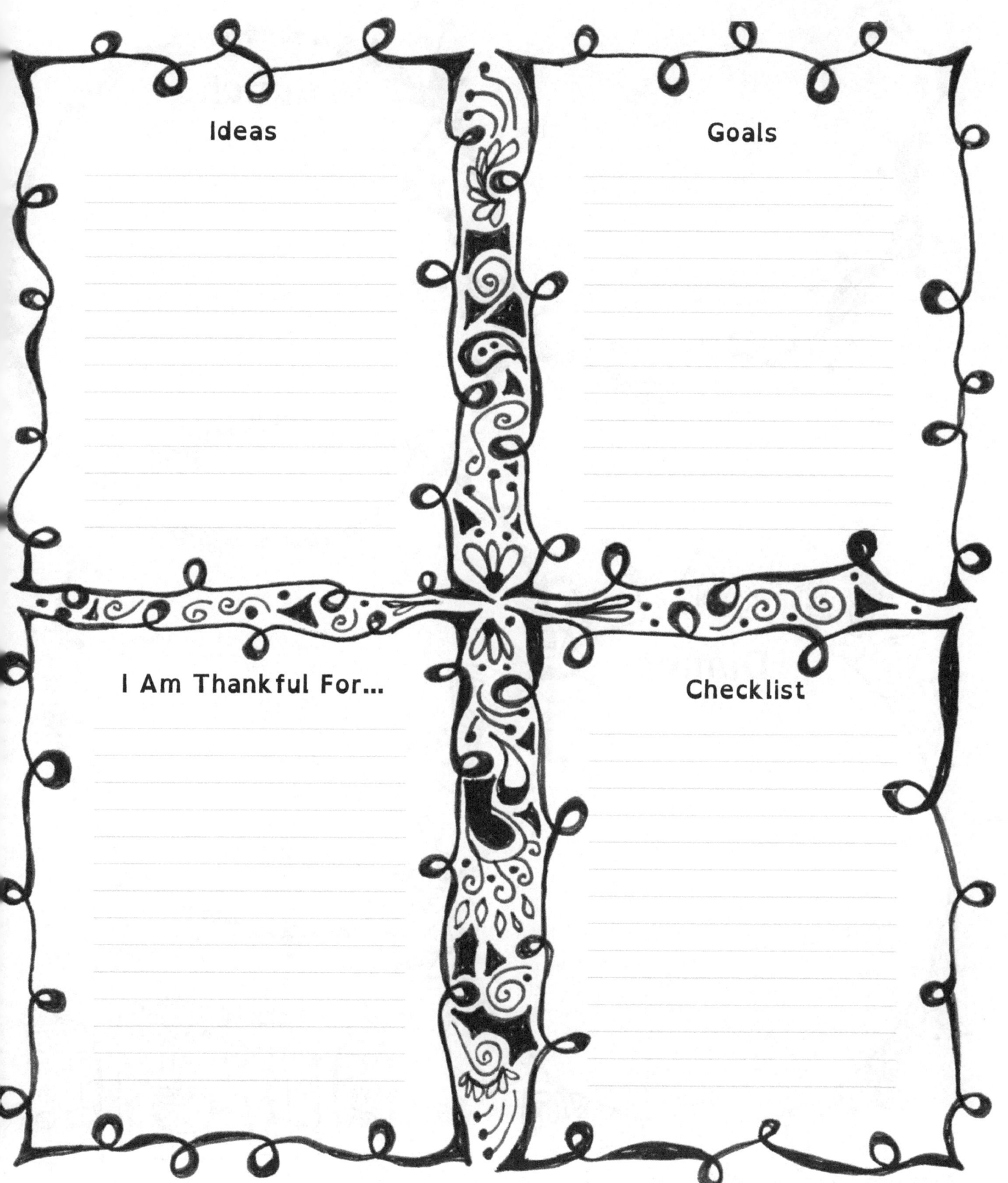

Ideas

Goals

I Am Thankful For...

Checklist

Draw a Meal PLAN

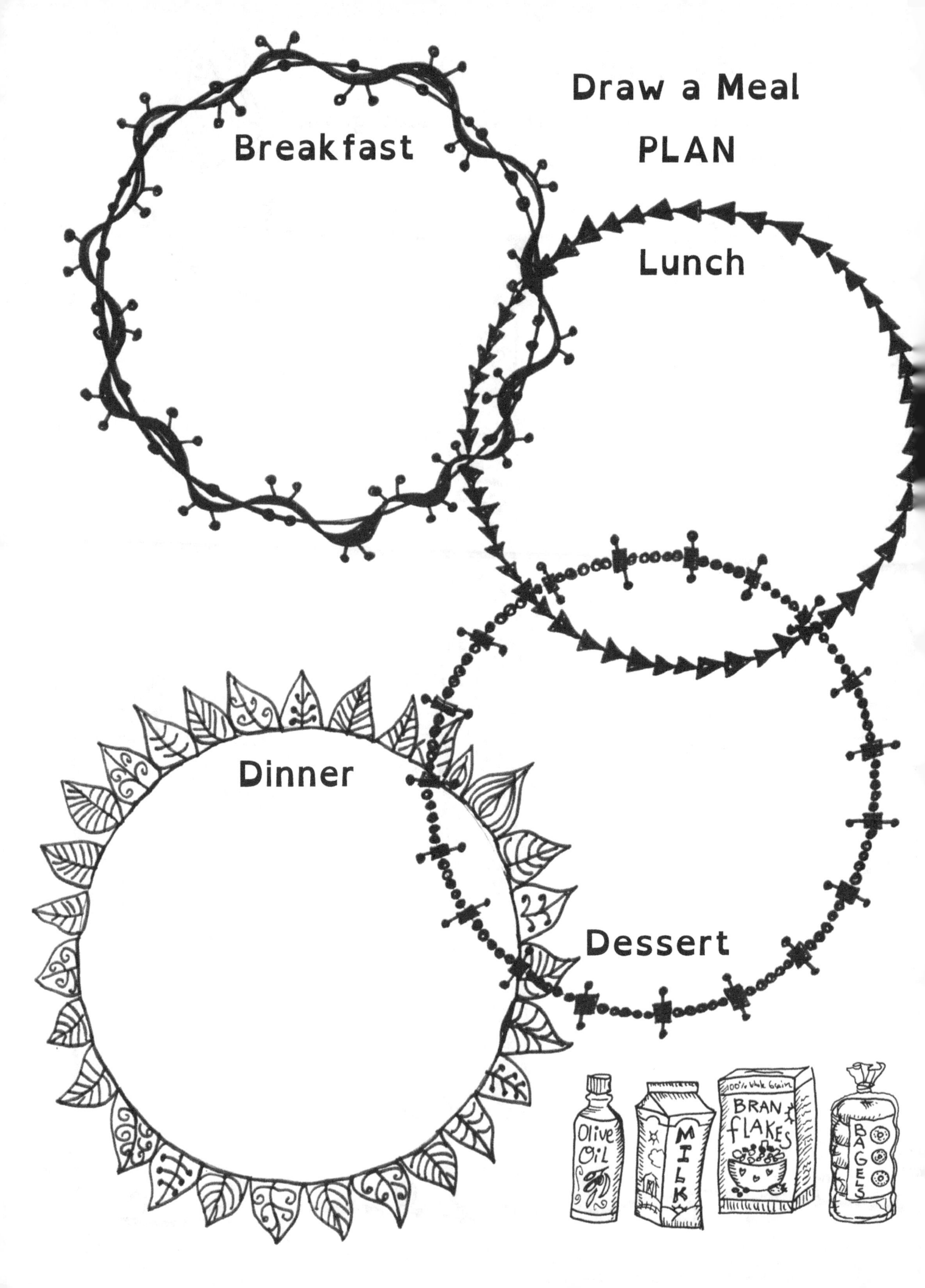

- Breakfast
- Lunch
- Dinner
- Dessert

Recipe:

_____

Serves:

Prep Time:

Ingredients:

Instructions:

Shopping List:

Open a cookbook, learn from mom or look online for some wonderful recipes!

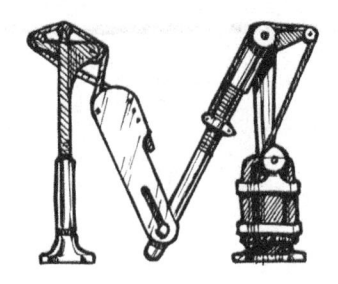

Math Practice

Watch a math tutorial or open up a math book.
You can practice math problems here.

Write & Draw about something that really happened.

_____
_____
_____
_____
_____
_____
_____
_____
_____

Reading Time - 1 Hour

Choose Four Books - Read from each book for 15 minutes.
Copy a sentence or picture from each book here:

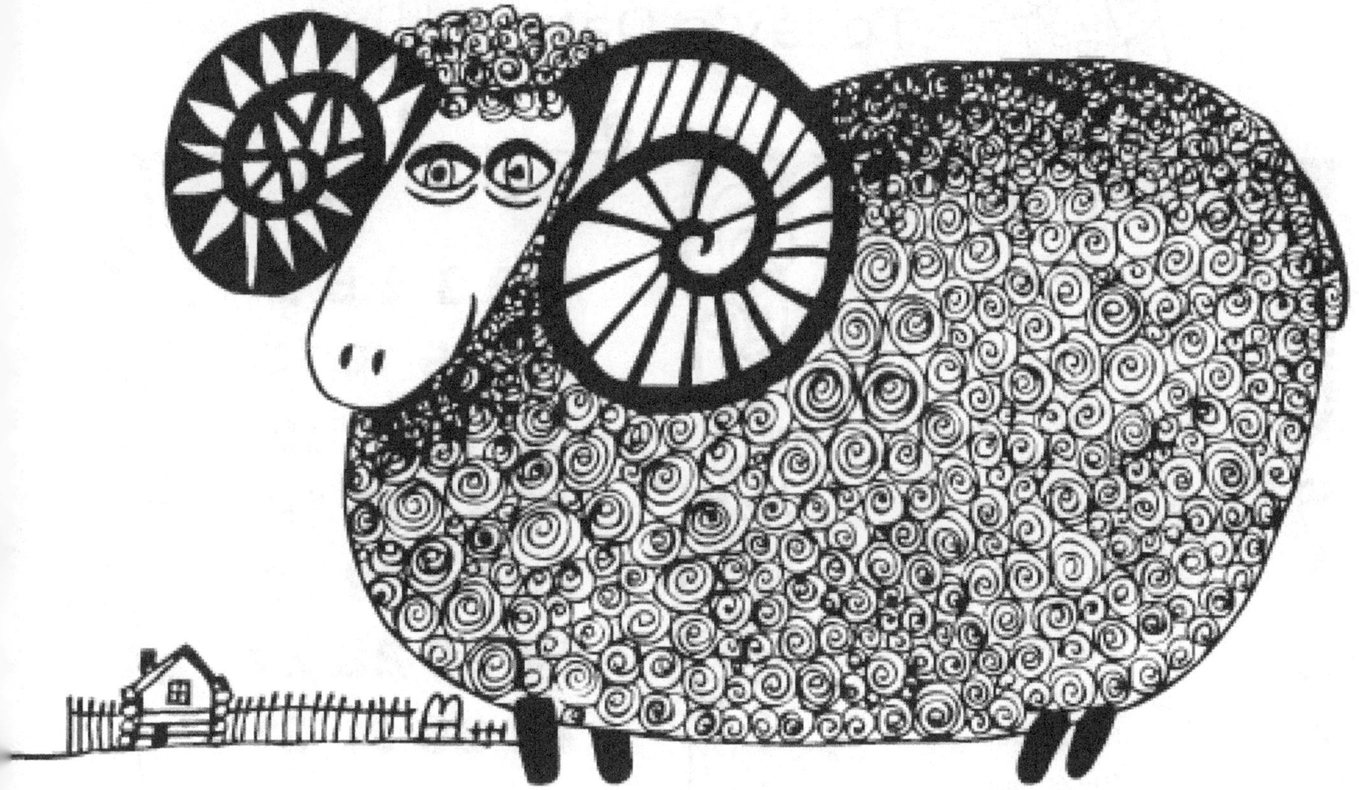

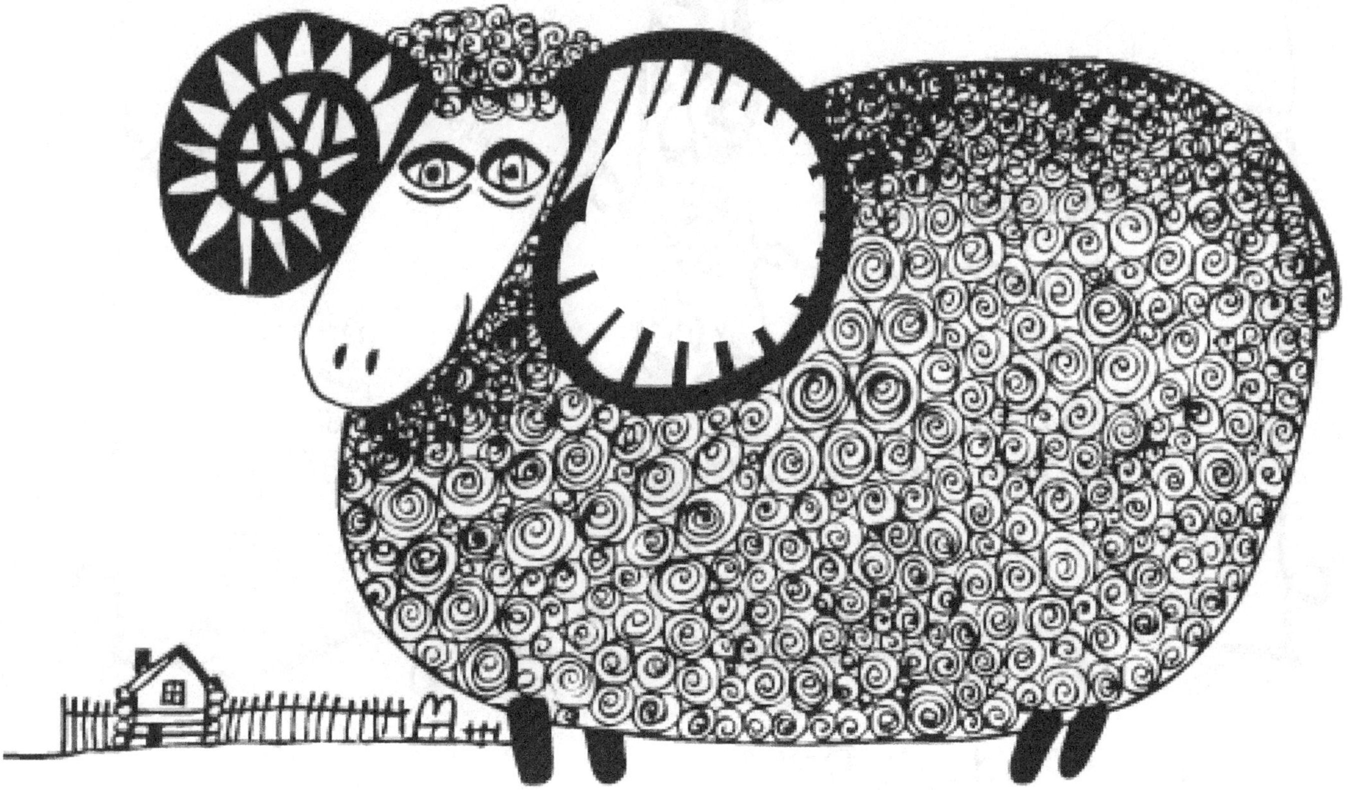

Circle Today's Date

January
February
March
April
May
June
July
August
September
October
November
December

1 2 3 4 5 6
7 8 9 10 11
12 13 14 15
16 17 18 19
20 21 22 23
24 25 26 27
28 29 30 31

MONDAY
TUESDAY
WEDNESDAY
THURSDAY
FRIDAY
SATURDAY
SUNDAY

2015
2016
2017
2018
2019
2020
2021
2022
2023
2024
2025
2026
2027
2028
2029

Write Today's Date: _____

My Illustrated TO-DO List

Film Study

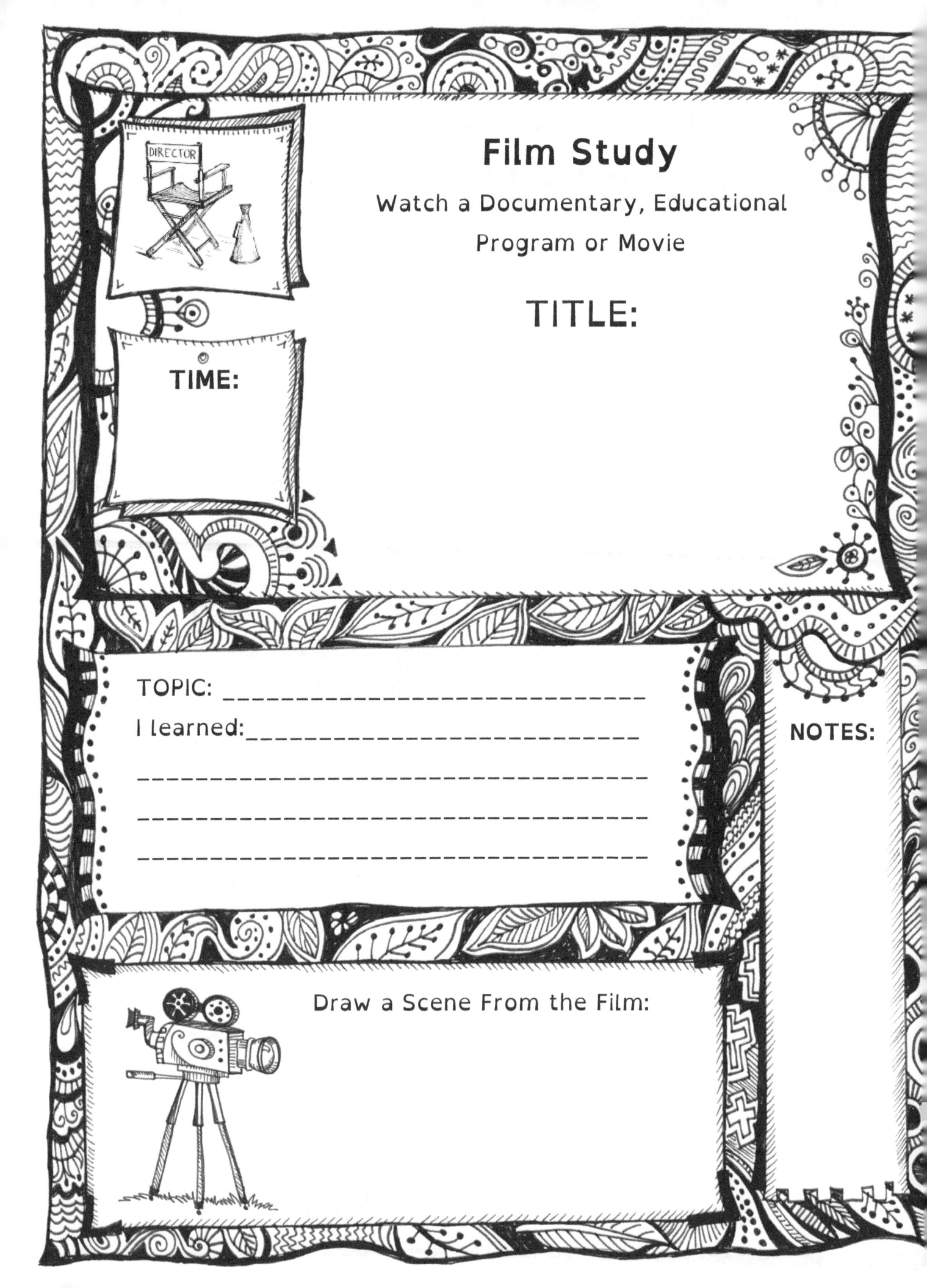

Watch a Documentary, Educational Program or Movie

TITLE:

TIME:

TOPIC: _____

I learned: _____

_____

_____

_____

NOTES:

Draw a Scene From the Film:

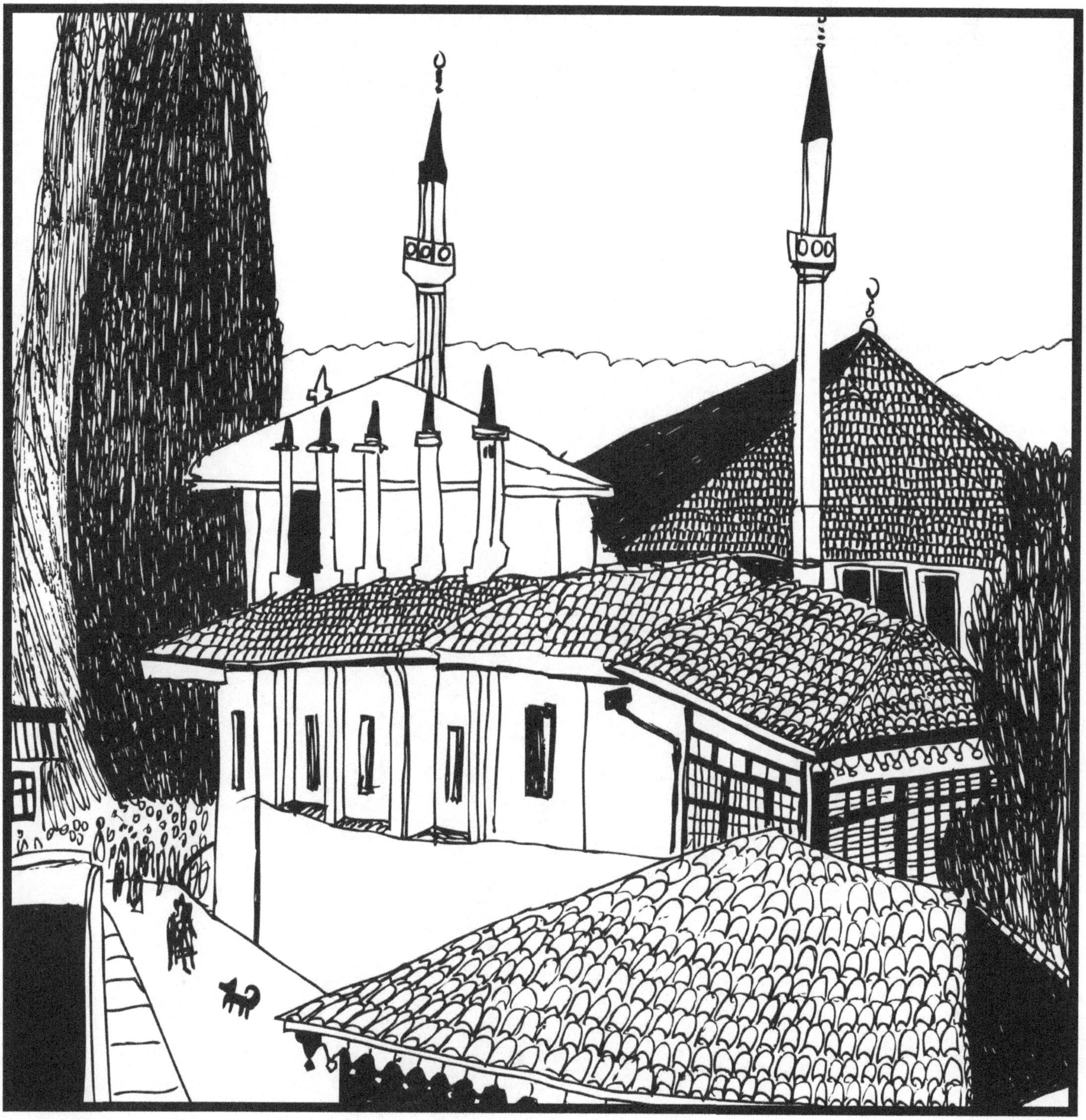

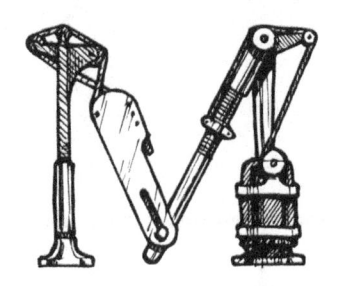

Math Practice

Watch a math tutorial or open up a math book.
You can practice math problems here.

Copywork

Find an interesting paragraph in one of your books and copy it. Be diligent to make your writing look exactly like it does in the book.

TITLE:_____ **Page Number:**_____

Sketch a Picture

Look through your library books and find something to draw.

Circle Today's Date

January
February
March
April
May
June
July
August
September
October
November
December

1 2 3 4 5 6
7 8 9 10 11
12 13 14 15
16 17 18 19
20 21 22 23
24 25 26 27
28 29 30 31

MONDAY
TUESDAY
WEDNESDAY
THURSDAY
FRIDAY
SATURDAY
SUNDAY

2015
2016
2017
2018
2019
2020
2021
2022
2023
2024
2025
2026
2027
2028
2029

Write Today's Date: _____

My Thinking Page

This is where you write down your ideas, goals, and plans - with a thankful heart!

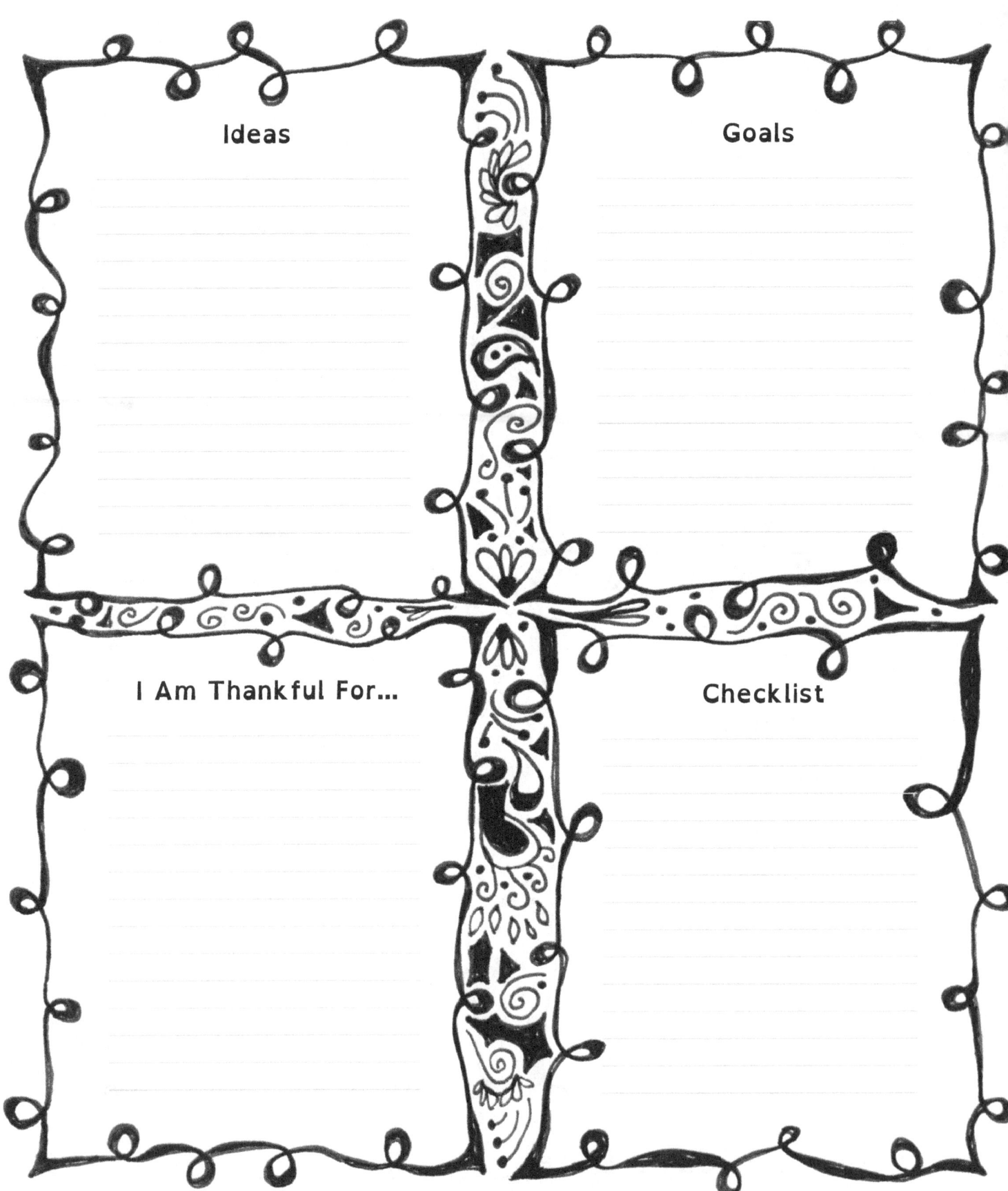

Ideas

Goals

I Am Thankful For...

Checklist

Nature Study

Go outside and make a realistic drawing of something you find in nature.

Creative Writing

Draw a picture below.
Write a poem or short story about it.

TITLE: _____

_____
_____
_____
_____
_____
_____
_____
_____
_____
_____
_____
_____
_____
_____

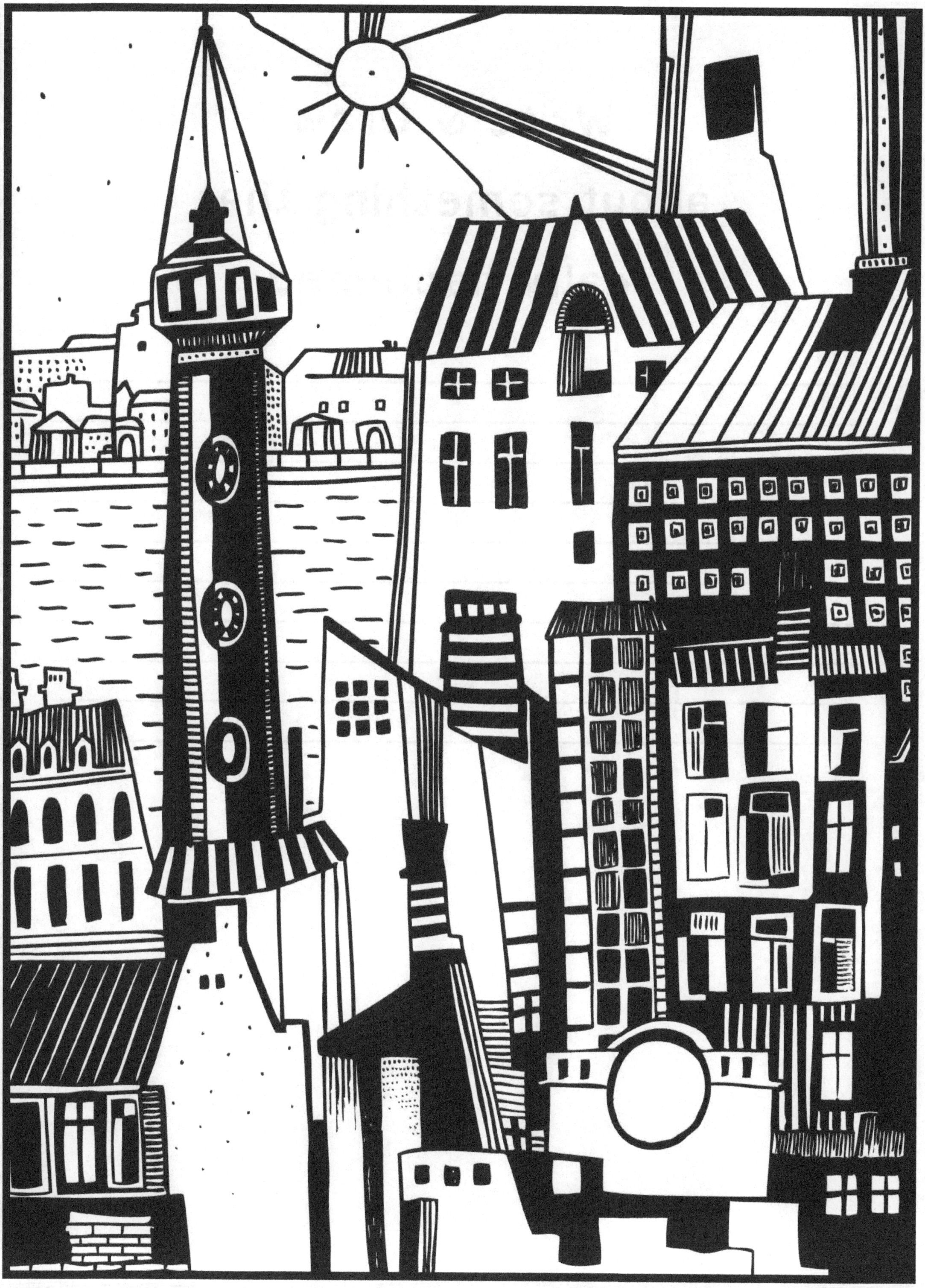

Write & Draw about something that really happened.

_____
_____
_____
_____
_____
_____
_____
_____
_____

Reading Time - 1 Hour

Choose Four Books - Read from each book for 15 minutes.
Copy a sentence or picture from each book here:

Circle Today's Date

January
February
March
April
May
June
July
August
September
October
November
December

1 2 3 4 5 6
7 8 9 10 11
12 13 14 15
16 17 18 19
20 21 22 23
24 25 26 27
28 29 30 31

MONDAY
TUESDAY
WEDNESDAY
THURSDAY
FRIDAY
SATURDAY
SUNDAY

2015
2016
2017
2018
2019
2020
2021
2022
2023
2024
2025
2026
2027
2028
2029

Write Today's Date: _____

Art & Creativity Time

Creative Writing

Draw a picture below.
Write a poem or short story about it.

TITLE: _____

_____
_____
_____
_____
_____
_____
_____
_____
_____
_____
_____
_____
_____
_____

Spelling Time

Find 20 Words with 7 letters each.
Look in your books for words.
Write the words here:

_____ _____

_____ _____

_____ _____

_____ _____

_____ _____

_____ _____

_____ _____

_____ _____

_____ _____

_____ _____

Film Study

Watch a Documentary, Educational Program or Movie

TITLE:

TIME:

TOPIC: _____

I learned: _____

_____

_____

_____

NOTES:

Draw a Scene From the Film:

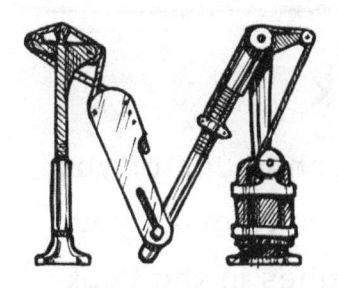

Math Practice

Watch a math tutorial or open up a math book.
You can practice math problems here.

Copywork

Find an interesting paragraph in one of your books and copy it. Be diligent to make your writing look exactly like it does in the book.

TITLE:_____ Page Number:_____

Sketch a Picture

Look through your library books and find something to draw.

Circle Today's Date

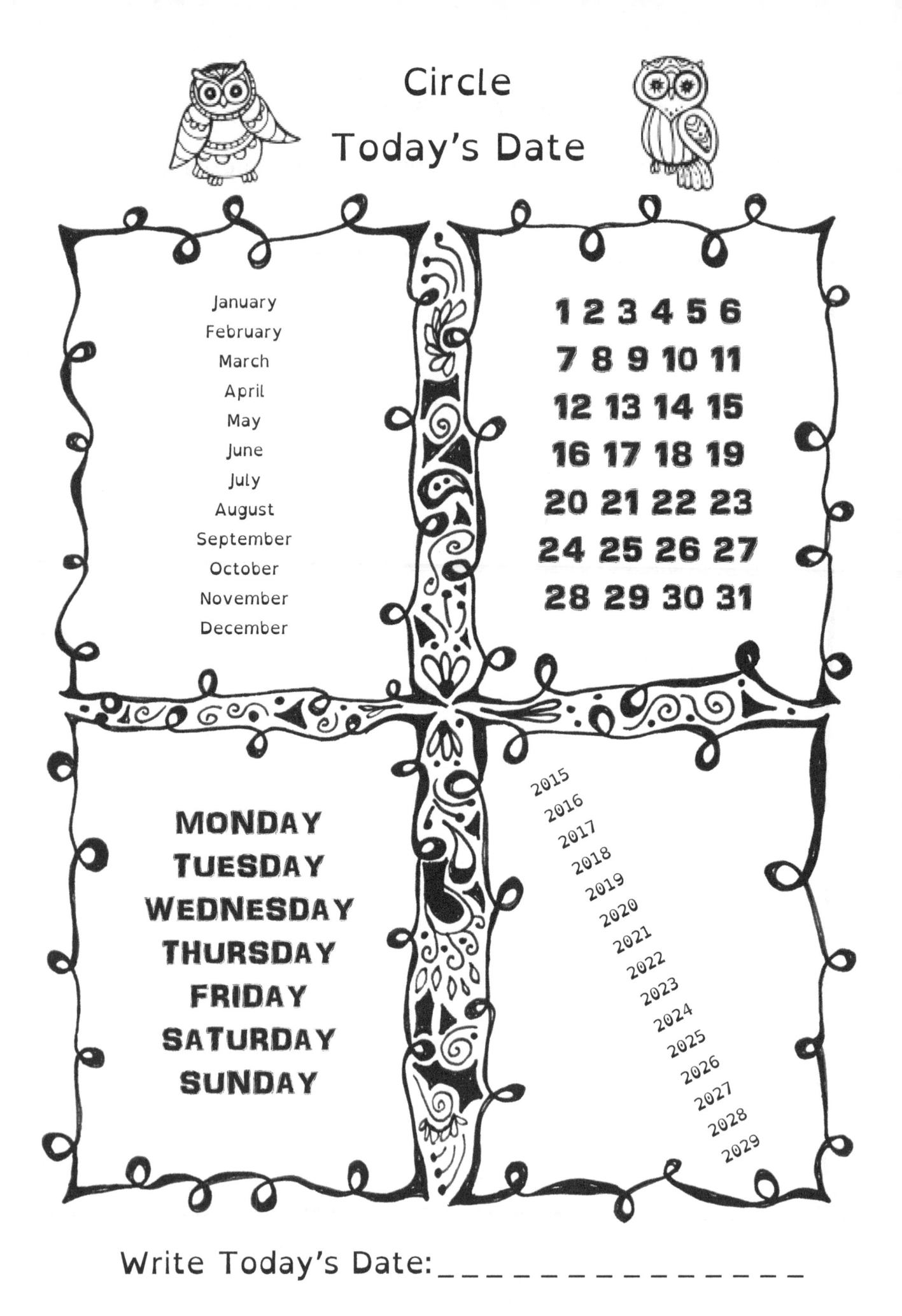

January
February
March
April
May
June
July
August
September
October
November
December

1 2 3 4 5 6
7 8 9 10 11
12 13 14 15
16 17 18 19
20 21 22 23
24 25 26 27
28 29 30 31

MONDAY
TUESDAY
WEDNESDAY
THURSDAY
FRIDAY
SATURDAY
SUNDAY

2015
2016
2017
2018
2019
2020
2021
2022
2023
2024
2025
2026
2027
2028
2029

Write Today's Date: _____

My Thinking Page

This is where you write down your ideas, goals, and plans - with a thankful heart!

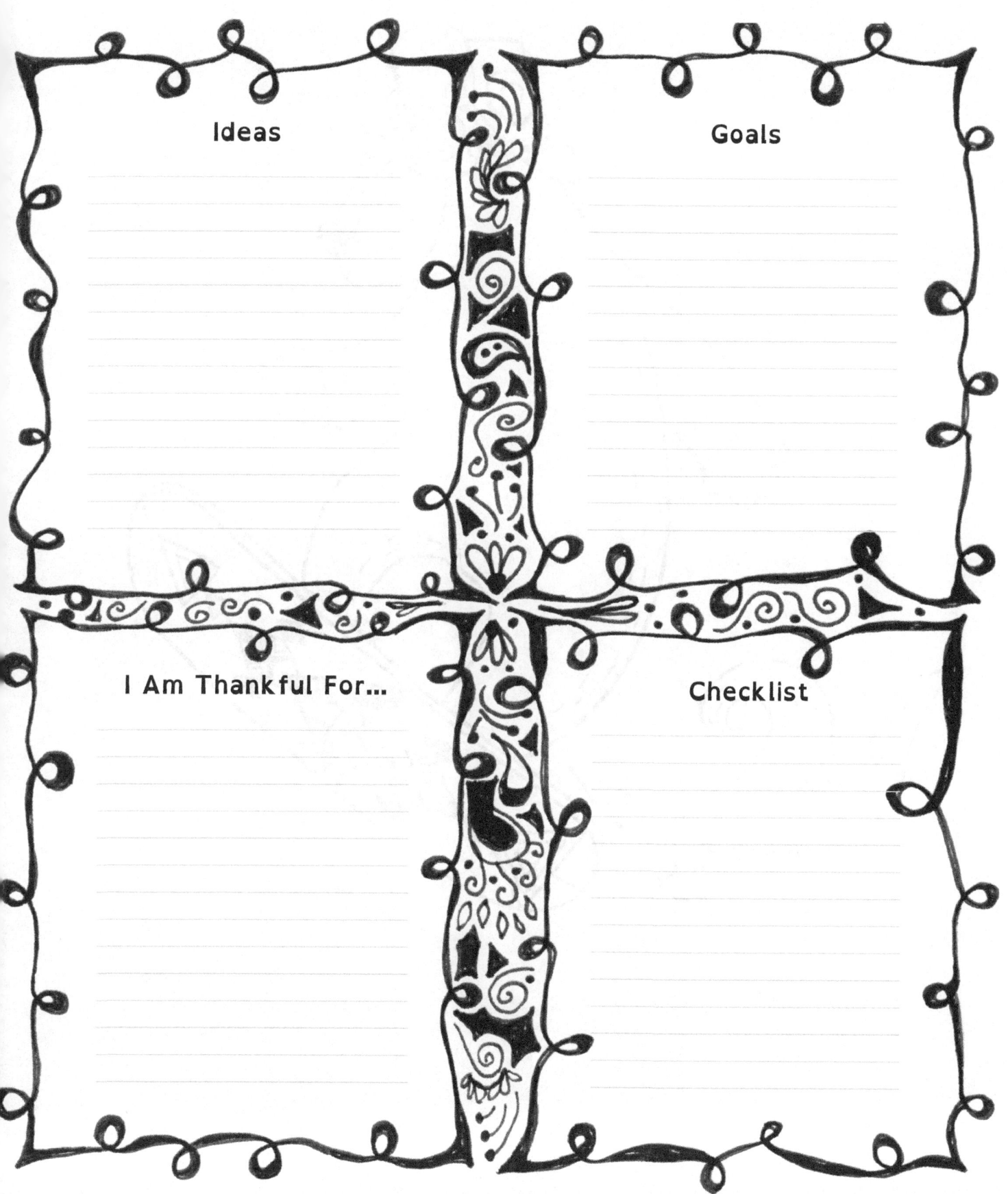

Ideas

Goals

I Am Thankful For...

Checklist

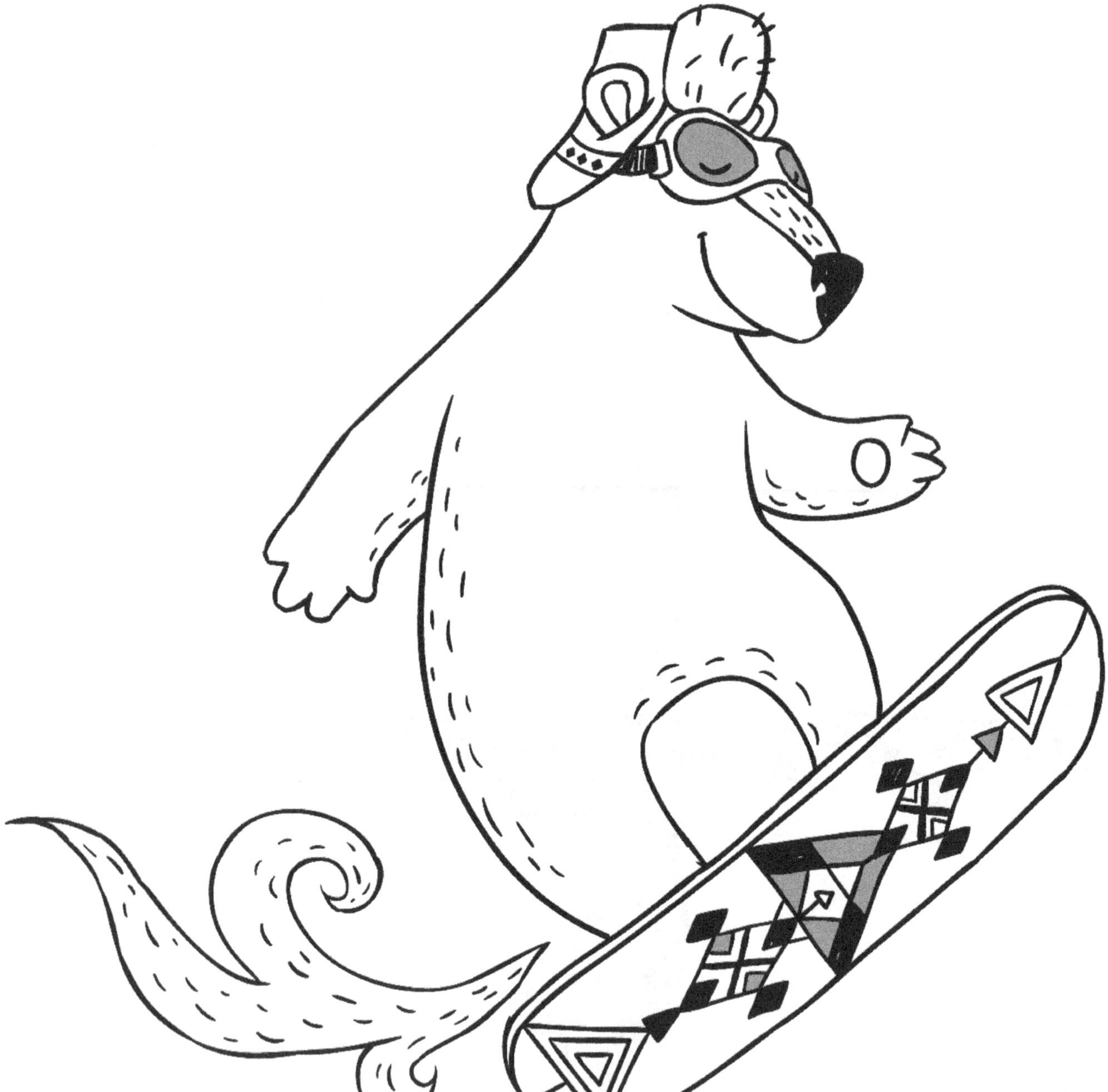

Nature Study

Go outside and make a realistic drawing of something you find in nature.

Creative Writing

Draw a picture below.
Write a poem or short story about it.

TITLE: _____

_____
_____
_____
_____
_____
_____
_____
_____
_____
_____
_____
_____
_____
_____
_____

My Illustrated TO-DO List

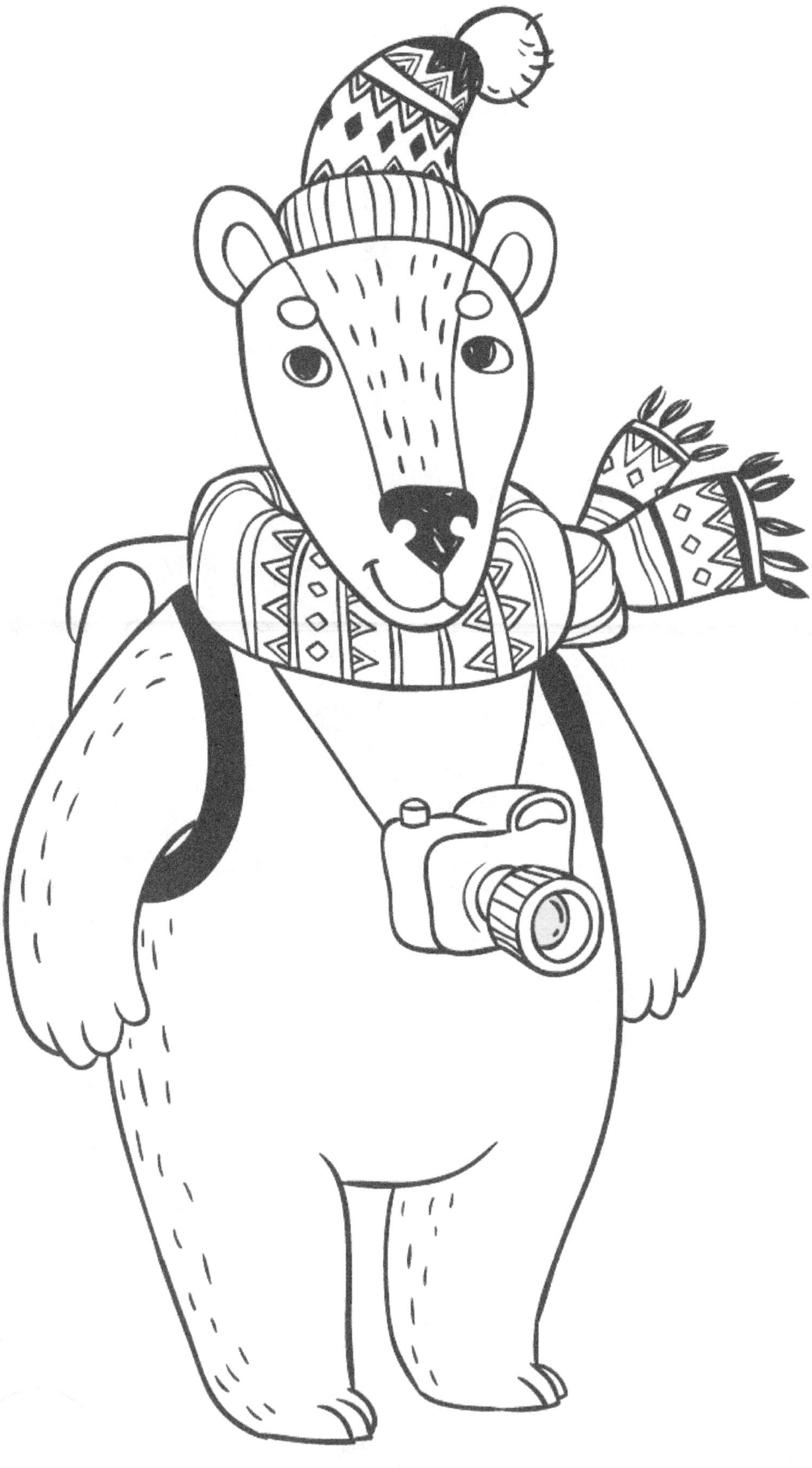

Circle Today's Date

January
February
March
April
May
June
July
August
September
October
November
December

1 2 3 4 5 6
7 8 9 10 11
12 13 14 15
16 17 18 19
20 21 22 23
24 25 26 27
28 29 30 31

MONDAY
TUESDAY
WEDNESDAY
THURSDAY
FRIDAY
SATURDAY
SUNDAY

2015
2016
2017
2018
2019
2020
2021
2022
2023
2024
2025
2026
2027
2028
2029

Write Today's Date: _____

Sketch a Picture

Look through your library books and find something to draw.

Film Study

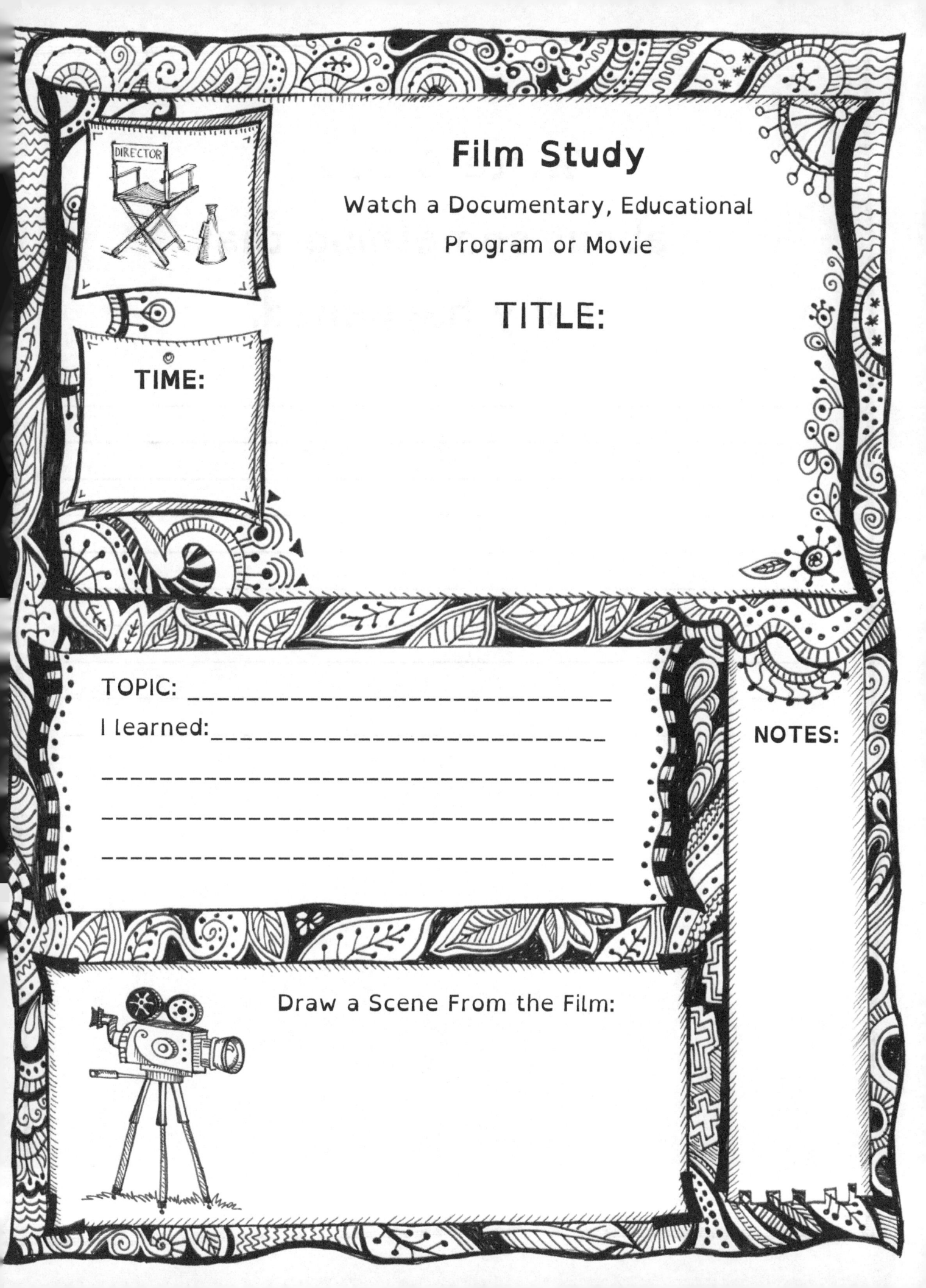

Watch a Documentary, Educational Program or Movie

TITLE:

TIME:

TOPIC: _____

I learned: _____

_____

_____

_____

NOTES:

Draw a Scene From the Film:

Write & Draw about something that really happened.

_____
_____
_____
_____
_____
_____
_____
_____

Spelling Time

Find 20 Words with **6** letters each.
Look in your books for words.
Write the words here:

_____   _____
_____   _____
_____   _____
_____   _____
_____   _____
_____   _____
_____   _____
_____   _____
_____   _____
_____   _____

Learning a Skill

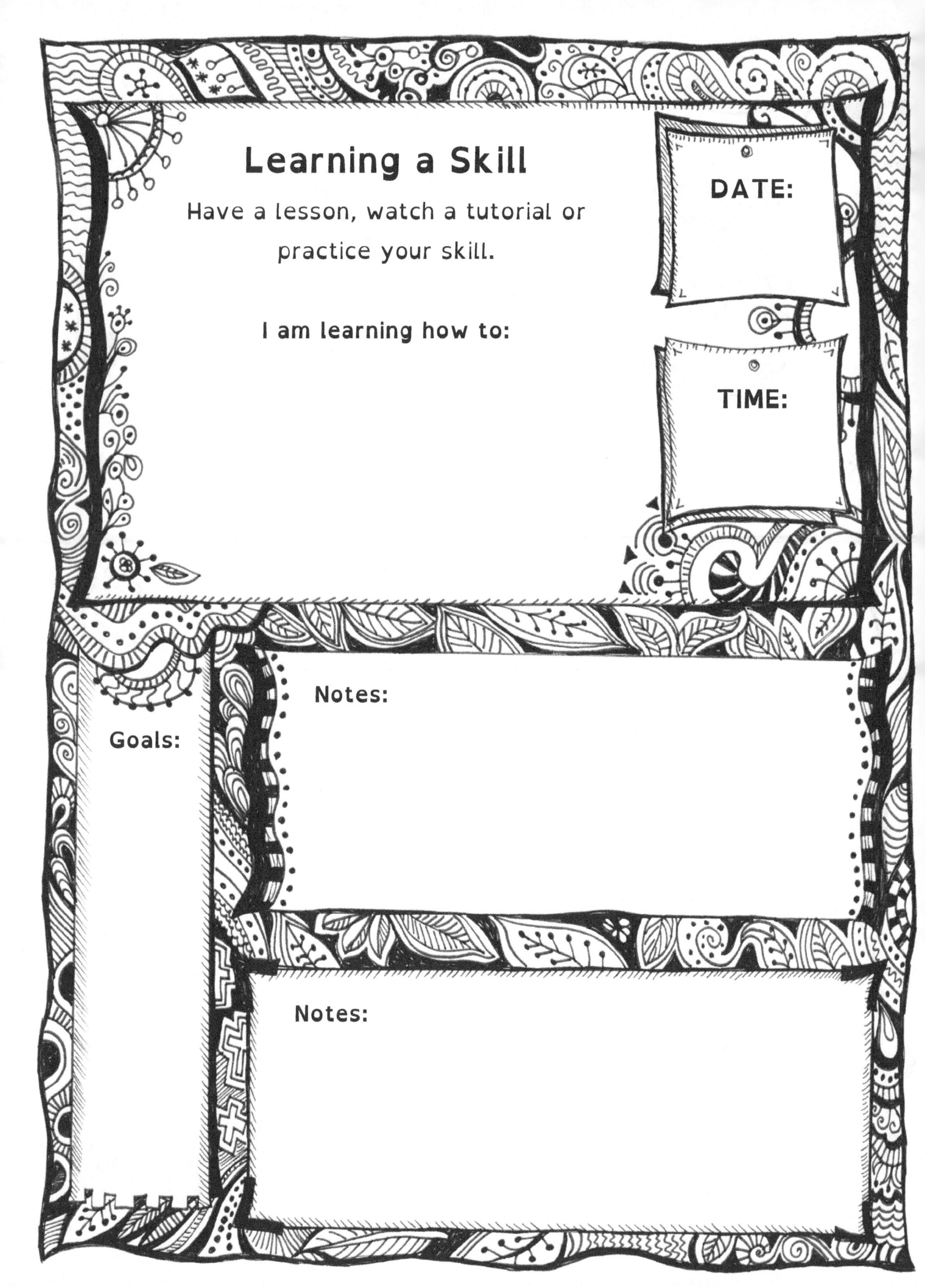

Have a lesson, watch a tutorial or practice your skill.

I am learning how to:

DATE:

TIME:

Goals:

Notes:

Notes:

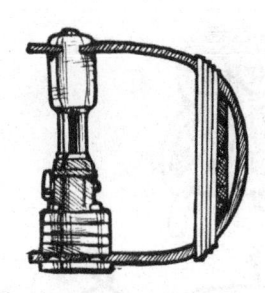

Design Something

Use this graph paper to design something.
If you can't think of anything design a house.

Circle Today's Date

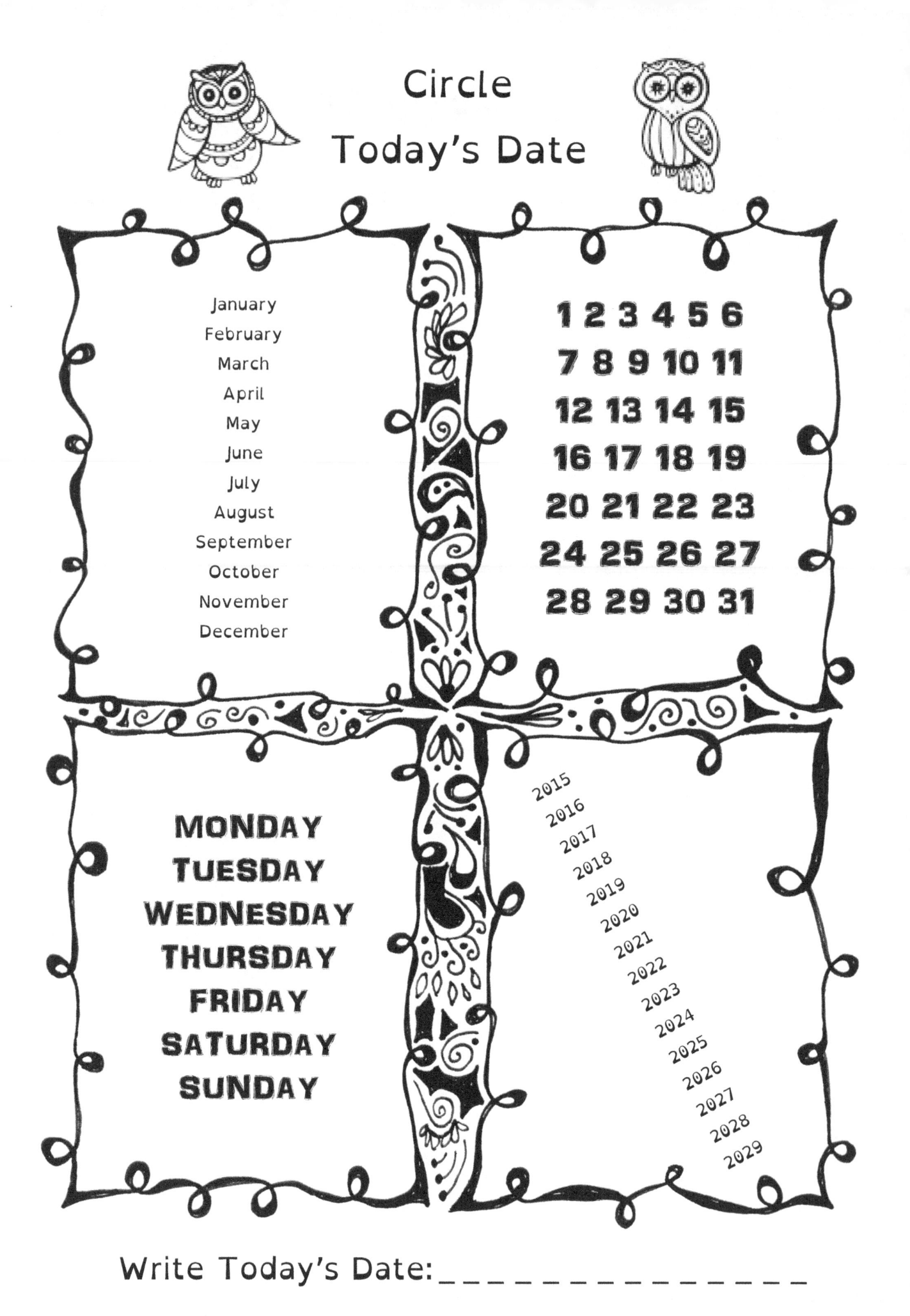

January
February
March
April
May
June
July
August
September
October
November
December

1 2 3 4 5 6
7 8 9 10 11
12 13 14 15
16 17 18 19
20 21 22 23
24 25 26 27
28 29 30 31

MONDAY
TUESDAY
WEDNESDAY
THURSDAY
FRIDAY
SATURDAY
SUNDAY

2015
2016
2017
2018
2019
2020
2021
2022
2023
2024
2025
2026
2027
2028
2029

Write Today's Date: _____

My Thinking Page

This is where you write down your ideas, goals, and plans - with a thankful heart!

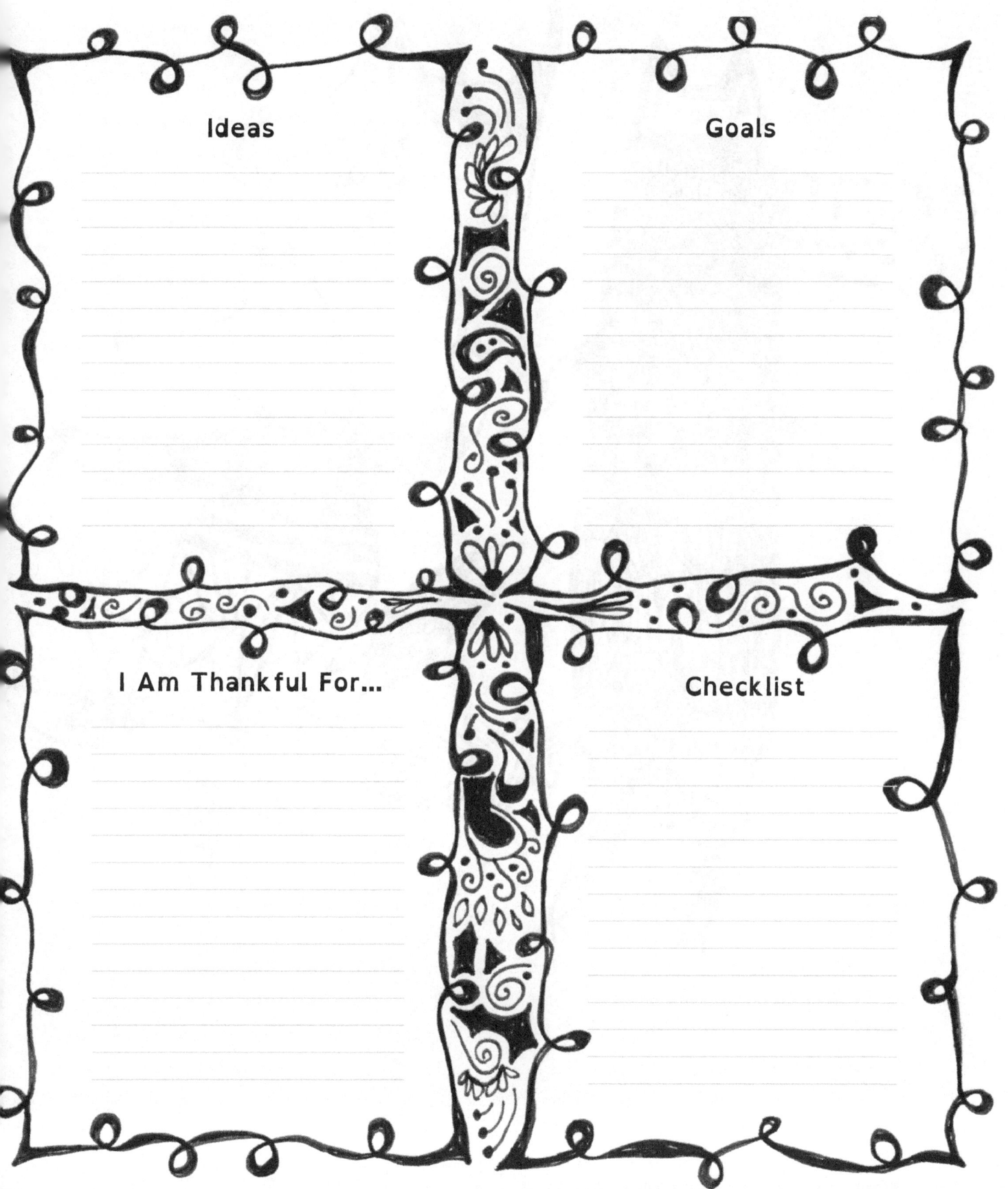

Ideas

Goals

I Am Thankful For...

Checklist

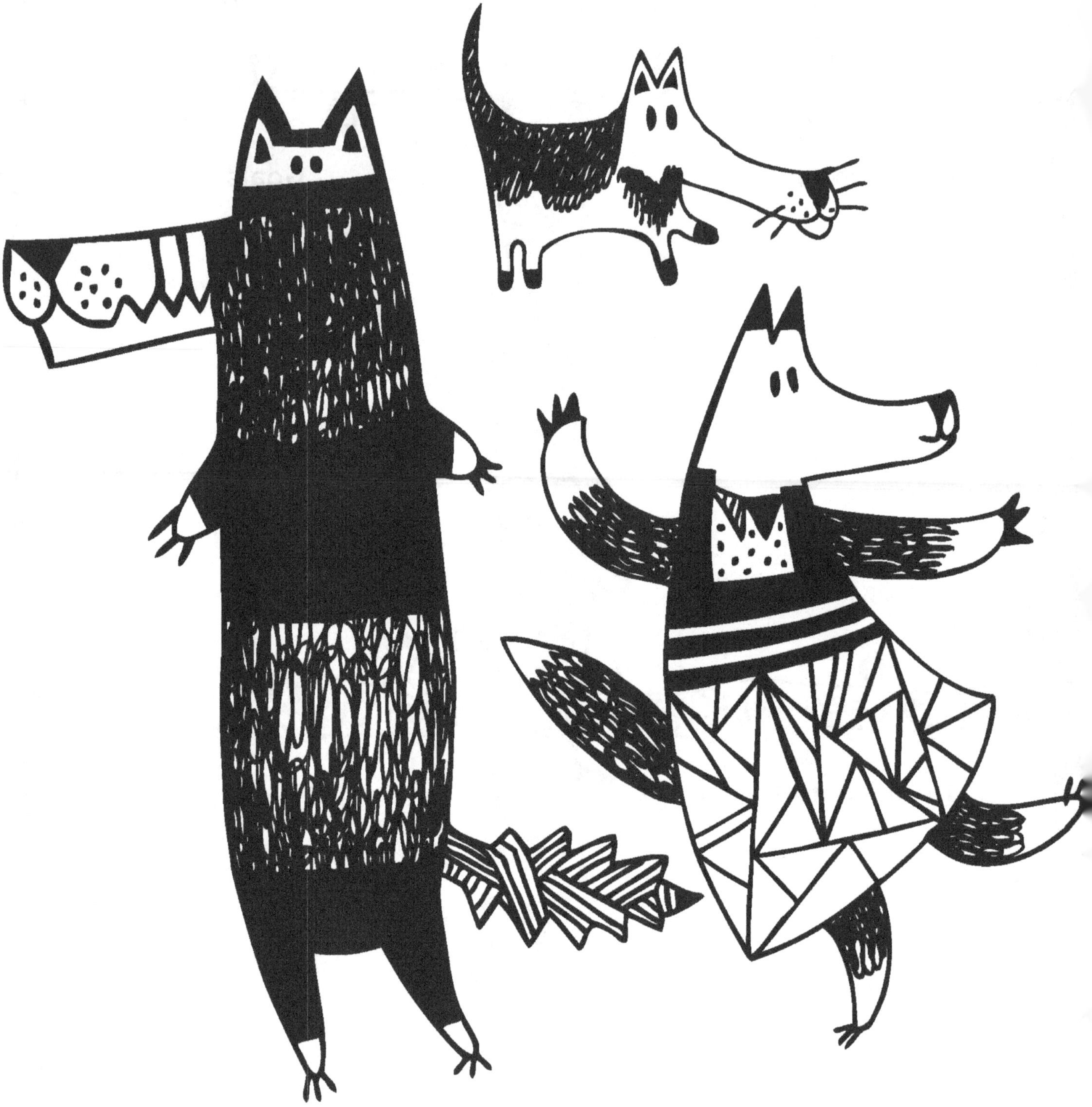

Learning a Skill

Have a lesson, watch a tutorial or practice your skill.

I am learning how to:

DATE:

TIME:

Goals:

Notes:

Notes:

Write & Draw about something that really happened.

Nature Study

Go outside and make a realistic drawing of something you find in nature.

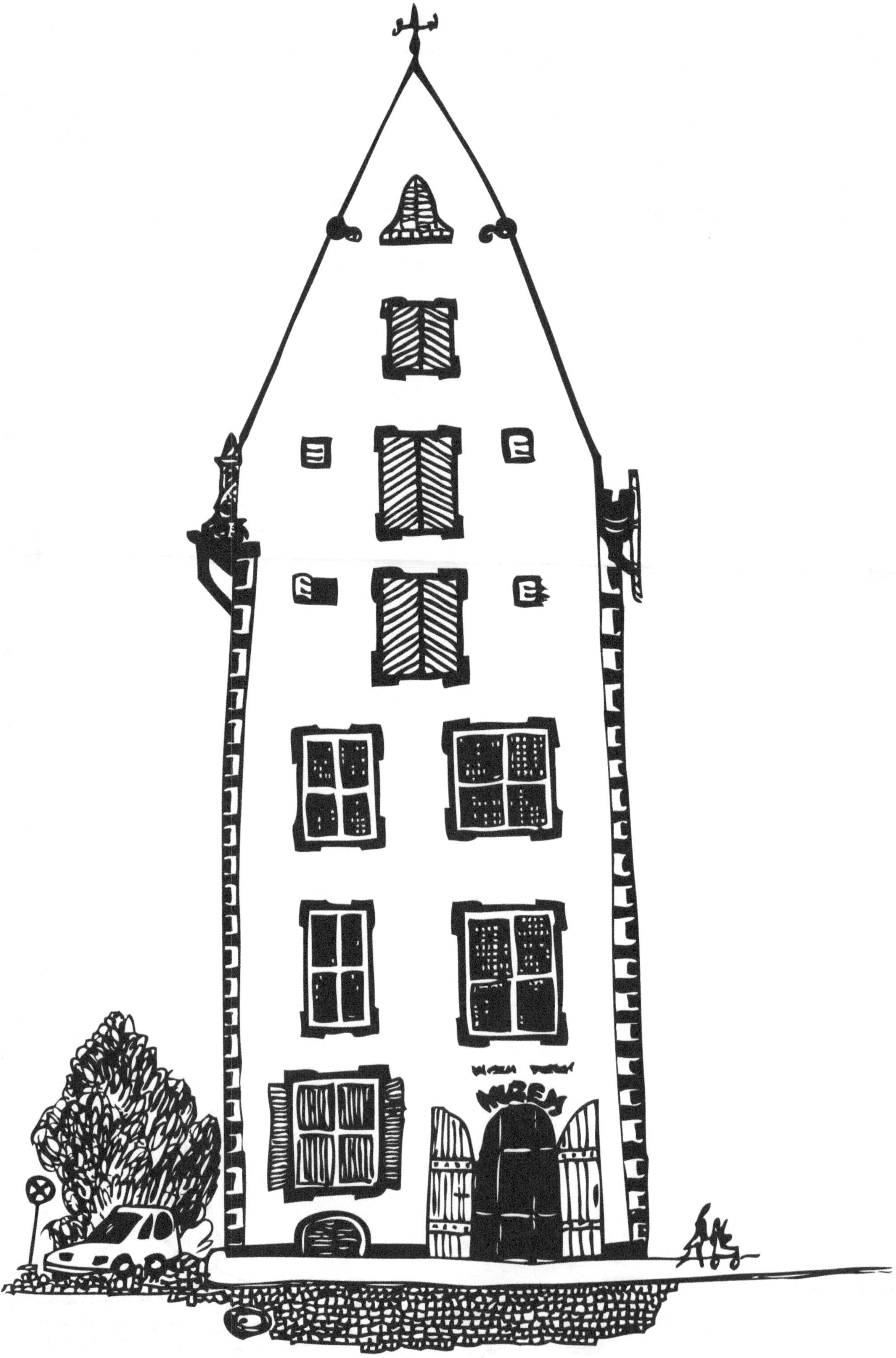

Reading Time - 1 Hour

Choose Four Books - Read from each book for 15 minutes.
Copy a sentence or picture from each book here:

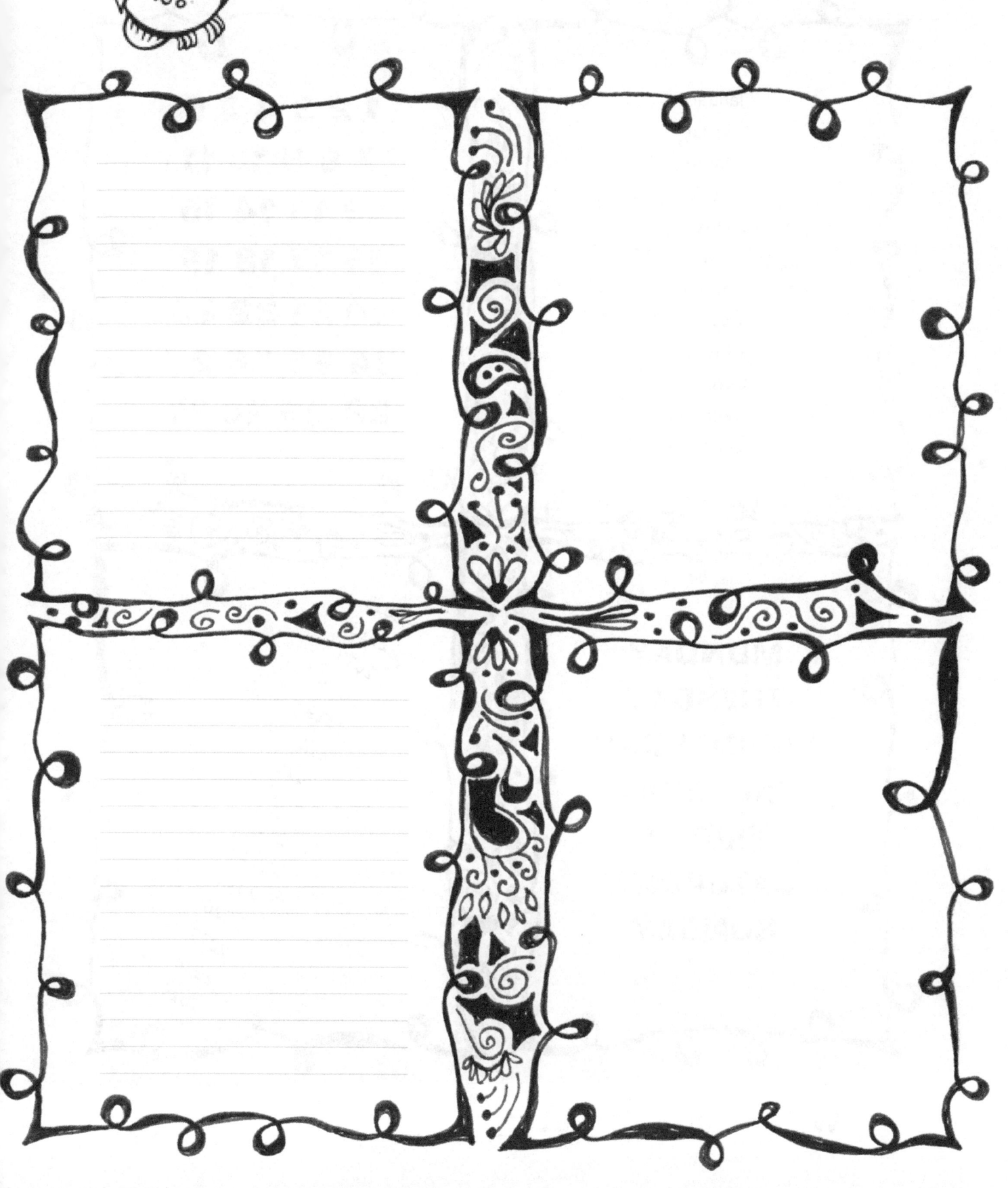

Circle Today's Date

January
February
March
April
May
June
July
August
September
October
November
December

1 2 3 4 5 6
7 8 9 10 11
12 13 14 15
16 17 18 19
20 21 22 23
24 25 26 27
28 29 30 31

MONDAY
TUESDAY
WEDNESDAY
THURSDAY
FRIDAY
SATURDAY
SUNDAY

2015
2016
2017
2018
2019
2020
2021
2022
2023
2024
2025
2026
2027
2028
2029

Write Today's Date: _____

My Illustrated TO-DO List

Film Study

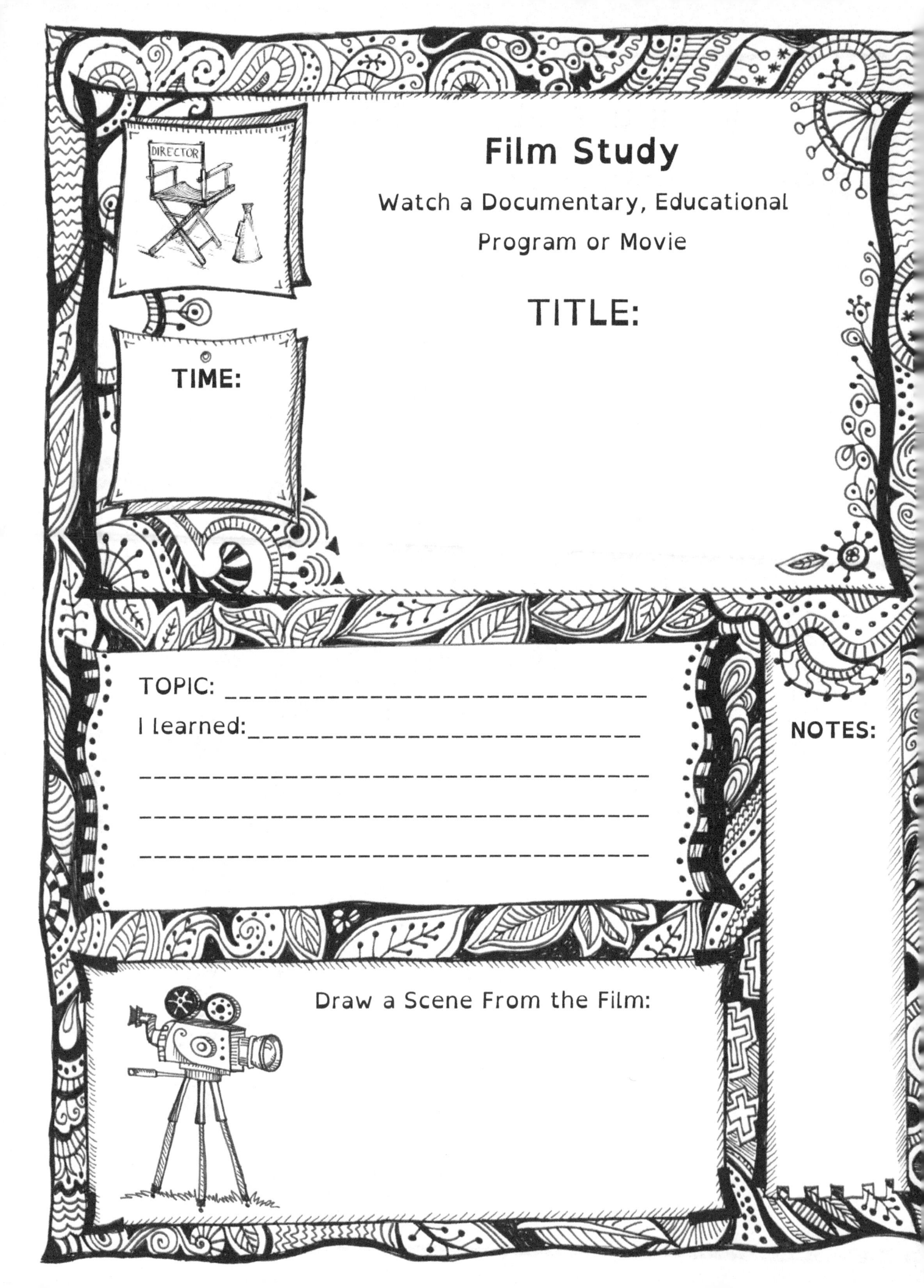

Watch a Documentary, Educational Program or Movie

TITLE:

TIME:

TOPIC: _____

I learned: _____

_____

_____

_____

NOTES:

Draw a Scene From the Film:

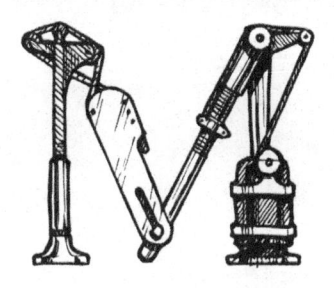

Math Practice

Watch a math tutorial or open up a math book.
You can practice math problems here.

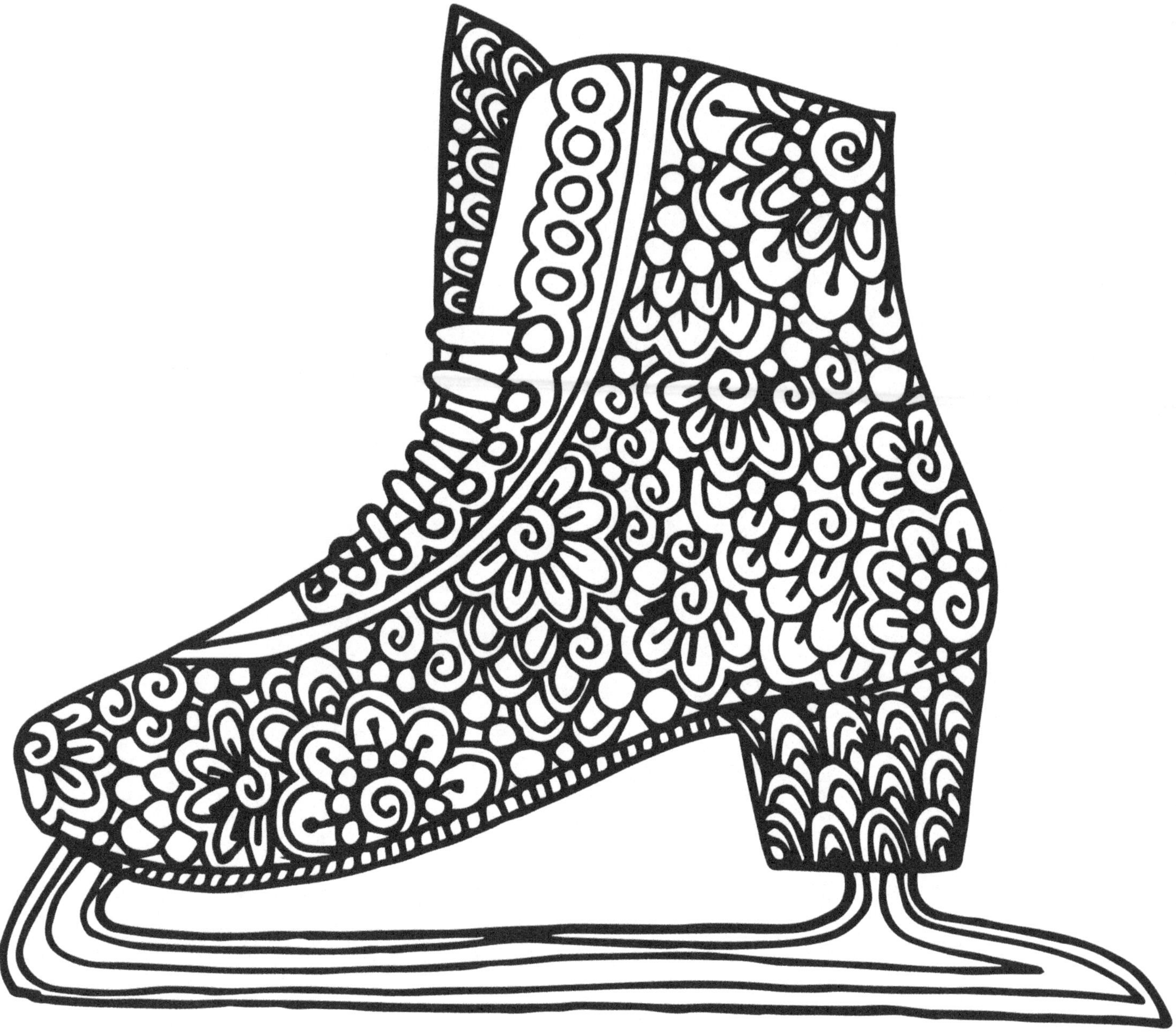

Copywork

Find an interesting paragraph in one of your books and copy it. Be diligent to make your writing look exactly like it does in the book.

TITLE:_____   Page Number:_____

Learning a Skill

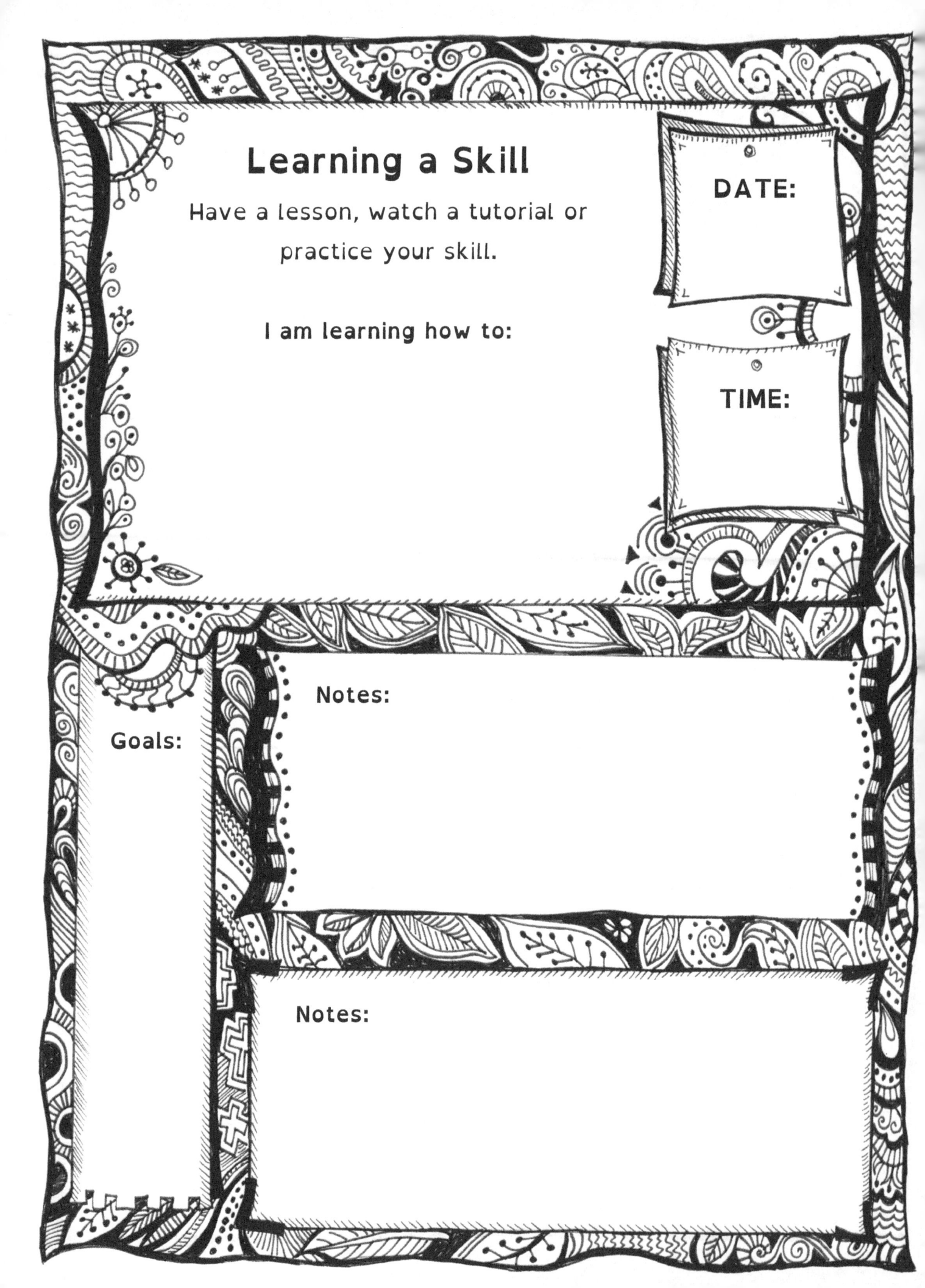

Have a lesson, watch a tutorial or practice your skill.

I am learning how to:

DATE:

TIME:

Goals:

Notes:

Notes:

Circle Today's Date

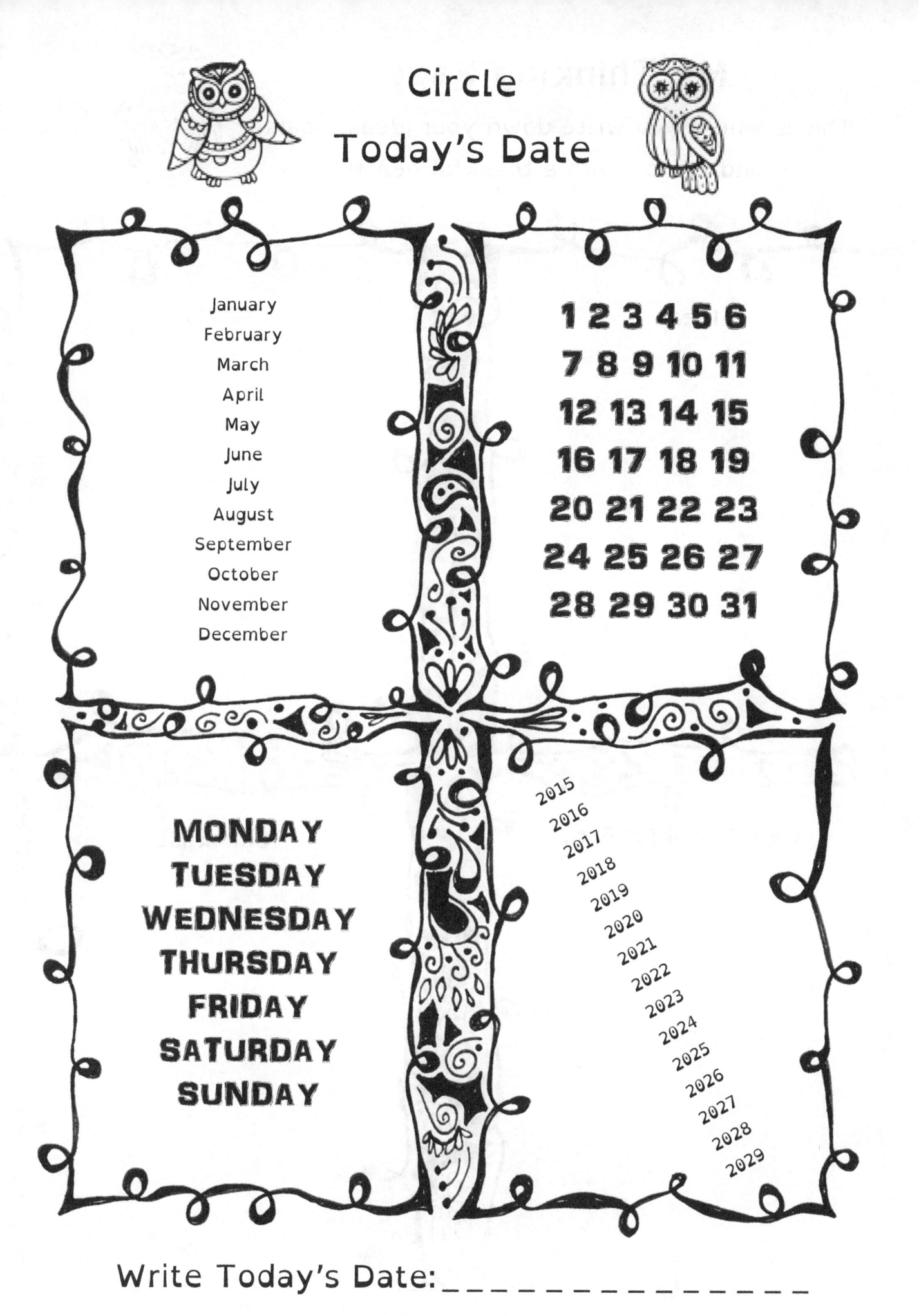

January
February
March
April
May
June
July
August
September
October
November
December

1 2 3 4 5 6
7 8 9 10 11
12 13 14 15
16 17 18 19
20 21 22 23
24 25 26 27
28 29 30 31

MONDAY
TUESDAY
WEDNESDAY
THURSDAY
FRIDAY
SATURDAY
SUNDAY

2015
2016
2017
2018
2019
2020
2021
2022
2023
2024
2025
2026
2027
2028
2029

Write Today's Date: _____

My Thinking Page

This is where you write down your ideas, goals, and plans - with a thankful heart!

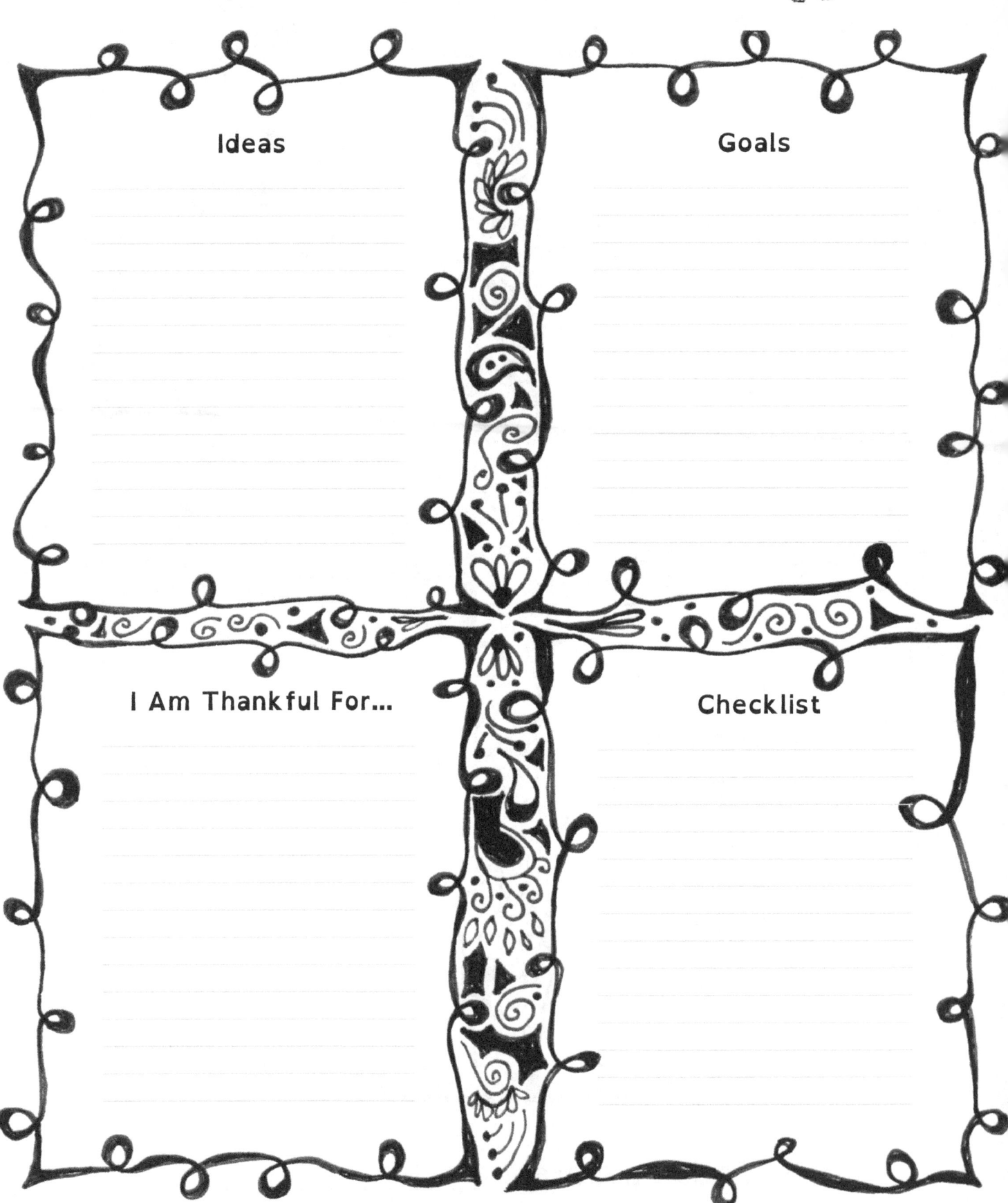

Ideas

Goals

I Am Thankful For...

Checklist

My Illustrated TO-DO List

Write & Draw about something that really happened.

_____
_____
_____
_____
_____
_____
_____
_____
_____
_____

Nature Study

Go outside and make a realistic drawing of something you find in nature.

Reading Time - 1 Hour

Choose Four Books - Read from each book for 15 minutes.
Copy a sentence or picture from each book here:

Circle Today's Date

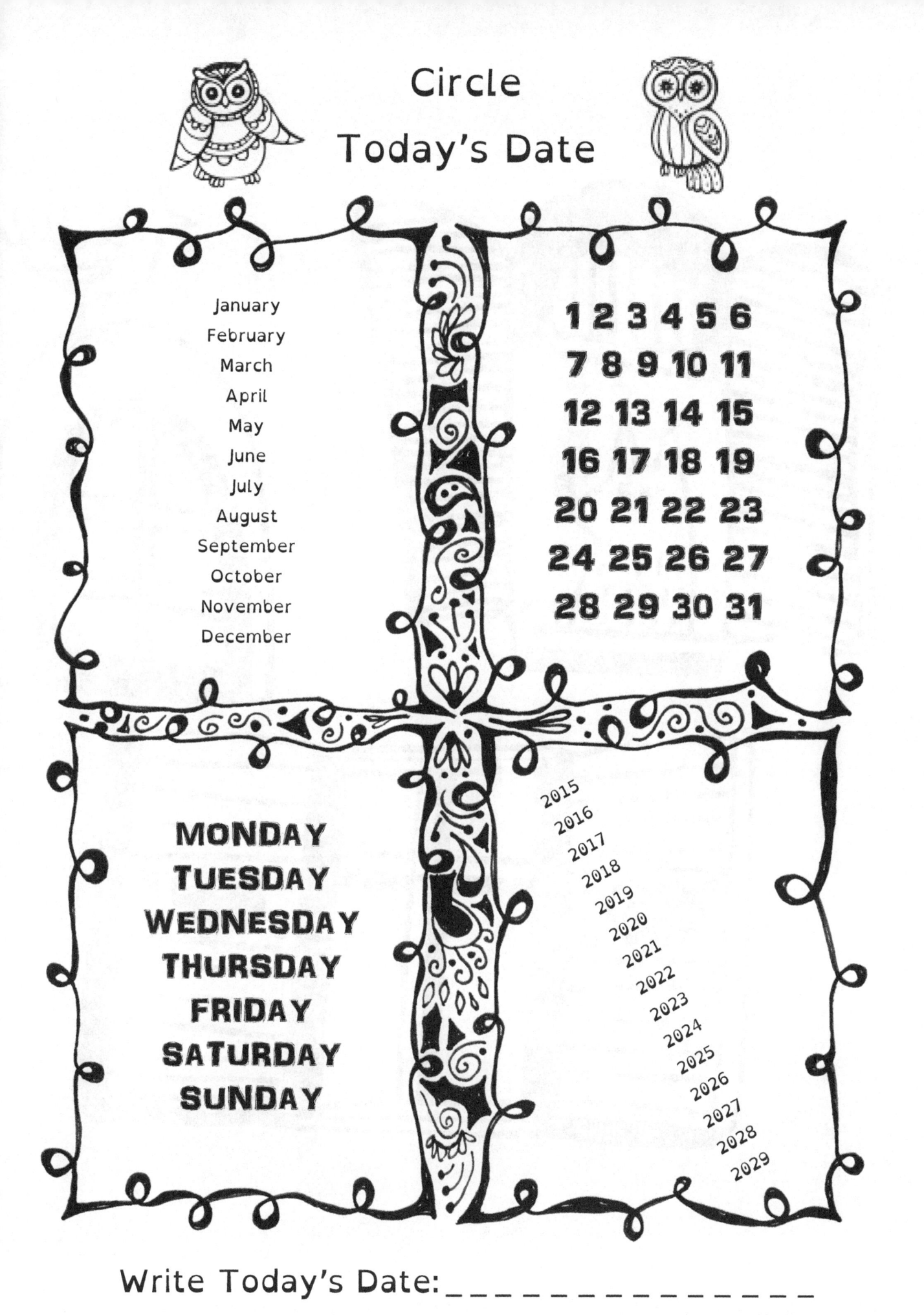

January
February
March
April
May
June
July
August
September
October
November
December

1 2 3 4 5 6
7 8 9 10 11
12 13 14 15
16 17 18 19
20 21 22 23
24 25 26 27
28 29 30 31

MONDAY
TUESDAY
WEDNESDAY
THURSDAY
FRIDAY
SATURDAY
SUNDAY

2015
2016
2017
2018
2019
2020
2021
2022
2023
2024
2025
2026
2027
2028
2029

Write Today's Date: _____

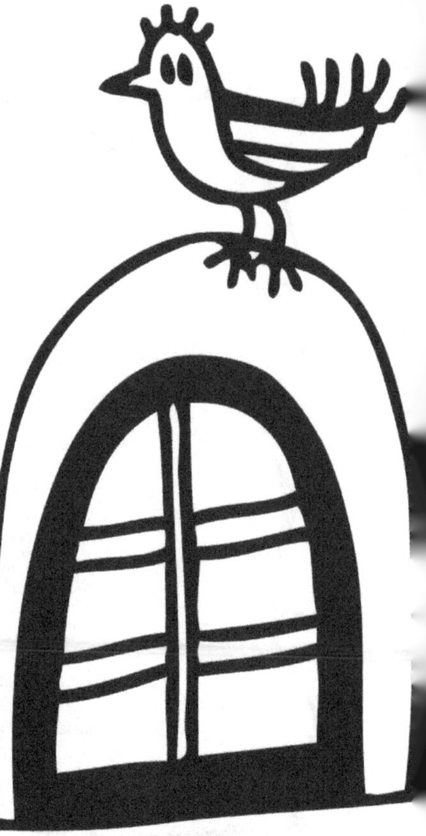

Spelling Time

Find 20 Words with 5 letters each.
Look in your books for words.
Write the words here:

_____   _____

_____   _____

_____   _____

_____   _____

_____   _____

_____   _____

_____   _____

_____   _____

_____   _____

_____   _____

Film Study

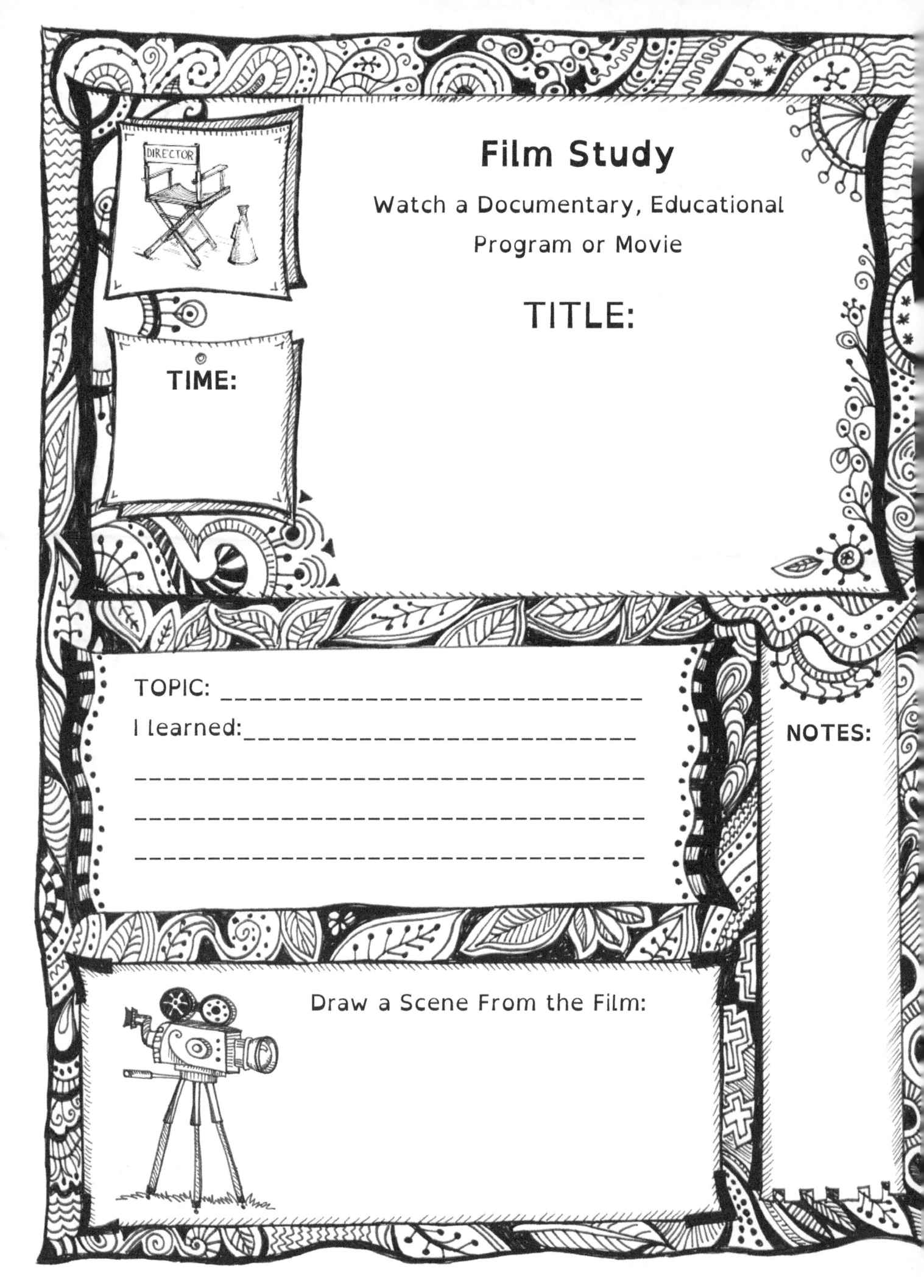

Watch a Documentary, Educational Program or Movie

TITLE:

TIME:

TOPIC: _____

I learned: _____

_____

_____

_____

NOTES:

Draw a Scene From the Film:

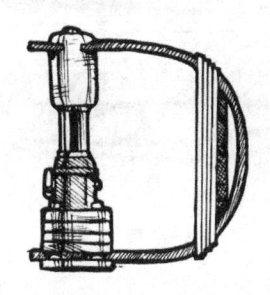

Design Something

Use this graph paper to design something.
If you can't think of anything design a house.

Learning a Skill

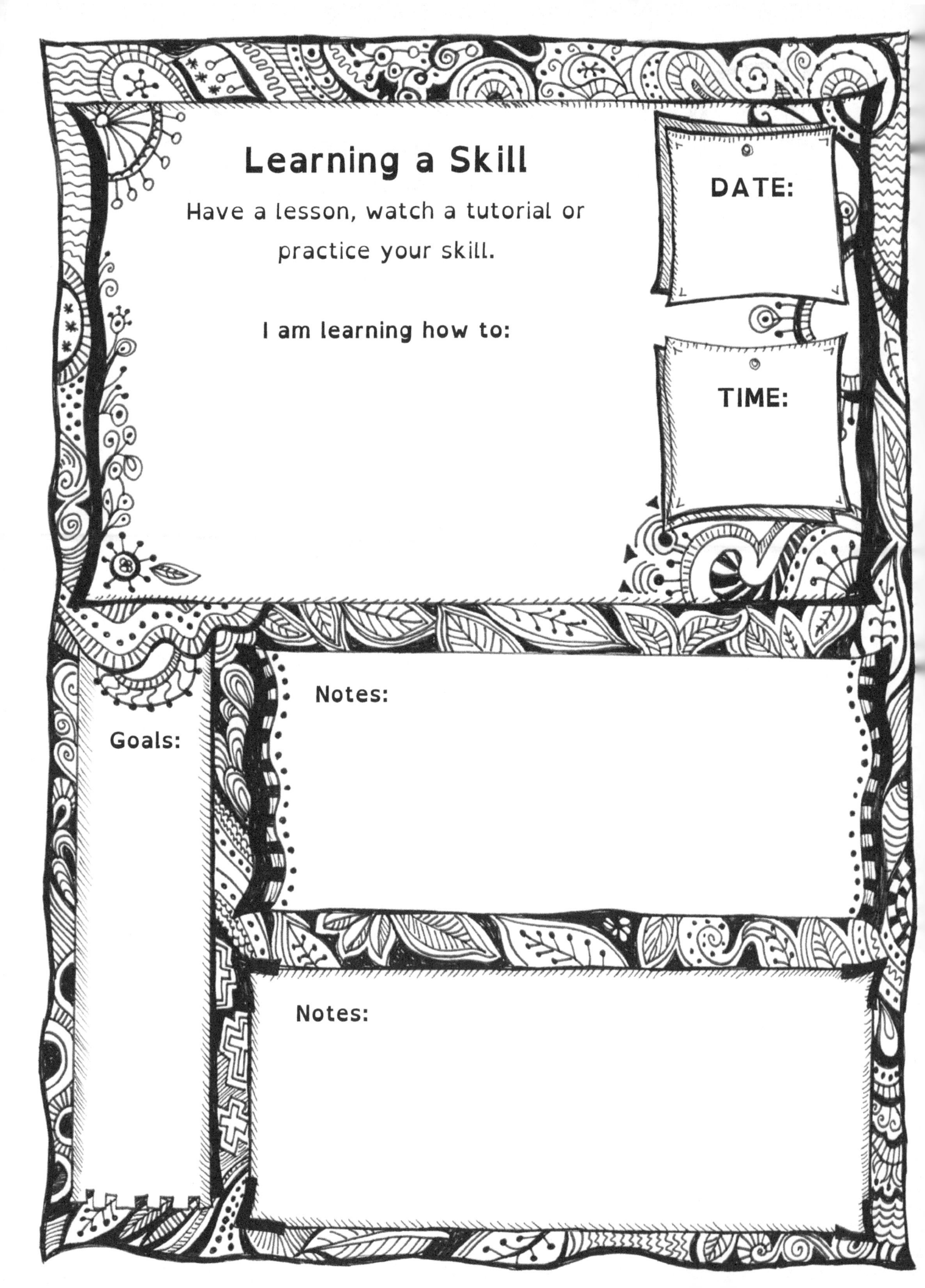

Have a lesson, watch a tutorial or practice your skill.

I am learning how to:

DATE:

TIME:

Goals:

Notes:

Notes:

Sketch a Picture

Look through your library books and find something to draw.

Circle Today's Date

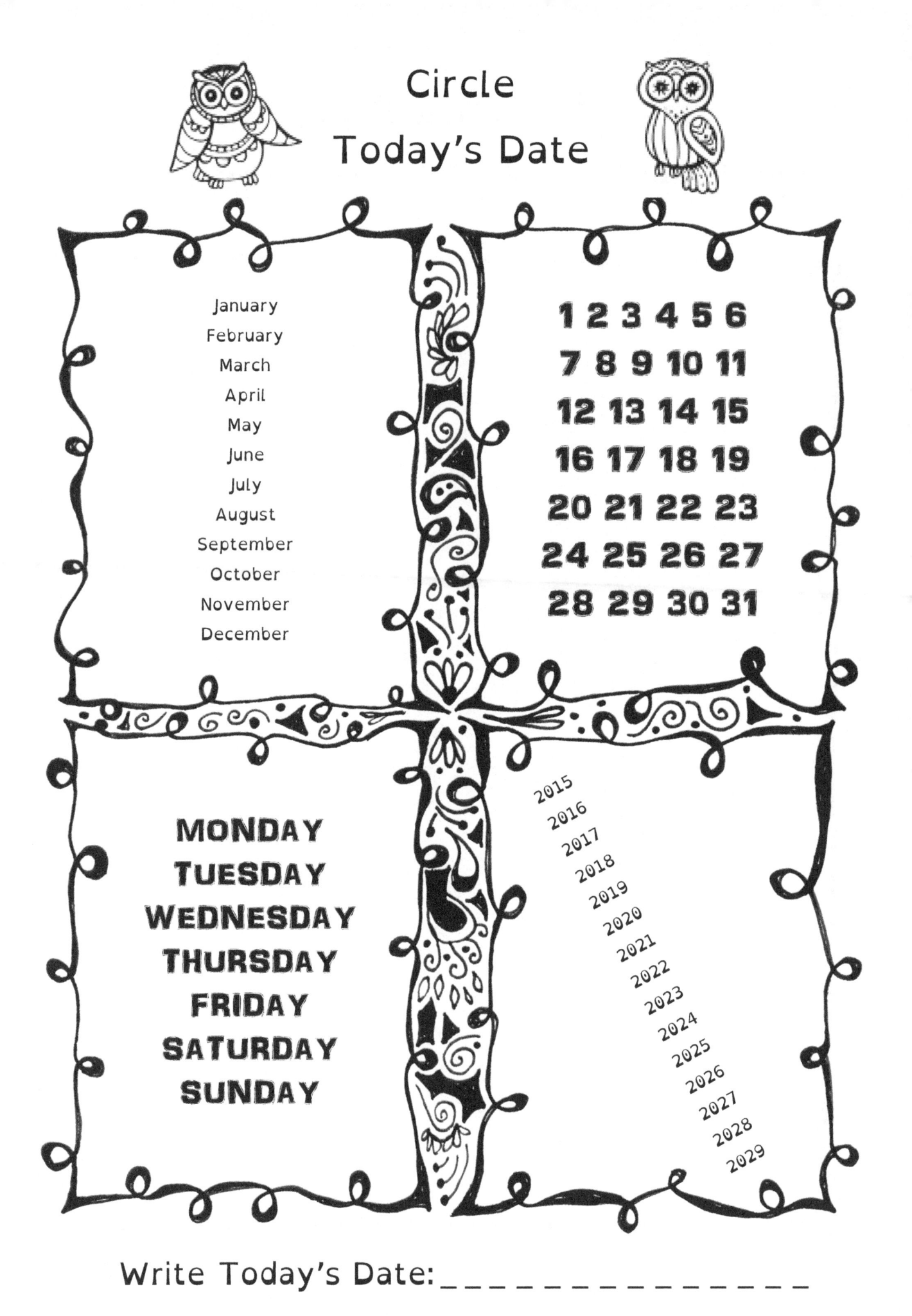

January
February
March
April
May
June
July
August
September
October
November
December

1 2 3 4 5 6
7 8 9 10 11
12 13 14 15
16 17 18 19
20 21 22 23
24 25 26 27
28 29 30 31

MONDAY
TUESDAY
WEDNESDAY
THURSDAY
FRIDAY
SATURDAY
SUNDAY

2015
2016
2017
2018
2019
2020
2021
2022
2023
2024
2025
2026
2027
2028
2029

Write Today's Date: _____

My Thinking Page

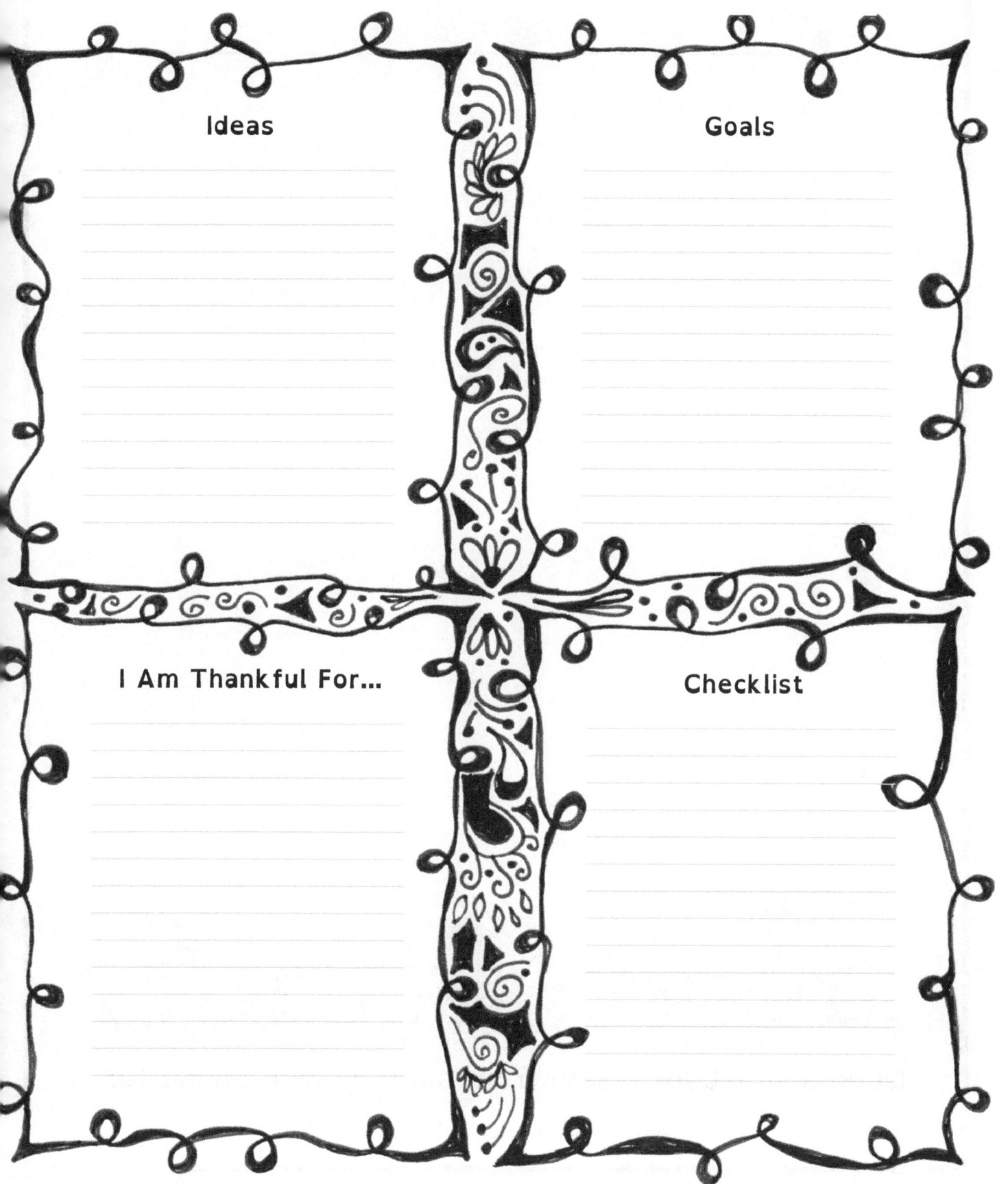

This is where you write down your ideas, goals, and plans - with a thankful heart!

Ideas

Goals

I Am Thankful For...

Checklist

Recipe:

_____

Serves:

Prep Time:

Ingredients:

Instructions:

Shopping List:

Open a cookbook, learn from mom or look online for some wonderful recipes!

Creative Writing

Draw a picture below.
Write a poem or short story about it.

TITLE: _____

_____
_____
_____
_____
_____
_____
_____
_____
_____
_____
_____
_____
_____

Write & Draw about something that really happened.

_____
_____
_____
_____
_____
_____
_____
_____

Nature Study

Go outside and make a realistic drawing of something you find in nature.

Reading Time - 1 Hour

Choose Four Books - Read from each book for 15 minutes.
Copy a sentence or picture from each book here:

Circle Today's Date

January
February
March
April
May
June
July
August
September
October
November
December

1 2 3 4 5 6
7 8 9 10 11
12 13 14 15
16 17 18 19
20 21 22 23
24 25 26 27
28 29 30 31

MONDAY
TUESDAY
WEDNESDAY
THURSDAY
FRIDAY
SATURDAY
SUNDAY

2015
2016
2017
2018
2019
2020
2021
2022
2023
2024
2025
2026
2027
2028
2029

Write Today's Date: _____

Spelling Time

Find 20 Words with **4** letters each.
Look in your books for words.
Write the words here:

_____   _____

_____   _____

_____   _____

_____   _____

_____   _____

_____   _____

_____   _____

_____   _____

_____   _____

_____   _____

Film Study

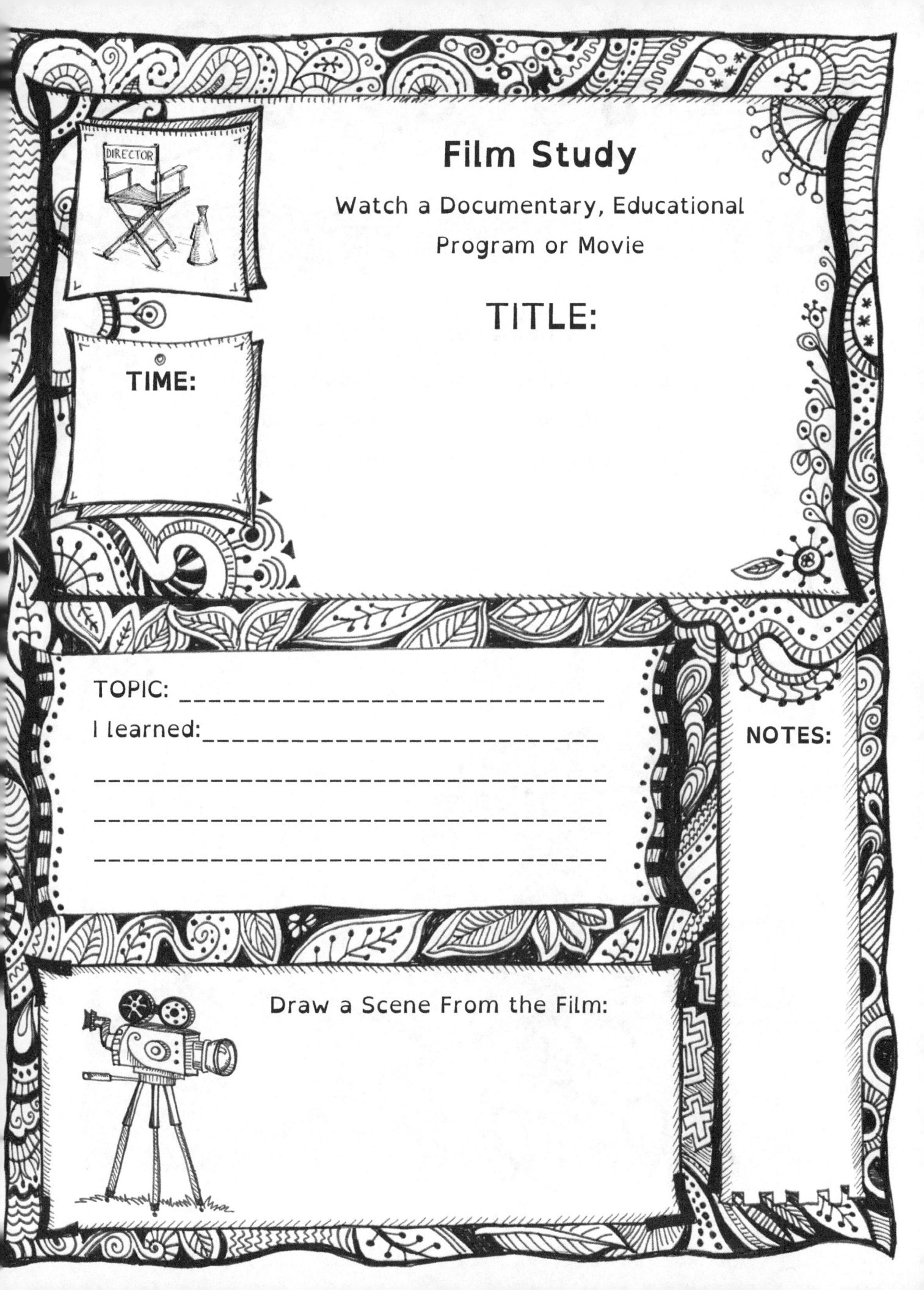

Watch a Documentary, Educational Program or Movie

TITLE:

TIME:

TOPIC: _____

I learned: _____

_____

_____

_____

NOTES:

Draw a Scene From the Film:

Listening Time

Listen to an audio book or classical music or ask someone to read a story to you while you color and draw on the next page.

What are you listening to?

_____

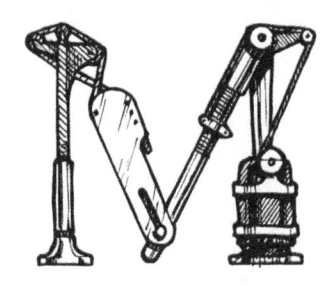

Math Practice

Watch a math tutorial or open up a math book.
You can practice math problems here.

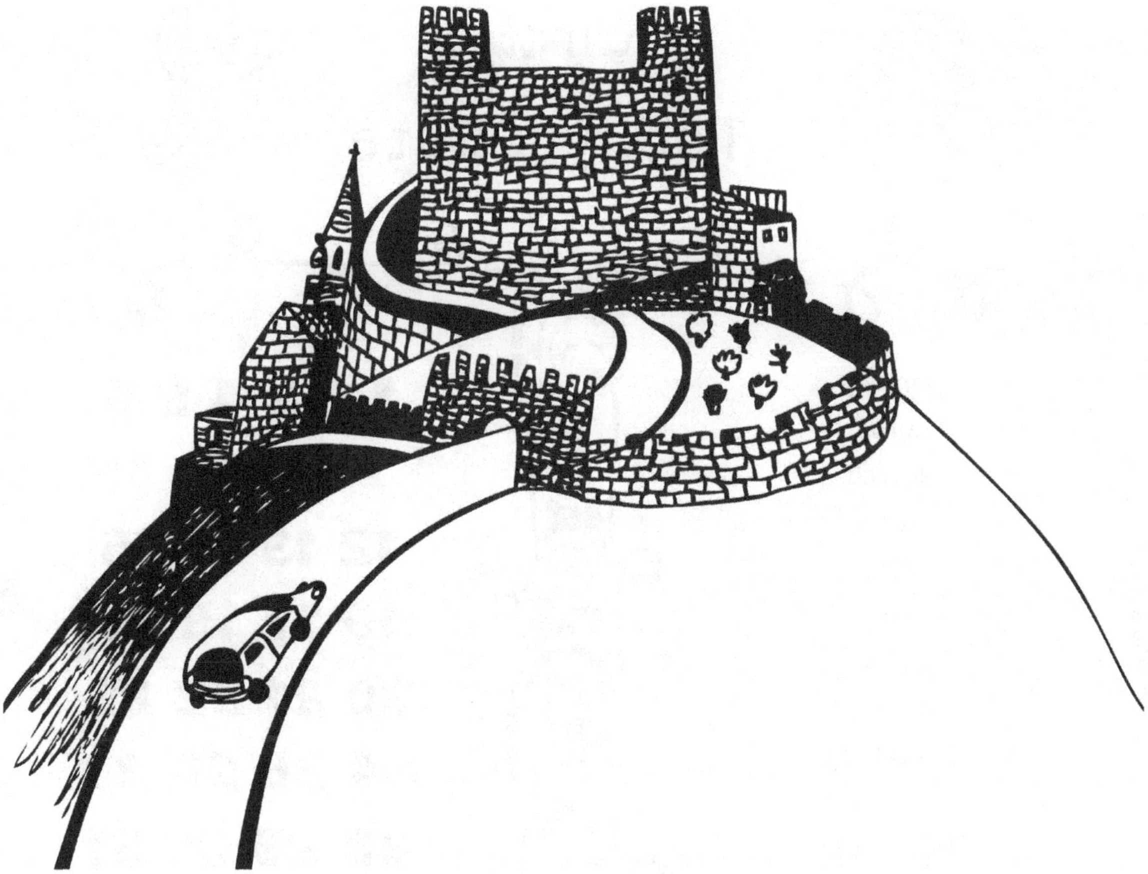

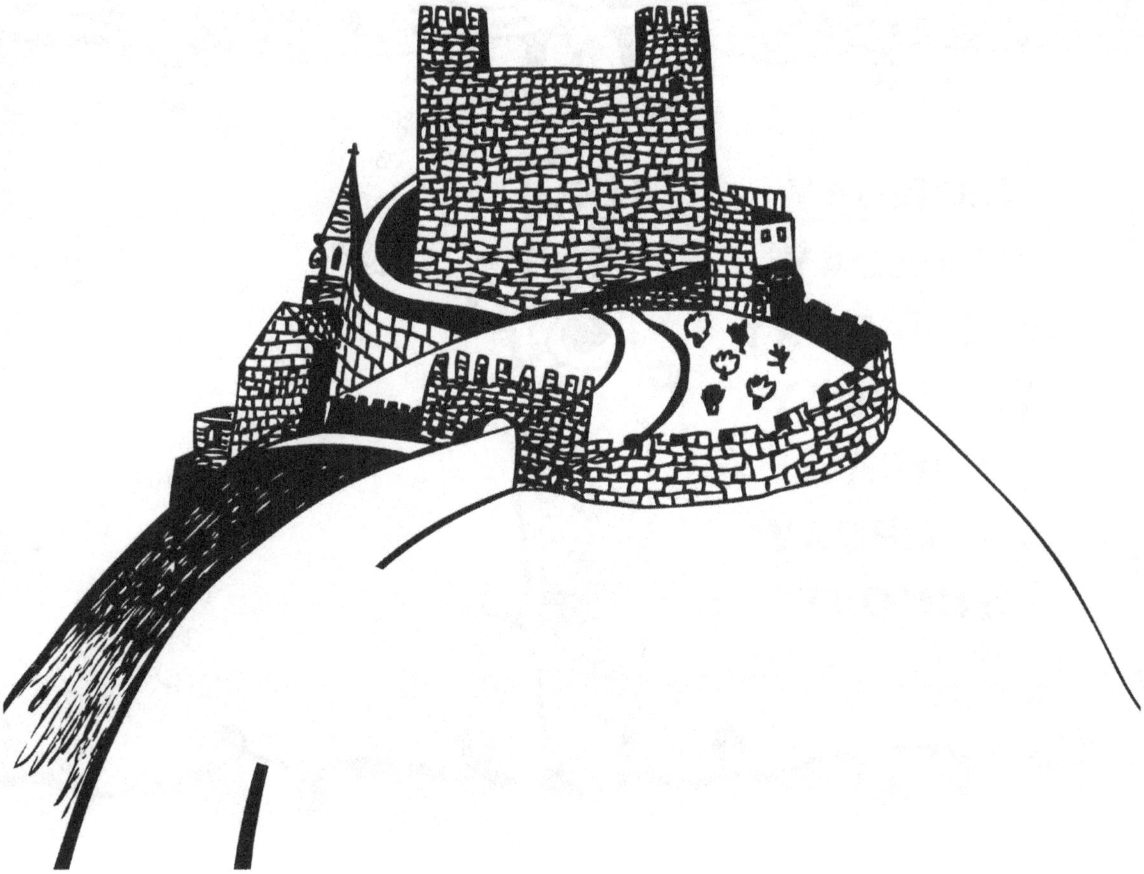

Circle Today's Date

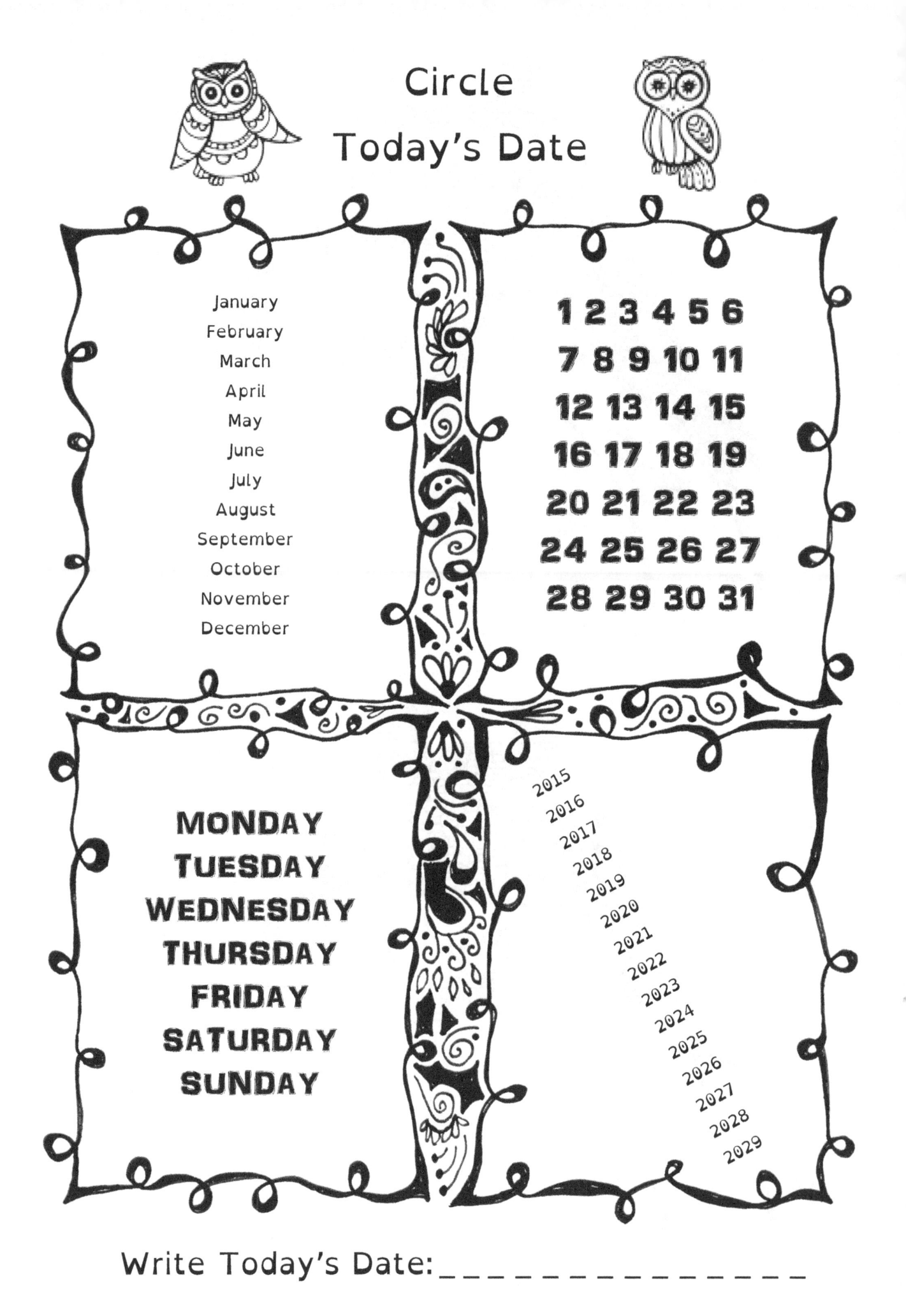

January
February
March
April
May
June
July
August
September
October
November
December

1 2 3 4 5 6
7 8 9 10 11
12 13 14 15
16 17 18 19
20 21 22 23
24 25 26 27
28 29 30 31

MONDAY
TUESDAY
WEDNESDAY
THURSDAY
FRIDAY
SATURDAY
SUNDAY

2015
2016
2017
2018
2019
2020
2021
2022
2023
2024
2025
2026
2027
2028
2029

Write Today's Date: _____

My Thinking Page

This is where you write down your ideas, goals, and plans - with a thankful heart!

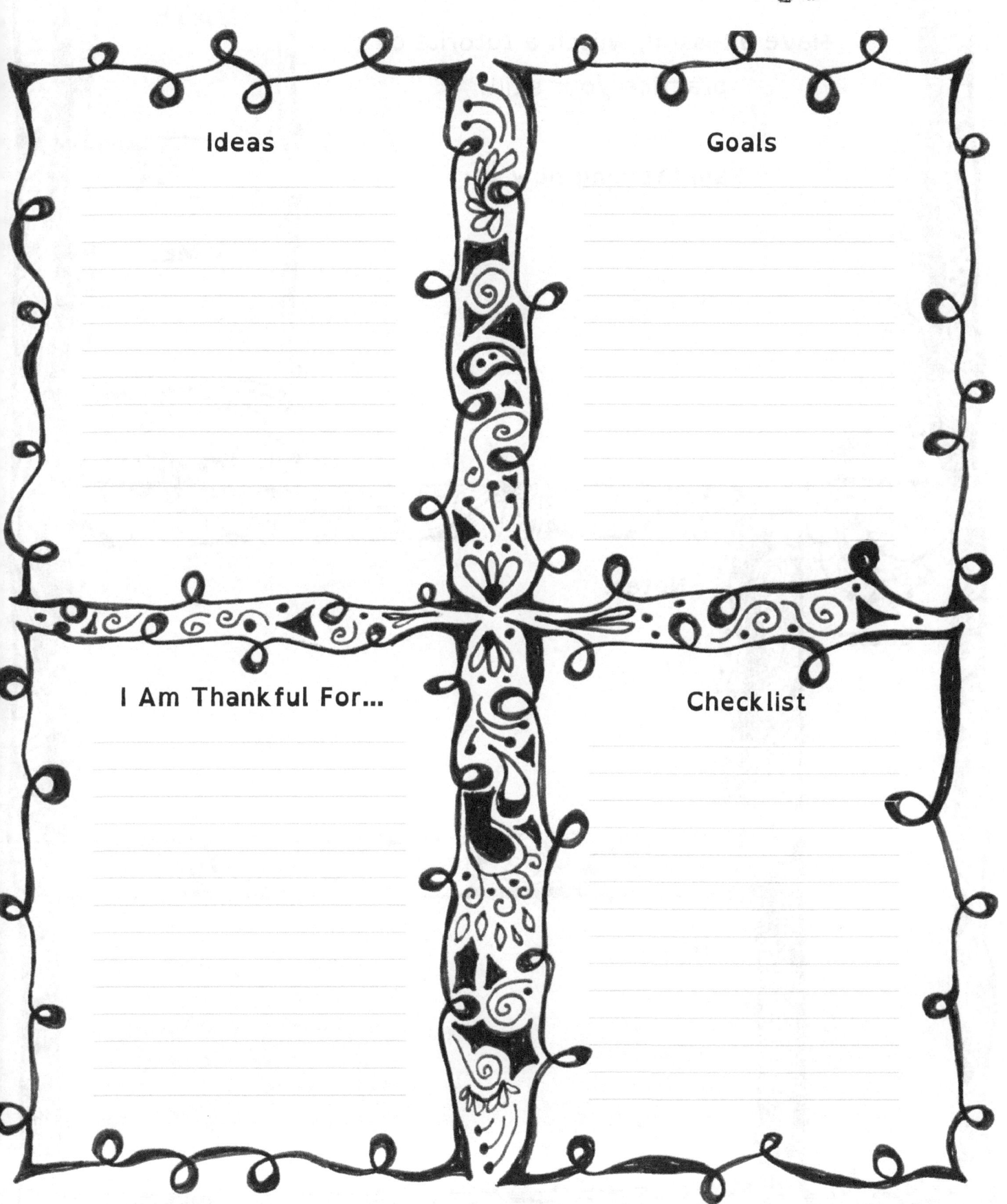

Ideas

Goals

I Am Thankful For...

Checklist

Learning a Skill

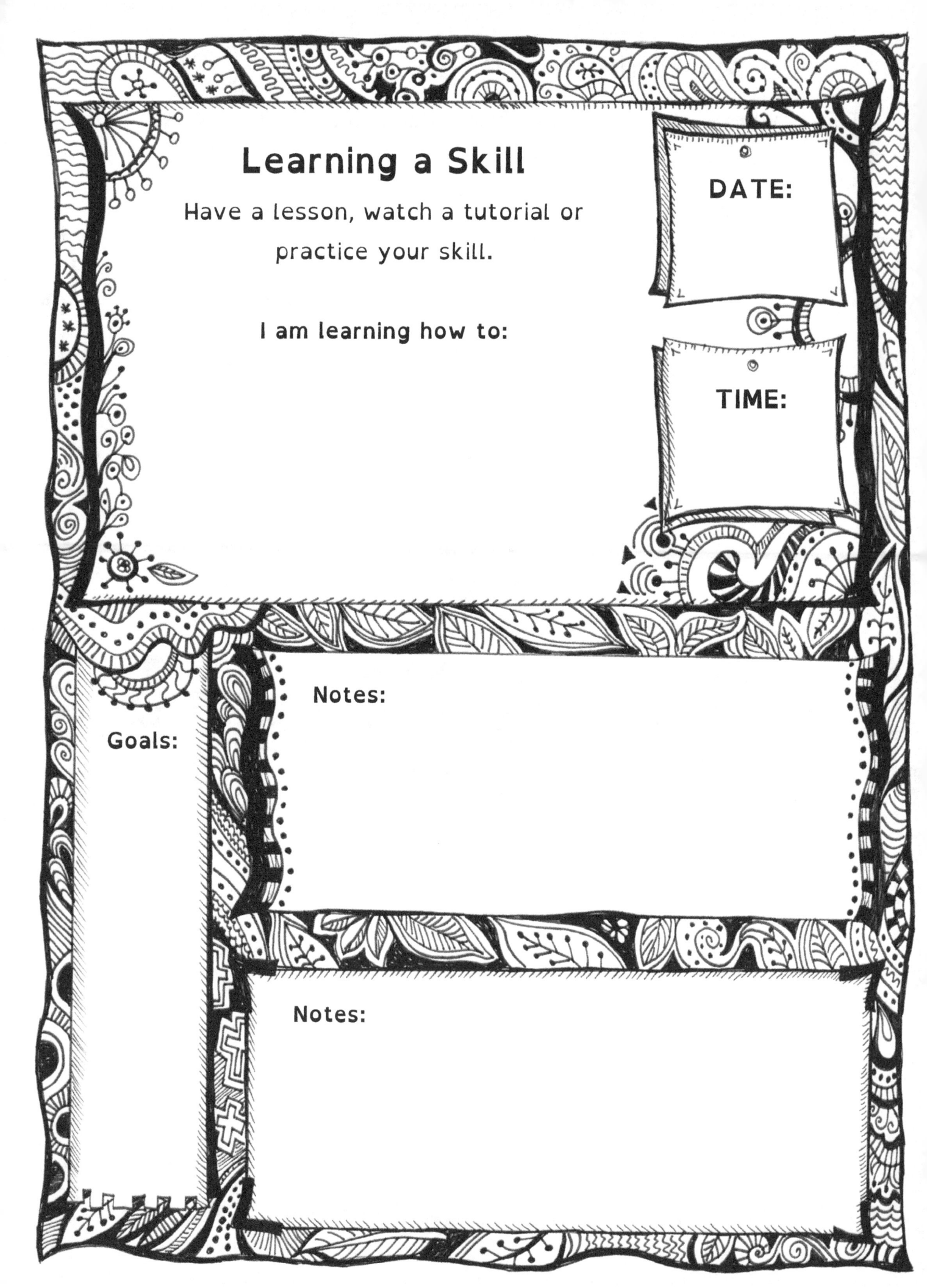

Have a lesson, watch a tutorial or practice your skill.

I am learning how to:

DATE:

TIME:

Goals:

Notes:

Notes:

Creative Writing

Draw a picture below.
Write a poem or short story about it.

TITLE: _____

_____
_____
_____
_____
_____
_____
_____
_____
_____
_____
_____
_____

Write & Draw about something that really happened.

_____
_____
_____
_____
_____
_____
_____
_____
_____

Nature Study

Go outside and make a realistic drawing of something you find in nature.

Reading Time - 1 Hour

Choose Four Books - Read from each book for 15 minutes.
Copy a sentence or picture from each book here:

Circle Today's Date

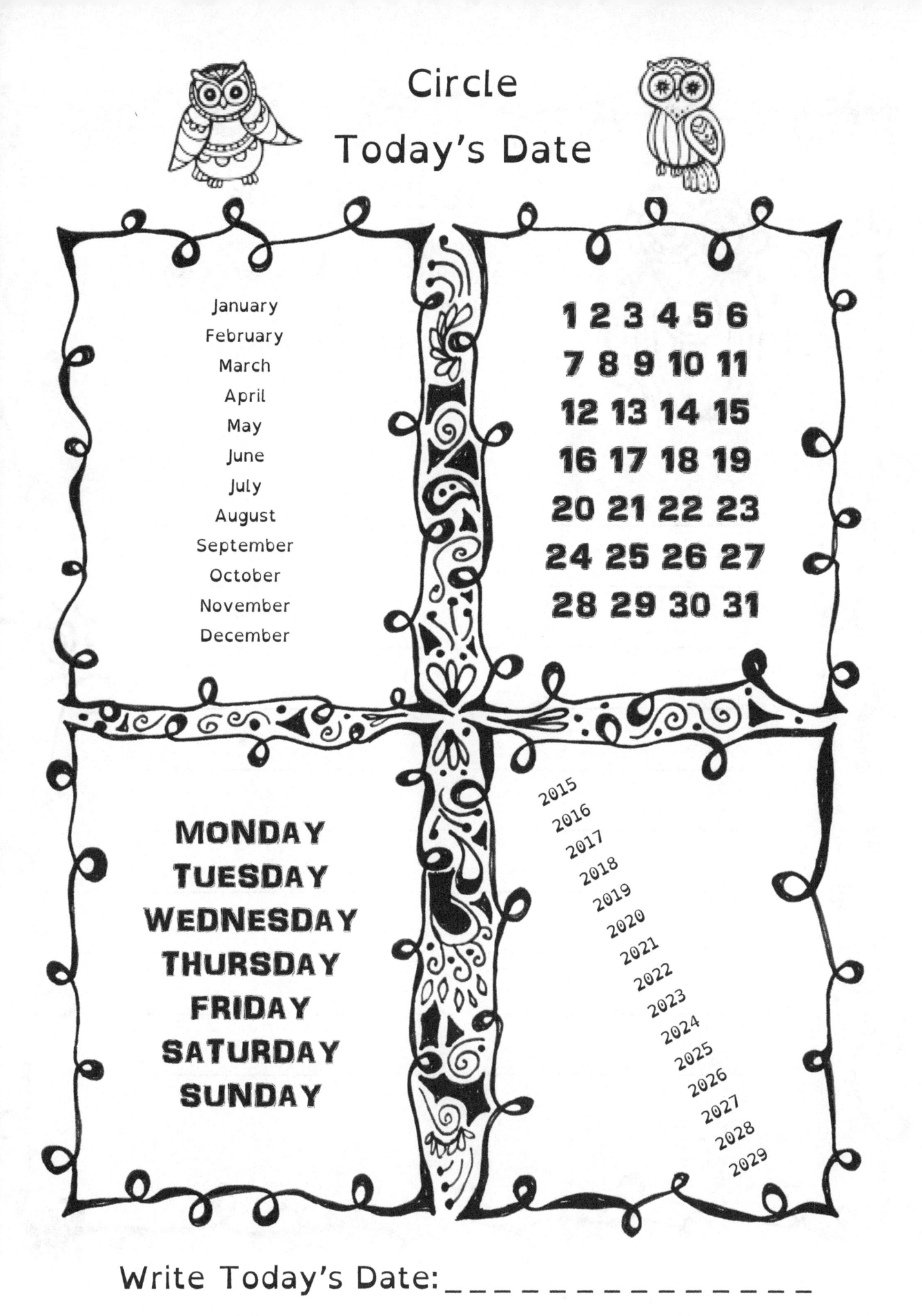

January
February
March
April
May
June
July
August
September
October
November
December

1 2 3 4 5 6
7 8 9 10 11
12 13 14 15
16 17 18 19
20 21 22 23
24 25 26 27
28 29 30 31

MONDAY
TUESDAY
WEDNESDAY
THURSDAY
FRIDAY
SATURDAY
SUNDAY

2015
2016
2017
2018
2019
2020
2021
2022
2023
2024
2025
2026
2027
2028
2029

Write Today's Date: _____

Spelling Time

Find 20 Words with 3 letters each.
Look in your books for words.
Write the words here:

_____   _____

_____   _____

_____   _____

_____   _____

_____   _____

_____   _____

_____   _____

_____   _____

_____   _____

_____   _____

Film Study

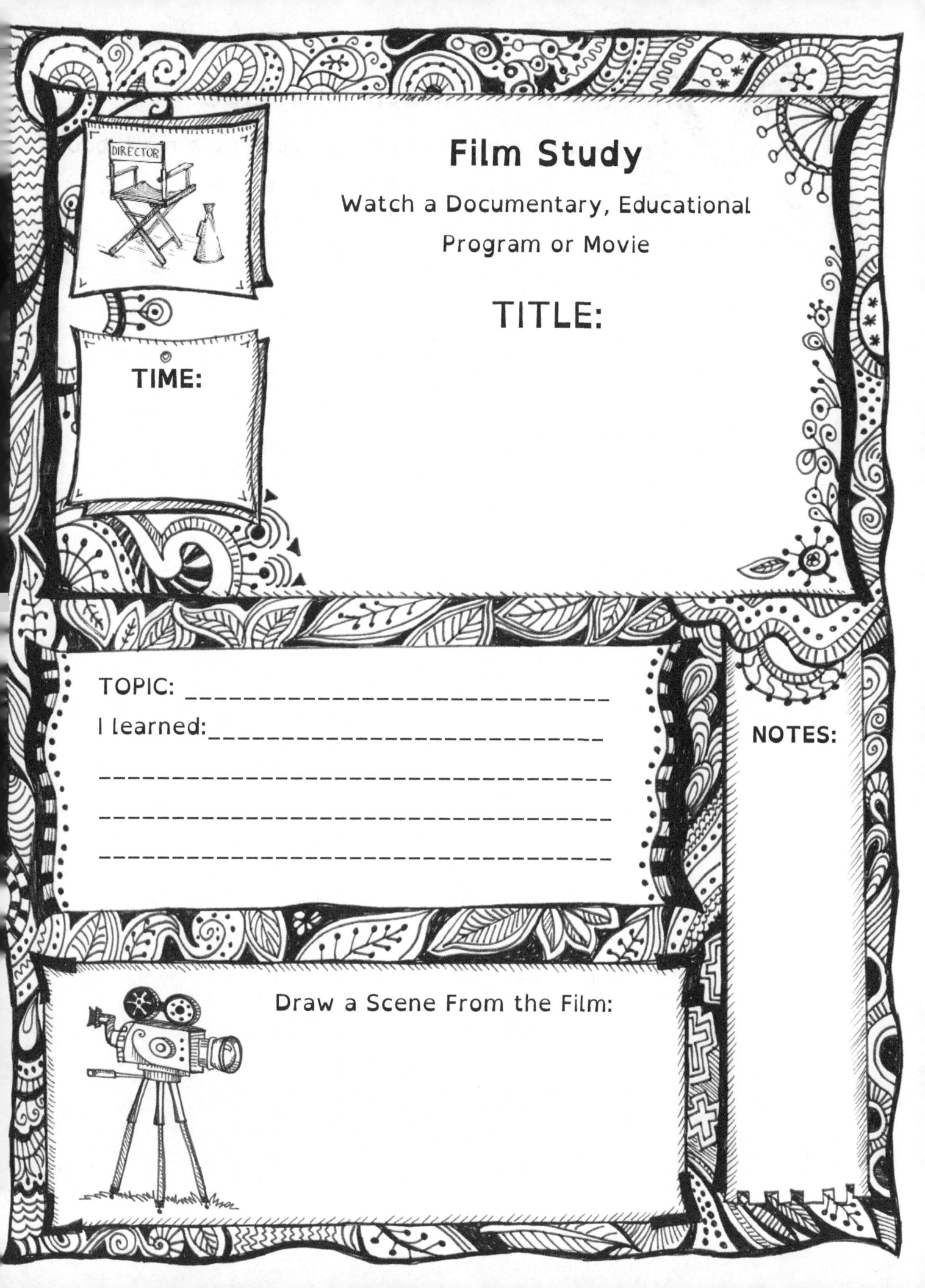

Watch a Documentary, Educational Program or Movie

TITLE:

TIME:

TOPIC: _____

I learned: _____

_____

_____

_____

NOTES:

Draw a Scene From the Film:

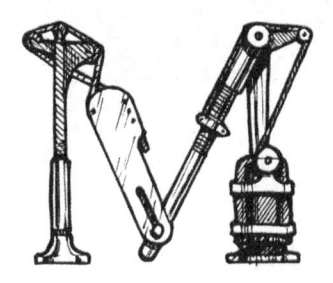

Math Practice

Watch a math tutorial or open up a math book.
You can practice math problems here.

Draw a Meal PLAN

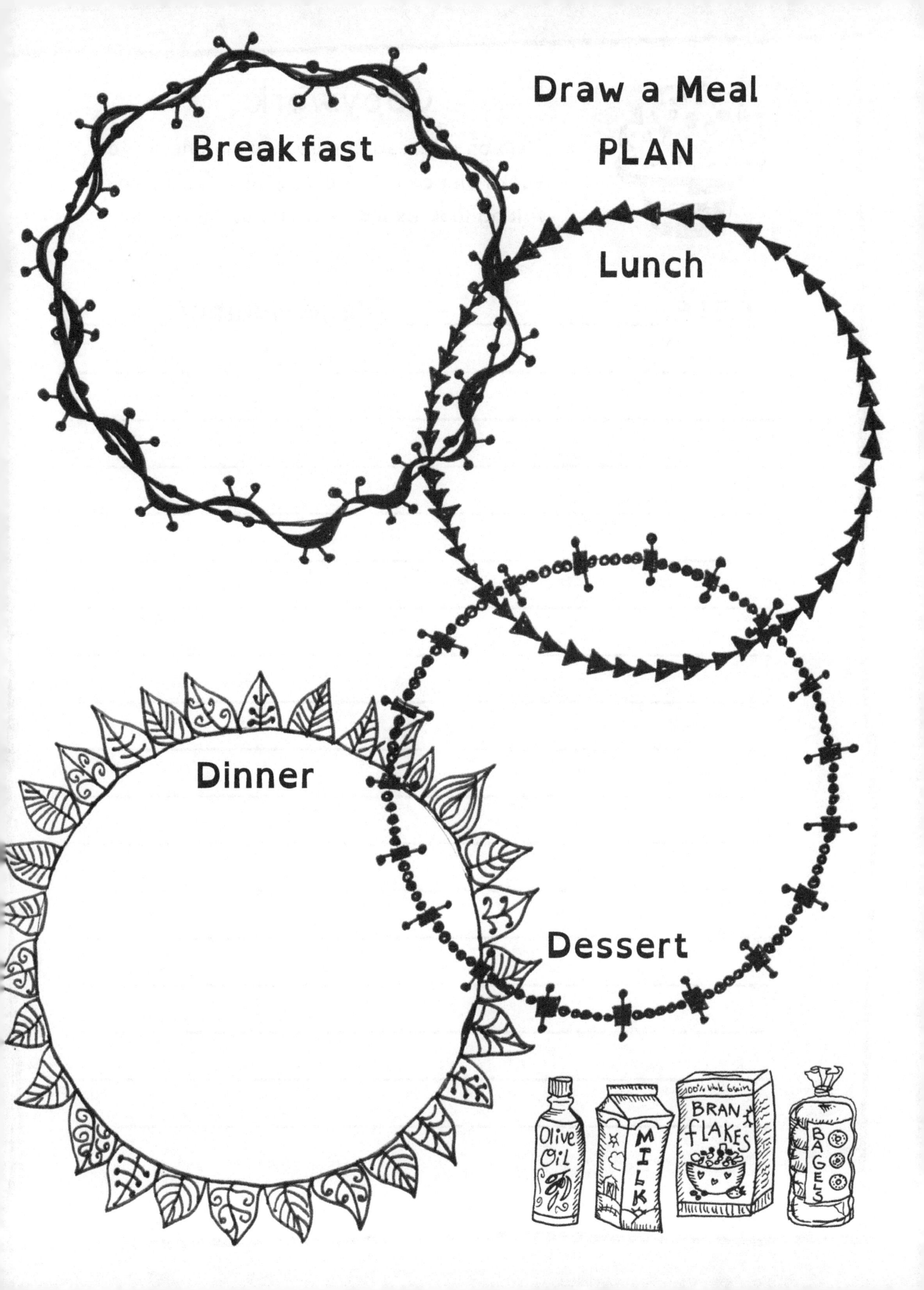

- Breakfast
- Lunch
- Dinner
- Dessert

Olive Oil | Milk | Bran Flakes | Bagels

Copywork

Find an interesting paragraph in one of your books and copy it. Be diligent to make your writing look exactly like it does in the book.

TITLE: _____ **Page Number:** _____

Sketch a Picture
Look through your library books and find something to draw.

Circle Today's Date

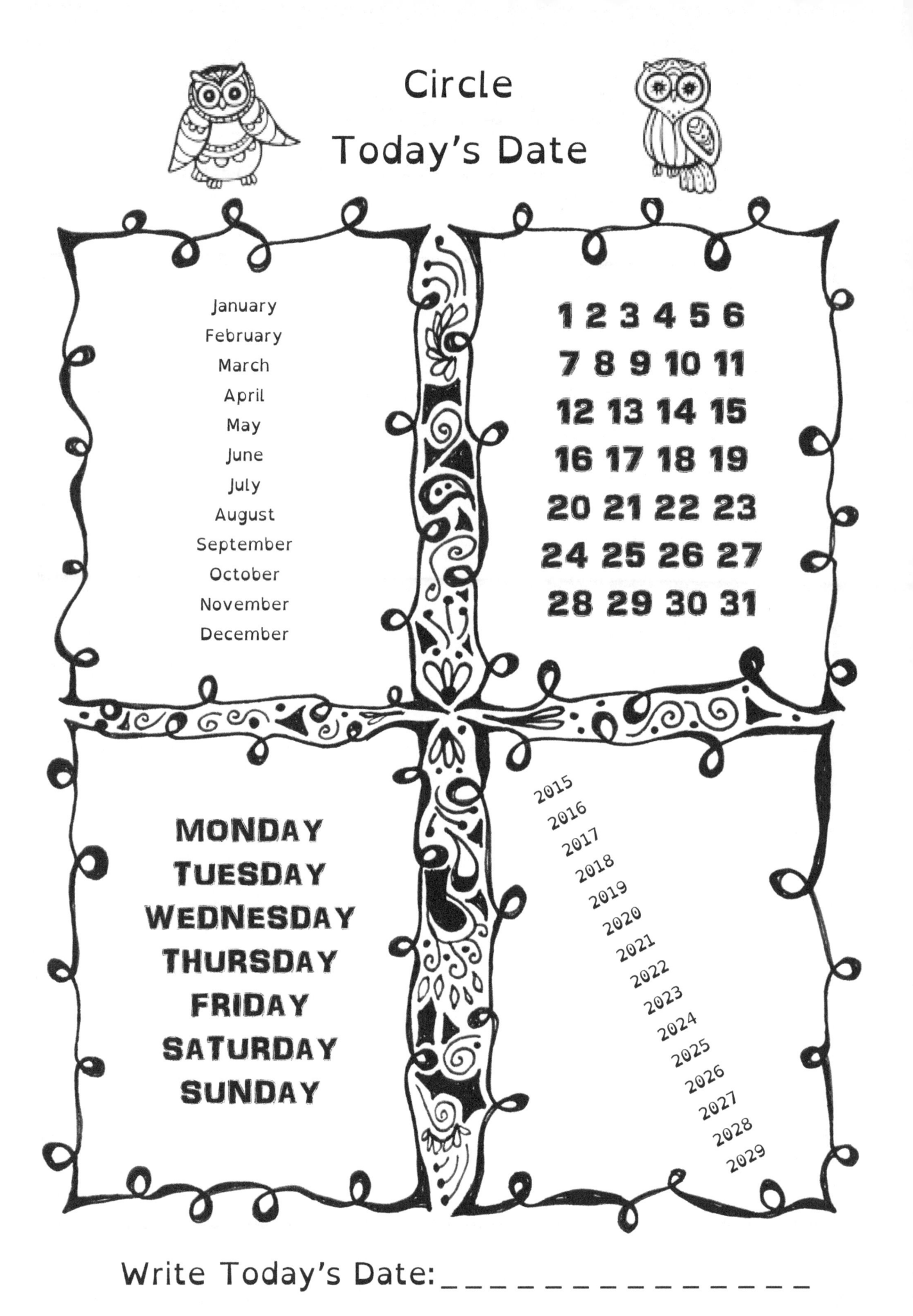

January
February
March
April
May
June
July
August
September
October
November
December

1 2 3 4 5 6
7 8 9 10 11
12 13 14 15
16 17 18 19
20 21 22 23
24 25 26 27
28 29 30 31

MONDAY
TUESDAY
WEDNESDAY
THURSDAY
FRIDAY
SATURDAY
SUNDAY

2015
2016
2017
2018
2019
2020
2021
2022
2023
2024
2025
2026
2027
2028
2029

Write Today's Date: _____

My Thinking Page

This is where you write down your ideas, goals, and plans - with a thankful heart!

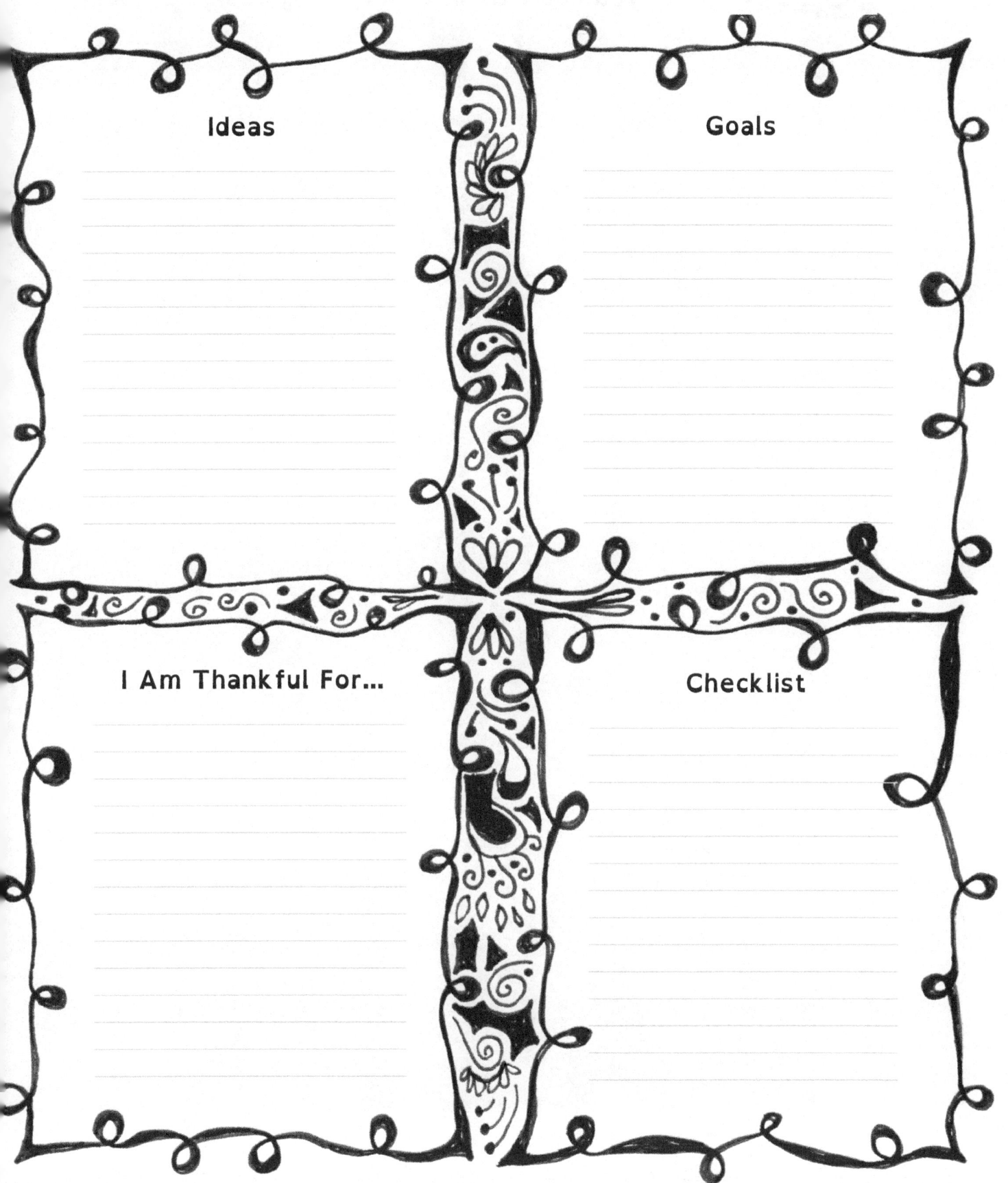

Ideas

Goals

I Am Thankful For...

Checklist

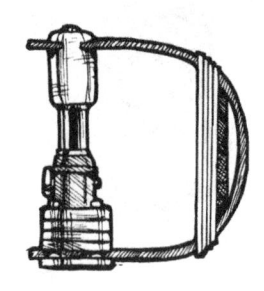

Design Something

Use this graph paper to design something.
If you can't think of anything design a house.

Creative Writing

Draw a picture below.
Write a poem or short story about it.

TITLE: _____

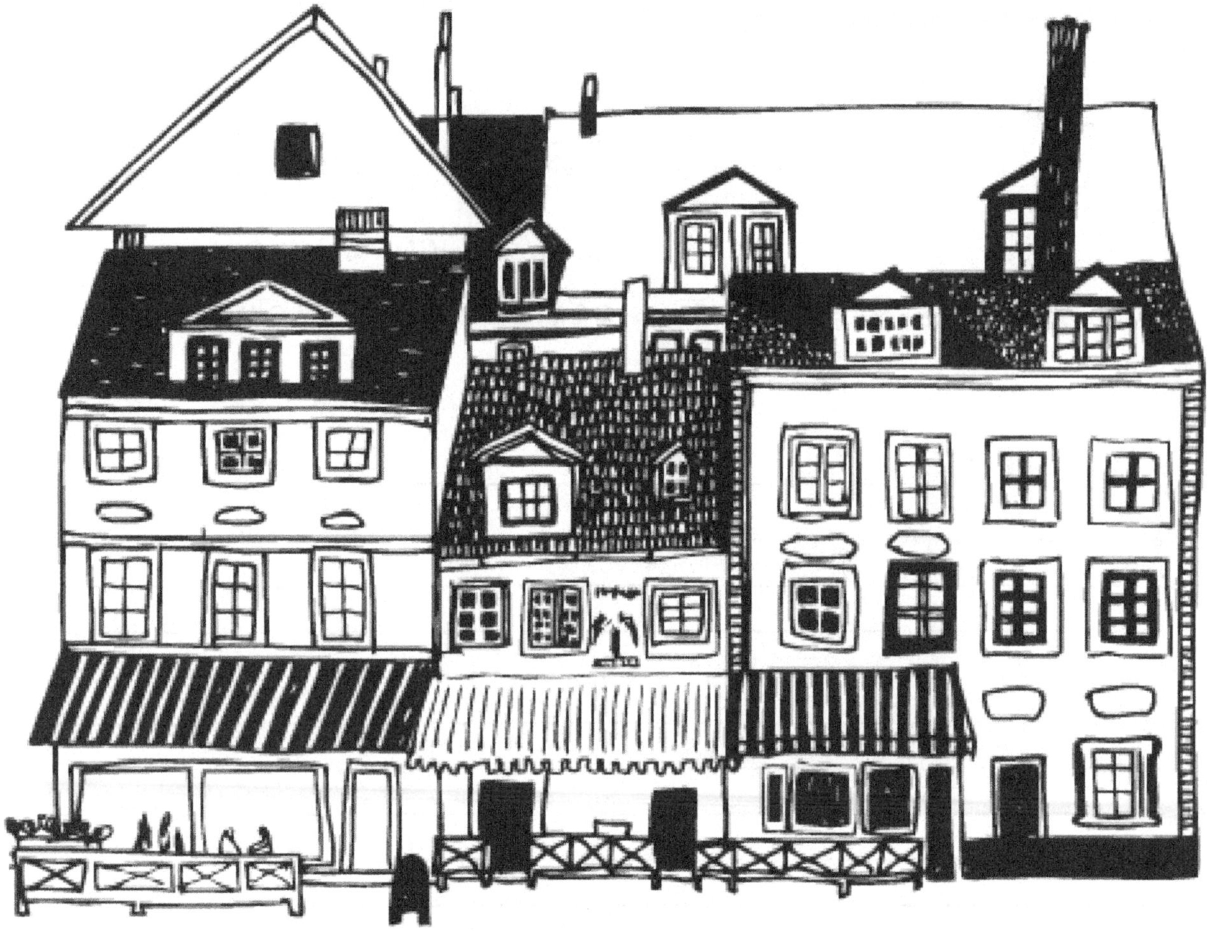

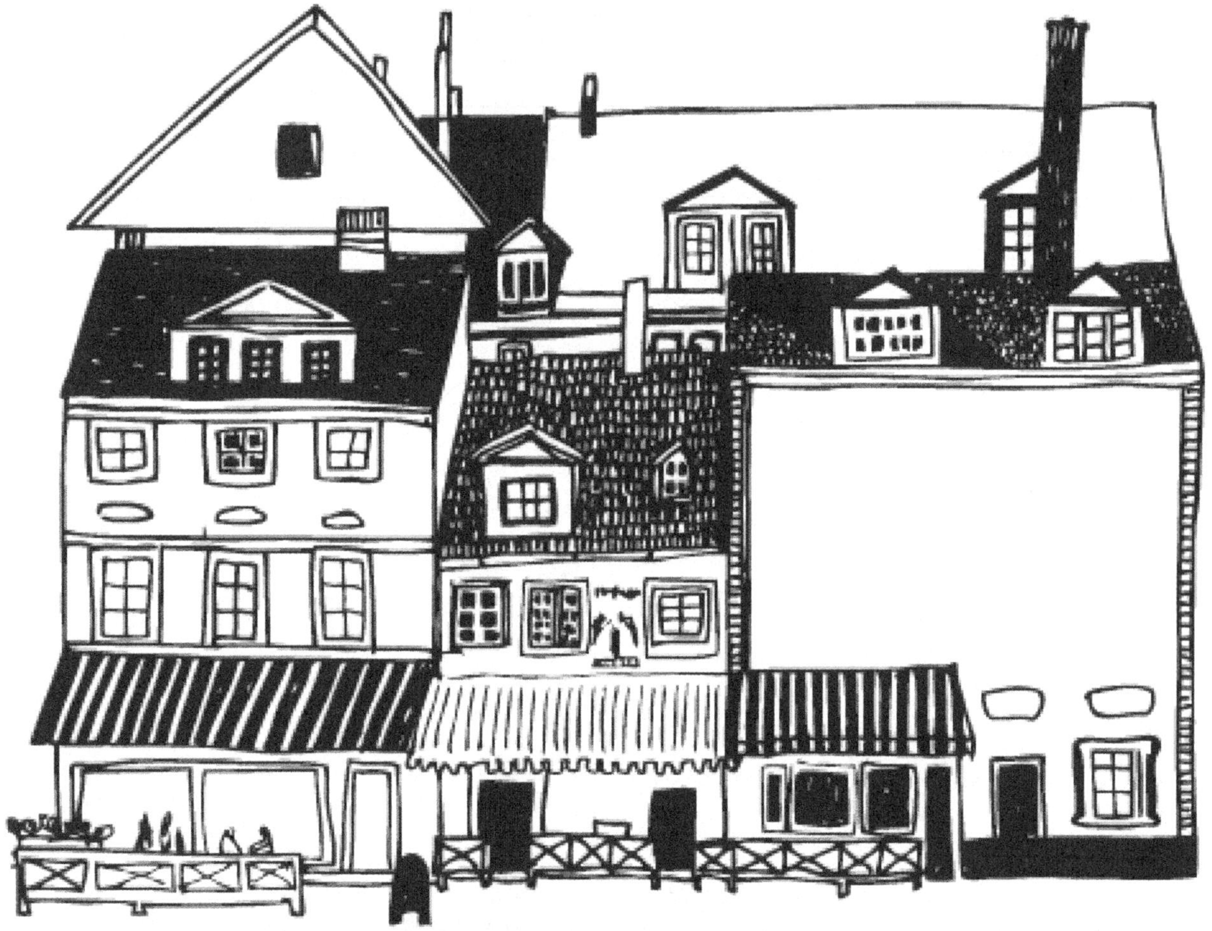

Write & Draw about something that really happened.

_____
_____
_____
_____
_____
_____
_____
_____

Nature Study

Go outside and make a realistic drawing of something you find in nature.

Reading Time - 1 Hour

Choose Four Books - Read from each book for 15 minutes.
Copy a sentence or picture from each book here:

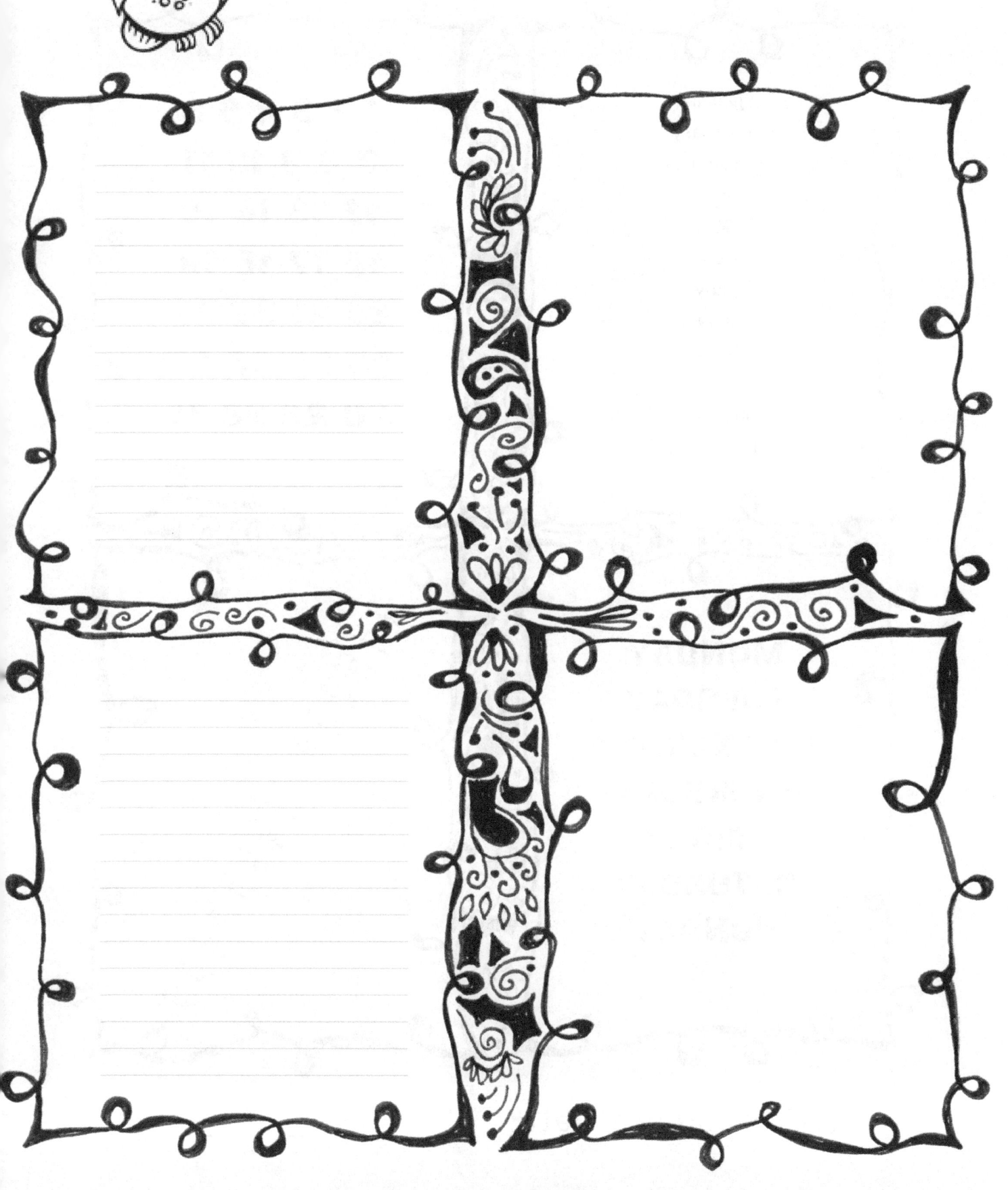

Circle Today's Date

January
February
March
April
May
June
July
August
September
October
November
December

1 2 3 4 5 6
7 8 9 10 11
12 13 14 15
16 17 18 19
20 21 22 23
24 25 26 27
28 29 30 31

MONDAY
TUESDAY
WEDNESDAY
THURSDAY
FRIDAY
SATURDAY
SUNDAY

2015
2016
2017
2018
2019
2020
2021
2022
2023
2024
2025
2026
2027
2028
2029

Write Today's Date: _____

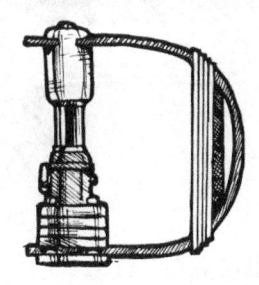

Design Something

Use this graph paper to design something.
If you can't think of anything design a house.

4

Film Study

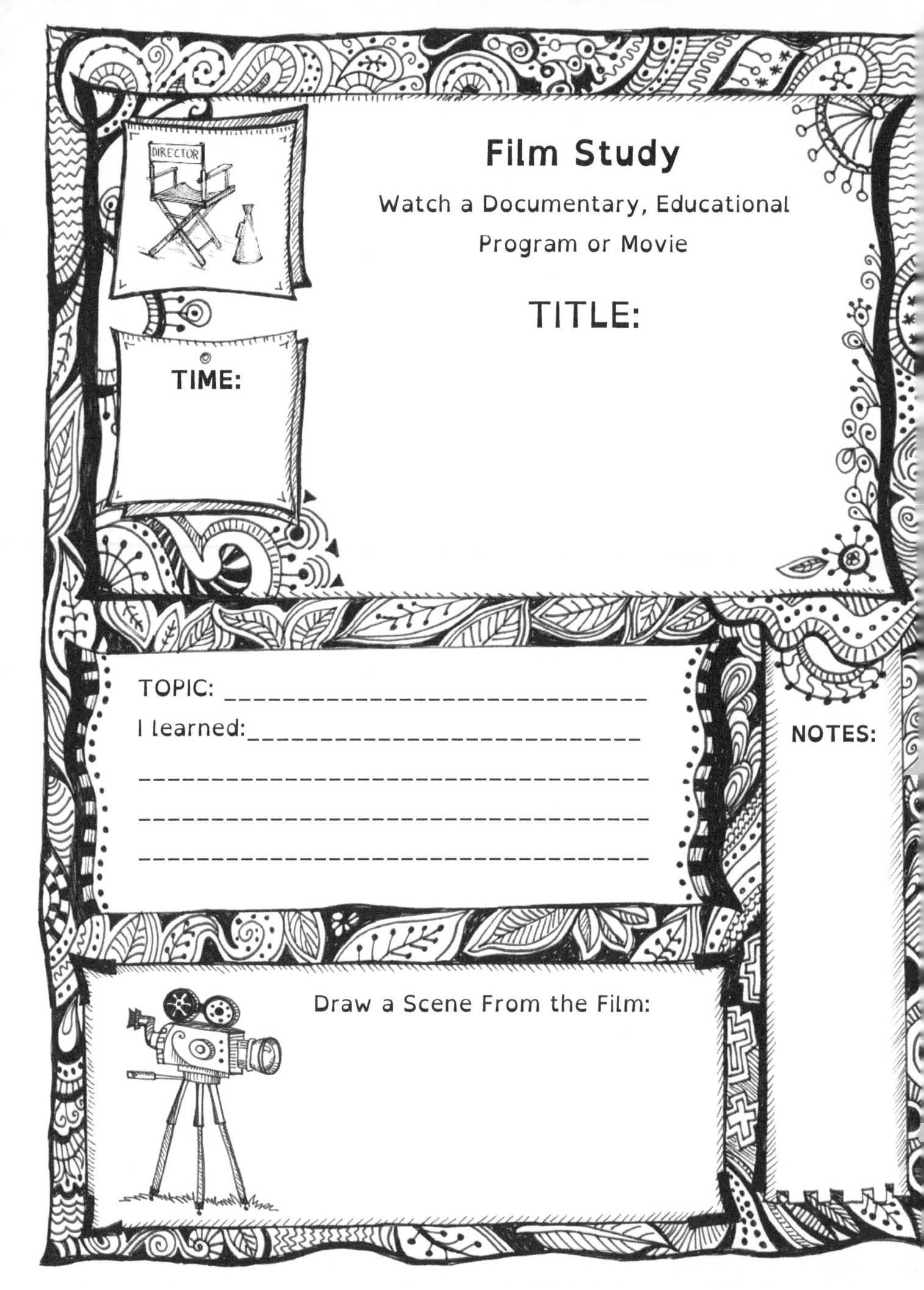

Watch a Documentary, Educational Program or Movie

TITLE:

TIME:

TOPIC: _____

I learned: _____

_____

_____

_____

NOTES:

Draw a Scene From the Film:

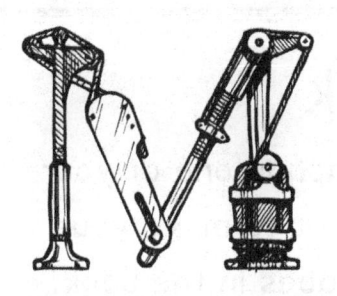

Math Practice

Watch a math tutorial or open up a math book.
You can practice math problems here.

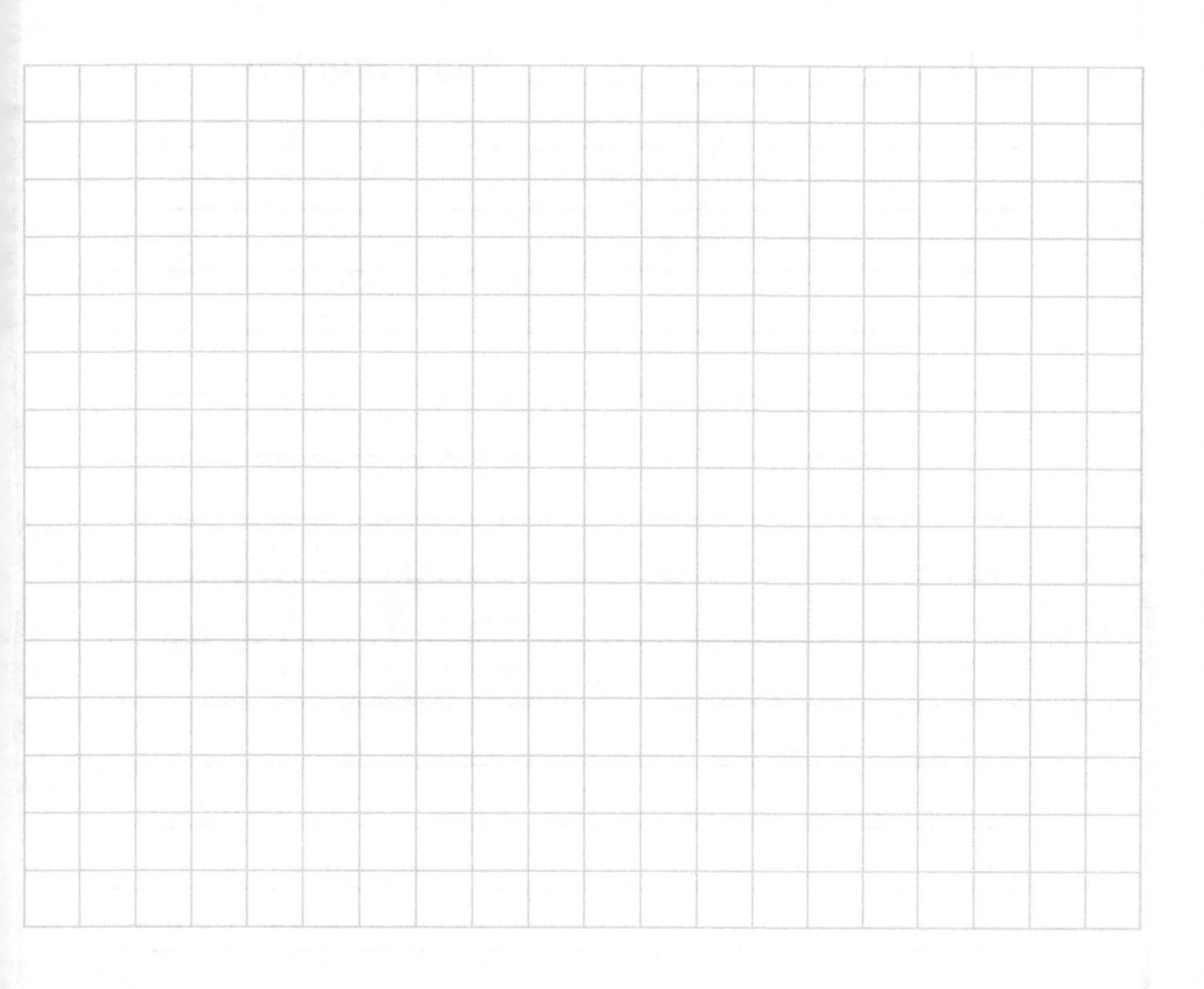

Copywork

Find an interesting paragraph in one of your books and copy it. Be diligent to make your writing look exactly like it does in the book.

TITLE:_____ **Page Number:_____**

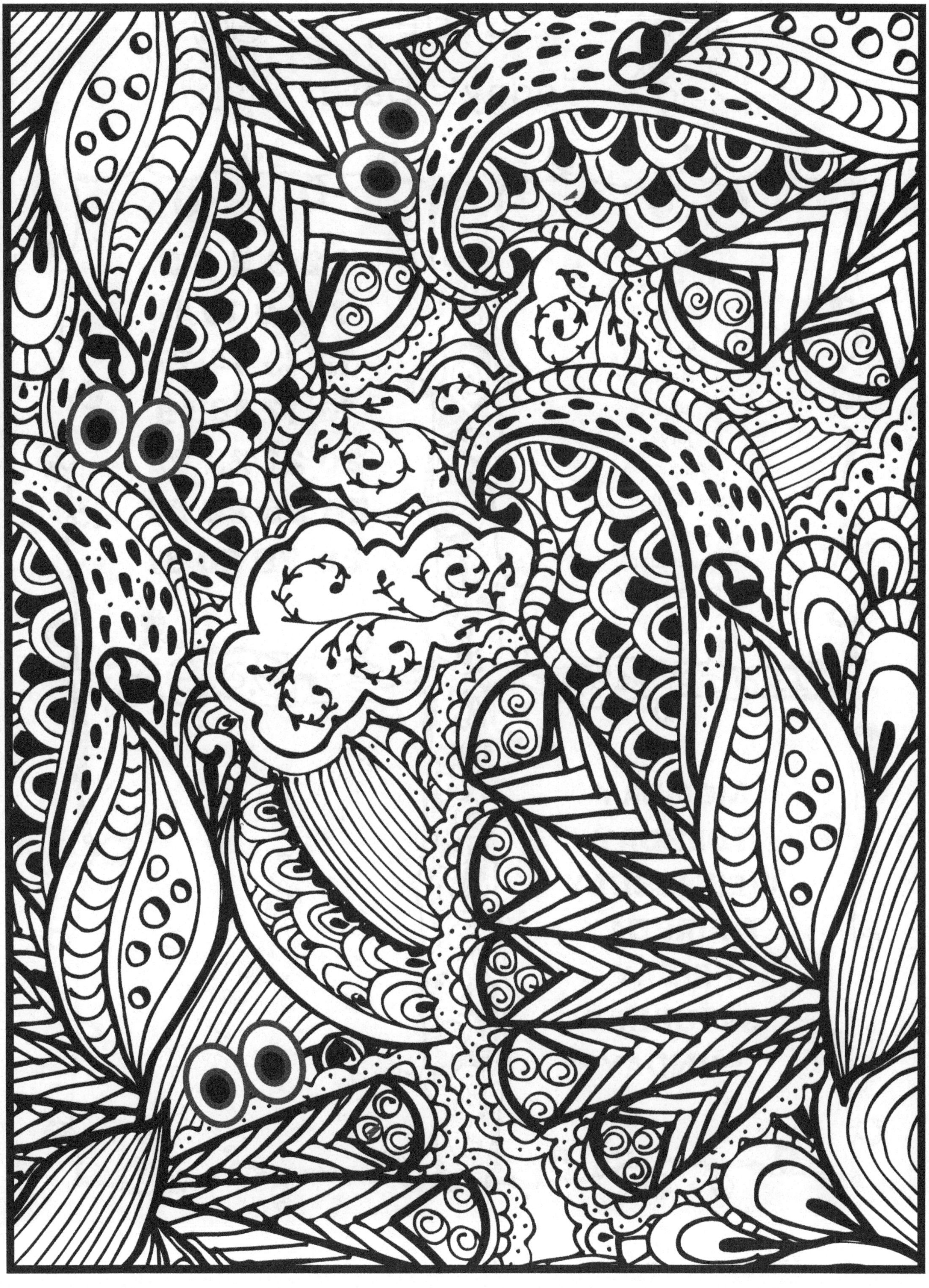

Circle Today's Date

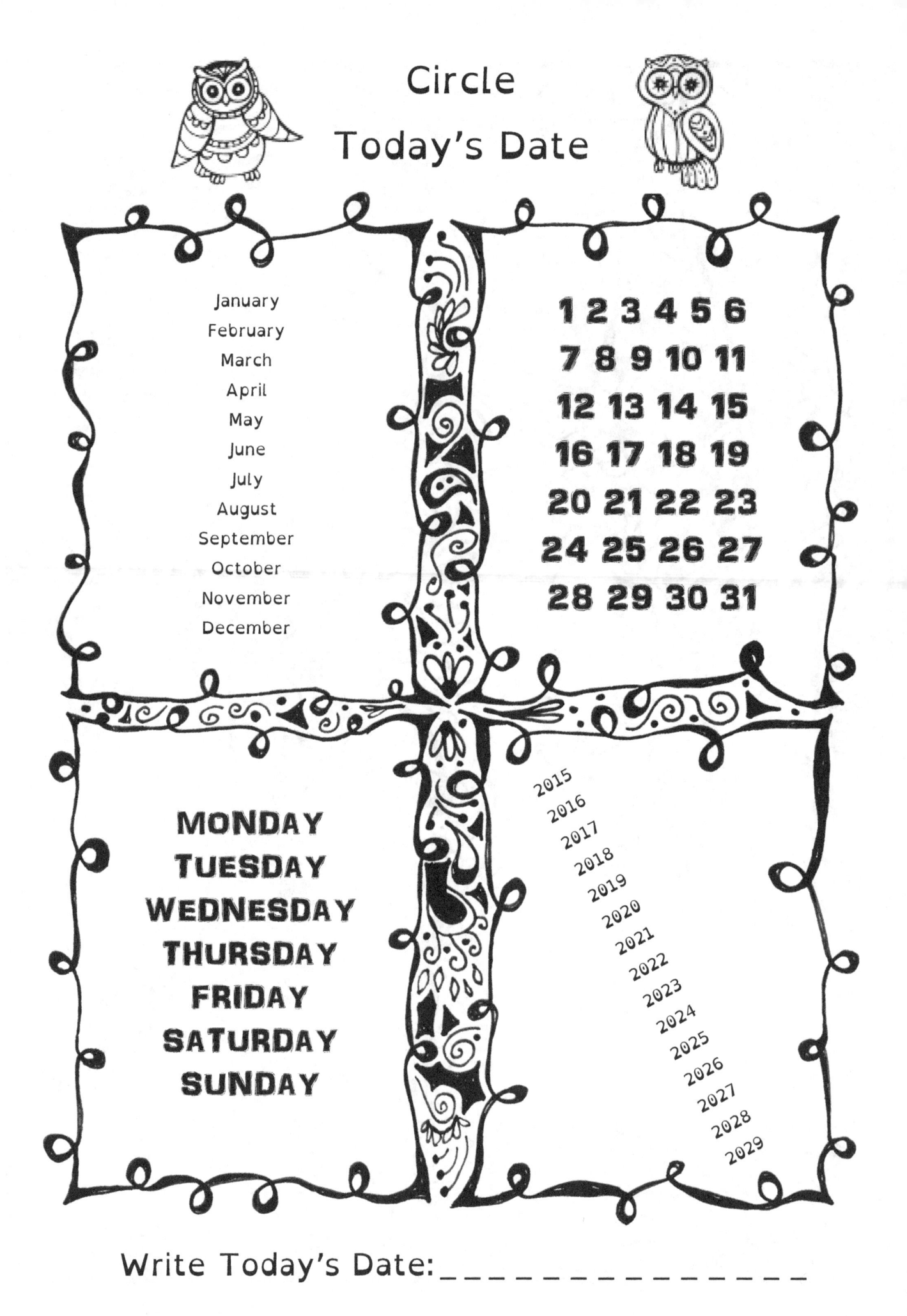

January
February
March
April
May
June
July
August
September
October
November
December

1 2 3 4 5 6
7 8 9 10 11
12 13 14 15
16 17 18 19
20 21 22 23
24 25 26 27
28 29 30 31

MONDAY
TUESDAY
WEDNESDAY
THURSDAY
FRIDAY
SATURDAY
SUNDAY

2015
2016
2017
2018
2019
2020
2021
2022
2023
2024
2025
2026
2027
2028
2029

Write Today's Date: _____

My Thinking Page

This is where you write down your ideas, goals, and plans - with a thankful heart!

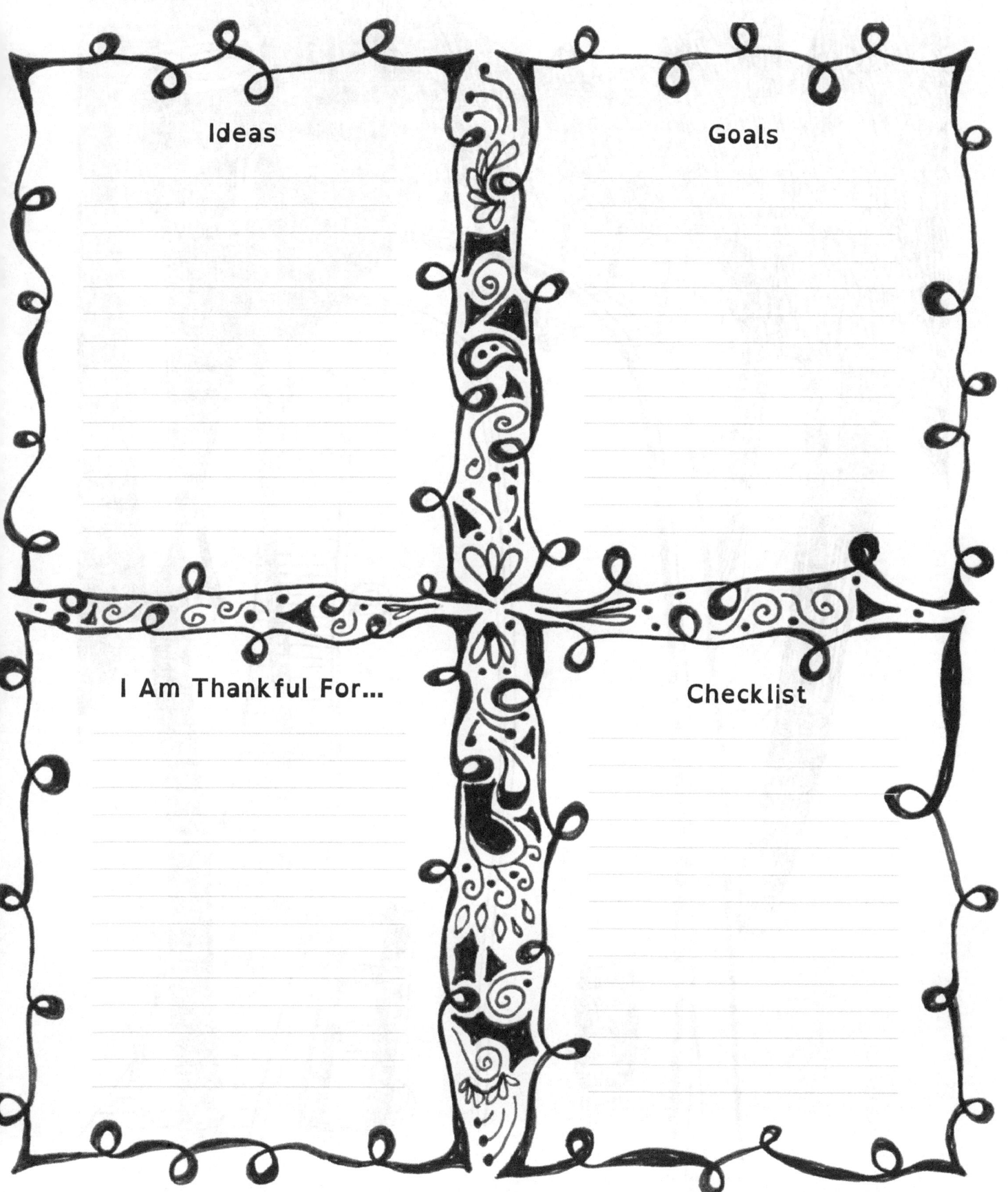

Ideas

Goals

I Am Thankful For...

Checklist

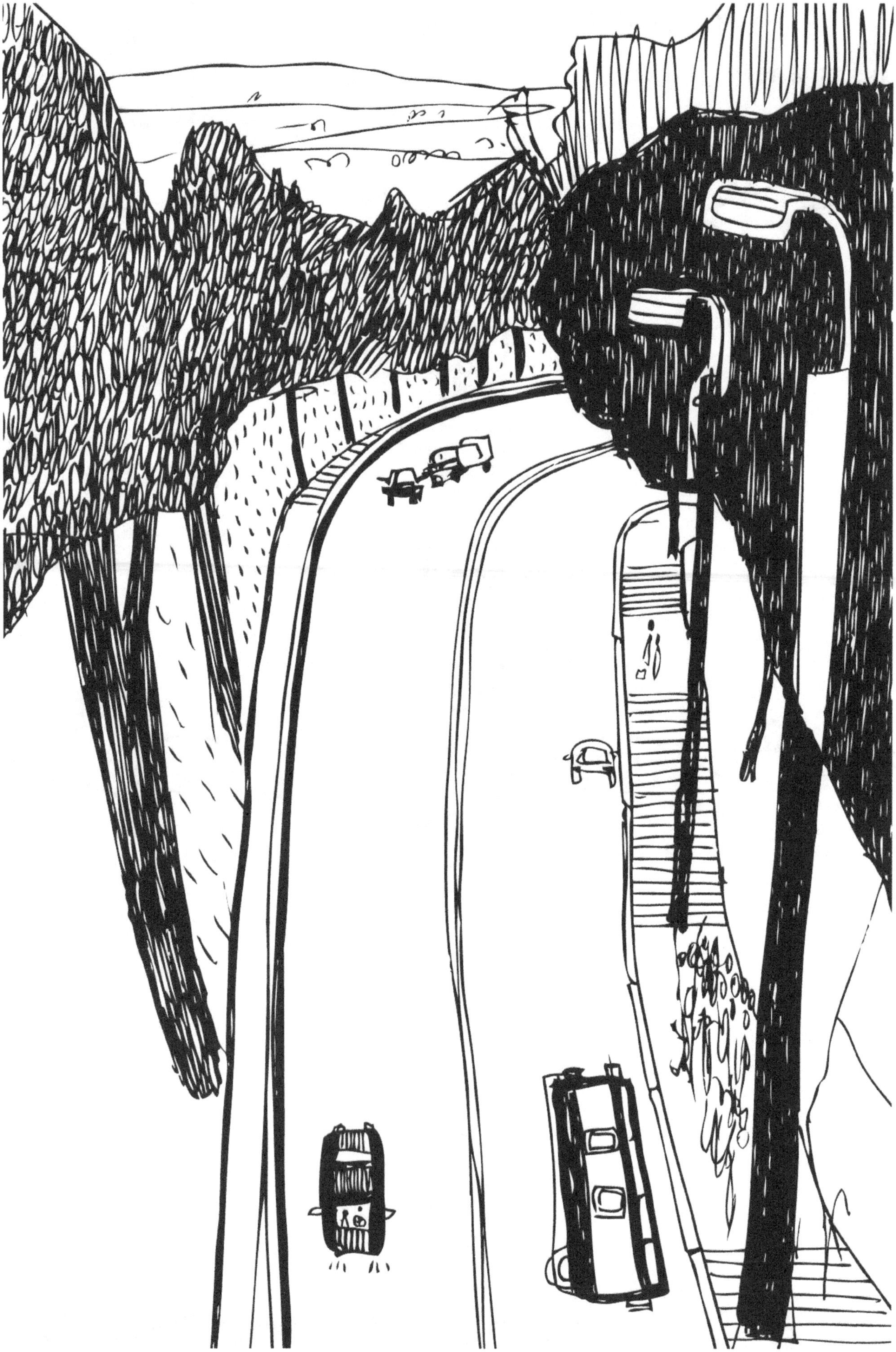

Write & Draw about something that really happened.

Nature Study

Go outside and make a realistic drawing of something you find in nature.

Reading Time - 1 Hour

Choose Four Books - Read from each book for 15 minutes.
Copy a sentence or picture from each book here:

Spelling Time

Find 20 Words with 5 letters each.
Look in your books for words.
Write the words here:

_____   _____

_____   _____

_____   _____

_____   _____

_____   _____

_____   _____

_____   _____

_____   _____

_____   _____

_____   _____

Circle Today's Date

January
February
March
April
May
June
July
August
September
October
November
December

1 2 3 4 5 6
7 8 9 10 11
12 13 14 15
16 17 18 19
20 21 22 23
24 25 26 27
28 29 30 31

MONDAY
TUESDAY
WEDNESDAY
THURSDAY
FRIDAY
SATURDAY
SUNDAY

2015
2016
2017
2018
2019
2020
2021
2022
2023
2024
2025
2026
2027
2028
2029

Write Today's Date: _____

Film Study

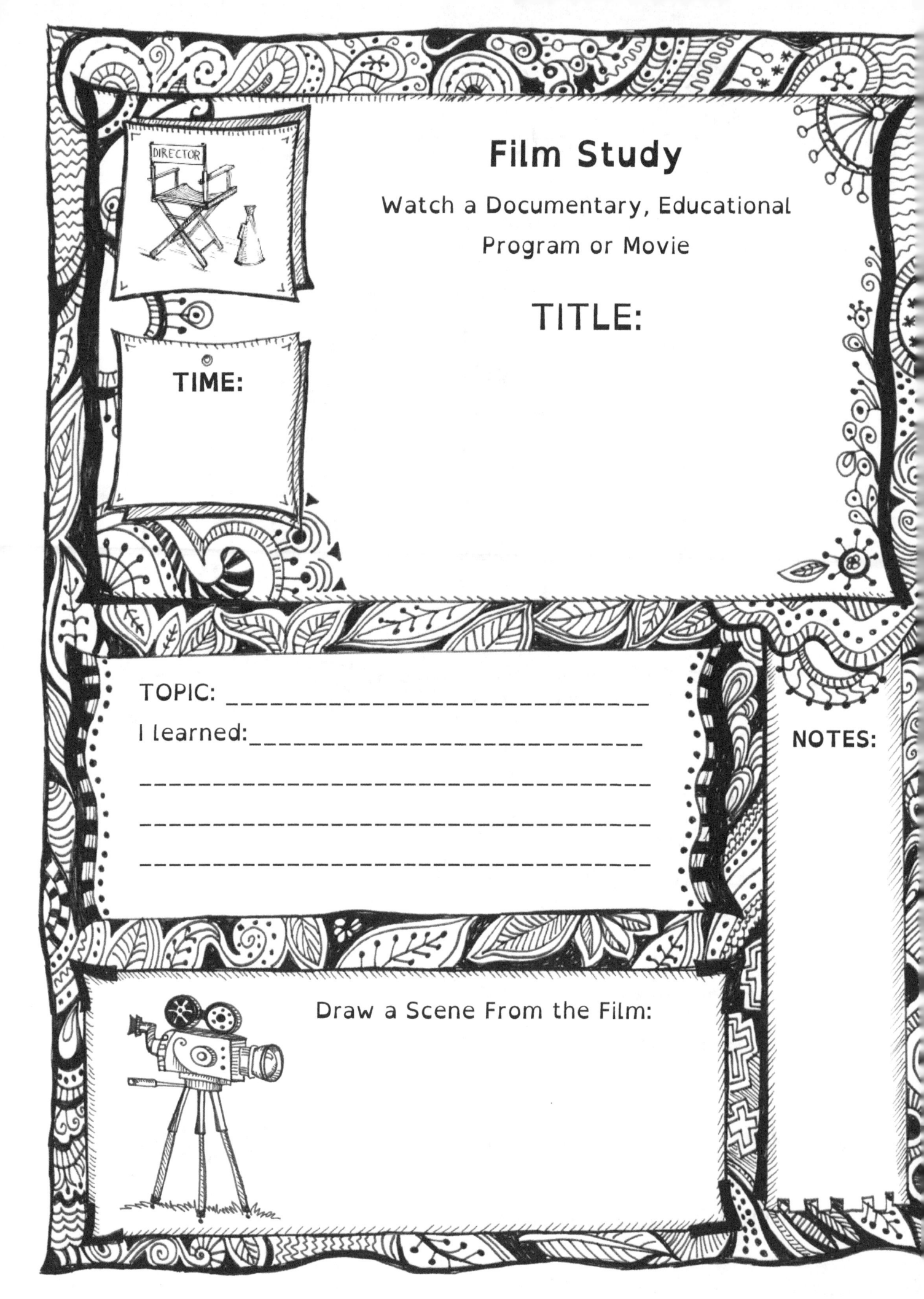

Watch a Documentary, Educational Program or Movie

TITLE:

TIME:

TOPIC: _____
I learned: _____
_____
_____
_____

NOTES:

Draw a Scene From the Film:

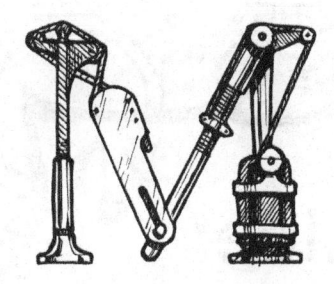

Math Practice

Watch a math tutorial or open up a math book.
You can practice math problems here.

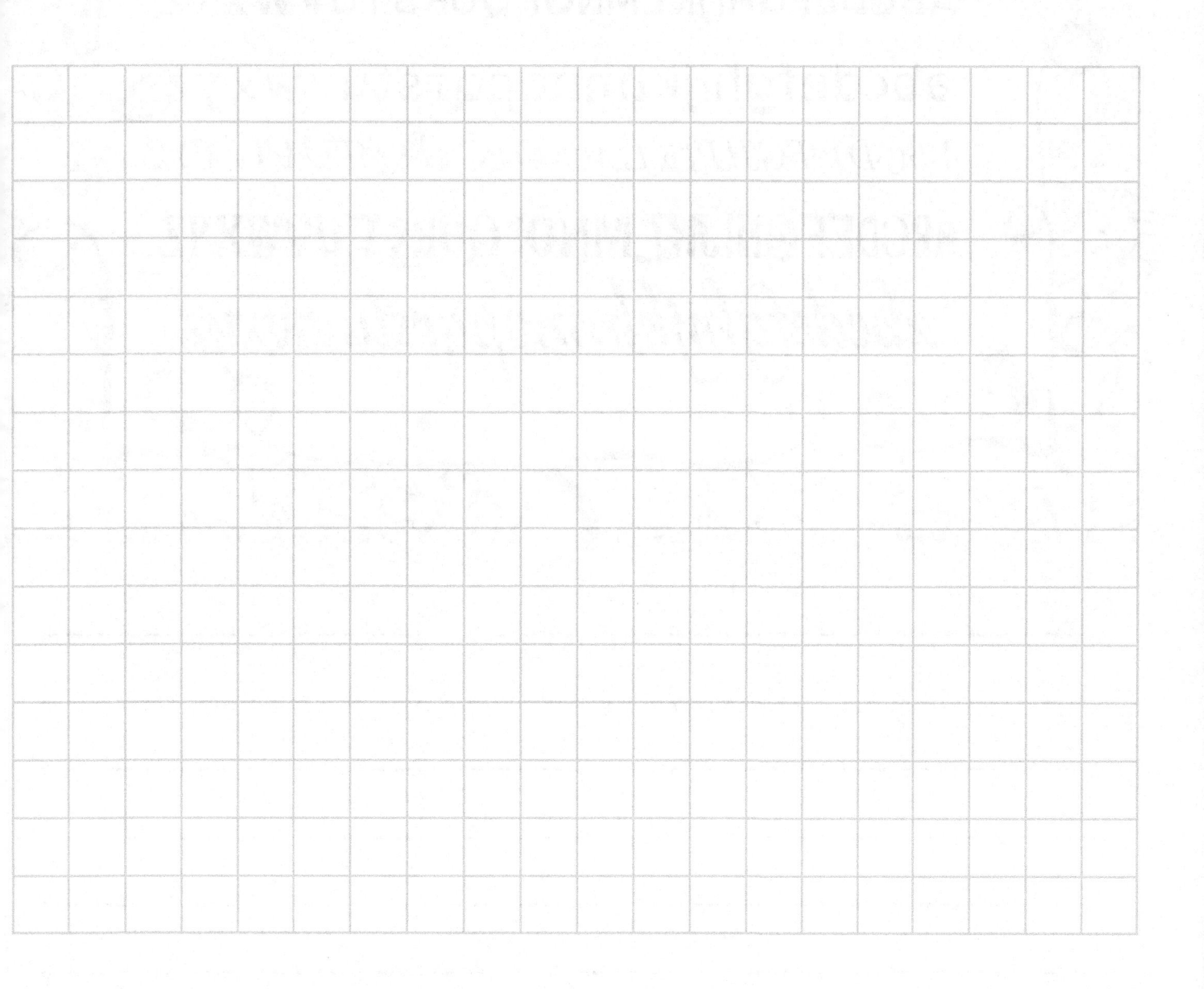

Fun Writing Practice:

ABCDEFGHIJKLMNOPQURSTUVWXYZ

abcdefghijklmnopqrstuvwxyz

ABCDEFGHIJKLMNOPQURSTUVWXYZ

ABCDEFGHIJKLMNOPQURSTUVWXYZ

abcdefghijklmnopqrstuvwxyz

A B C
D F
E G

Copywork

Find an interesting paragraph in one of your books and copy it. Be diligent to make your writing look exactly like it does in the book.

TITLE:_____ **Page Number:**____

Circle Today's Date

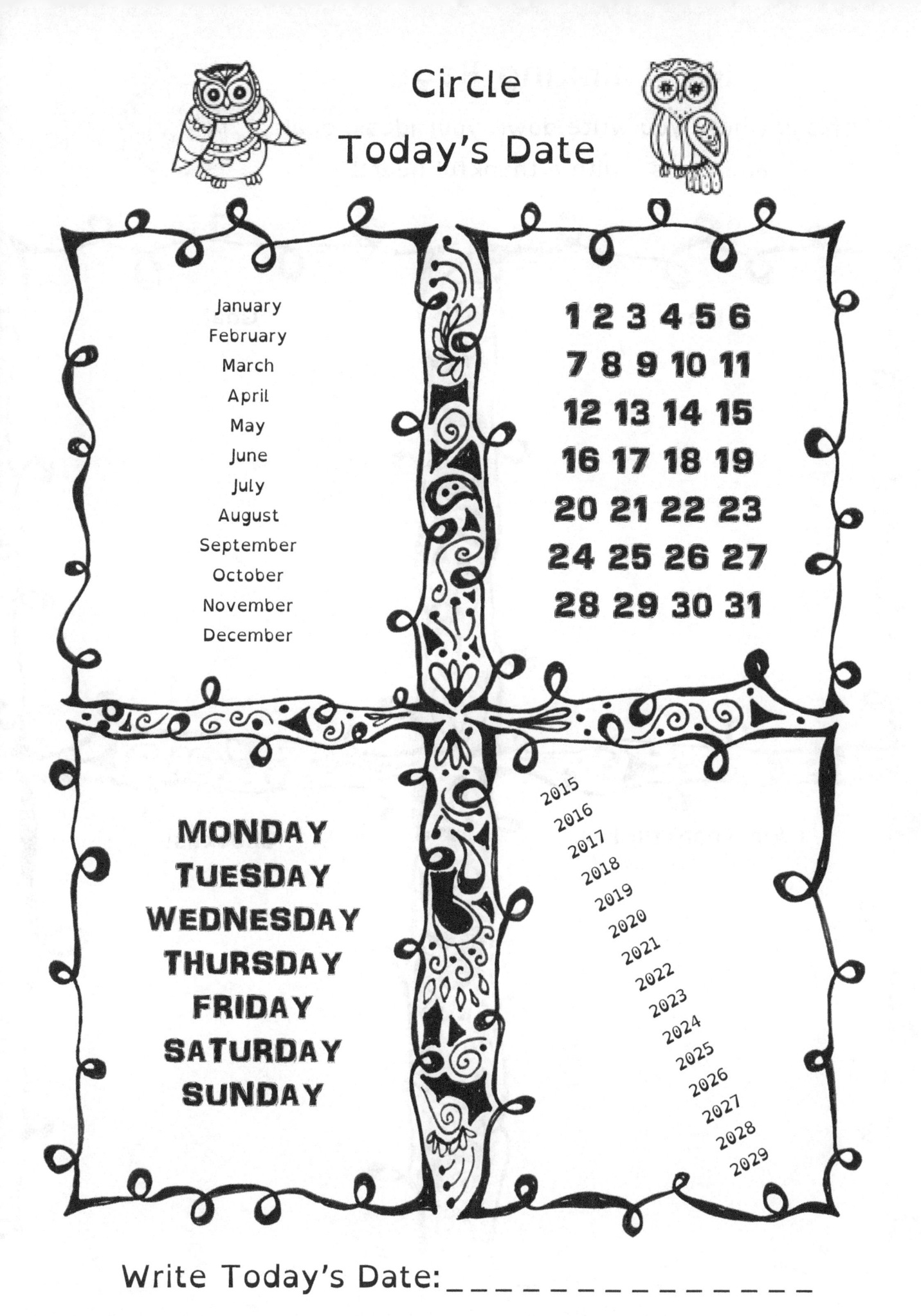

January
February
March
April
May
June
July
August
September
October
November
December

1 2 3 4 5 6
7 8 9 10 11
12 13 14 15
16 17 18 19
20 21 22 23
24 25 26 27
28 29 30 31

MONDAY
TUESDAY
WEDNESDAY
THURSDAY
FRIDAY
SATURDAY
SUNDAY

2015
2016
2017
2018
2019
2020
2021
2022
2023
2024
2025
2026
2027
2028
2029

Write Today's Date: _____

My Thinking Page

This is where you write down your ideas, goals, and plans - with a thankful heart!

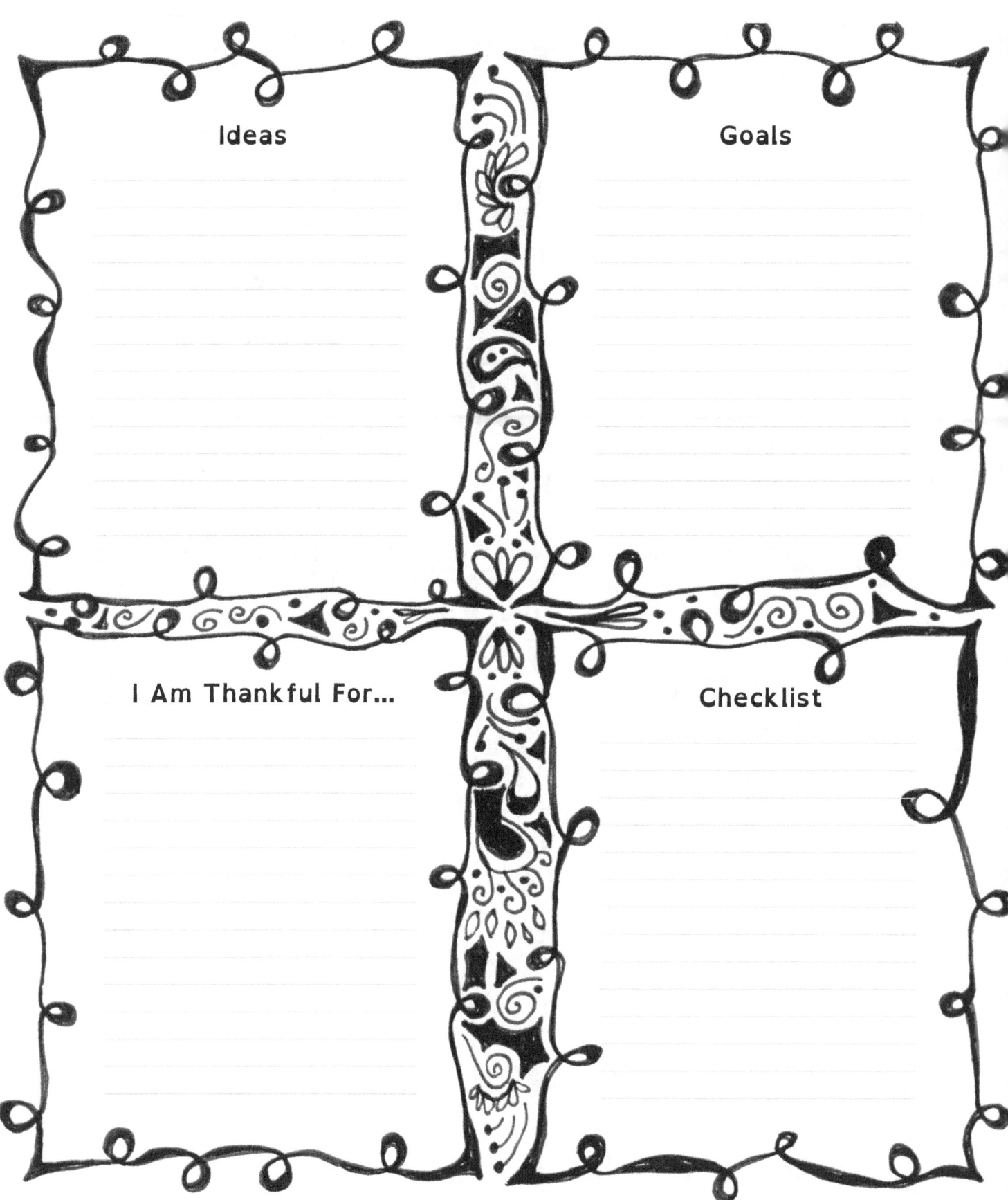

Ideas

Goals

I Am Thankful For...

Checklist

Write & Draw about something that really happened.

_____
_____
_____
_____
_____
_____
_____
_____

Nature Study

Go outside and make a realistic drawing of something you find in nature.

Reading Time - 1 Hour

Choose Four Books - Read from each book for 15 minutes.
Copy a sentence or picture from each book here:

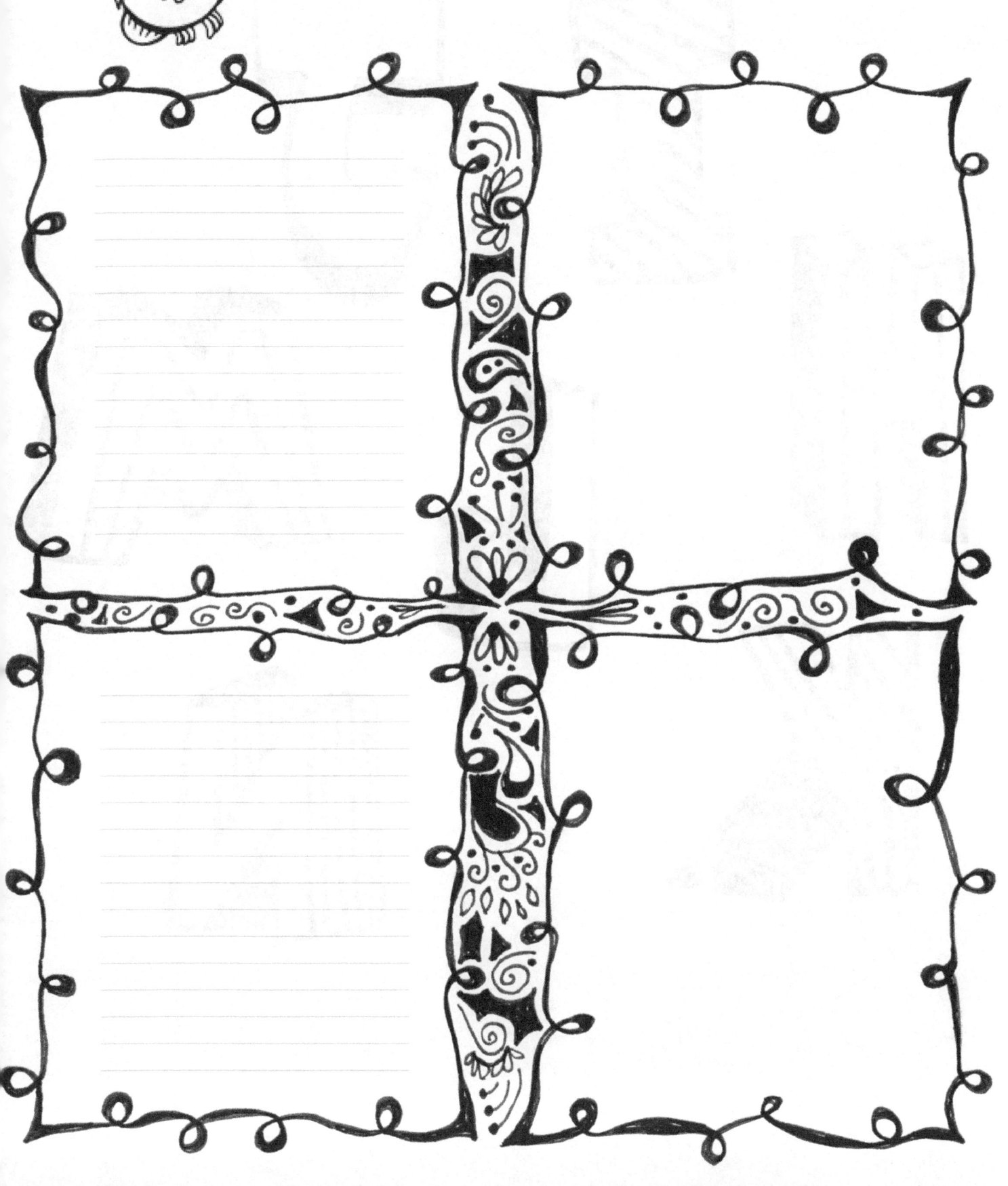

H I J K L M N

Circle Today's Date

January
February
March
April
May
June
July
August
September
October
November
December

1 2 3 4 5 6
7 8 9 10 11
12 13 14 15
16 17 18 19
20 21 22 23
24 25 26 27
28 29 30 31

MONDAY
TUESDAY
WEDNESDAY
THURSDAY
FRIDAY
SATURDAY
SUNDAY

2015
2016
2017
2018
2019
2020
2021
2022
2023
2024
2025
2026
2027
2028
2029

Write Today's Date: _____

Spelling Time

Find 20 Words with 6 letters each.
Look in your books for words.
Write the words here:

_____   _____

_____   _____

_____   _____

_____   _____

_____   _____

_____   _____

_____   _____

_____   _____

_____   _____

_____   _____

Film Study

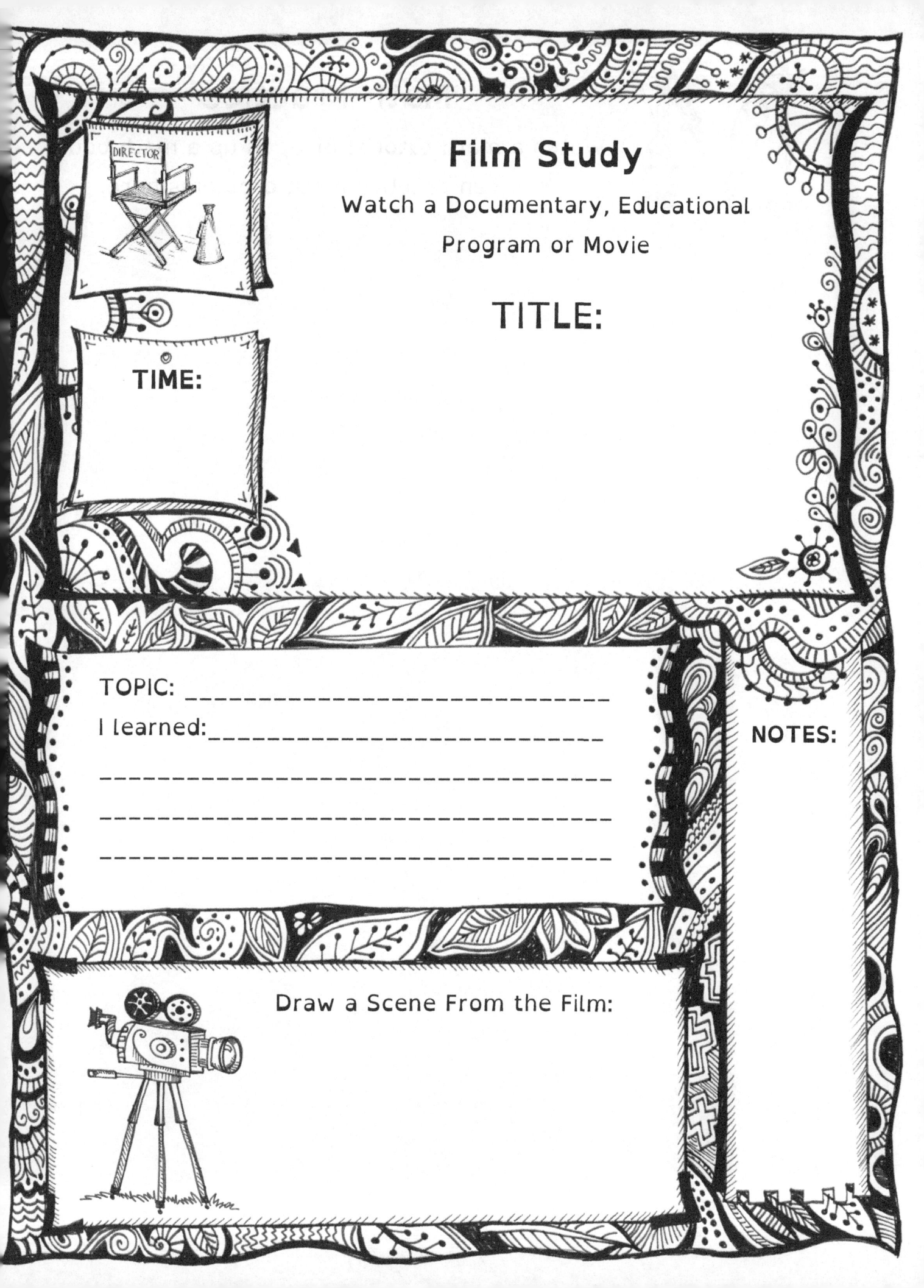

Watch a Documentary, Educational Program or Movie

TITLE:

TIME:

TOPIC: _____

I learned: _____

_____

_____

_____

NOTES:

Draw a Scene From the Film:

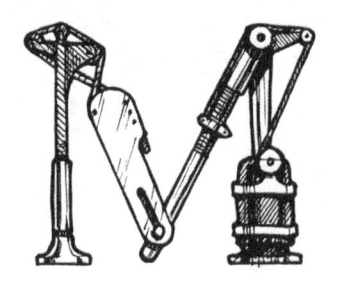

Math Practice

Watch a math tutorial or open up a math book.
You can practice math problems here.

My Illustrated TO-DO List

Copywork

Find an interesting paragraph in one of your books and copy it. Be diligent to make your writing look exactly like it does in the book.

TITLE:_____ **Page Number:**_____

Sketch a Picture

Look through your library books and find something to draw.

Circle Today's Date

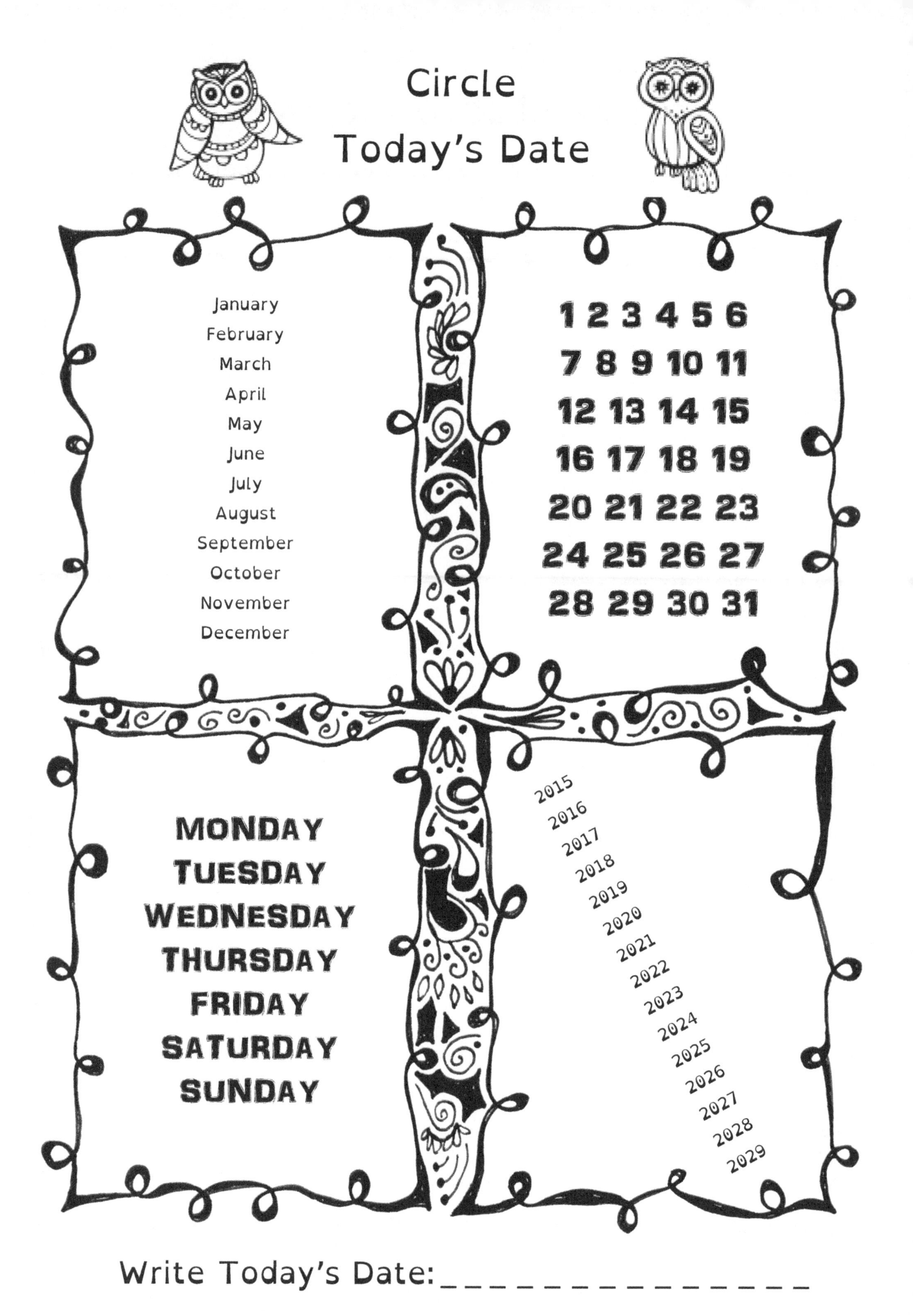

January
February
March
April
May
June
July
August
September
October
November
December

1 2 3 4 5 6
7 8 9 10 11
12 13 14 15
16 17 18 19
20 21 22 23
24 25 26 27
28 29 30 31

MONDAY
TUESDAY
WEDNESDAY
THURSDAY
FRIDAY
SATURDAY
SUNDAY

2015
2016
2017
2018
2019
2020
2021
2022
2023
2024
2025
2026
2027
2028
2029

Write Today's Date: _____

My Thinking Page

This is where you write down your ideas, goals, and plans - with a thankful heart!

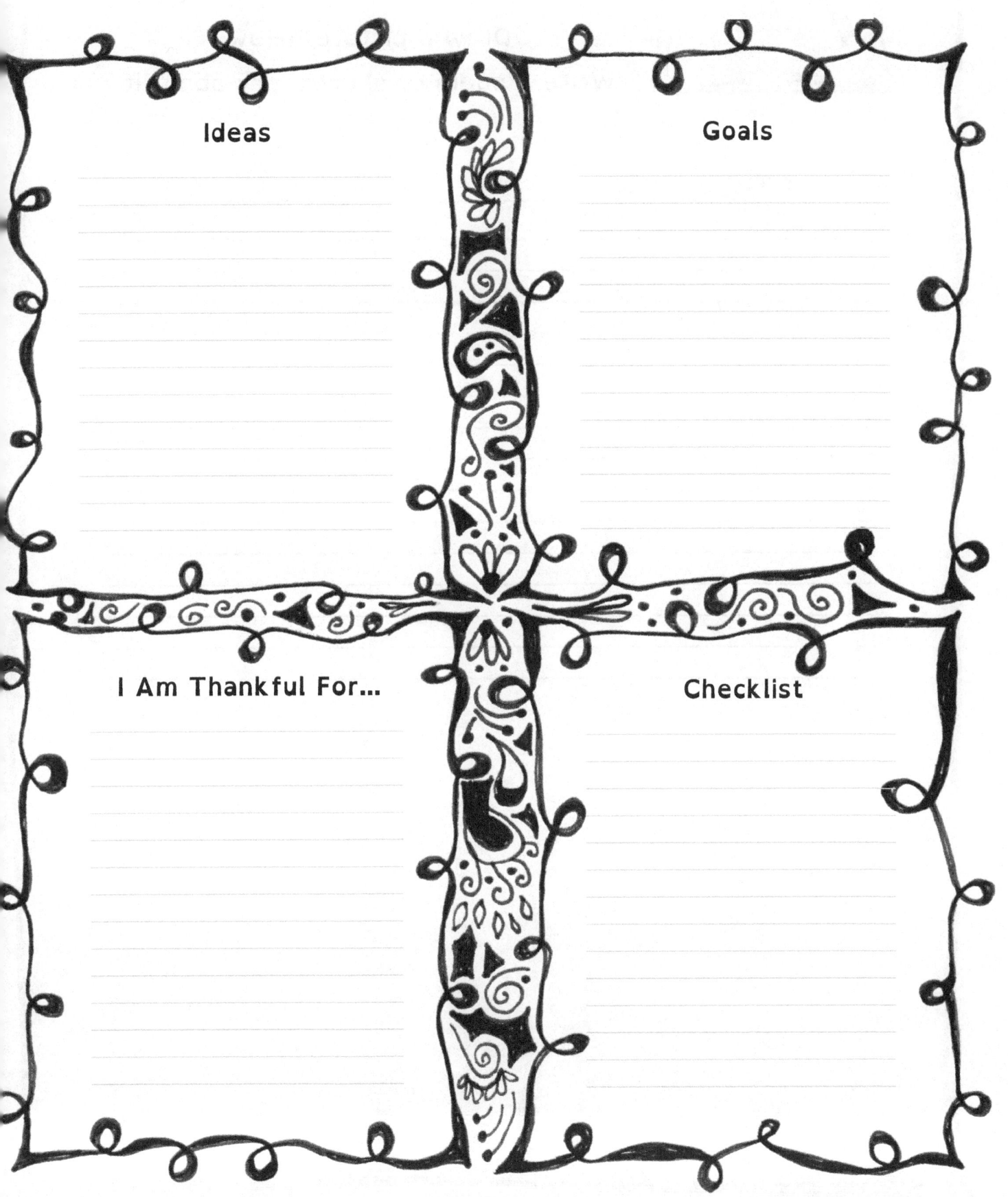

Ideas

Goals

I Am Thankful For...

Checklist

Creative Writing

Draw a picture below.
Write a poem or short story about it.

TITLE: _____

_____
_____
_____
_____
_____
_____
_____
_____
_____
_____
_____
_____
_____
_____
_____
_____

Nature Study

Go outside and make a realistic drawing of something you find in nature.

Reading Time - 1 Hour

Choose Four Books - Read from each book for 15 minutes.
Copy a sentence or picture from each book here:

O P Q
R T
S U

Circle Today's Date

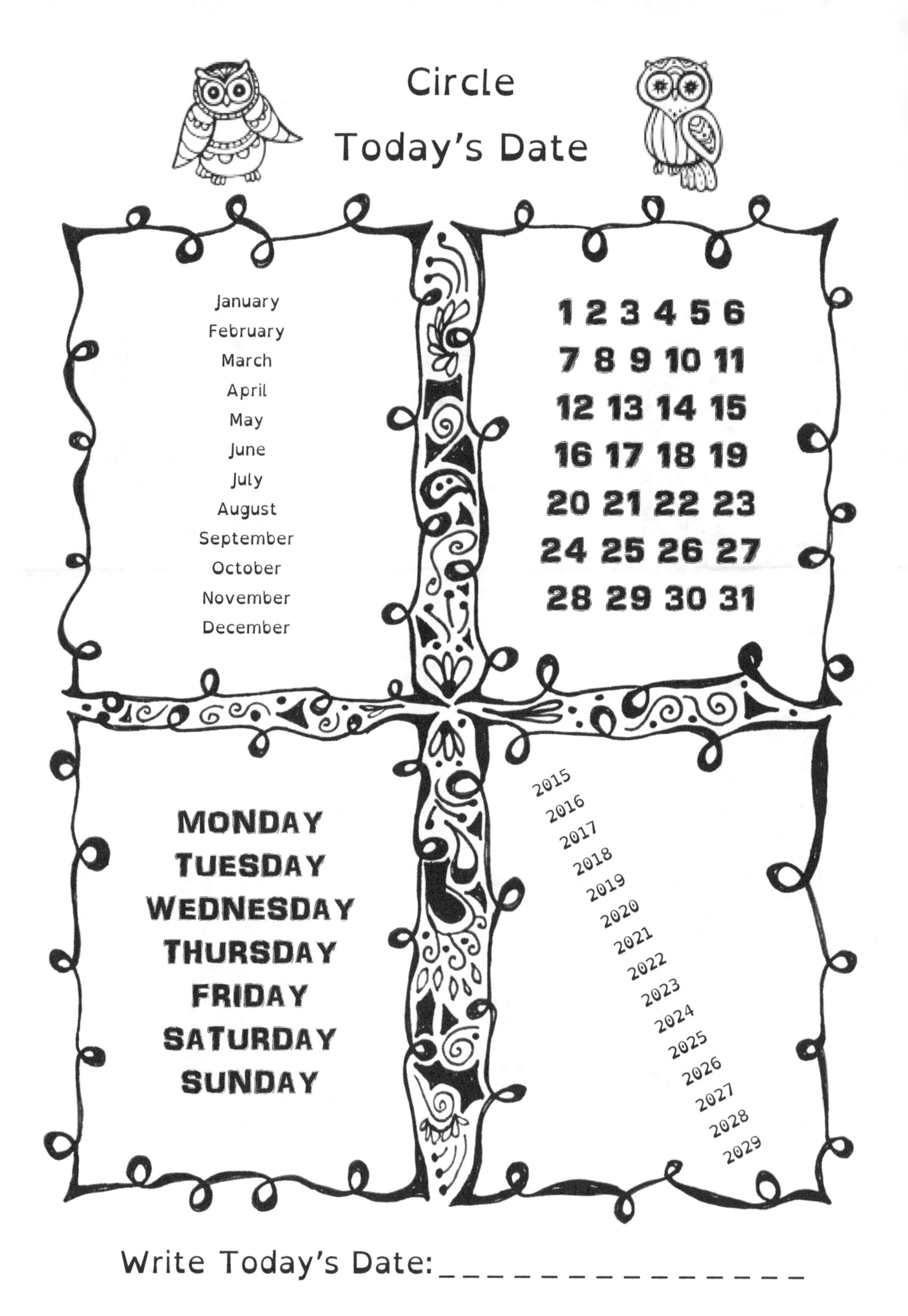

January
February
March
April
May
June
July
August
September
October
November
December

1 2 3 4 5 6
7 8 9 10 11
12 13 14 15
16 17 18 19
20 21 22 23
24 25 26 27
28 29 30 31

MONDAY
TUESDAY
WEDNESDAY
THURSDAY
FRIDAY
SATURDAY
SUNDAY

2015
2016
2017
2018
2019
2020
2021
2022
2023
2024
2025
2026
2027
2028
2029

Write Today's Date: _____

Spelling Time

Find 20 Words with 7 letters each.
Look in your books for words.
Write the words here:

_____ _____

_____ _____

_____ _____

_____ _____

_____ _____

_____ _____

_____ _____

_____ _____

_____ _____

_____ _____

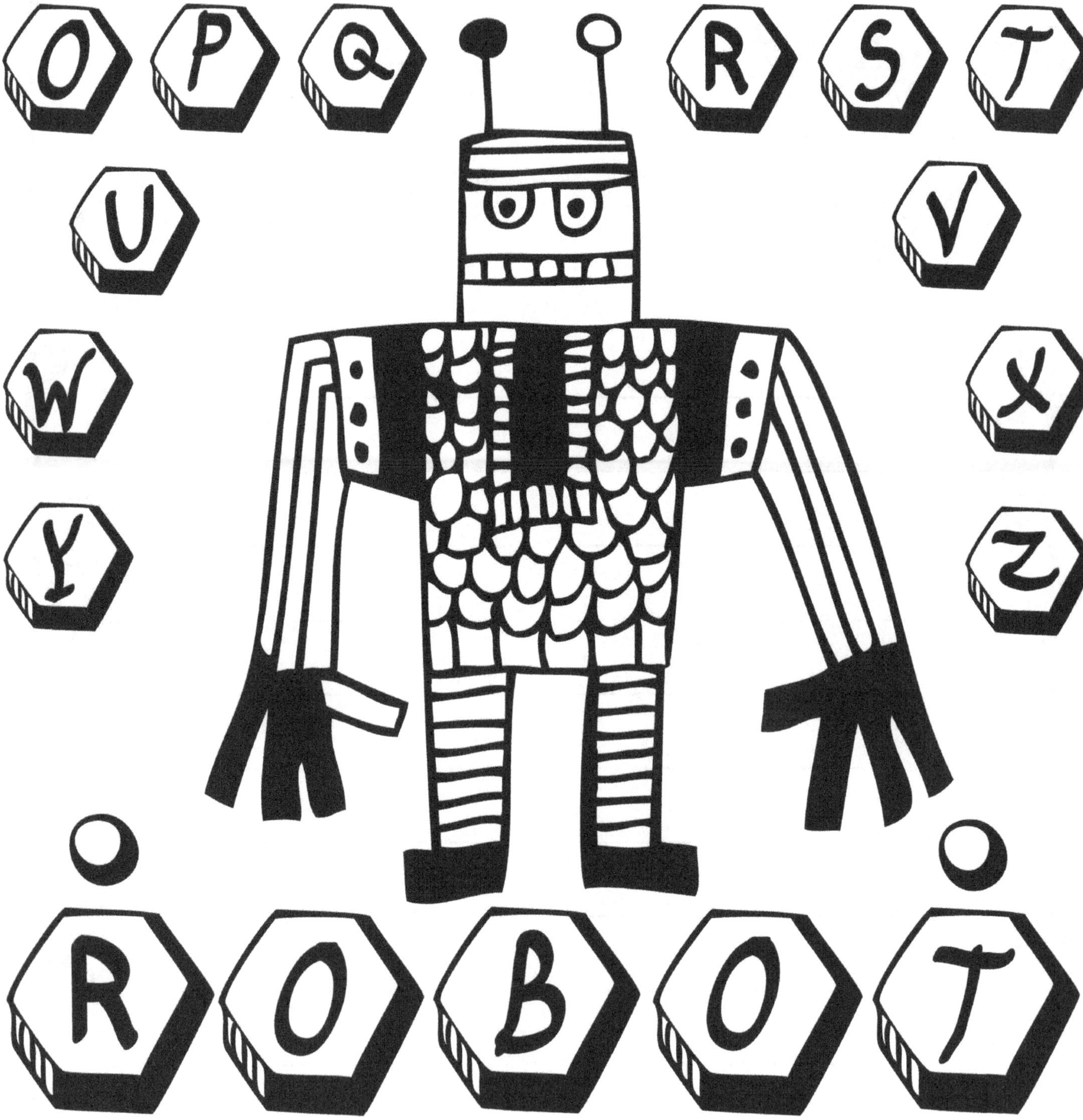
O P Q R S T
U V
W X
Y Z
ROBOT

Learning a Skill

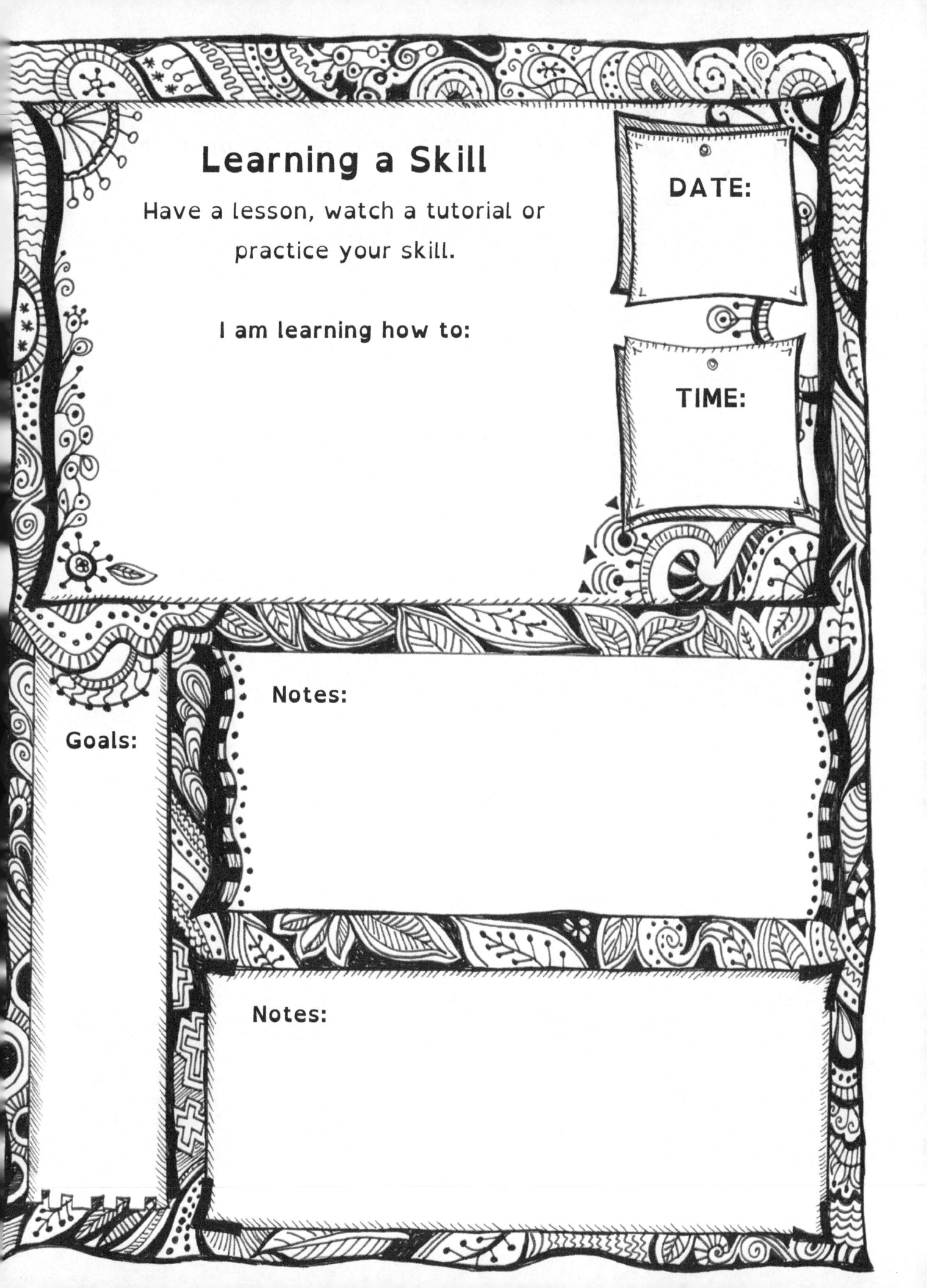

Have a lesson, watch a tutorial or practice your skill.

I am learning how to:

DATE:

TIME:

Goals:

Notes:

Notes:

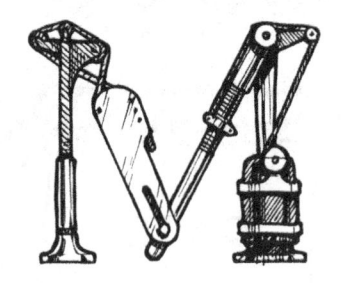

Math Practice

Watch a math tutorial or open up a math book.
You can practice math problems here.

Copywork

Find an interesting paragraph in one of your books and copy it. Be diligent to make your writing look exactly like it does in the book.

TITLE:_____ Page Number:_____

Circle Today's Date

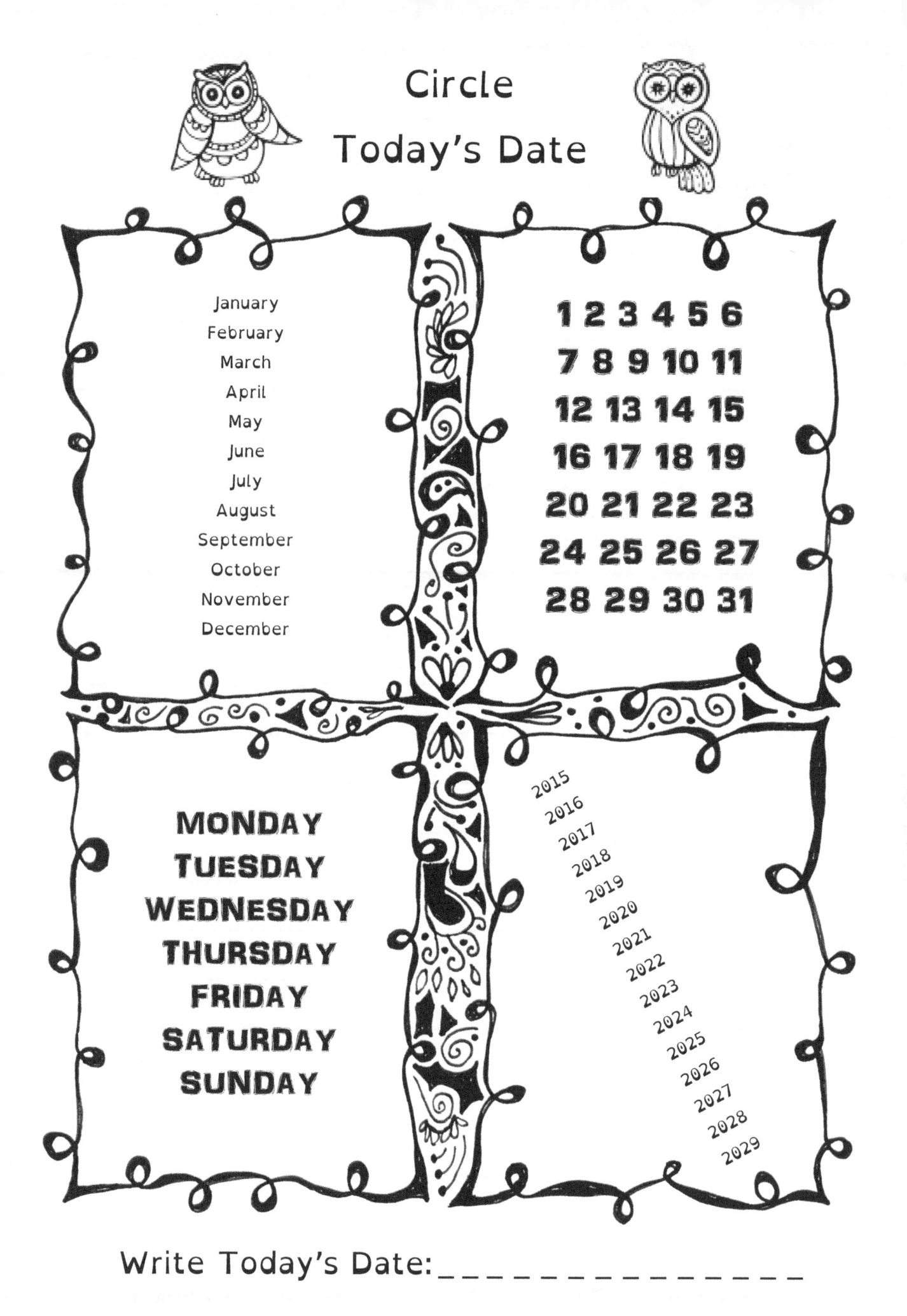

January
February
March
April
May
June
July
August
September
October
November
December

1 2 3 4 5 6
7 8 9 10 11
12 13 14 15
16 17 18 19
20 21 22 23
24 25 26 27
28 29 30 31

MONDAY
TUESDAY
WEDNESDAY
THURSDAY
FRIDAY
SATURDAY
SUNDAY

2015
2016
2017
2018
2019
2020
2021
2022
2023
2024
2025
2026
2027
2028
2029

Write Today's Date: _____

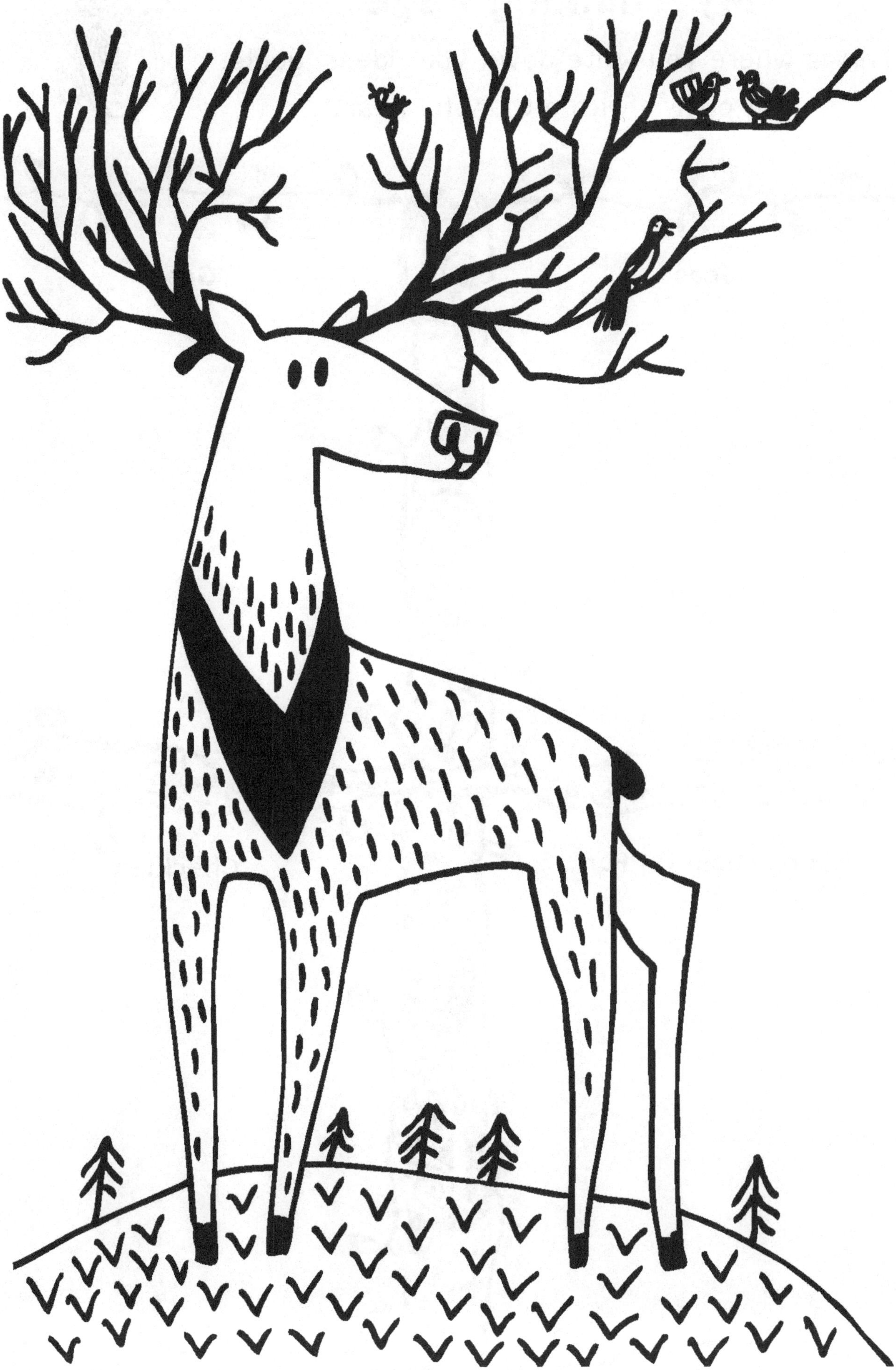

My Thinking Page

This is where you write down your ideas, goals, and plans - with a thankful heart!

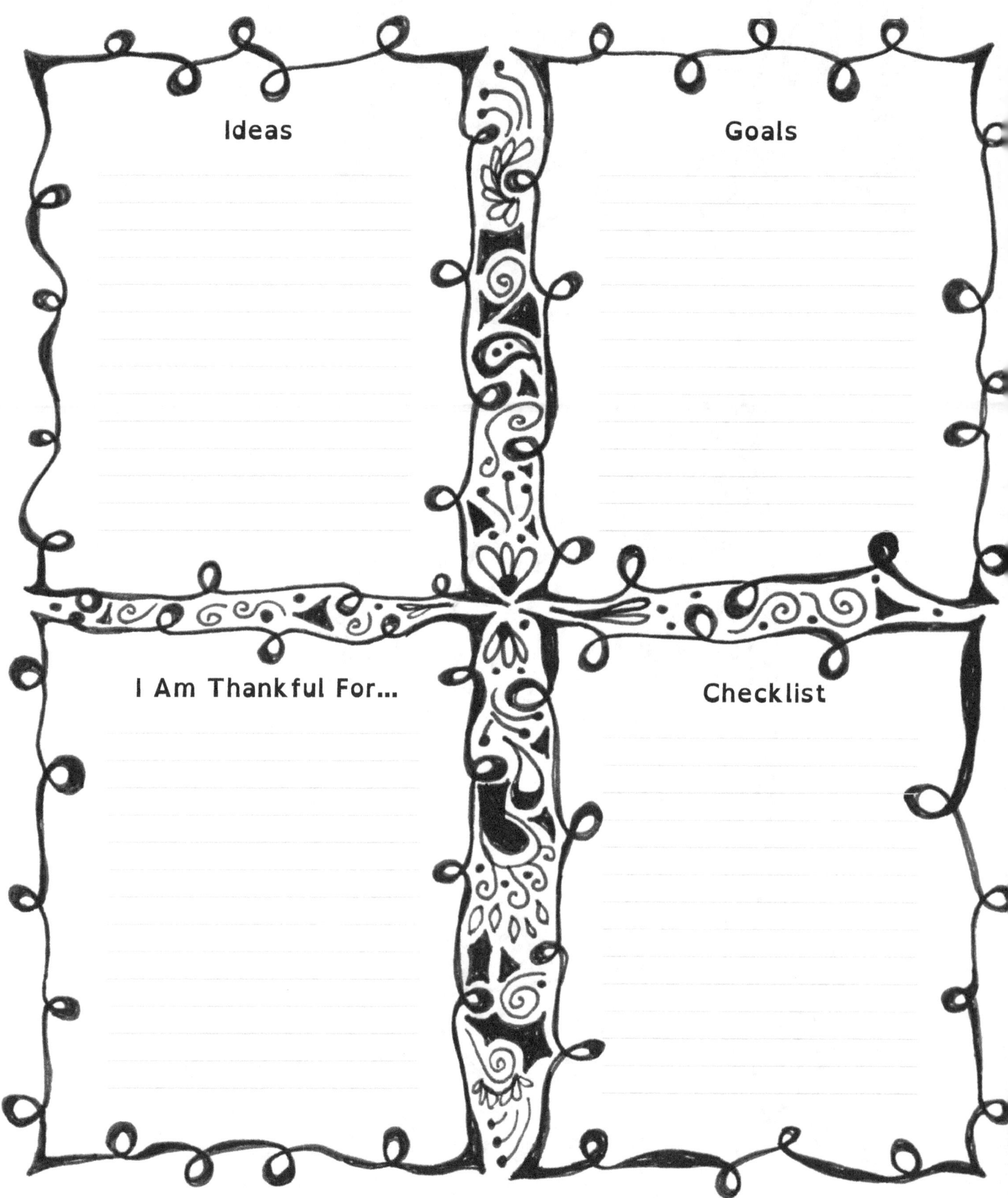

Ideas

Goals

I Am Thankful For...

Checklist

Creative Writing

Draw a picture below.
Write a poem or short story about it.

TITLE: _____

_____
_____
_____
_____
_____
_____
_____
_____
_____
_____
_____
_____

Learning a Skill

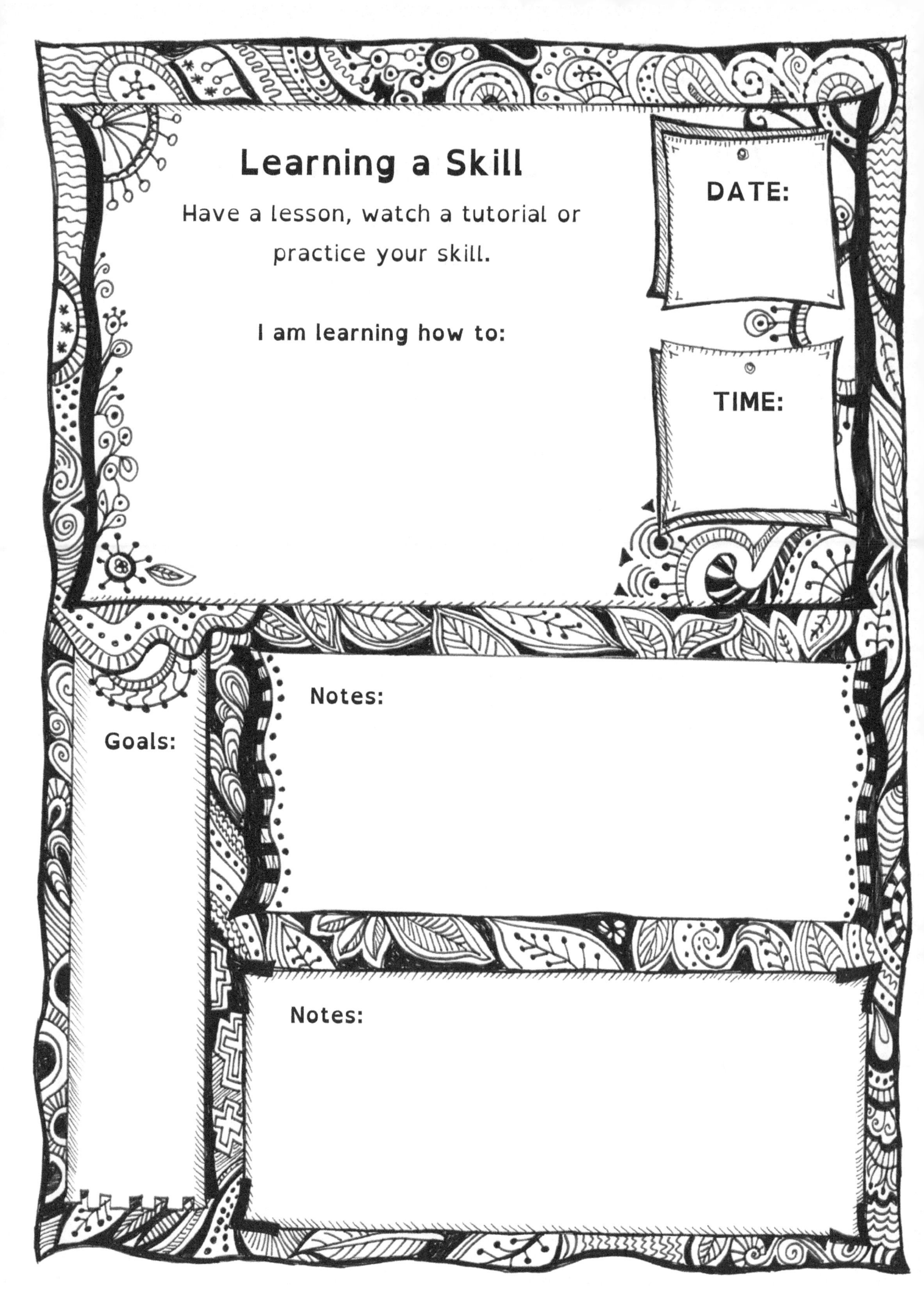

Have a lesson, watch a tutorial or practice your skill.

I am learning how to:

DATE:

TIME:

Goals:

Notes:

Notes:

Nature Study

Go outside and make a realistic drawing of something you find in nature.

Reading Time - 1 Hour

Choose Four Books - Read from each book for 15 minutes.
Copy a sentence or picture from each book here:

Circle Today's Date

January
February
March
April
May
June
July
August
September
October
November
December

1 2 3 4 5 6
7 8 9 10 11
12 13 14 15
16 17 18 19
20 21 22 23
24 25 26 27
28 29 30 31

MONDAY
TUESDAY
WEDNESDAY
THURSDAY
FRIDAY
SATURDAY
SUNDAY

2015
2016
2017
2018
2019
2020
2021
2022
2023
2024
2025
2026
2027
2028
2029

Write Today's Date: _____

Spelling Time

Find 20 Words with **8** letters each.
Look in your books for words.
Write the words here:

_____ _____

_____ _____

_____ _____

_____ _____

_____ _____

_____ _____

_____ _____

_____ _____

_____ _____

_____ _____

Film Study

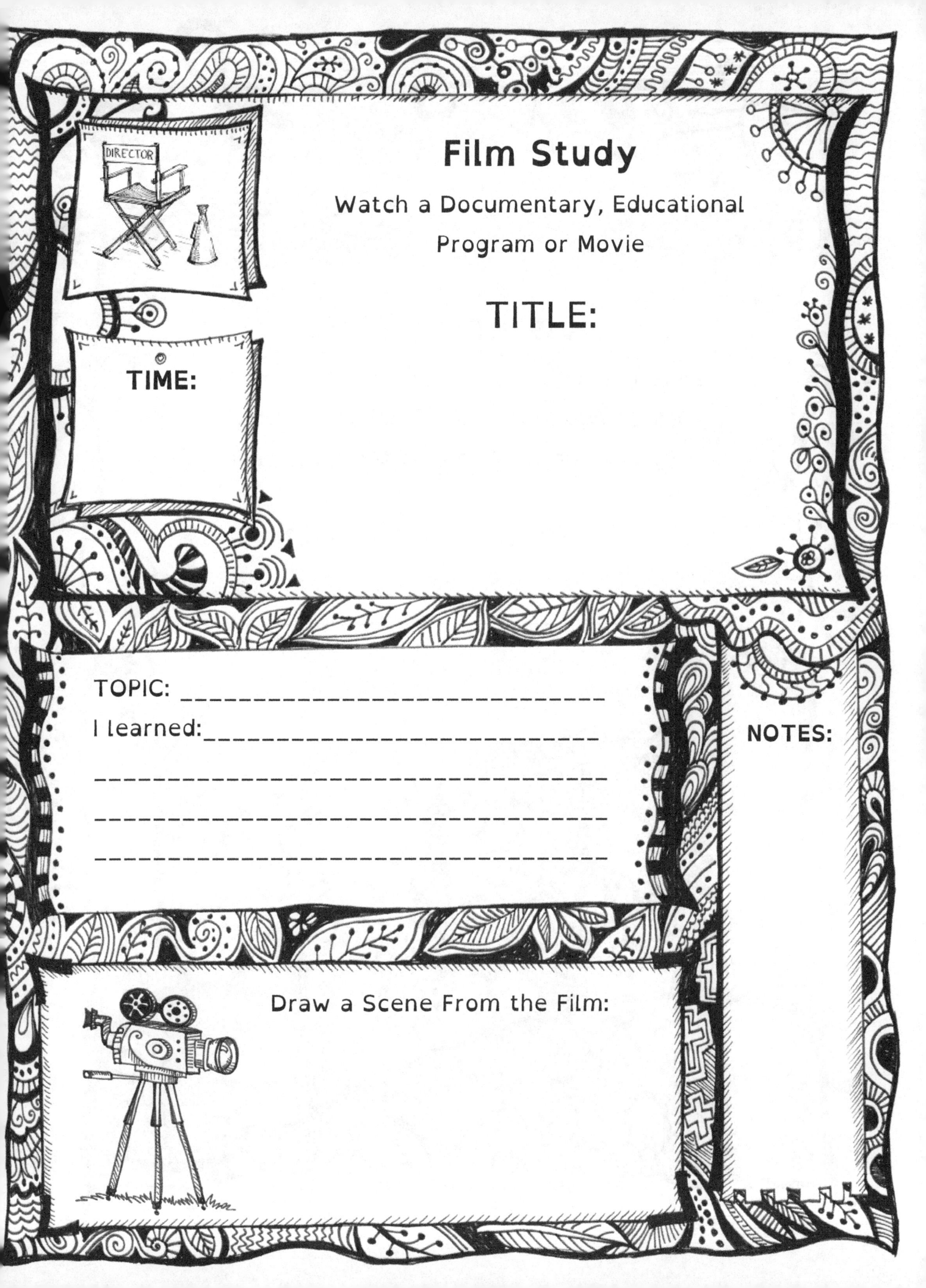

Watch a Documentary, Educational Program or Movie

TITLE:

TIME:

TOPIC: _____
I learned: _____
_____
_____
_____

NOTES:

Draw a Scene From the Film:

Listening Time

Listen to an audio book or classical music or ask someone to read a story to you while you color and draw on the next page.

What are you listening to?

_____

V W
X Y Z

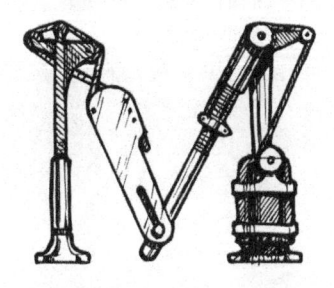

Math Practice

Watch a math tutorial or open up a math book.
You can practice math problems here.

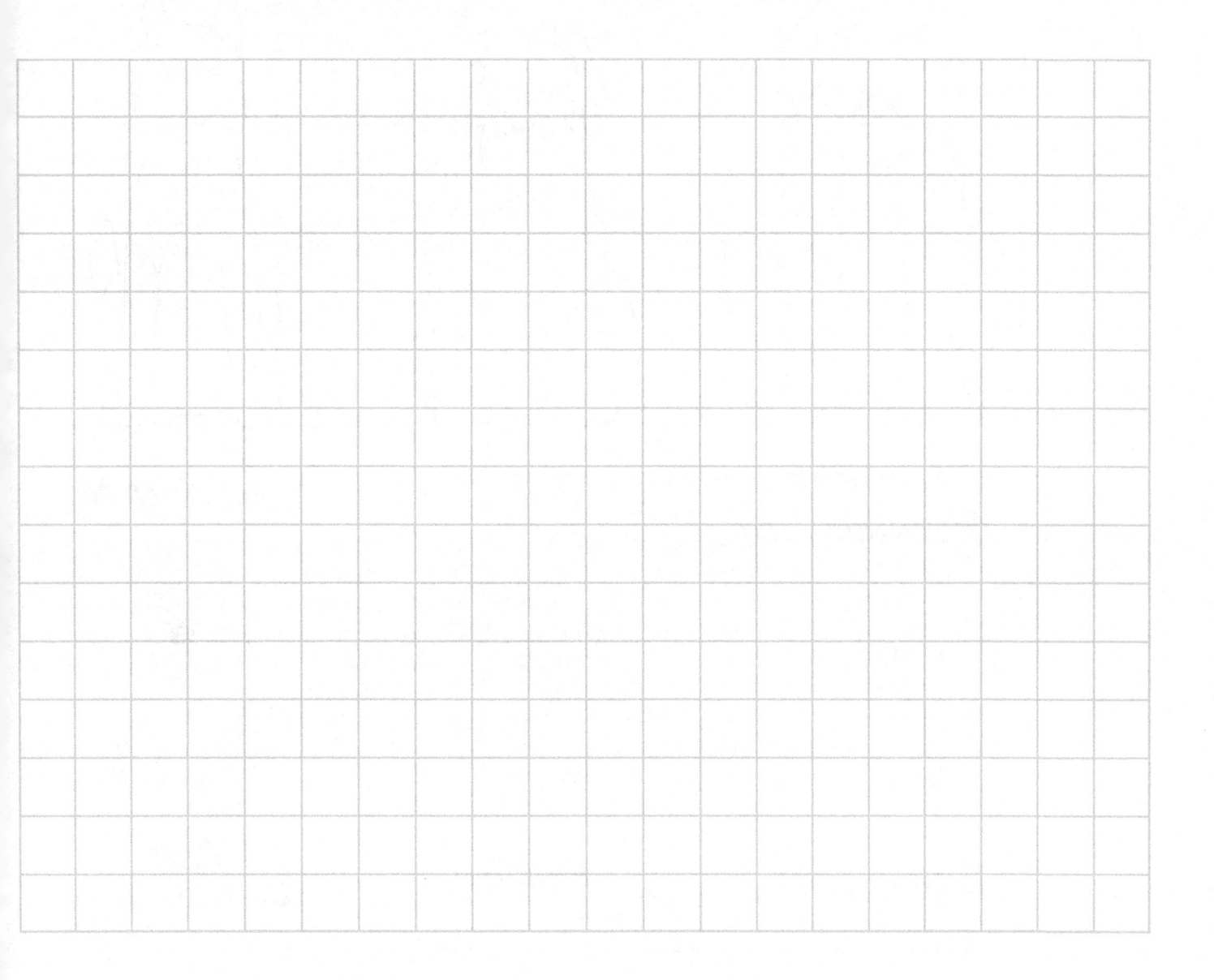

Pyrenean Mountain Dog	Briard	Beauce sheep dog
Bichon Frise	Papillon	Petit Basset Griffon

French dogs *(part 1)*

Bouvier des Flandres

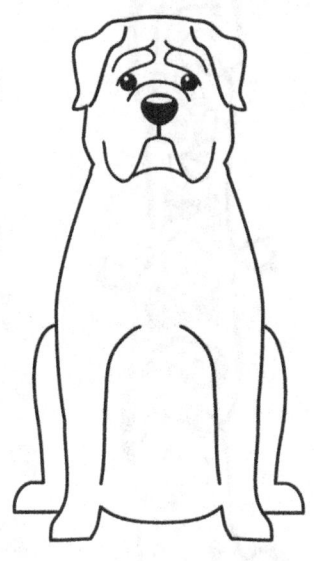

Dogue de Bordeaux (Bordeaux Mastiff)

Epagneul Breton

Lowchen (Little Dog Lion)

French Bulldog

Basset Hound

Pudel

French dogs (part 2)

Circle Today's Date

January
February
March
April
May
June
July
August
September
October
November
December

1 2 3 4 5 6
7 8 9 10 11
12 13 14 15
16 17 18 19
20 21 22 23
24 25 26 27
28 29 30 31

MONDAY
TUESDAY
WEDNESDAY
THURSDAY
FRIDAY
SATURDAY
SUNDAY

2015
2016
2017
2018
2019
2020
2021
2022
2023
2024
2025
2026
2027
2028
2029

Write Today's Date: _____

My Thinking Page

This is where you write down your ideas, goals, and plans - with a thankful heart!

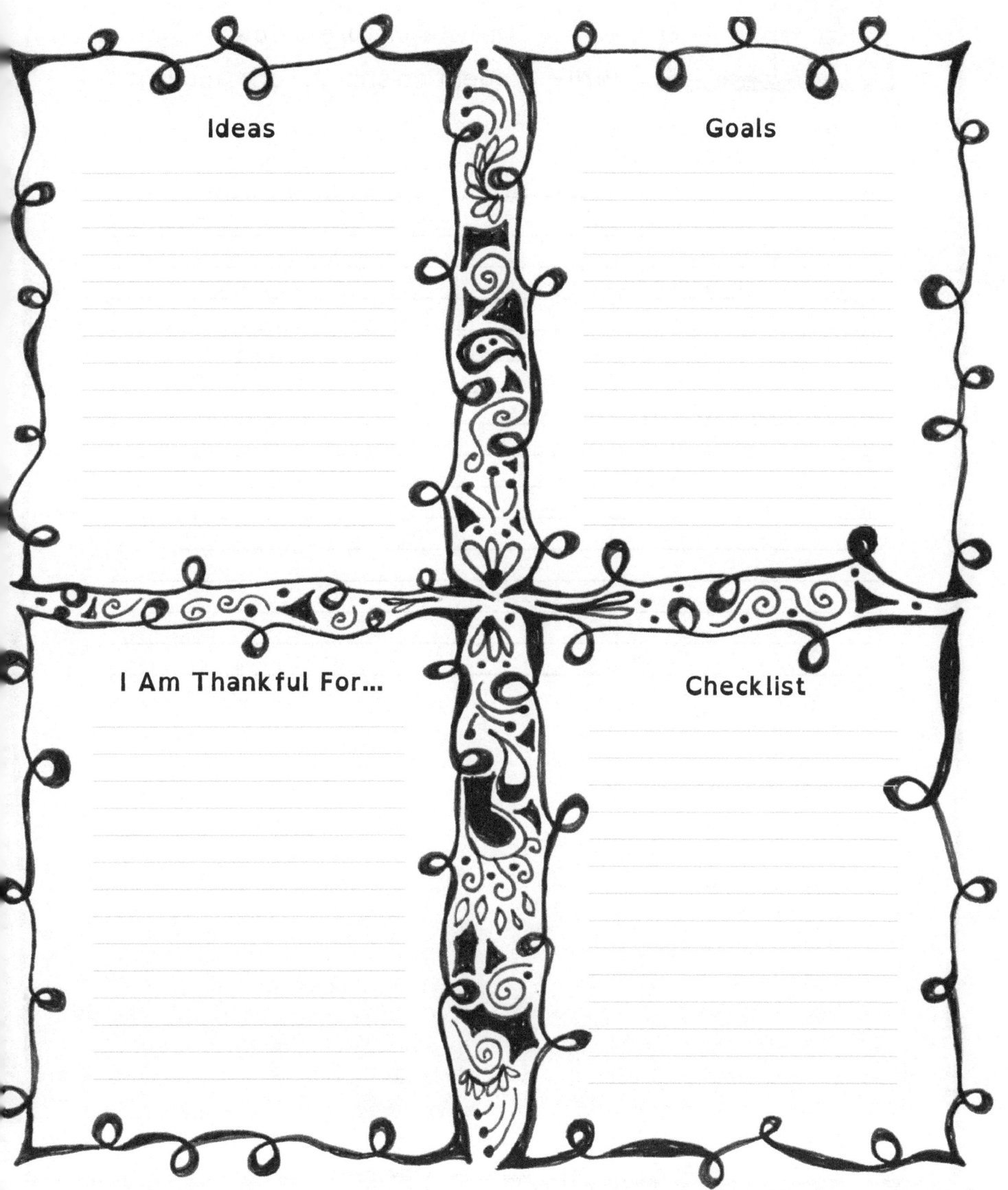

Ideas

Goals

I Am Thankful For...

Checklist

Creative Writing

Draw a picture below.
Write a poem or short story about it.

TITLE: _____

_____
_____
_____
_____
_____
_____
_____
_____
_____
_____
_____
_____
_____
_____

Learning a Skill

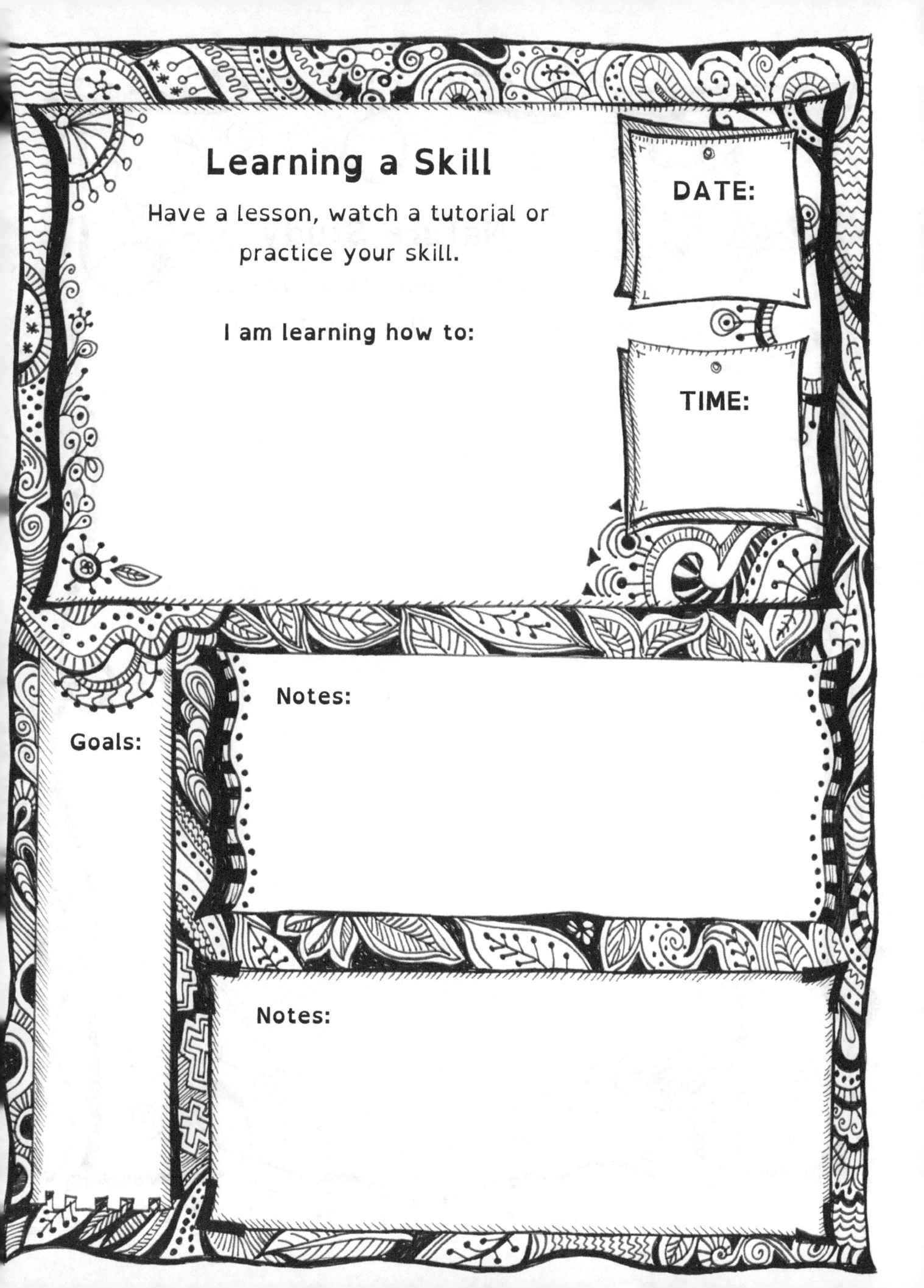

Have a lesson, watch a tutorial or practice your skill.

I am learning how to:

DATE:

TIME:

Goals:

Notes:

Notes:

Nature Study

Go outside and make a realistic drawing of something you find in nature.

Reading Time - 1 Hour

Choose Four Books - Read from each book for 15 minutes.
Copy a sentence or picture from each book here:

Circle Today's Date

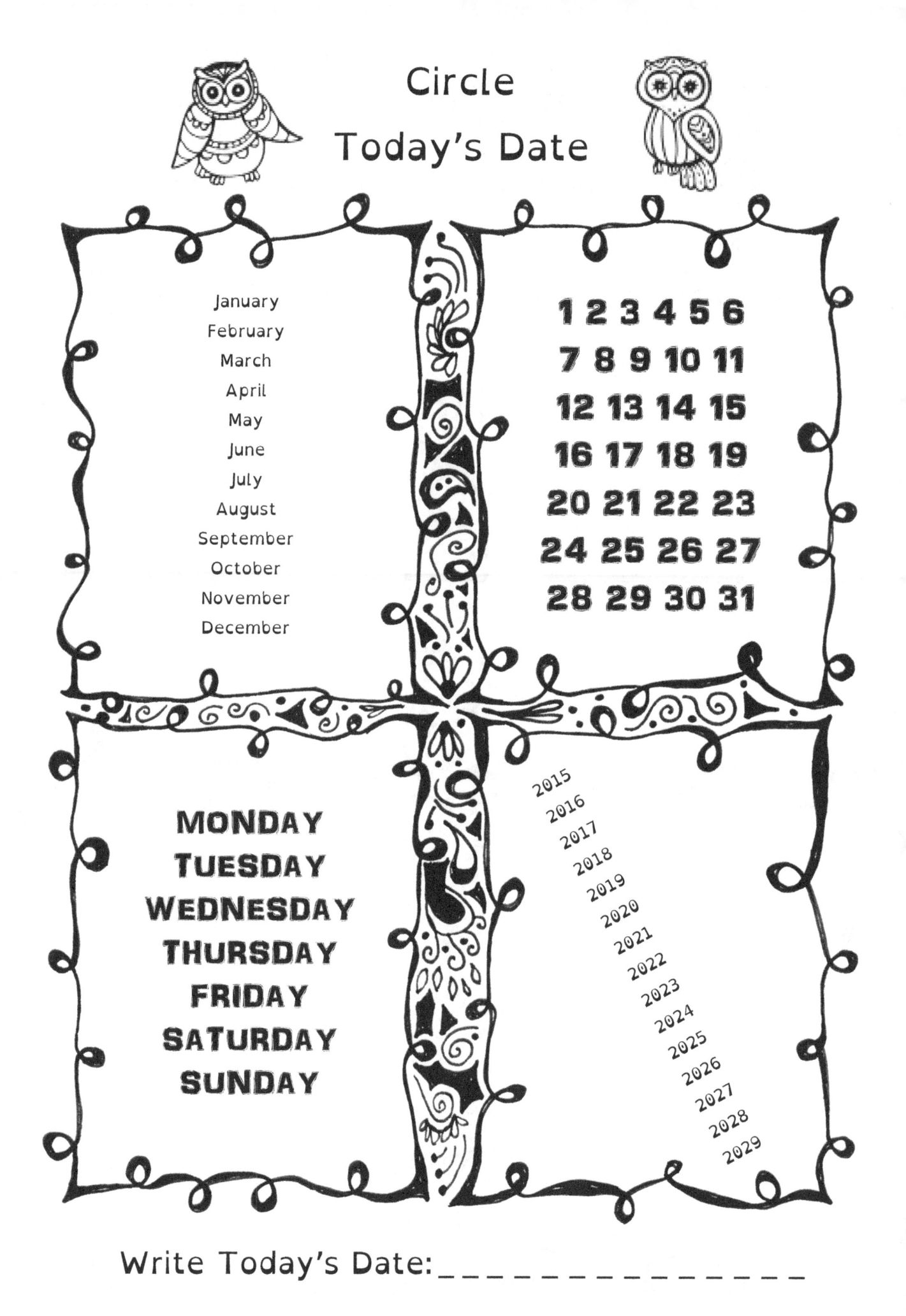

January
February
March
April
May
June
July
August
September
October
November
December

1 2 3 4 5 6
7 8 9 10 11
12 13 14 15
16 17 18 19
20 21 22 23
24 25 26 27
28 29 30 31

MONDAY
TUESDAY
WEDNESDAY
THURSDAY
FRIDAY
SATURDAY
SUNDAY

2015
2016
2017
2018
2019
2020
2021
2022
2023
2024
2025
2026
2027
2028
2029

Write Today's Date: _____

My Illustrated TO-DO List

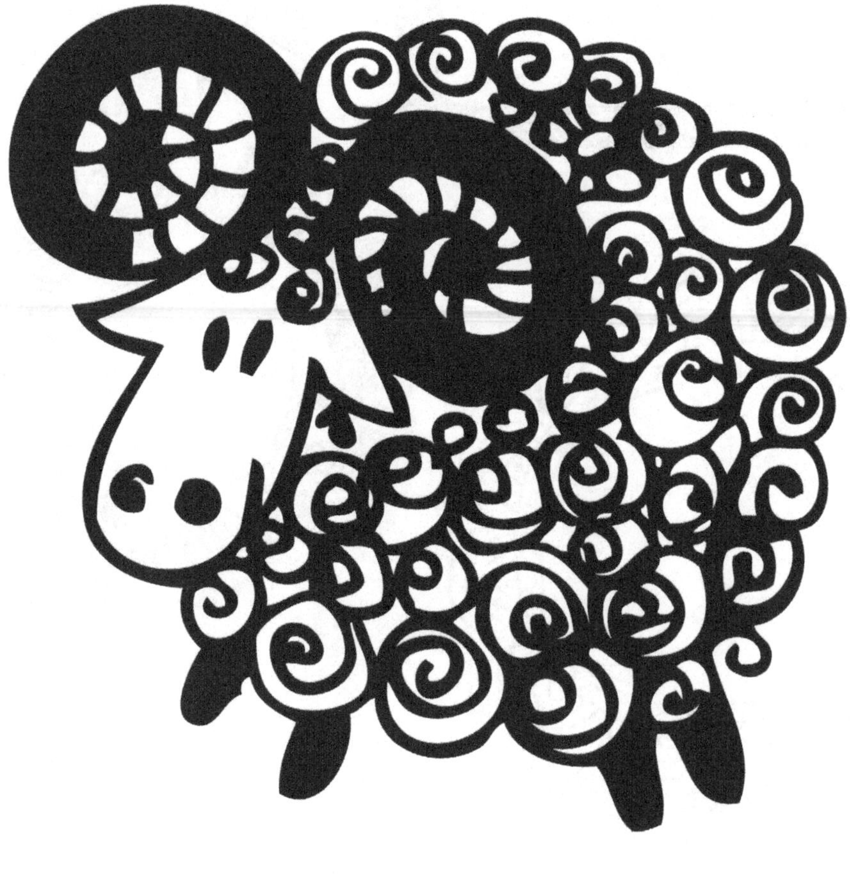

Film Study

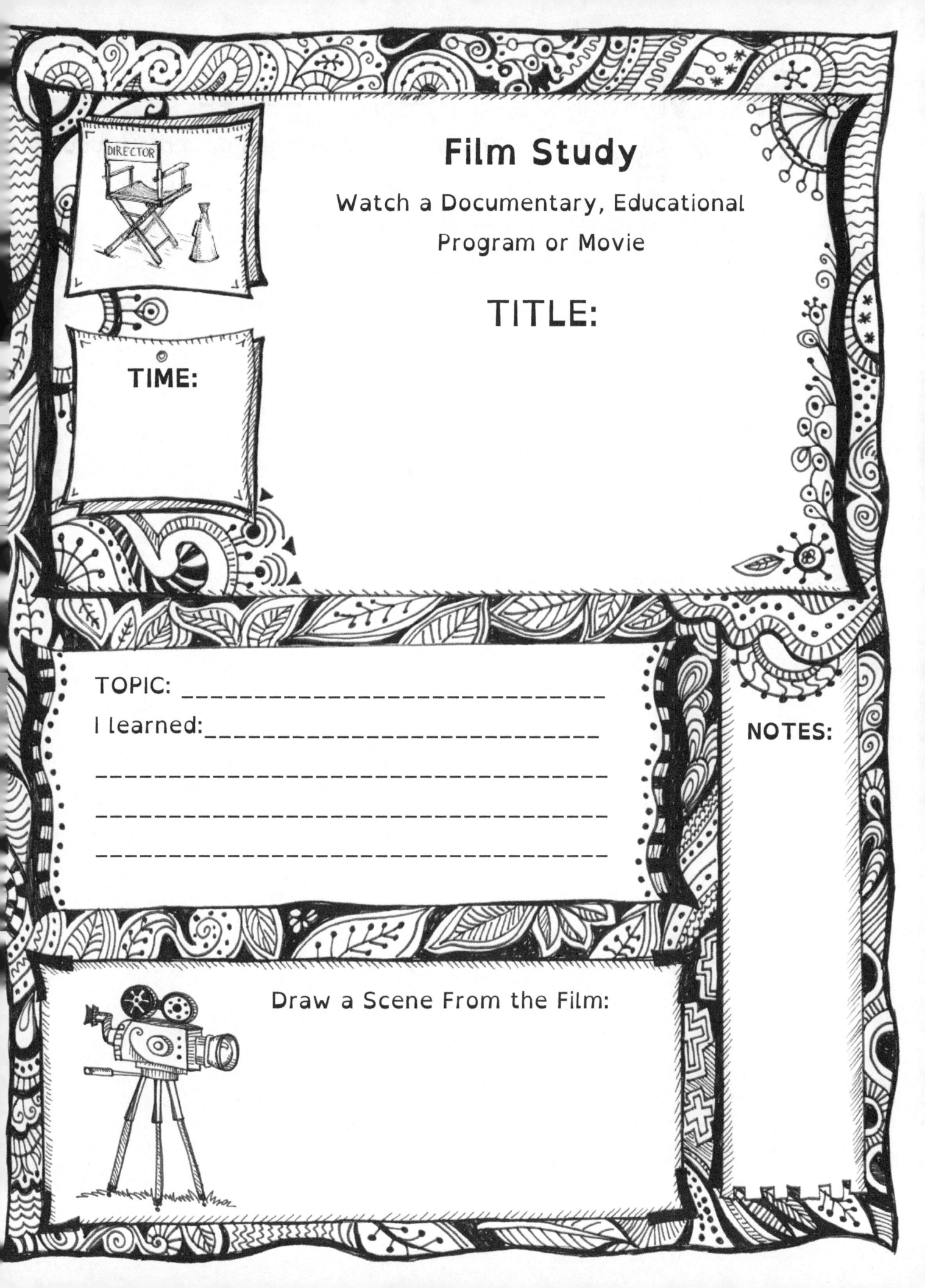

Watch a Documentary, Educational Program or Movie

TITLE:

TIME:

TOPIC: _____

I learned: _____

_____

_____

_____

NOTES:

Draw a Scene From the Film:

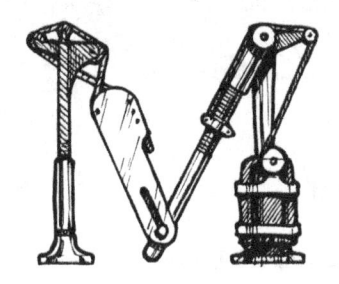

Math Practice

Watch a math tutorial or open up a math book.
You can practice math problems here.

Copywork

Find an interesting paragraph in one of your books and copy it. Be diligent to make your writing look exactly like it does in the book.

TITLE: _____ **Page Number:** _____

Sketch a Picture

Look through your library books and find something to draw.

Circle Today's Date

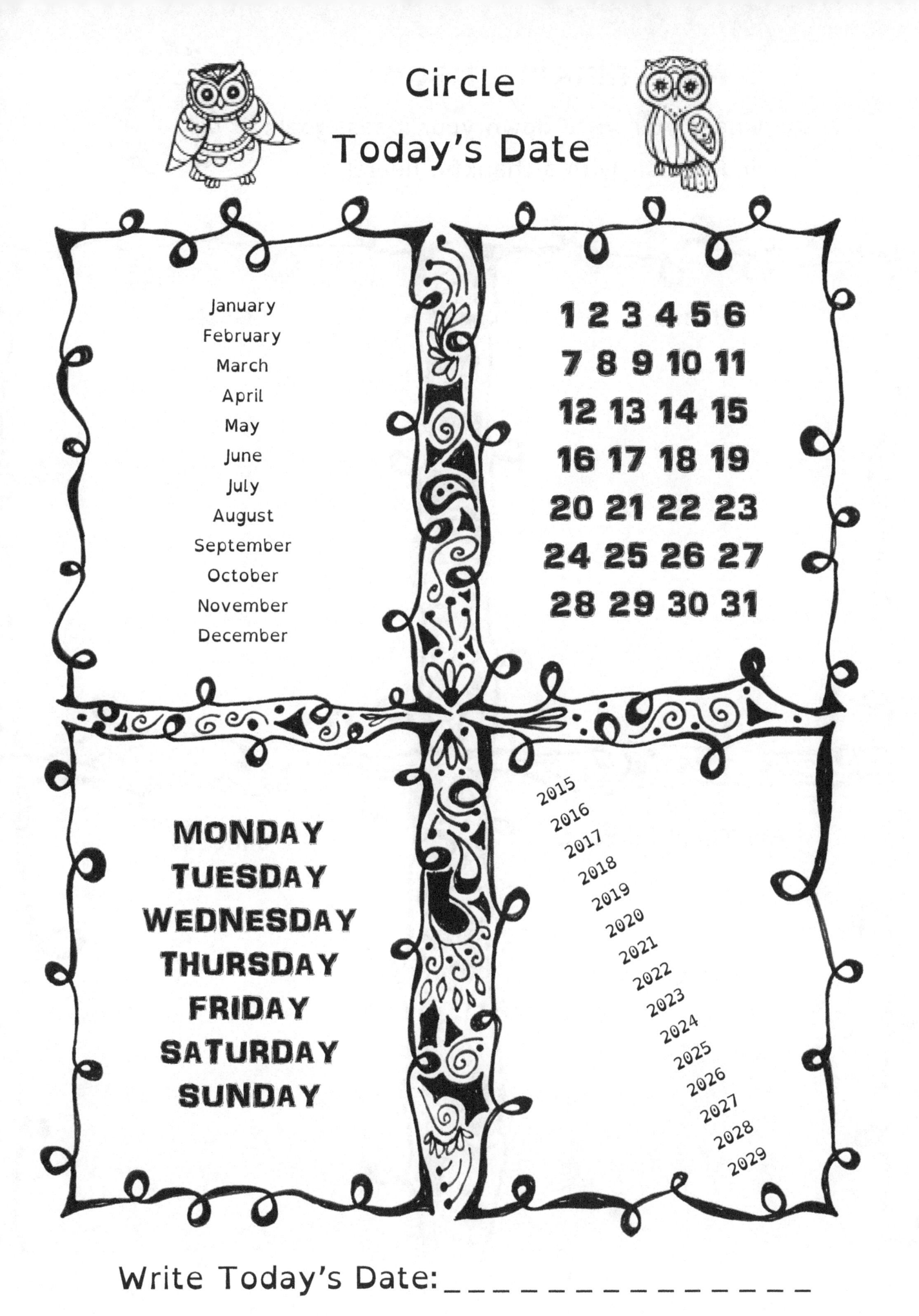

January
February
March
April
May
June
July
August
September
October
November
December

1 2 3 4 5 6
7 8 9 10 11
12 13 14 15
16 17 18 19
20 21 22 23
24 25 26 27
28 29 30 31

MONDAY
TUESDAY
WEDNESDAY
THURSDAY
FRIDAY
SATURDAY
SUNDAY

2015
2016
2017
2018
2019
2020
2021
2022
2023
2024
2025
2026
2027
2028
2029

Write Today's Date: _____

My Thinking Page

This is where you write down your ideas, goals, and plans - with a thankful heart!

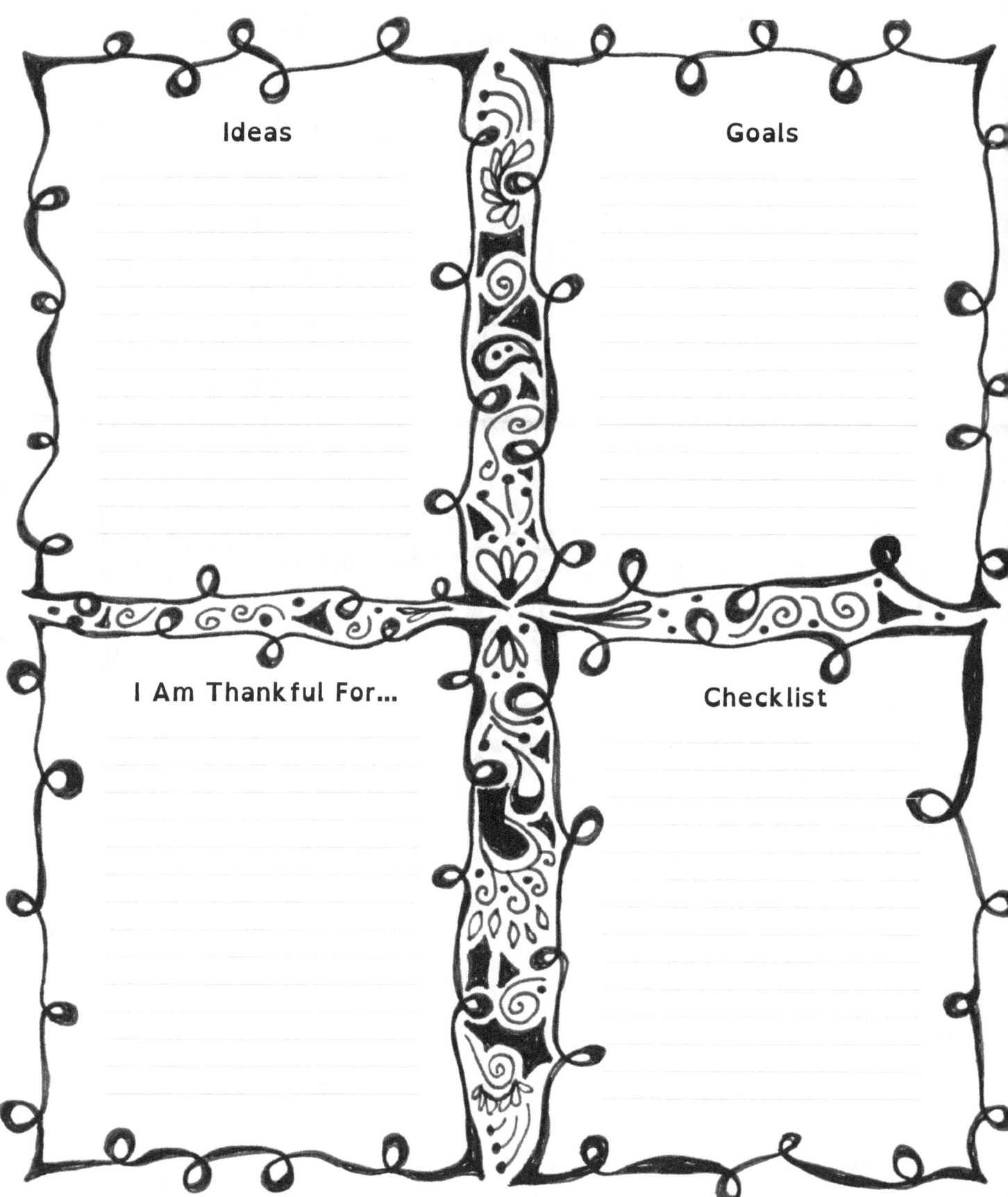

Ideas

Goals

I Am Thankful For...

Checklist

Creative Writing

Draw a picture below.
Write a poem or short story about it.

TITLE: _____

_____
_____
_____
_____
_____
_____
_____
_____
_____
_____
_____
_____

Nature Study

Go outside and make a realistic drawing of something you find in nature.

Reading Time - 1 Hour

Choose Four Books - Read from each book for 15 minutes.
Copy a sentence or picture from each book here:

Circle Today's Date

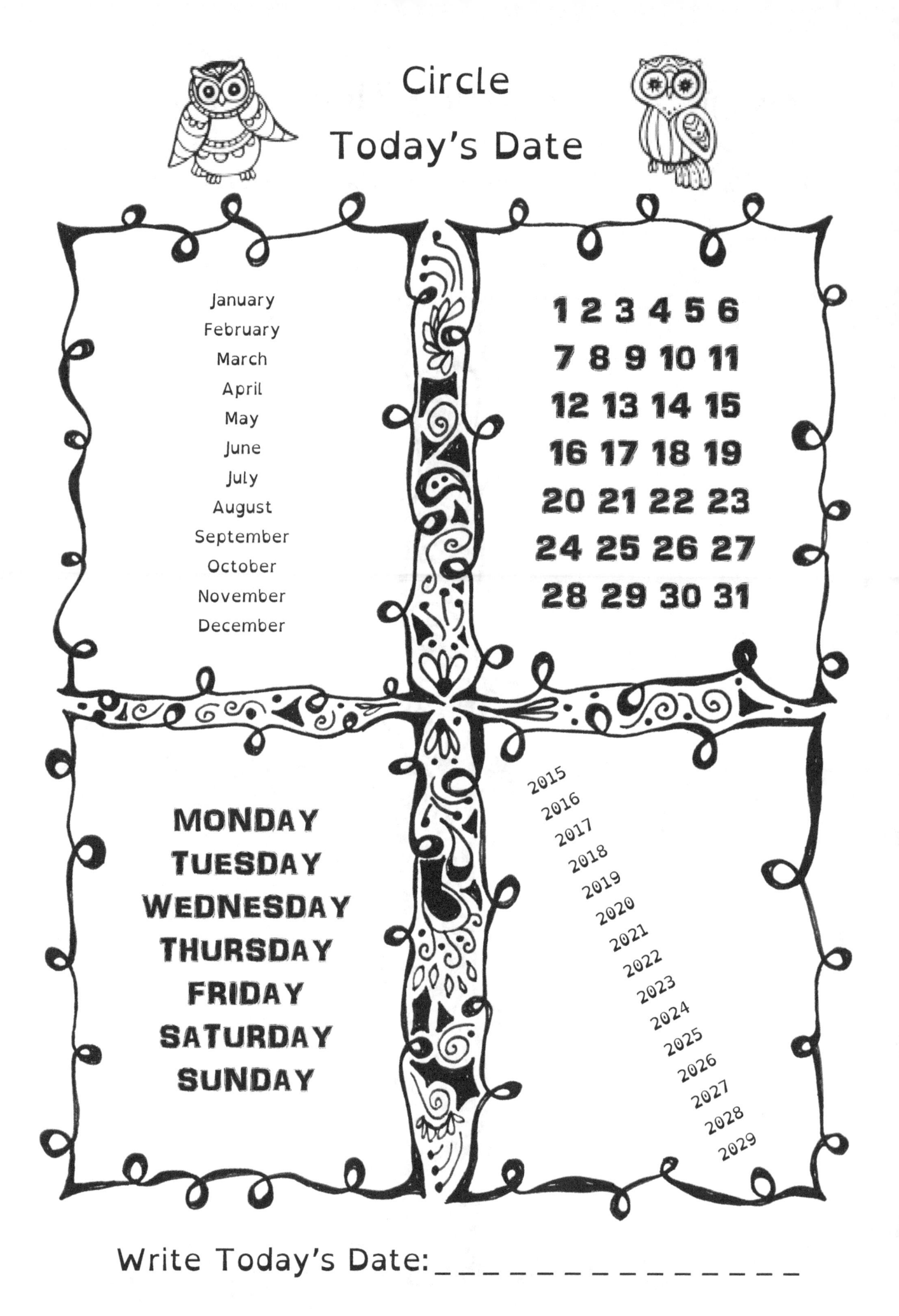

January
February
March
April
May
June
July
August
September
October
November
December

1 2 3 4 5 6
7 8 9 10 11
12 13 14 15
16 17 18 19
20 21 22 23
24 25 26 27
28 29 30 31

MONDAY
TUESDAY
WEDNESDAY
THURSDAY
FRIDAY
SATURDAY
SUNDAY

2015
2016
2017
2018
2019
2020
2021
2022
2023
2024
2025
2026
2027
2028
2029

Write Today's Date: _____

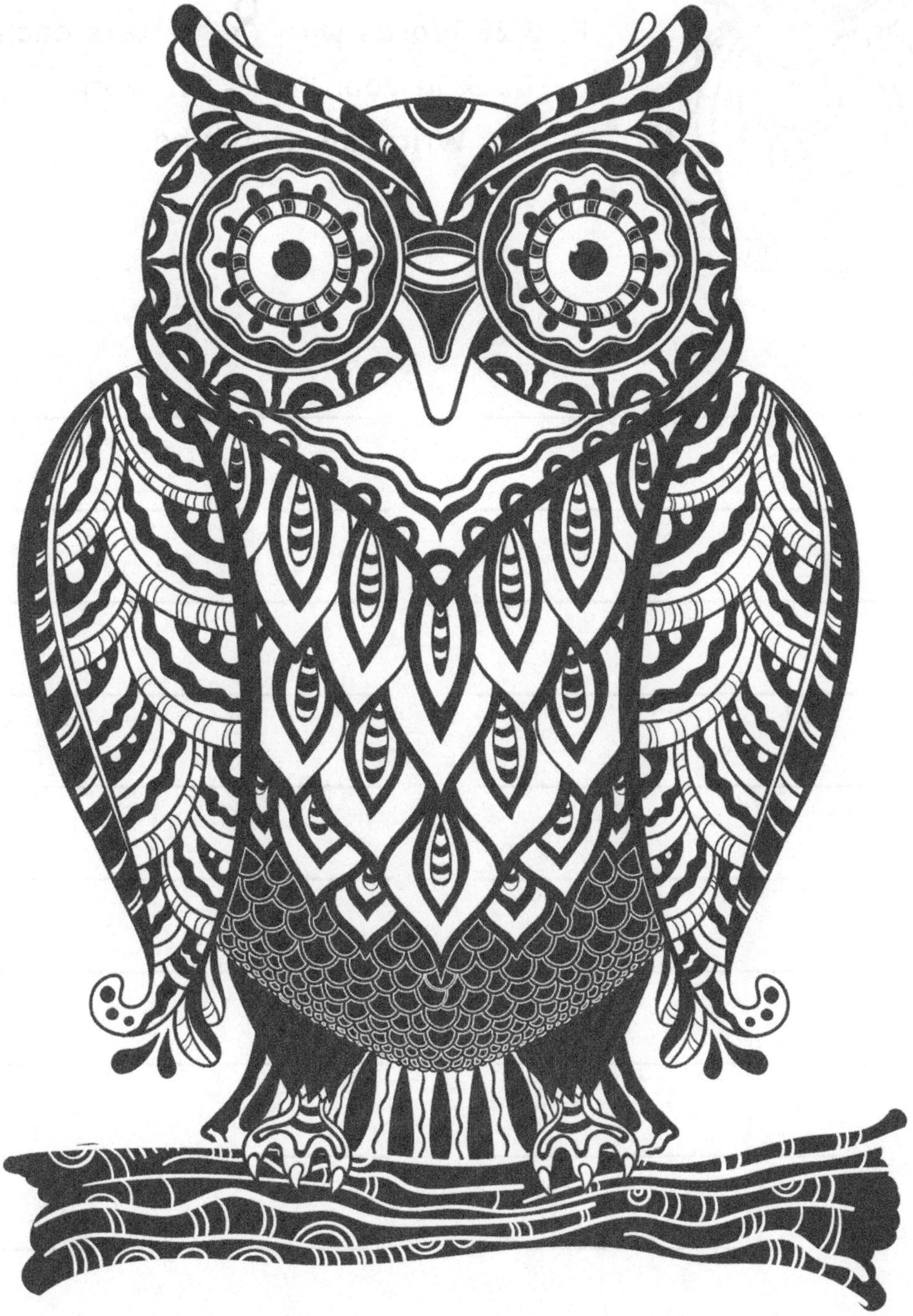

Spelling Time

Find 20 Words with **8** letters each.
Look in your books for words.
Write the words here:

Film Study

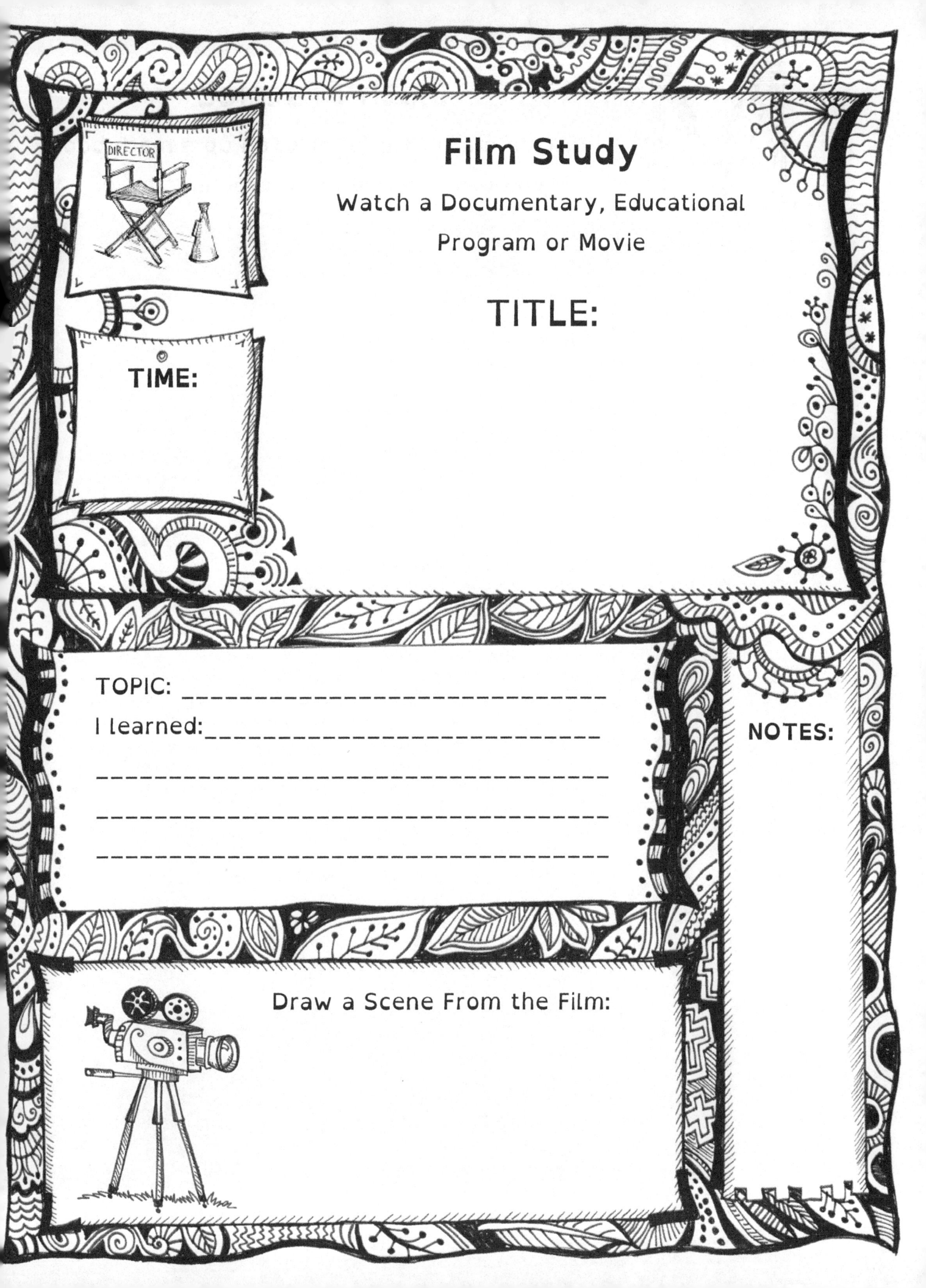

Watch a Documentary, Educational Program or Movie

TITLE:

TIME:

TOPIC: _____

I learned: _____

_____

_____

_____

NOTES:

Draw a Scene From the Film:

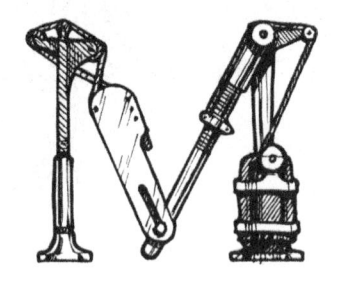

Math Practice

Watch a math tutorial or open up a math book.
You can practice math problems here.

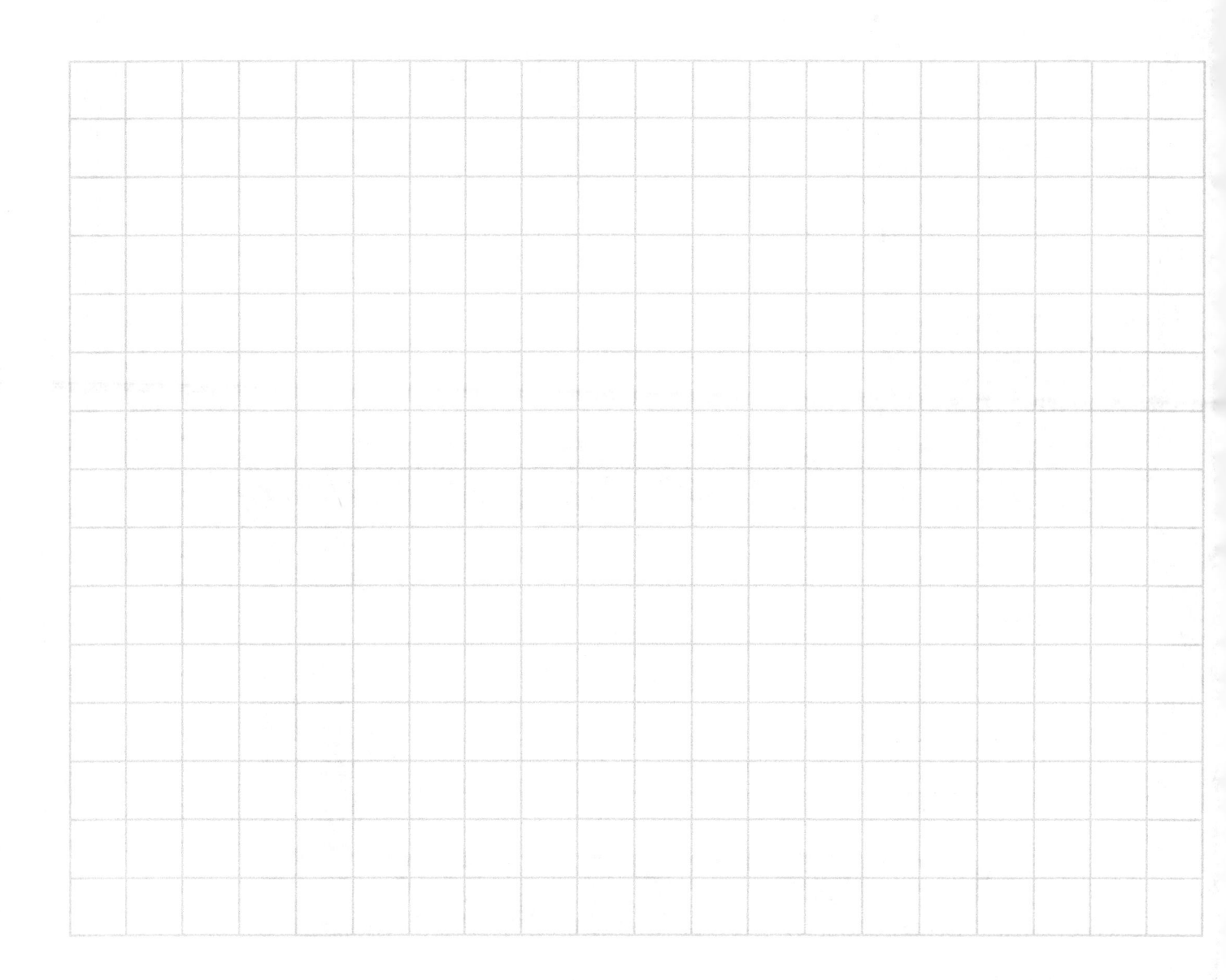

Draw a Meal PLAN

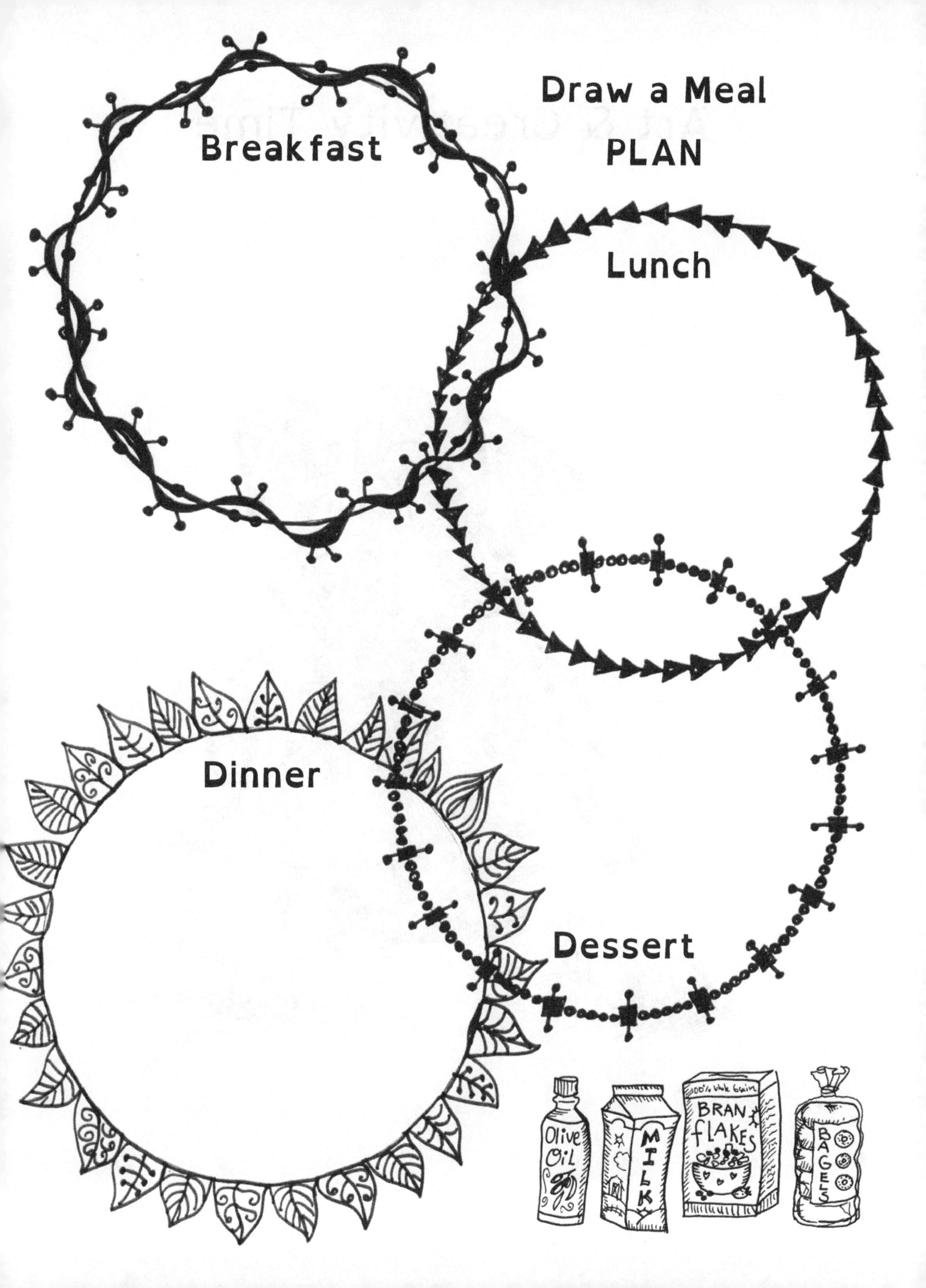

Breakfast

Lunch

Dinner

Dessert

Art & Creativity Time

Copywork

Find an interesting paragraph in one of your books and copy it. Be diligent to make your writing look exactly like it does in the book.

TITLE:_____ Page Number:_____

Circle Today's Date

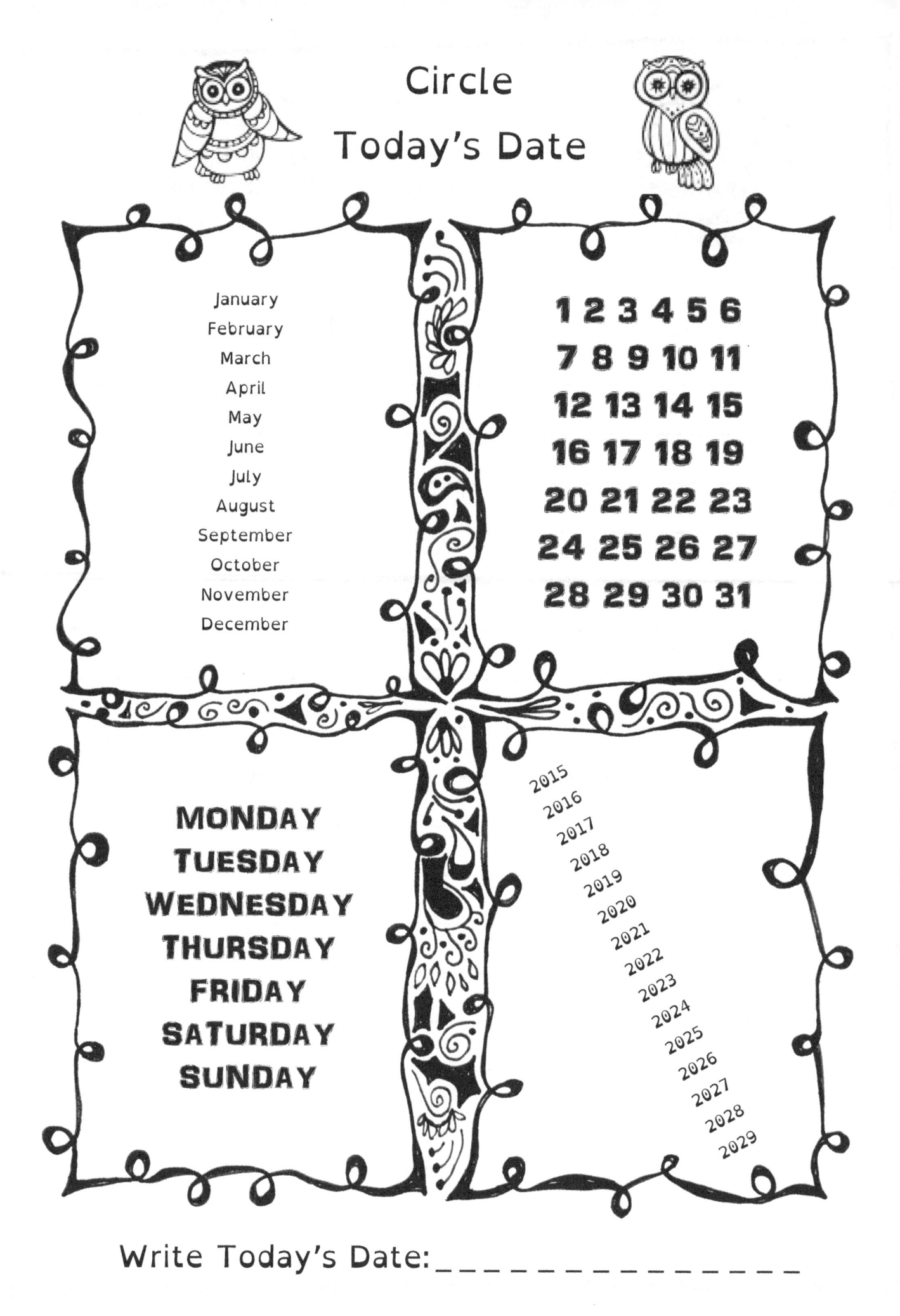

January
February
March
April
May
June
July
August
September
October
November
December

1 2 3 4 5 6
7 8 9 10 11
12 13 14 15
16 17 18 19
20 21 22 23
24 25 26 27
28 29 30 31

MONDAY
TUESDAY
WEDNESDAY
THURSDAY
FRIDAY
SATURDAY
SUNDAY

2015
2016
2017
2018
2019
2020
2021
2022
2023
2024
2025
2026
2027
2028
2029

Write Today's Date: _____

My Thinking Page

This is where you write down your ideas, goals, and plans - with a thankful heart!

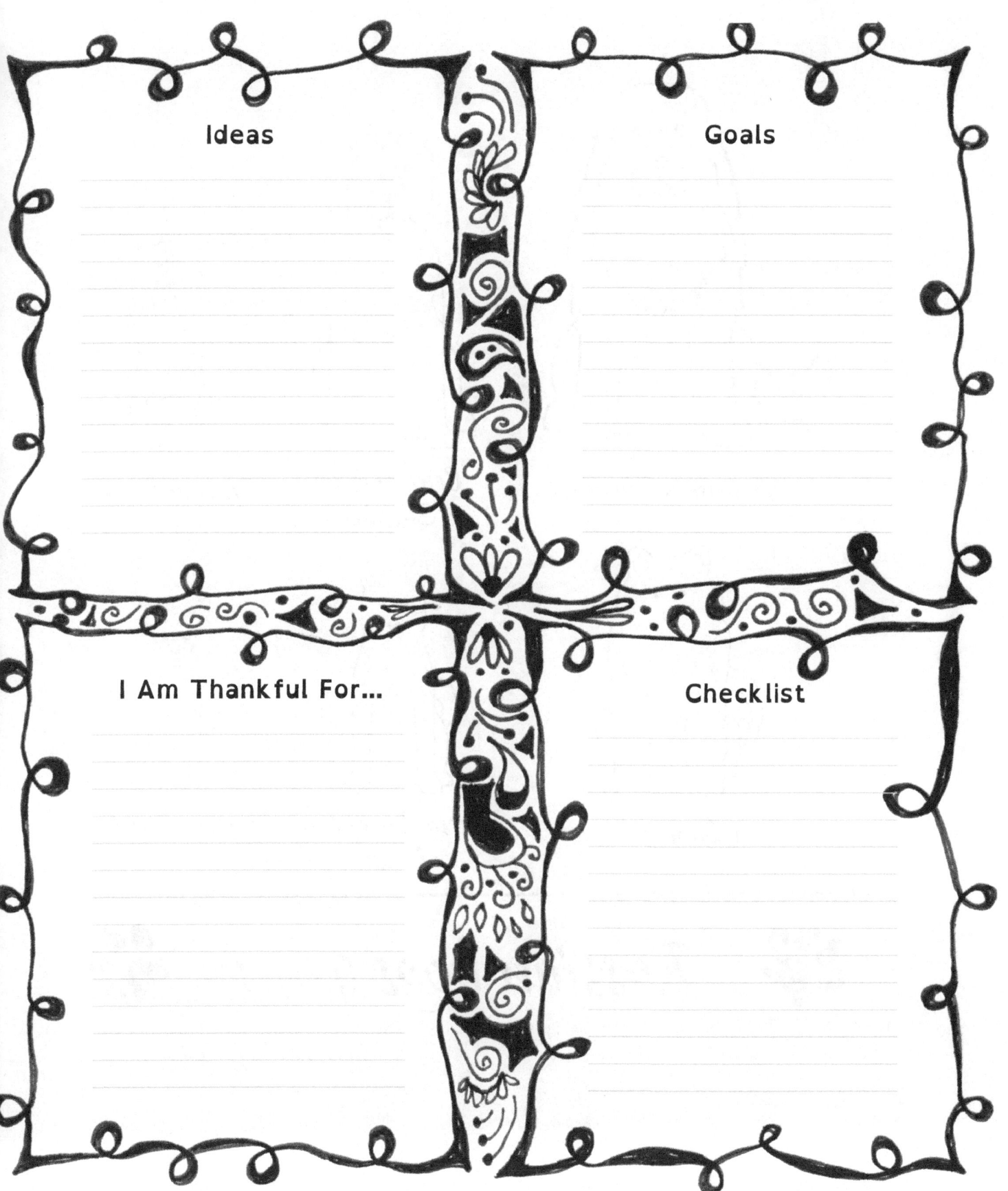

Ideas

Goals

I Am Thankful For...

Checklist

Caucasian Shepherd

Central Asian Shepherd

Russian Spaniel

Samoyed

Russo European Laika

Russian Toy Terrier

Russian dogs (part 1)

Moscow watch

Black Russian Terrier

West Siberian Laika

South Russian Shepherd Dog

Russian wolfhound

Karelian Finnish Laika

Russian dogs (part 2)

Creative Writing

Draw a picture below.
Write a poem or short story about it.

TITLE: _____

_____
_____
_____
_____
_____
_____
_____
_____
_____
_____
_____
_____
_____
_____

Nature Study

Go outside and make a realistic drawing of something you find in nature.

Reading Time - 1 Hour

Choose Four Books - Read from each book for 15 minutes.
Copy a sentence or picture from each book here:

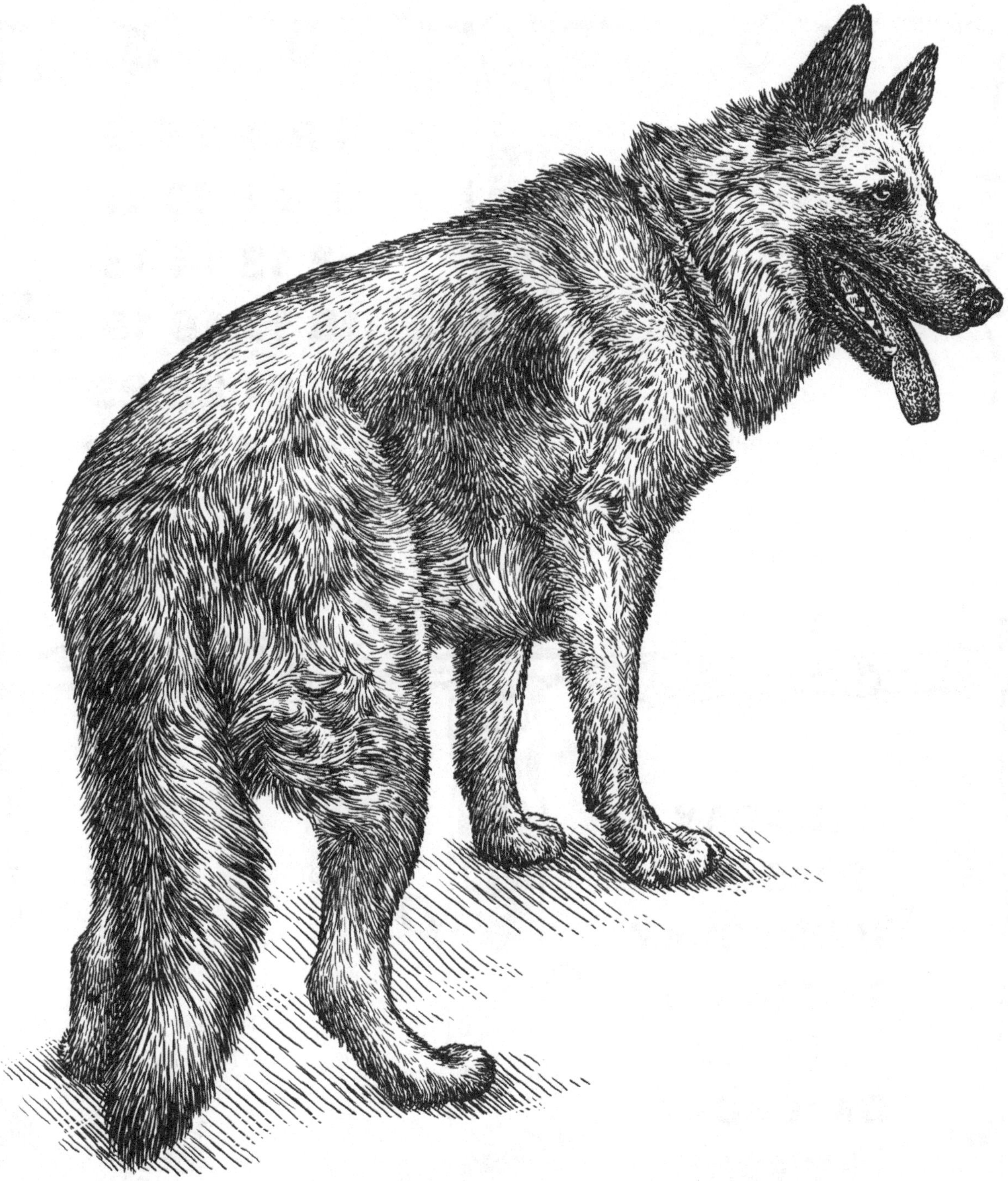

Circle Today's Date

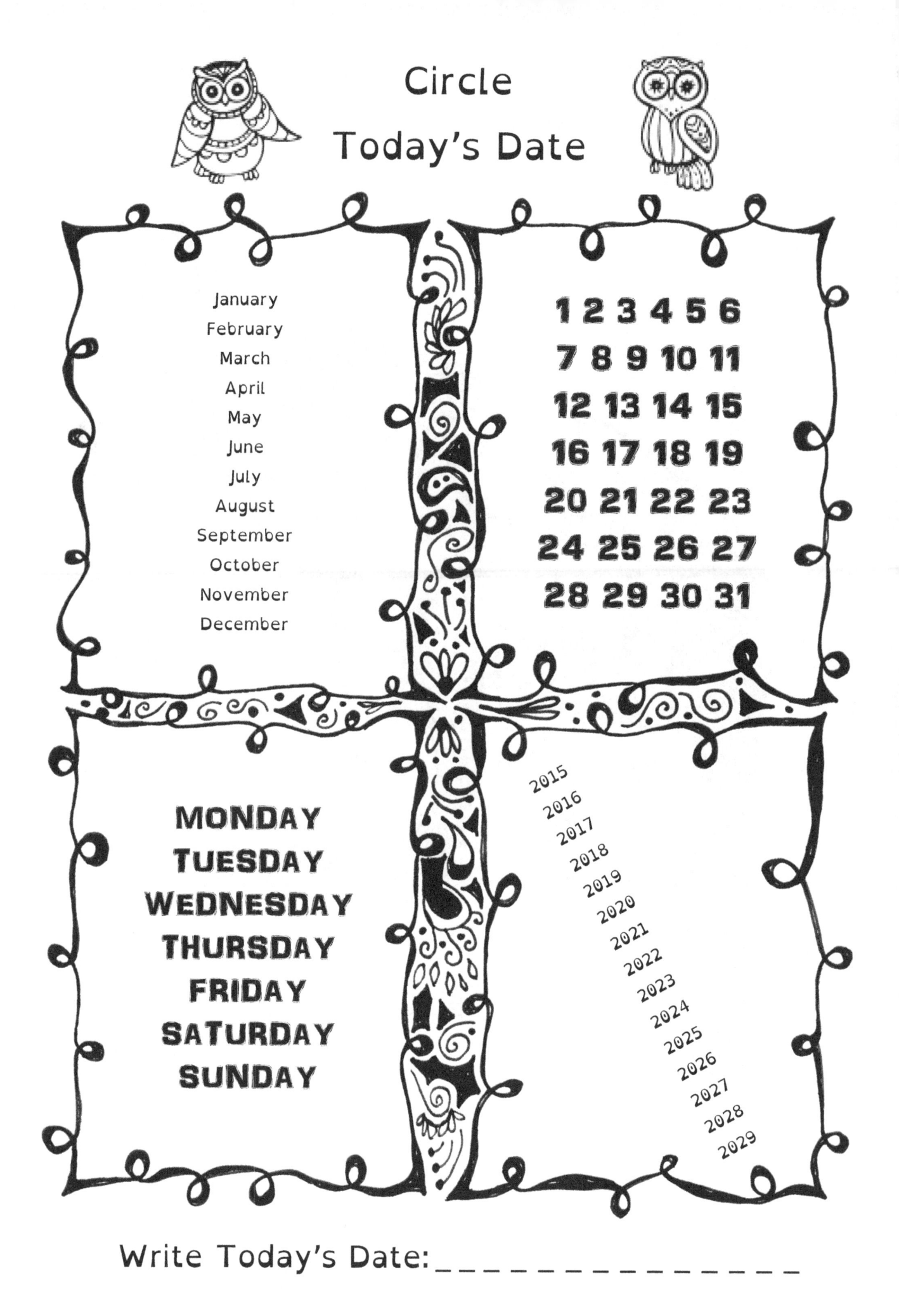

January
February
March
April
May
June
July
August
September
October
November
December

1 2 3 4 5 6
7 8 9 10 11
12 13 14 15
16 17 18 19
20 21 22 23
24 25 26 27
28 29 30 31

MONDAY
TUESDAY
WEDNESDAY
THURSDAY
FRIDAY
SATURDAY
SUNDAY

2015
2016
2017
2018
2019
2020
2021
2022
2023
2024
2025
2026
2027
2028
2029

Write Today's Date: _____

Spelling Time

Find 20 Words with **8** letters each.
Look in your books for words.
Write the words here:

_____   _____

_____   _____

_____   _____

_____   _____

_____   _____

_____   _____

_____   _____

_____   _____

_____   _____

_____   _____

Film Study

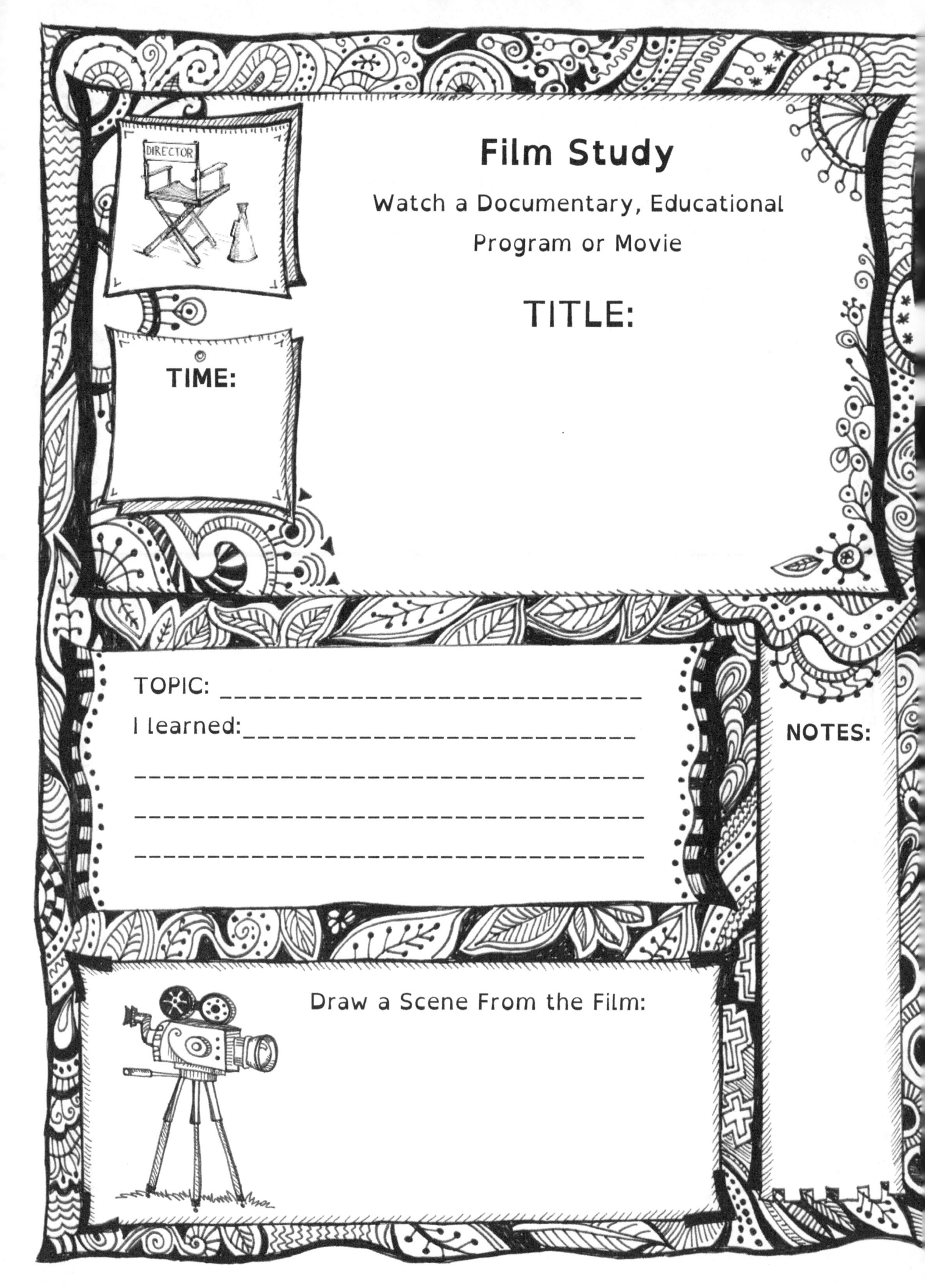

Watch a Documentary, Educational Program or Movie

TITLE:

TIME:

TOPIC: _____

I learned: _____

_____

_____

_____

NOTES:

Draw a Scene From the Film:

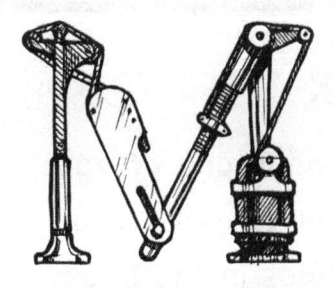

Math Practice

Watch a math tutorial or open up a math book.
You can practice math problems here.

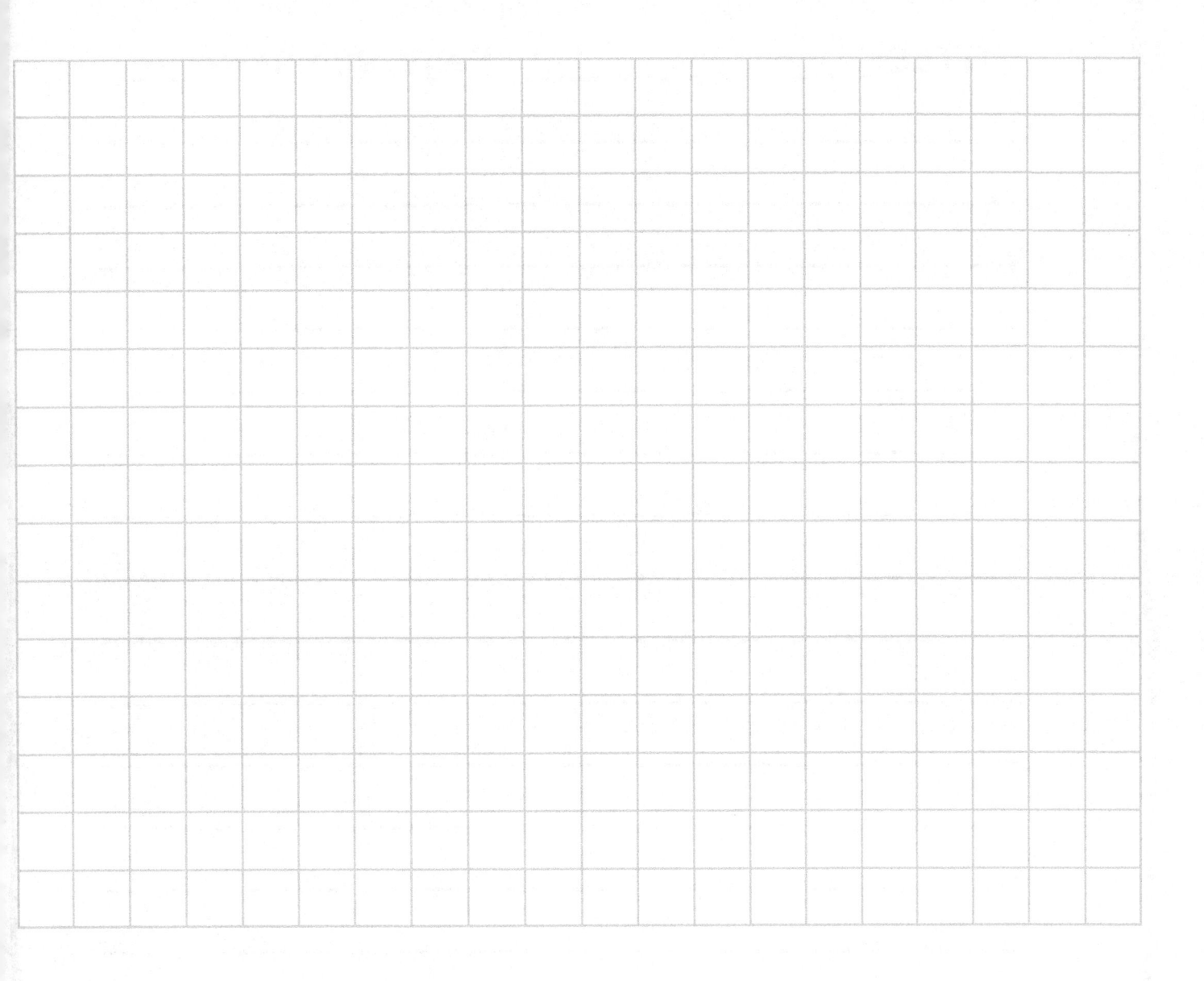

Copywork

Find an interesting paragraph in one of your books and copy it. Be diligent to make your writing look exactly like it does in the book.

TITLE:_____ **Page Number:**____

Sketch a Picture
Look through your library books and find something to draw.

Circle Today's Date

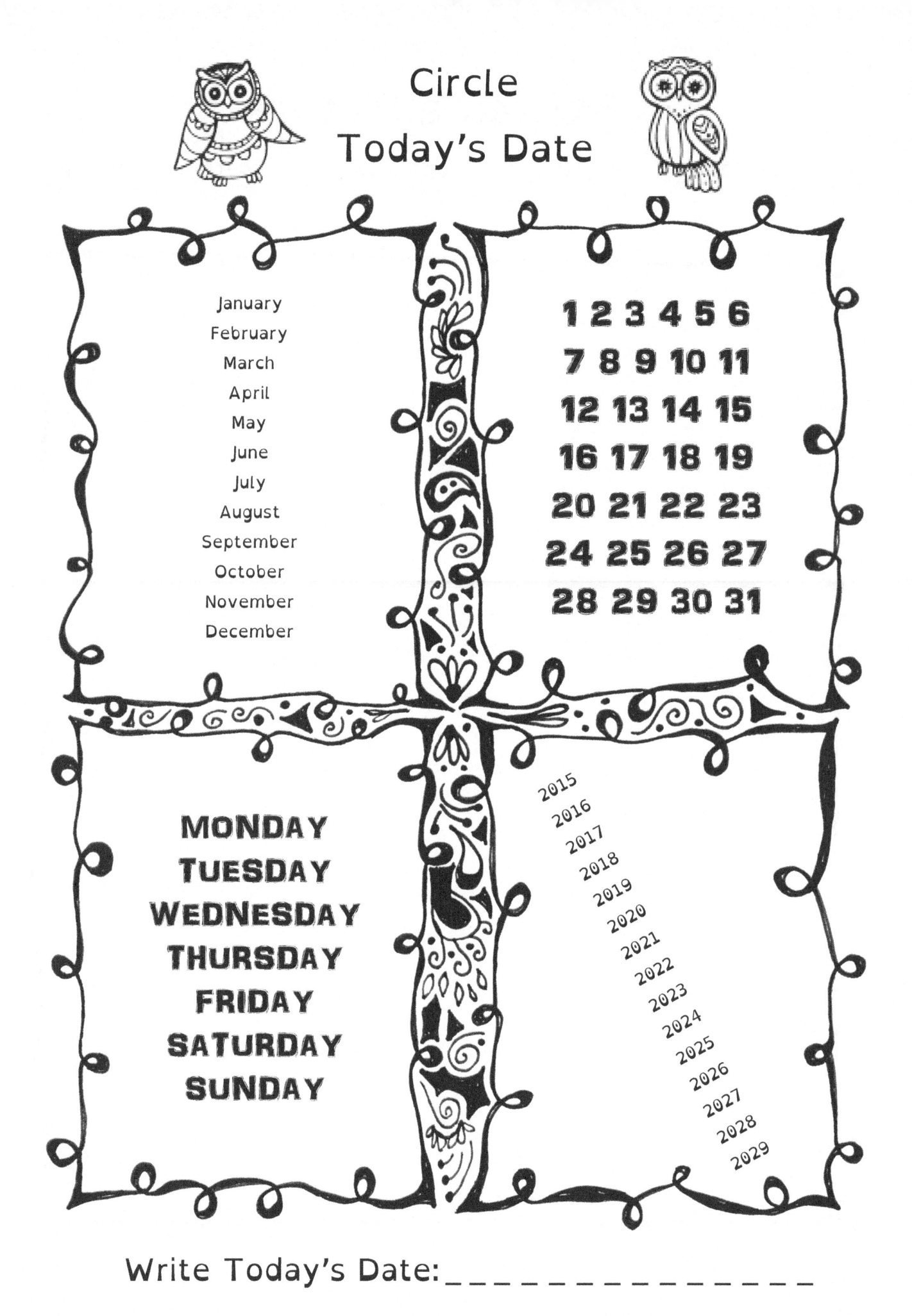

January
February
March
April
May
June
July
August
September
October
November
December

1 2 3 4 5 6
7 8 9 10 11
12 13 14 15
16 17 18 19
20 21 22 23
24 25 26 27
28 29 30 31

MONDAY
TUESDAY
WEDNESDAY
THURSDAY
FRIDAY
SATURDAY
SUNDAY

2015
2016
2017
2018
2019
2020
2021
2022
2023
2024
2025
2026
2027
2028
2029

Write Today's Date: _____

My Thinking Page

This is where you write down your ideas, goals, and plans - with a thankful heart!

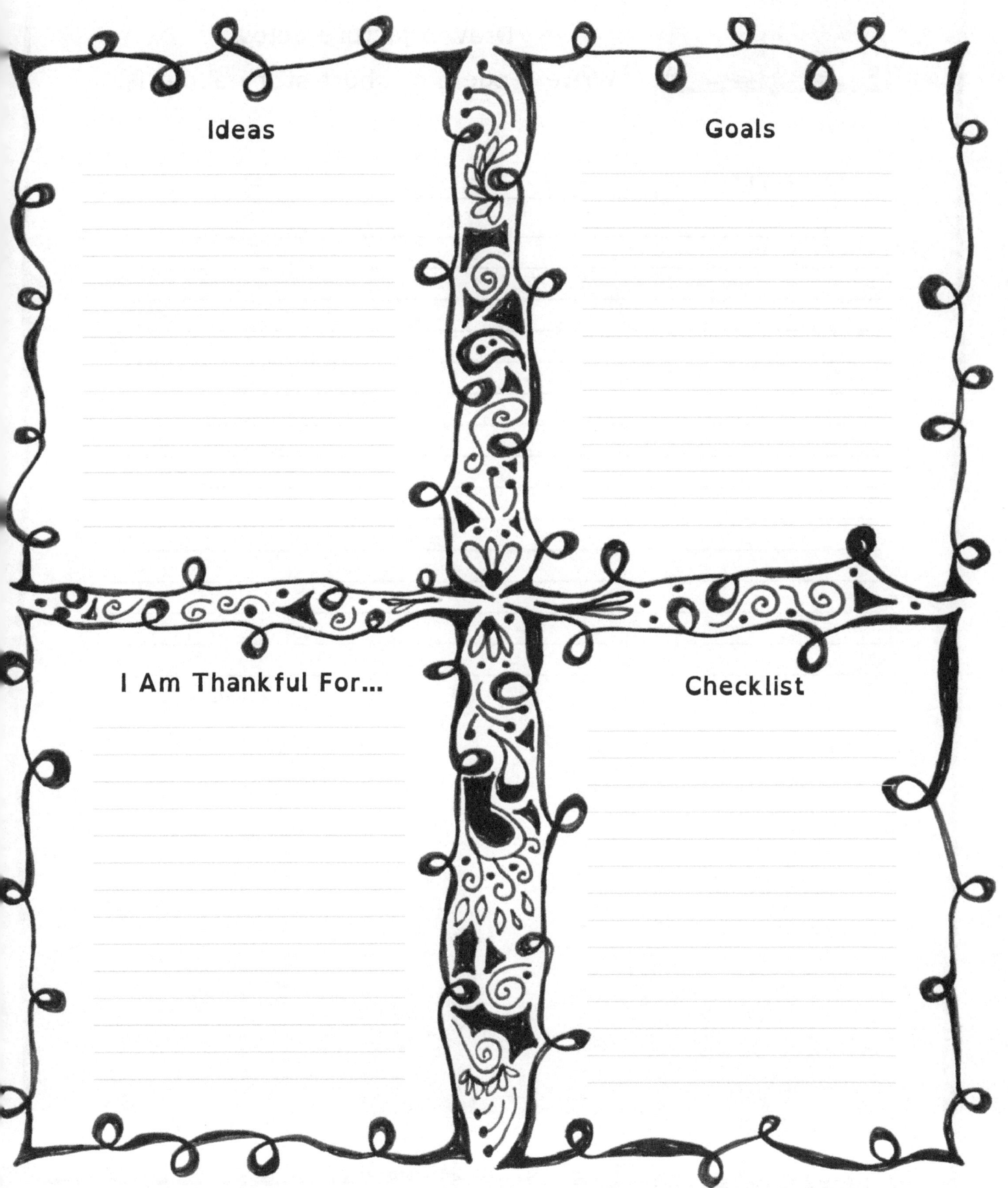

Ideas

Goals

I Am Thankful For...

Checklist

Creative Writing

Draw a picture below.
Write a poem or short story about it.

TITLE: _____

_____
_____
_____
_____
_____
_____
_____
_____
_____
_____
_____
_____
_____
_____

Nature Study

Go outside and make a realistic drawing of something you find in nature.

Reading Time - 1 Hour

Choose Four Books - Read from each book for 15 minutes.
Copy a sentence or picture from each book here:

Learning a Skill

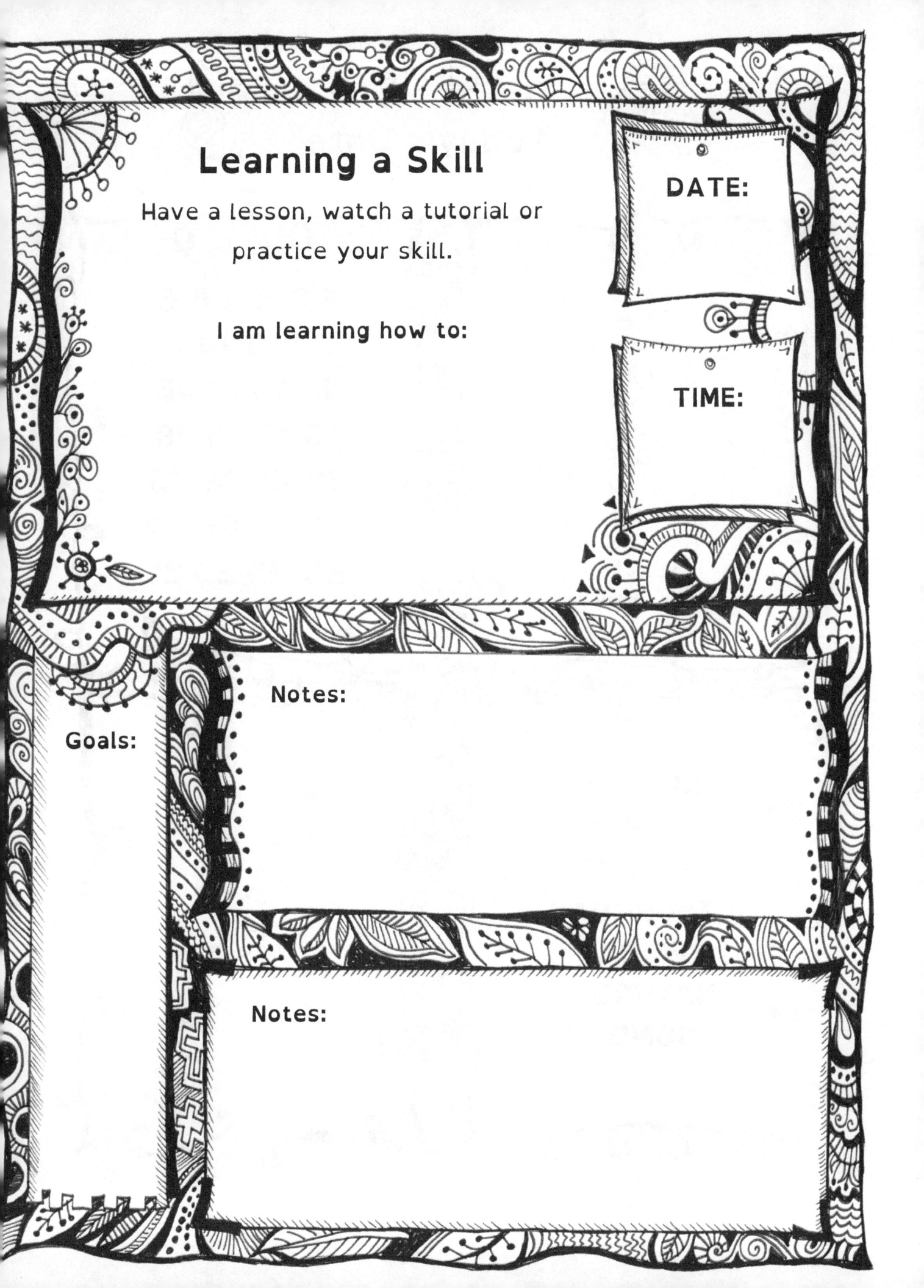

Have a lesson, watch a tutorial or practice your skill.

I am learning how to:

DATE:

TIME:

Goals:

Notes:

Notes:

Circle Today's Date

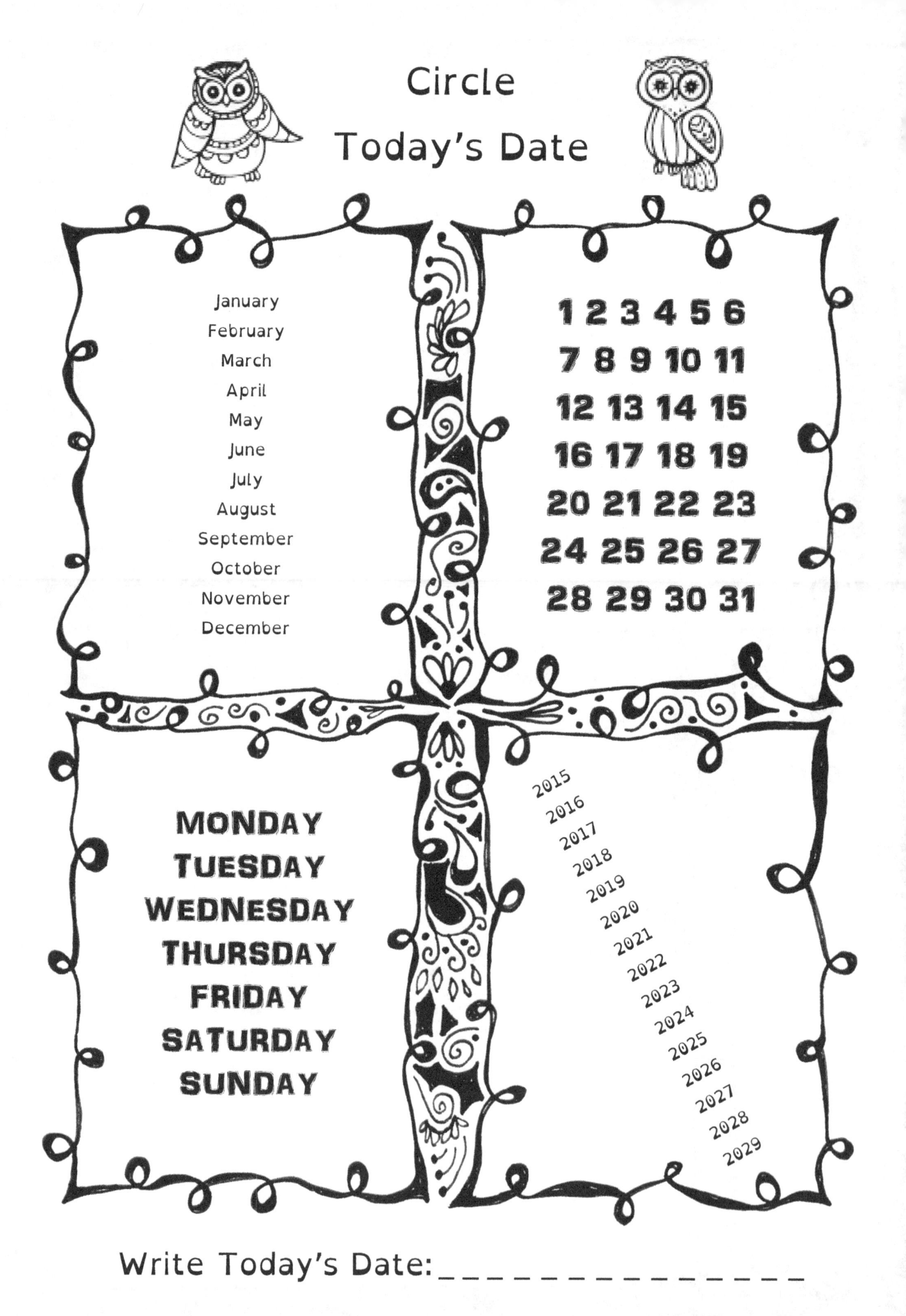

January
February
March
April
May
June
July
August
September
October
November
December

1 2 3 4 5 6
7 8 9 10 11
12 13 14 15
16 17 18 19
20 21 22 23
24 25 26 27
28 29 30 31

MONDAY
TUESDAY
WEDNESDAY
THURSDAY
FRIDAY
SATURDAY
SUNDAY

2015
2016
2017
2018
2019
2020
2021
2022
2023
2024
2025
2026
2027
2028
2029

Write Today's Date: _____

Spelling Time

Find 20 Words with 7 letters each.
Look in your books for words.
Write the words here:

Film Study

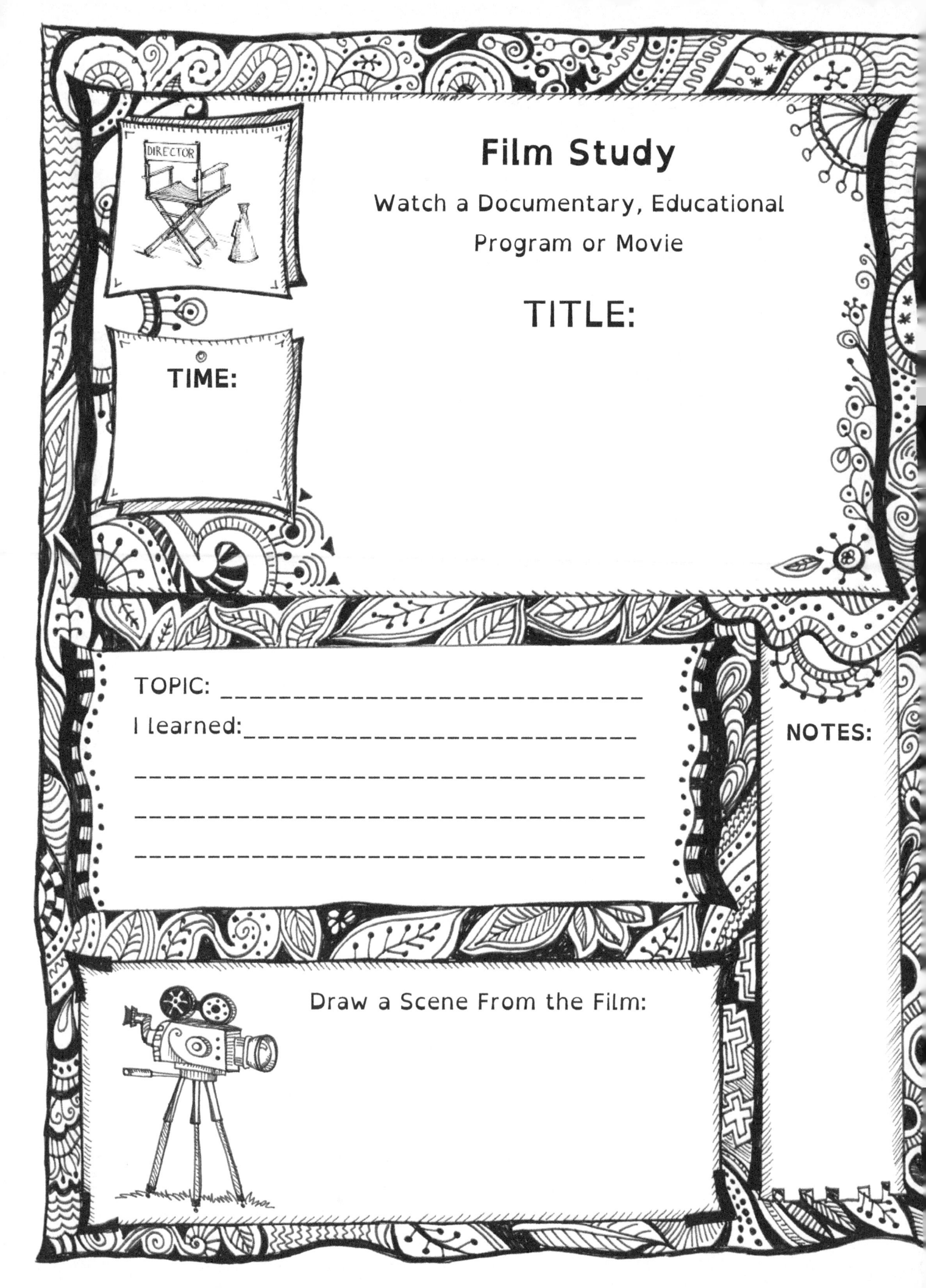

Watch a Documentary, Educational Program or Movie

TITLE:

TIME:

TOPIC: _____
I learned: _____
_____
_____
_____

NOTES:

Draw a Scene From the Film:

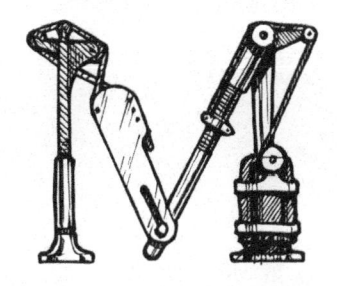

Math Practice

Watch a math tutorial or open up a math book.
You can practice math problems here.

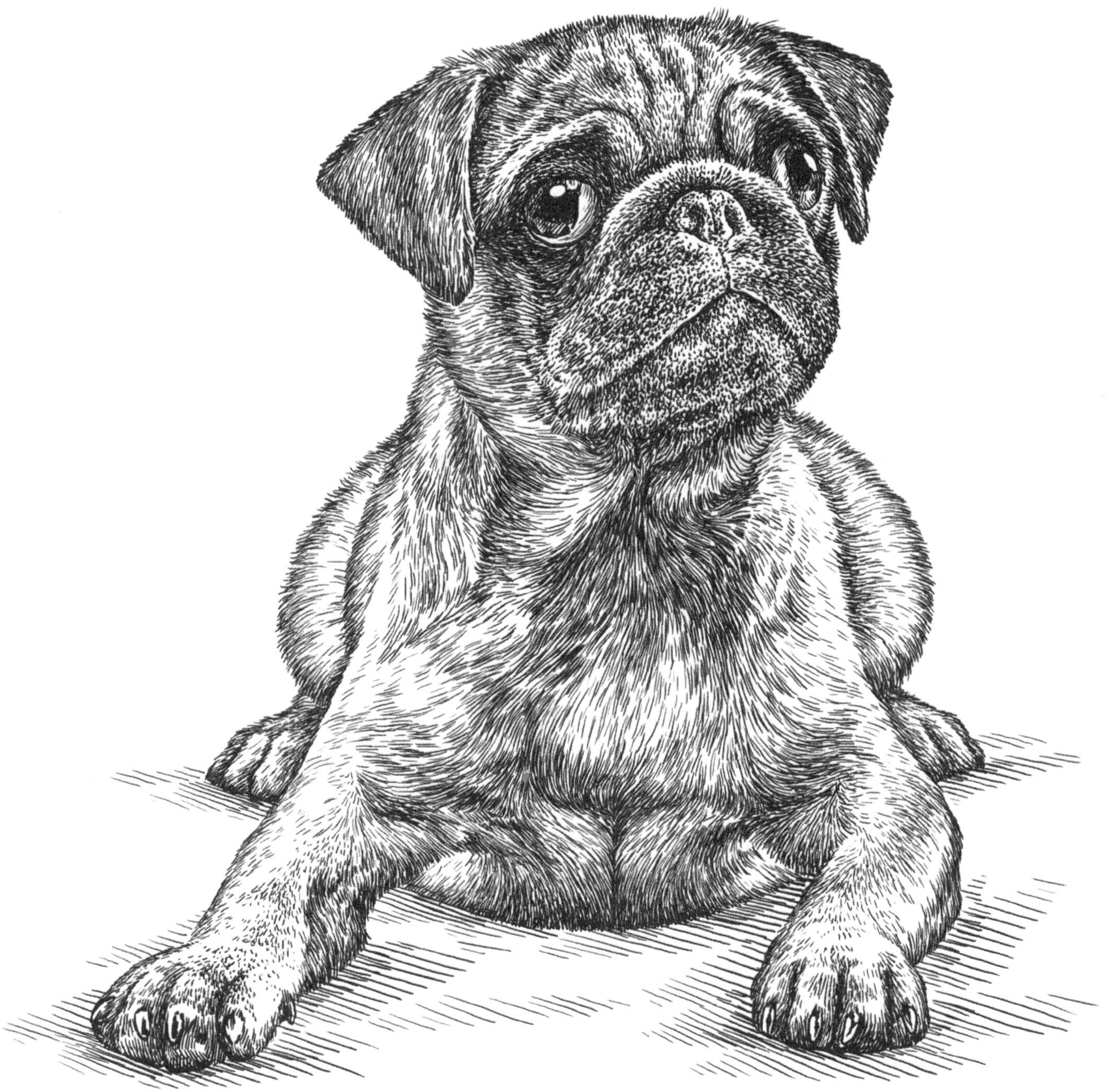

Copywork

Find an interesting paragraph in one of your books and copy it. Be diligent to make your writing look exactly like it does in the book.

TITLE:_____   Page Number:_____

Circle Today's Date

January
February
March
April
May
June
July
August
September
October
November
December

1 2 3 4 5 6
7 8 9 10 11
12 13 14 15
16 17 18 19
20 21 22 23
24 25 26 27
28 29 30 31

MONDAY
TUESDAY
WEDNESDAY
THURSDAY
FRIDAY
SATURDAY
SUNDAY

2015
2016
2017
2018
2019
2020
2021
2022
2023
2024
2025
2026
2027
2028
2029

Write Today's Date: _____

My Thinking Page

This is where you write down your ideas, goals, and plans - with a thankful heart!

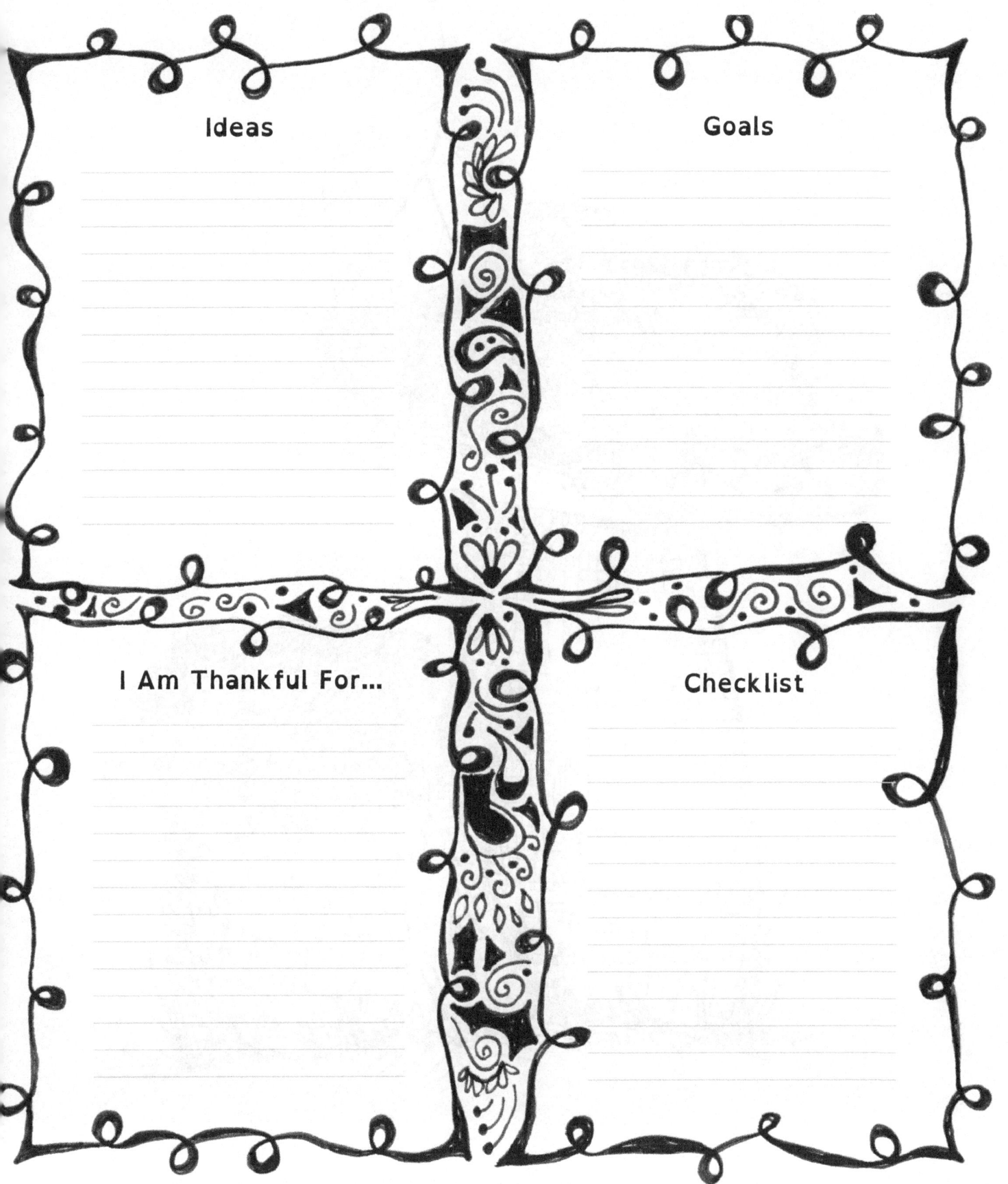

Ideas

Goals

I Am Thankful For...

Checklist

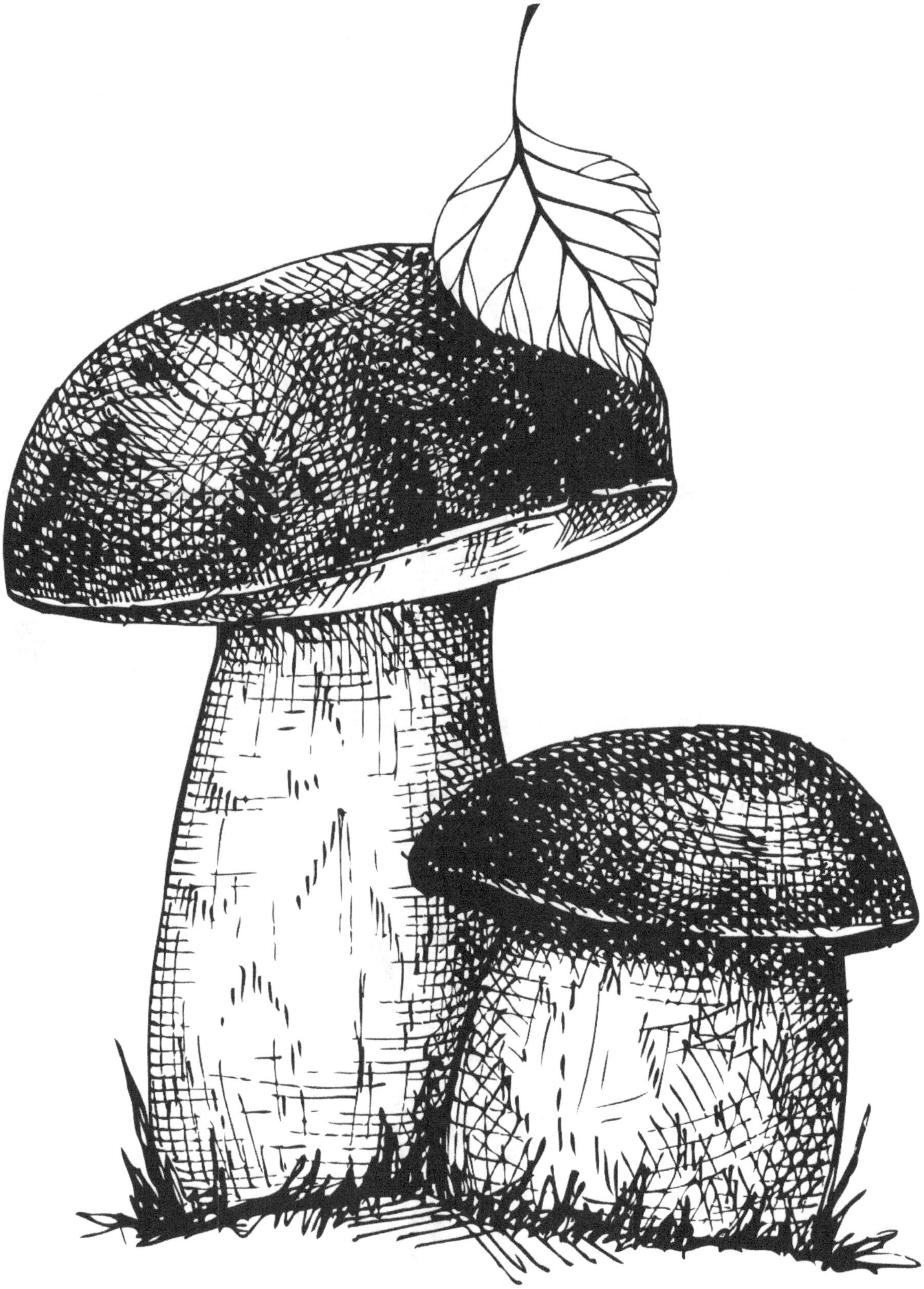

Creative Writing

Draw a picture below.

Write a poem or short story about it.

TITLE: _____

_____
_____
_____
_____
_____
_____
_____
_____
_____
_____
_____
_____
_____

Write & Draw about something that really happened.

___
___
___
___
___
___
___
___
___

Circle Today's Date

January
February
March
April
May
June
July
August
September
October
November
December

1 2 3 4 5 6
7 8 9 10 11
12 13 14 15
16 17 18 19
20 21 22 23
24 25 26 27
28 29 30 31

MONDAY
TUESDAY
WEDNESDAY
THURSDAY
FRIDAY
SATURDAY
SUNDAY

2015
2016
2017
2018
2019
2020
2021
2022
2023
2024
2025
2026
2027
2028
2029

Write Today's Date: _____

Nature Study

Go outside and make a realistic drawing of something you find in nature.

Reading Time - 1 Hour

Choose Four Books - Read from each book for 15 minutes.

Copy a sentence or picture from each book here:

Spelling Time

Find 20 Words with **6** letters each.
Look in your books for words.
Write the words here:

Film Study

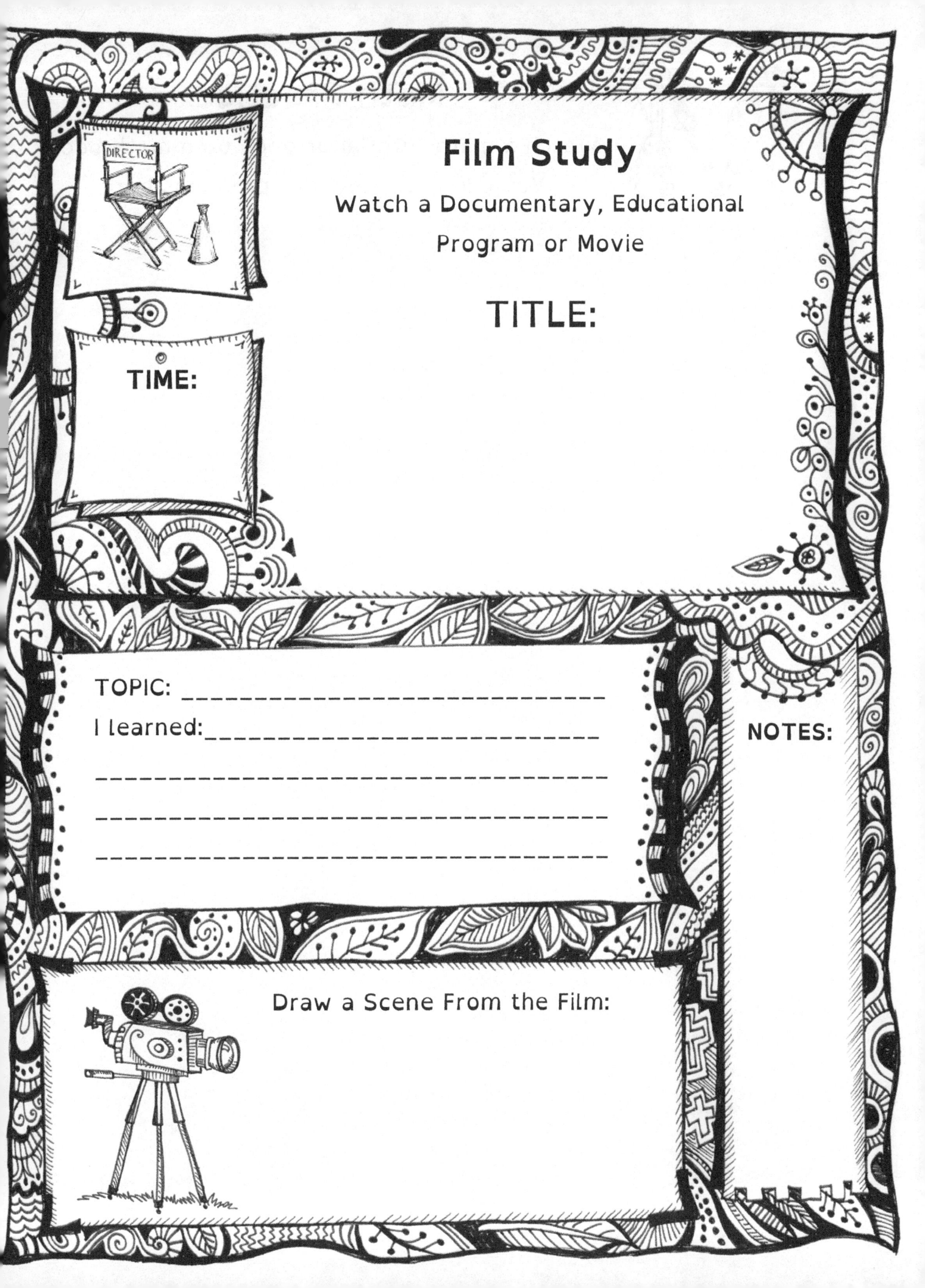

Watch a Documentary, Educational Program or Movie

TITLE:

TIME:

TOPIC: _____
I learned: _____
_____
_____
_____

NOTES:

Draw a Scene From the Film:

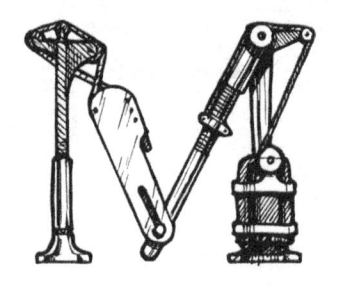

Math Practice

Watch a math tutorial or open up a math book.
You can practice math problems here.

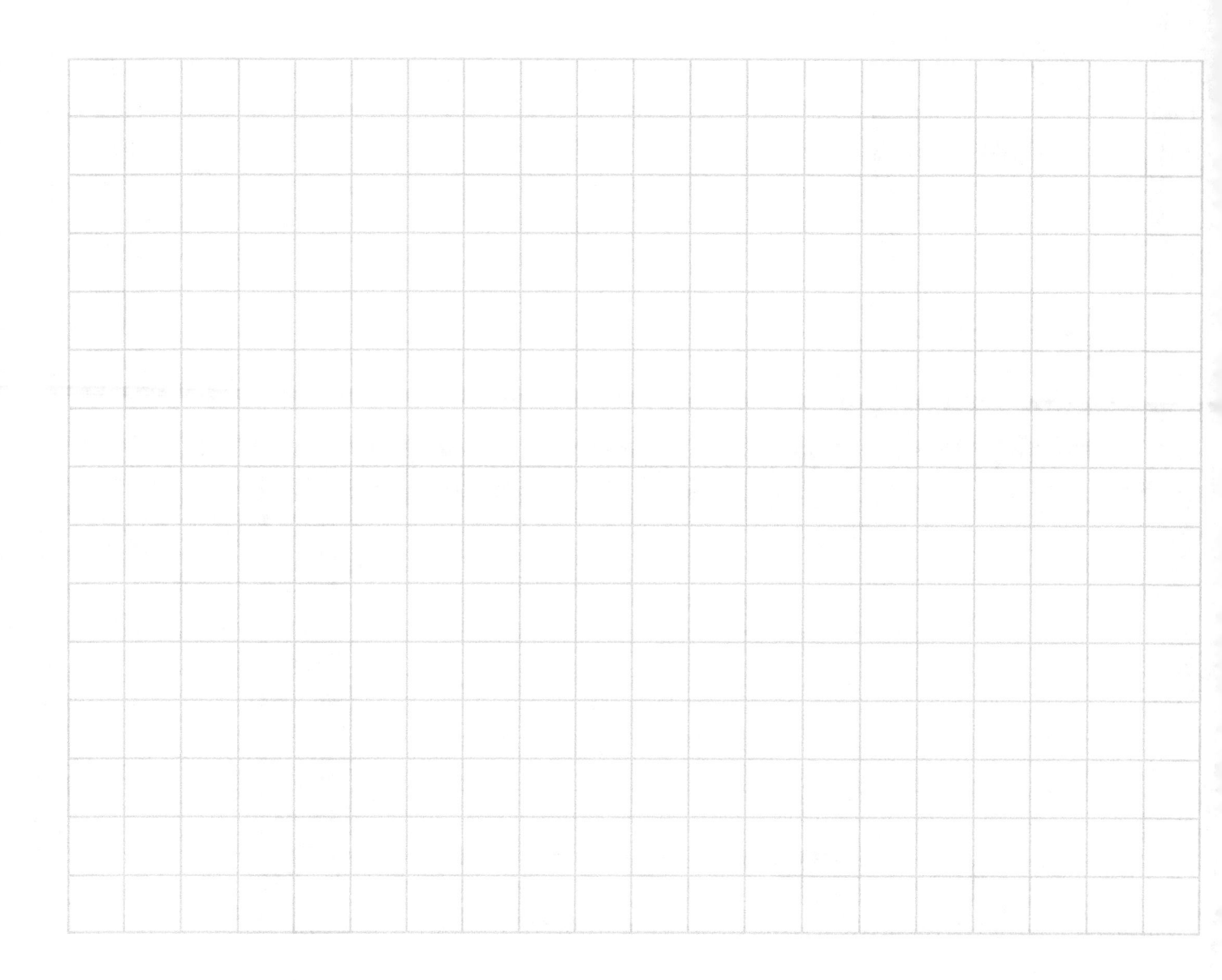

Copywork

Find an interesting paragraph in one of your books and copy it. Be diligent to make your writing look exactly like it does in the book.

TITLE:_____ **Page Number:**_____

Sketch a Picture

Look through your library books and find something to draw.

Circle Today's Date

January
February
March
April
May
June
July
August
September
October
November
December

1 2 3 4 5 6
7 8 9 10 11
12 13 14 15
16 17 18 19
20 21 22 23
24 25 26 27
28 29 30 31

MONDAY
TUESDAY
WEDNESDAY
THURSDAY
FRIDAY
SATURDAY
SUNDAY

2015
2016
2017
2018
2019
2020
2021
2022
2023
2024
2025
2026
2027
2028
2029

Write Today's Date: _____

My Thinking Page

This is where you write down your ideas, goals, and plans - with a thankful heart!

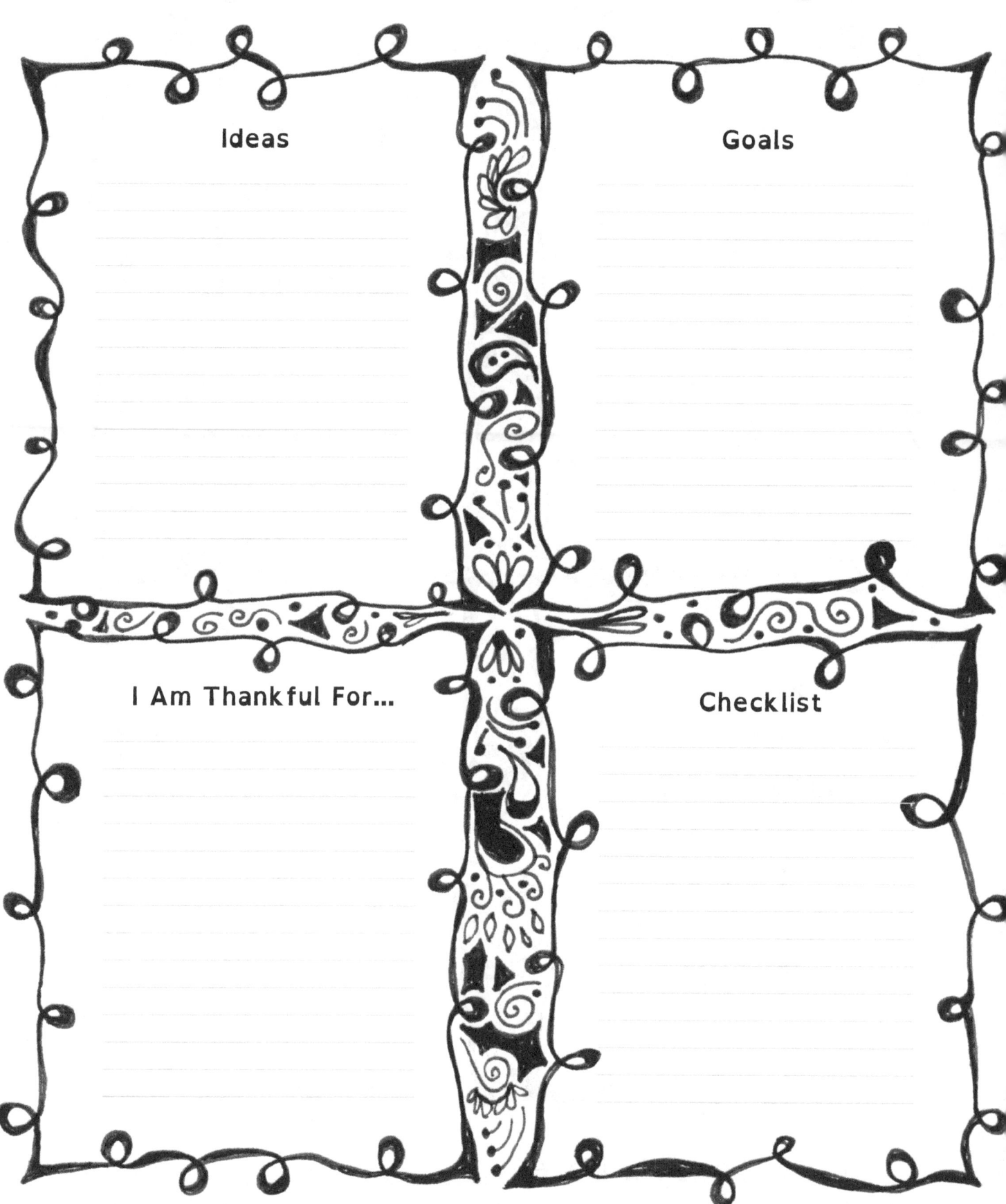

Ideas

Goals

I Am Thankful For...

Checklist

Write & Draw about something that really happened.

_____
_____
_____
_____
_____
_____
_____
_____

Nature Study

Go outside and make a realistic drawing of something you find in nature.

Circle Today's Date

January
February
March
April
May
June
July
August
September
October
November
December

1 2 3 4 5 6
7 8 9 10 11
12 13 14 15
16 17 18 19
20 21 22 23
24 25 26 27
28 29 30 31

MONDAY
TUESDAY
WEDNESDAY
THURSDAY
FRIDAY
SATURDAY
SUNDAY

2015
2016
2017
2018
2019
2020
2021
2022
2023
2024
2025
2026
2027
2028
2029

Write Today's Date: _____

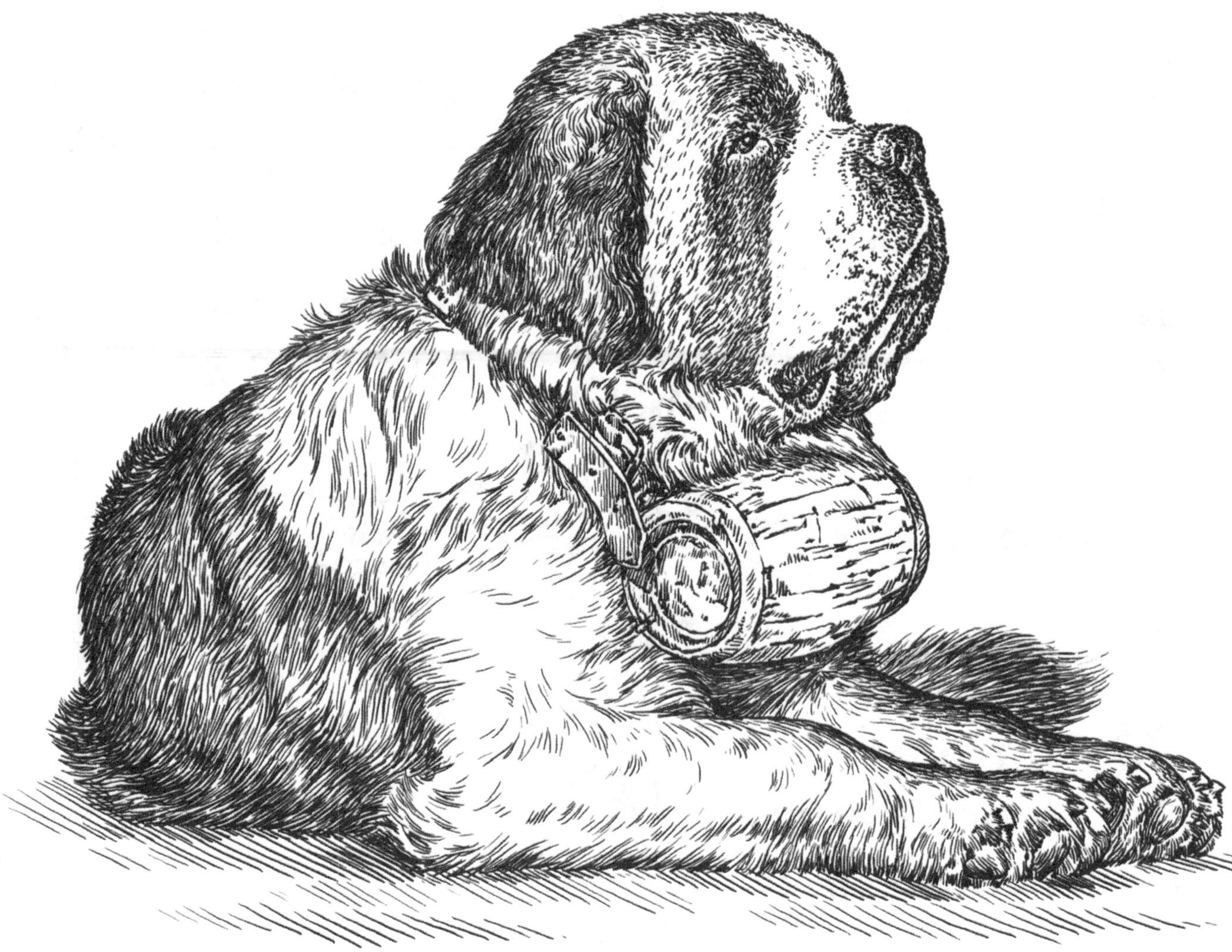

Reading Time - 1 Hour

Choose Four Books - Read from each book for 15 minutes.
Copy a sentence or picture from each book here:

Spelling Time

Find 20 Words with 5 letters each.
Look in your books for words.
Write the words here:

_____   _____

_____   _____

_____   _____

_____   _____

_____   _____

_____   _____

_____   _____

_____   _____

_____   _____

_____   _____

Film Study

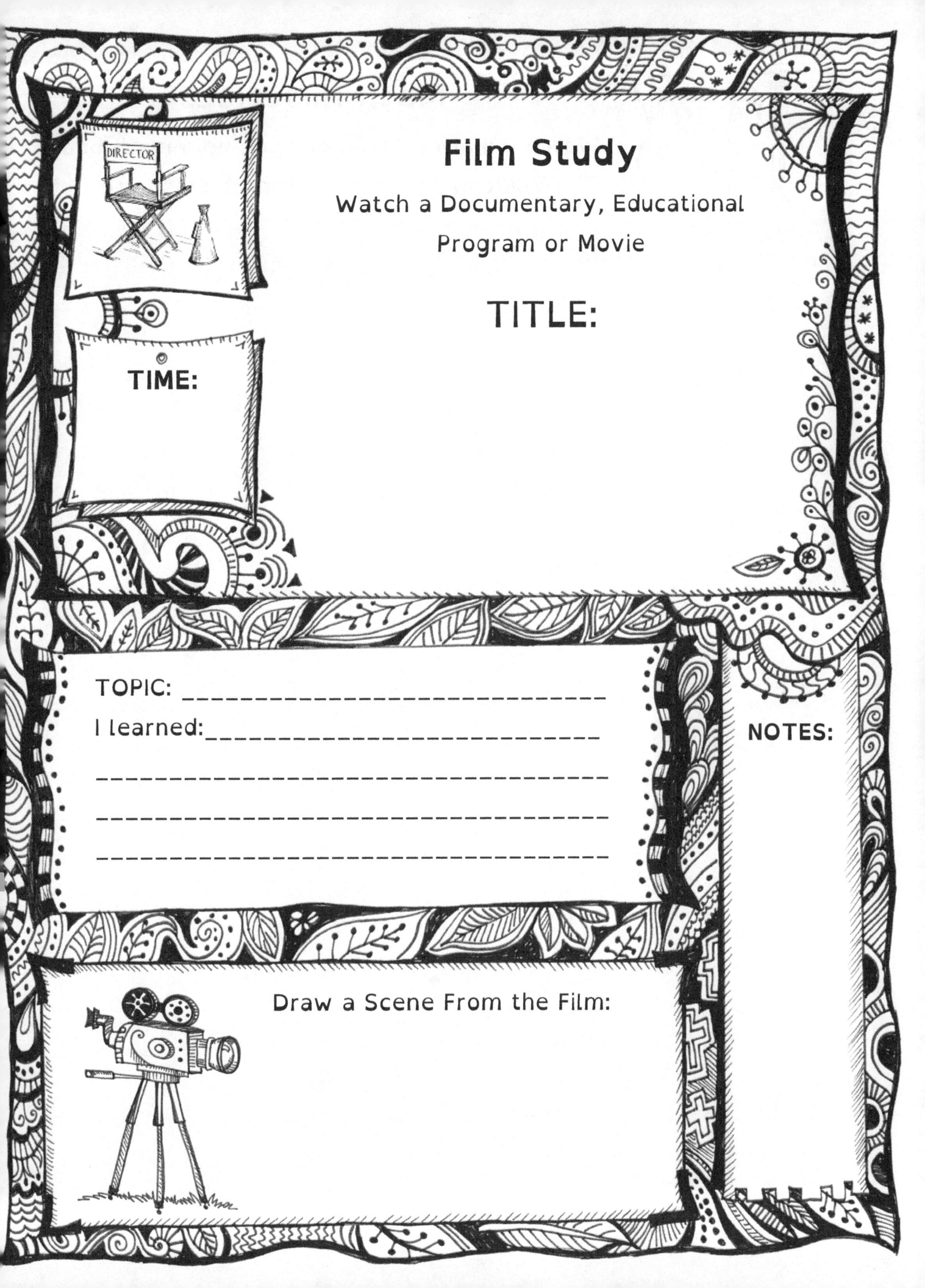

Watch a Documentary, Educational Program or Movie

TITLE:

TIME:

TOPIC: _____

I learned: _____

_____

_____

_____

NOTES:

Draw a Scene From the Film:

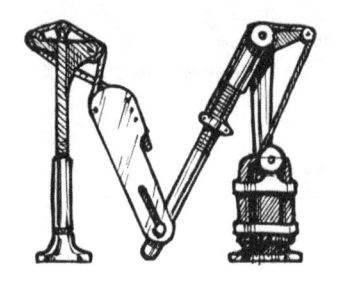

Math Practice

Watch a math tutorial or open up a math book. You can practice math problems here.

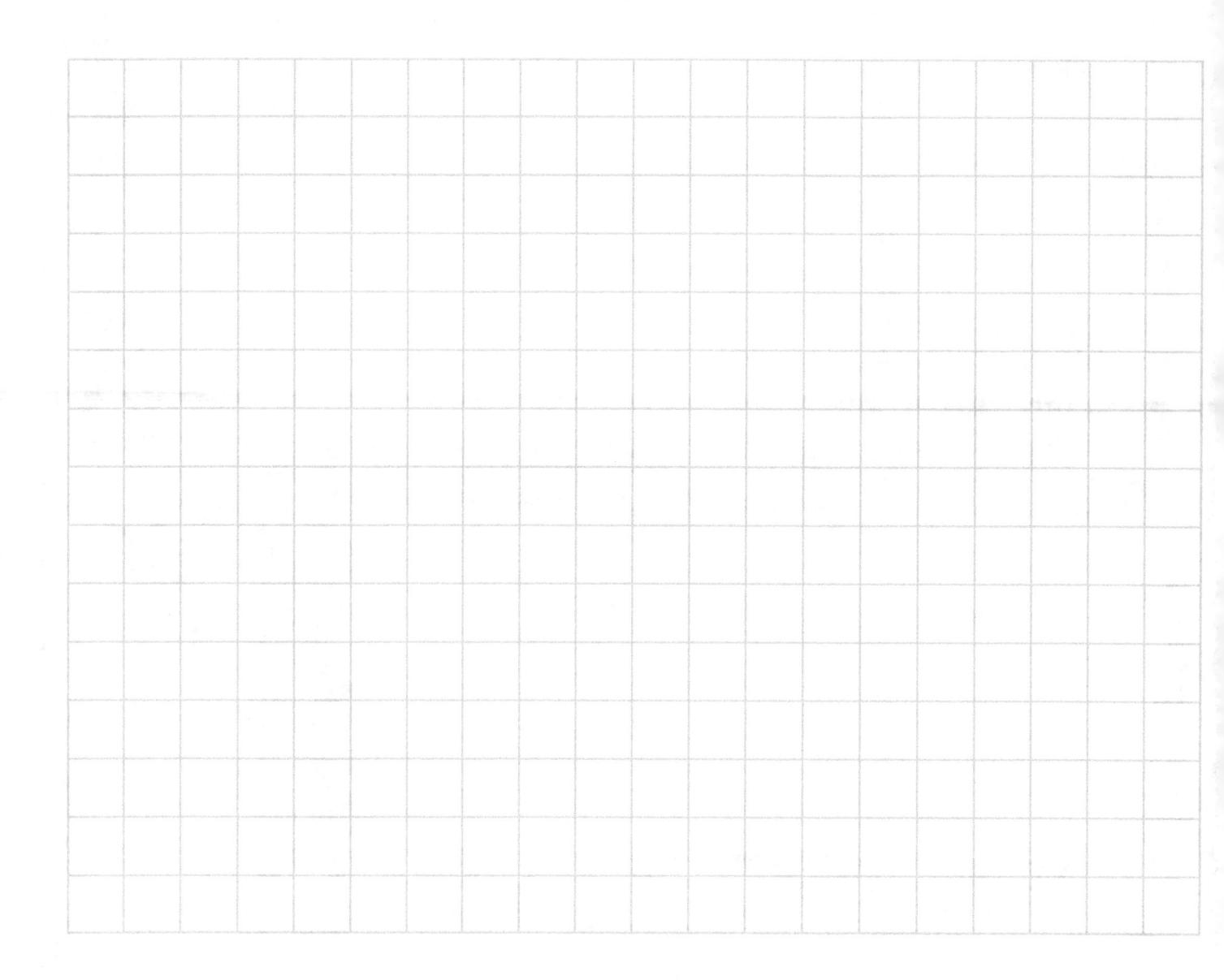

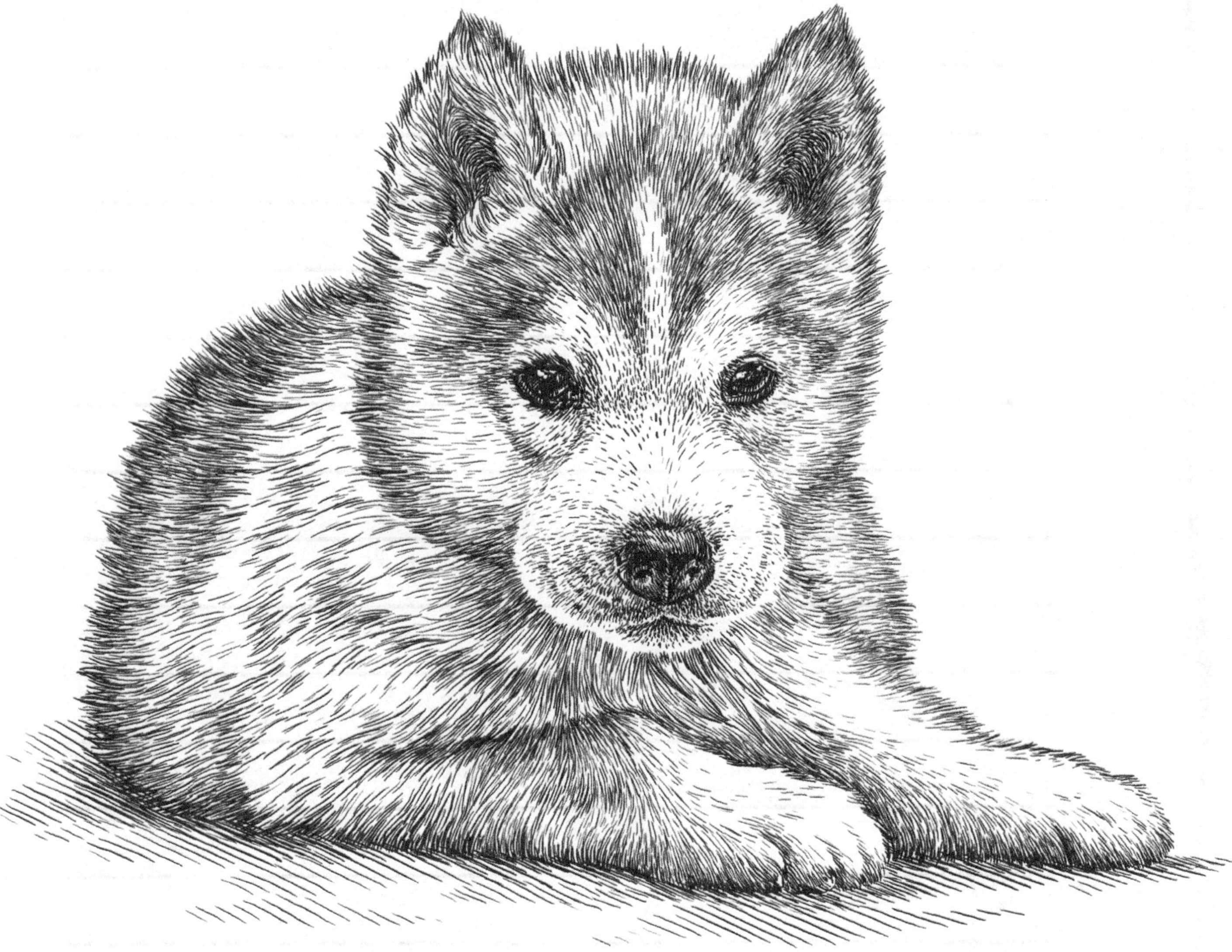

Copywork

Find an interesting paragraph in one of your books and copy it. Be diligent to make your writing look exactly like it does in the book.

TITLE:_____ **Page Number:**_____

Sketch a Picture
Look through your library books and find something to draw.

Circle Today's Date

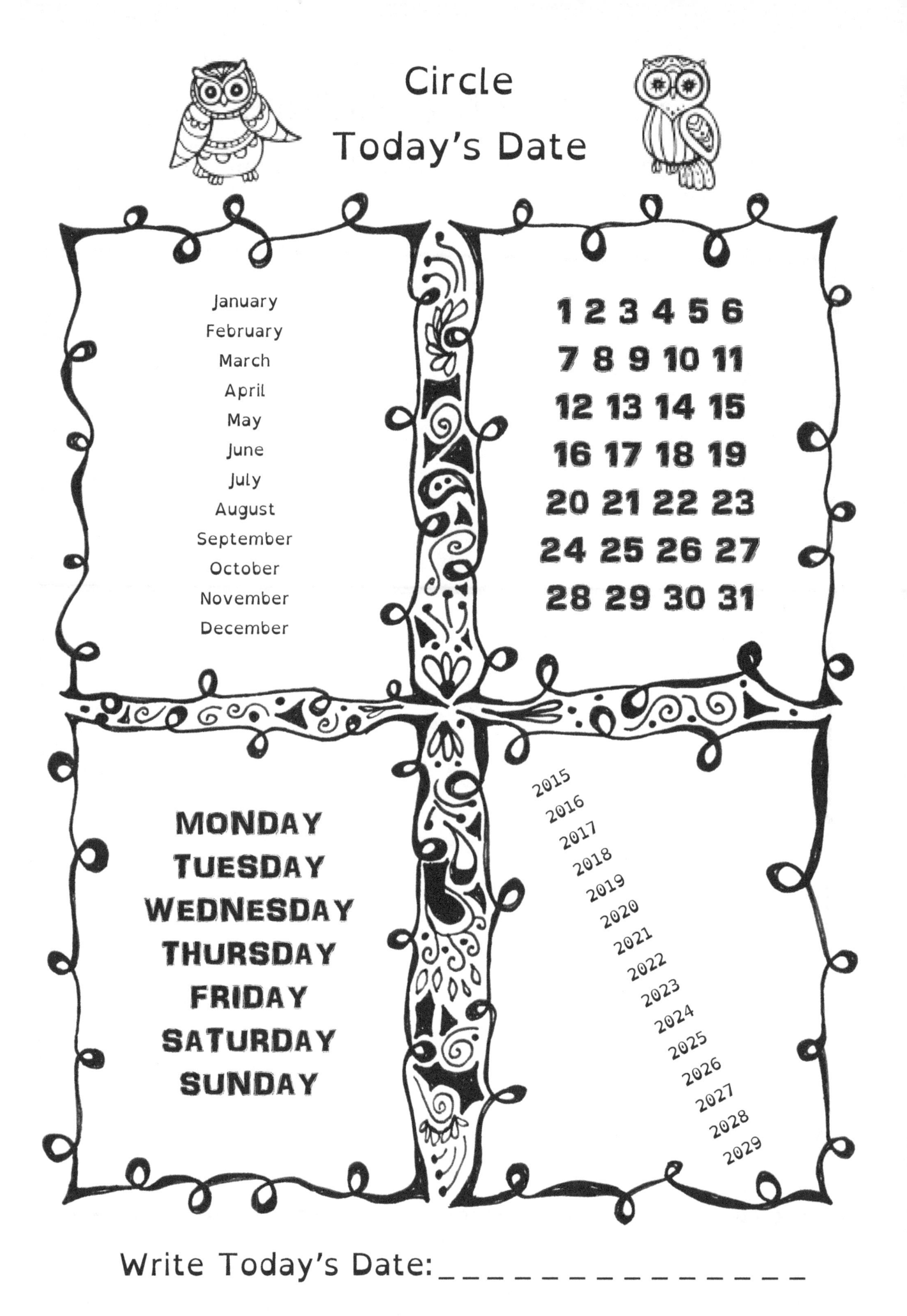

January
February
March
April
May
June
July
August
September
October
November
December

1 2 3 4 5 6
7 8 9 10 11
12 13 14 15
16 17 18 19
20 21 22 23
24 25 26 27
28 29 30 31

MONDAY
TUESDAY
WEDNESDAY
THURSDAY
FRIDAY
SATURDAY
SUNDAY

2015
2016
2017
2018
2019
2020
2021
2022
2023
2024
2025
2026
2027
2028
2029

Write Today's Date: _____

My Thinking Page

This is where you write down your ideas, goals, and plans - with a thankful heart!

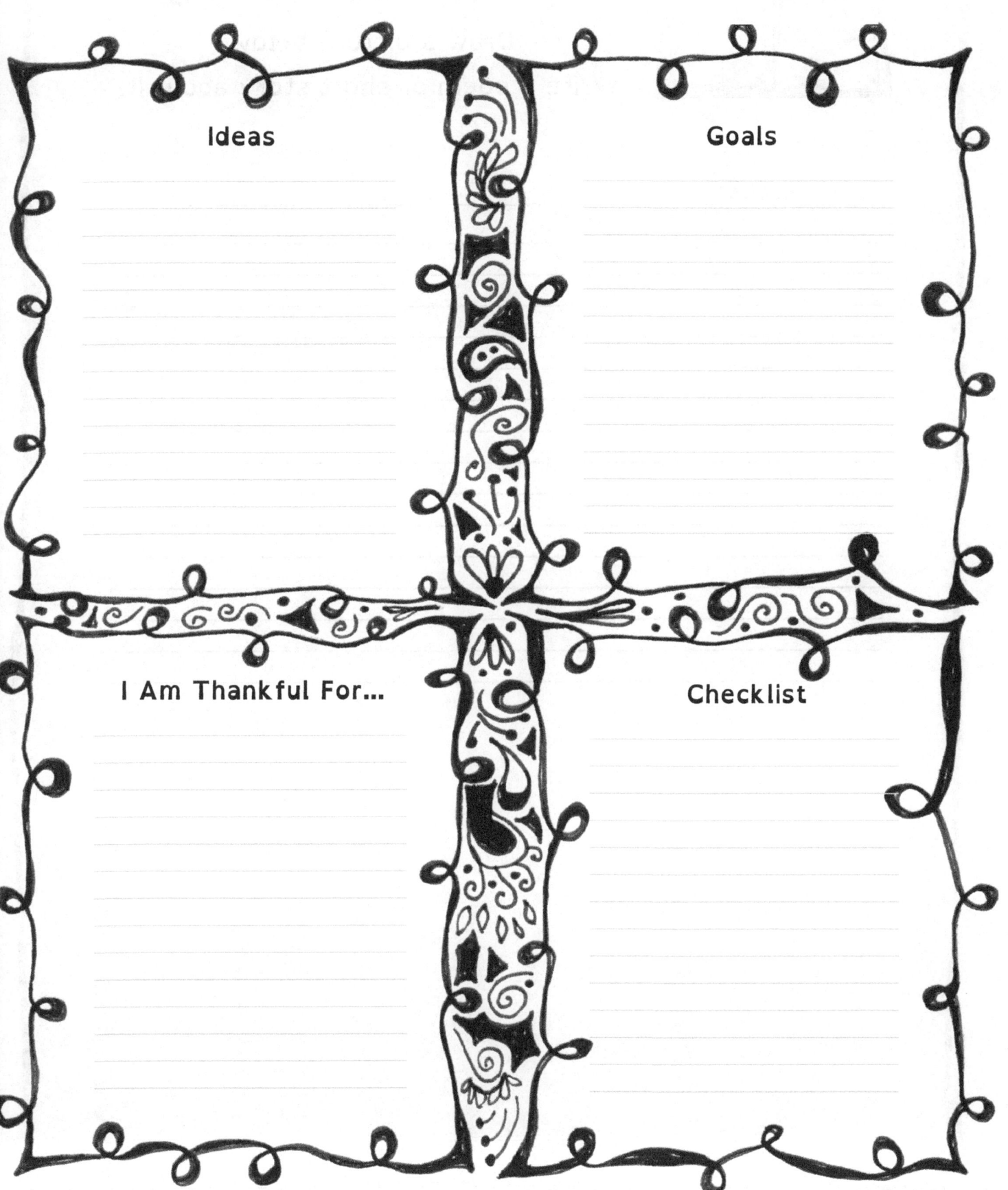

Ideas

Goals

I Am Thankful For...

Checklist

Creative Writing

Draw a picture below.
Write a poem or short story about it.

TITLE: _____
_____
_____
_____
_____
_____
_____
_____
_____
_____
_____
_____
_____
_____
_____

Write & Draw about something that really happened.

_____
_____
_____
_____
_____
_____
_____
_____

Nature Study

Go outside and make a realistic drawing of something you find in nature.

Circle Today's Date

January
February
March
April
May
June
July
August
September
October
November
December

1 2 3 4 5 6
7 8 9 10 11
12 13 14 15
16 17 18 19
20 21 22 23
24 25 26 27
28 29 30 31

MONDAY
TUESDAY
WEDNESDAY
THURSDAY
FRIDAY
SATURDAY
SUNDAY

2015
2016
2017
2018
2019
2020
2021
2022
2023
2024
2025
2026
2027
2028
2029

Write Today's Date: _____

Reading Time - 1 Hour

Choose Four Books - Read from each book for 15 minutes.
Copy a sentence or picture from each book here:

Spelling Time

Find 20 Words with **6** letters each.
Look in your books for words.
Write the words here:

Film Study

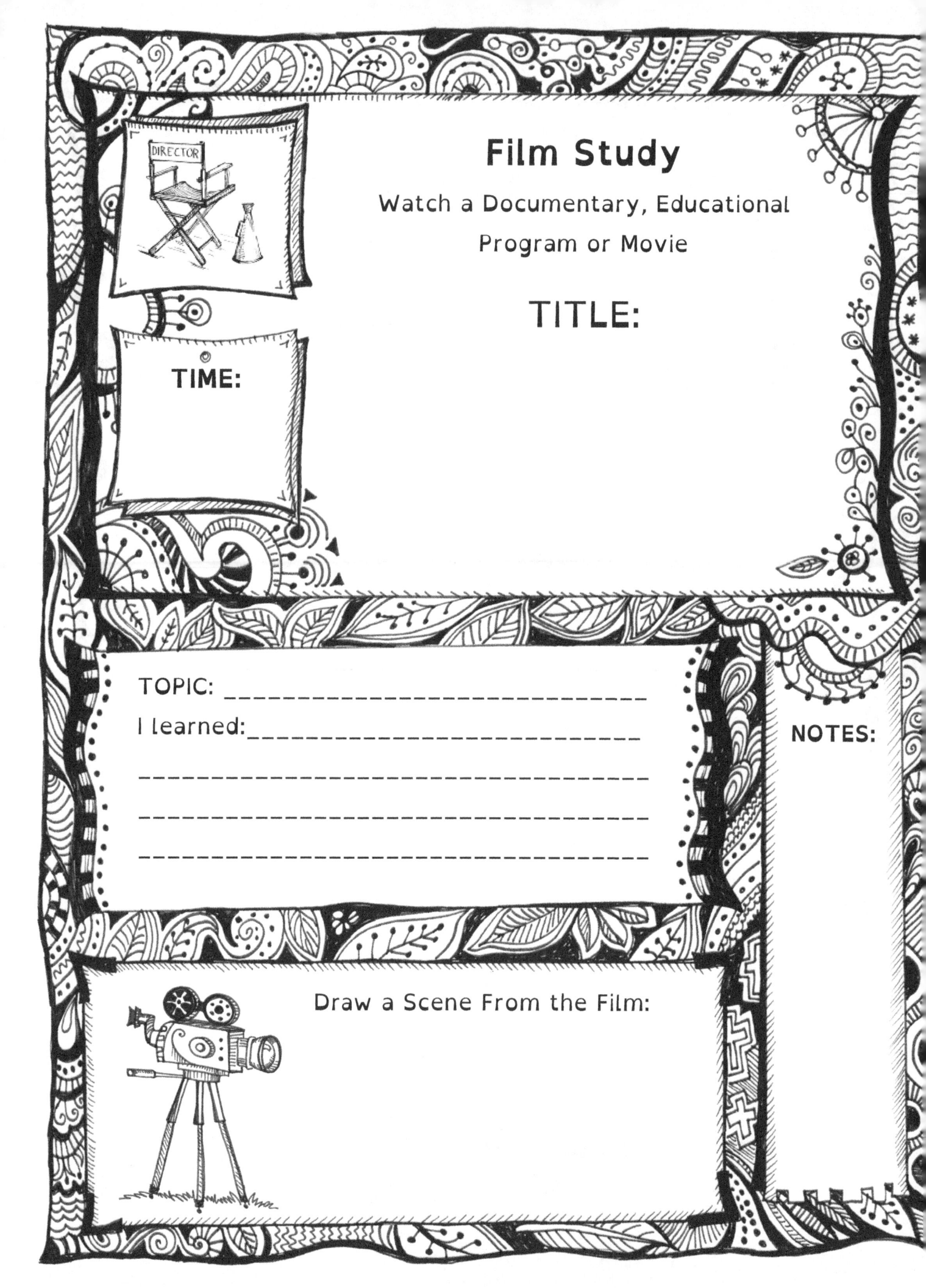

Watch a Documentary, Educational Program or Movie

TITLE:

TIME:

TOPIC: _____
I learned: _____
_____
_____
_____

NOTES:

Draw a Scene From the Film:

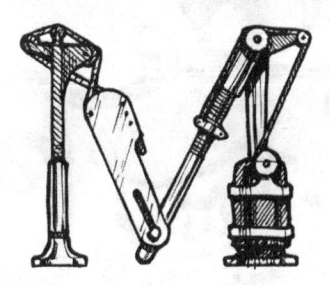

Math Practice

Watch a math tutorial or open up a math book.
You can practice math problems here.

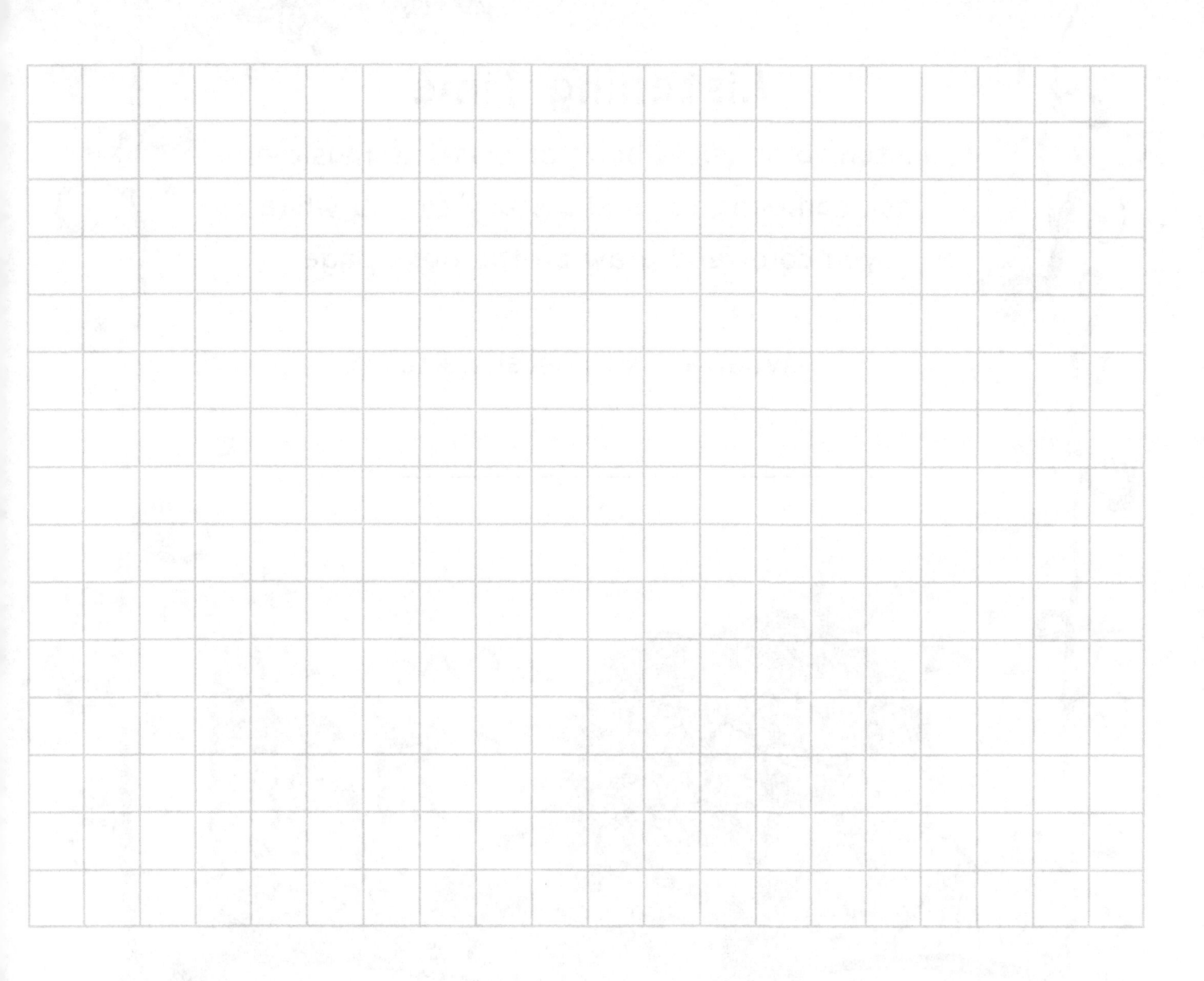

Listening Time

Listen to an audio book or classical music or ask someone to read a story to you while you color and draw on the next page.

What are you listening to?

_____

Draw a Meal PLAN

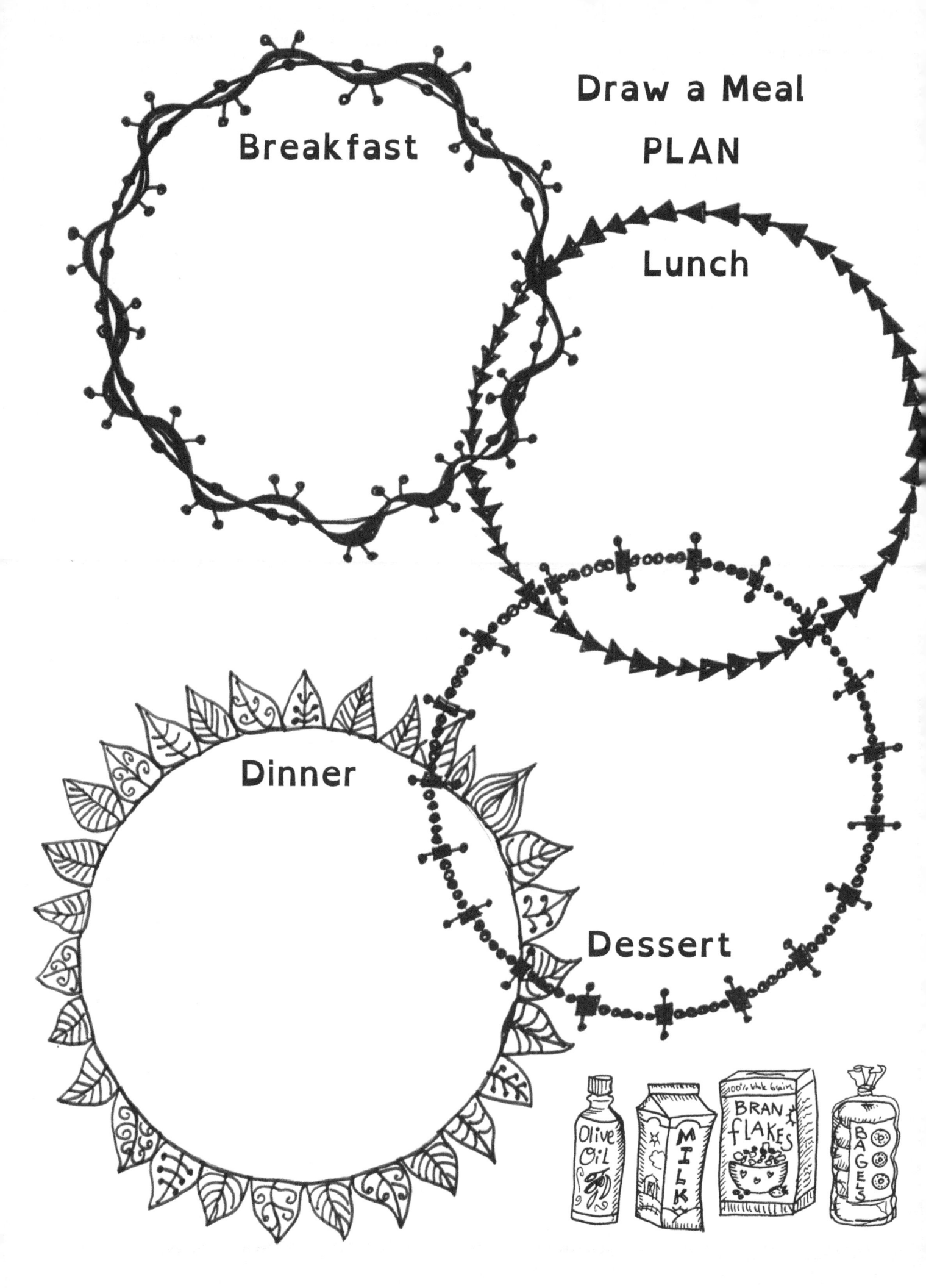

Breakfast

Lunch

Dinner

Dessert

Circle Today's Date

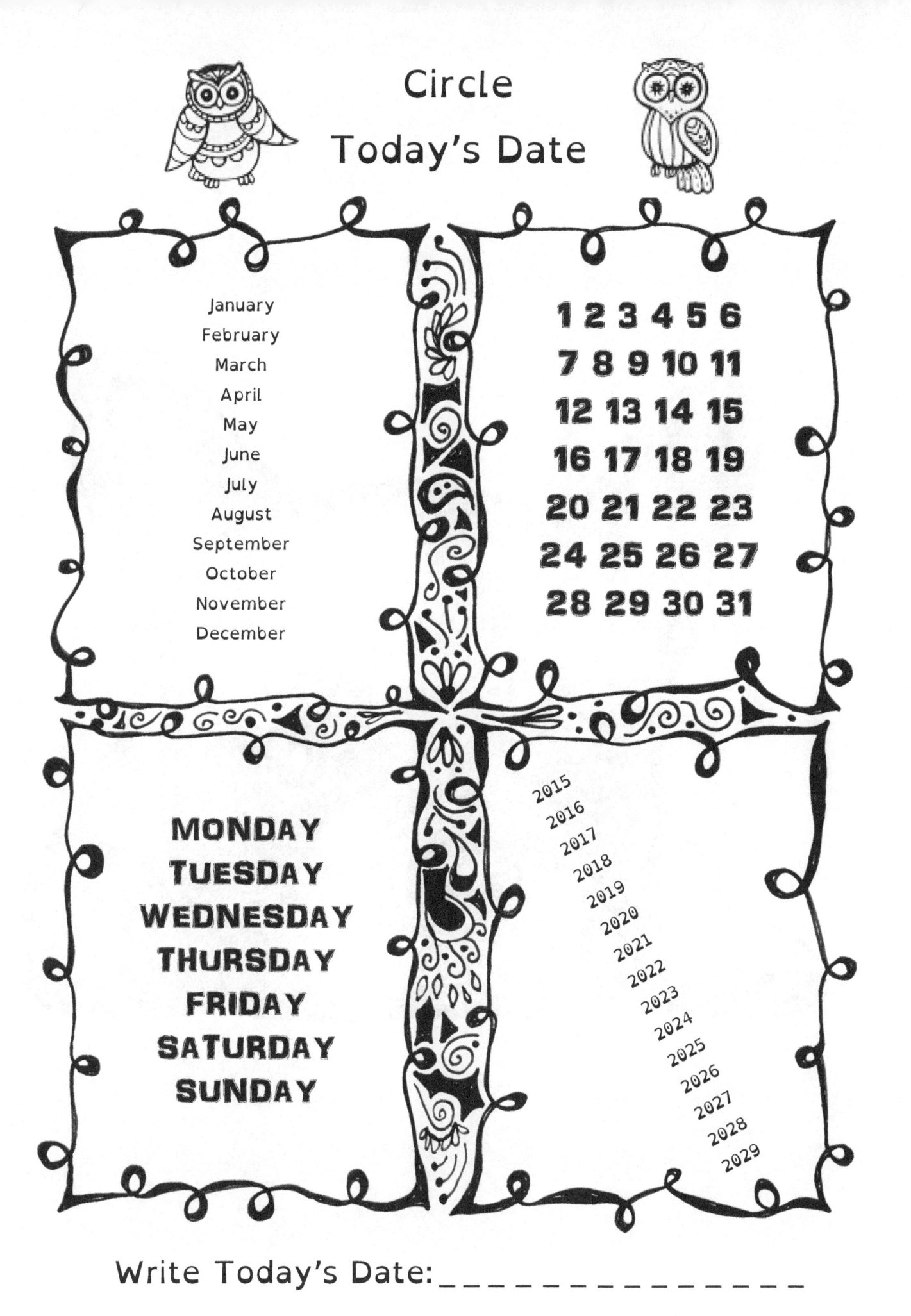

January
February
March
April
May
June
July
August
September
October
November
December

1 2 3 4 5 6
7 8 9 10 11
12 13 14 15
16 17 18 19
20 21 22 23
24 25 26 27
28 29 30 31

MONDAY
TUESDAY
WEDNESDAY
THURSDAY
FRIDAY
SATURDAY
SUNDAY

2015
2016
2017
2018
2019
2020
2021
2022
2023
2024
2025
2026
2027
2028
2029

Write Today's Date:_____

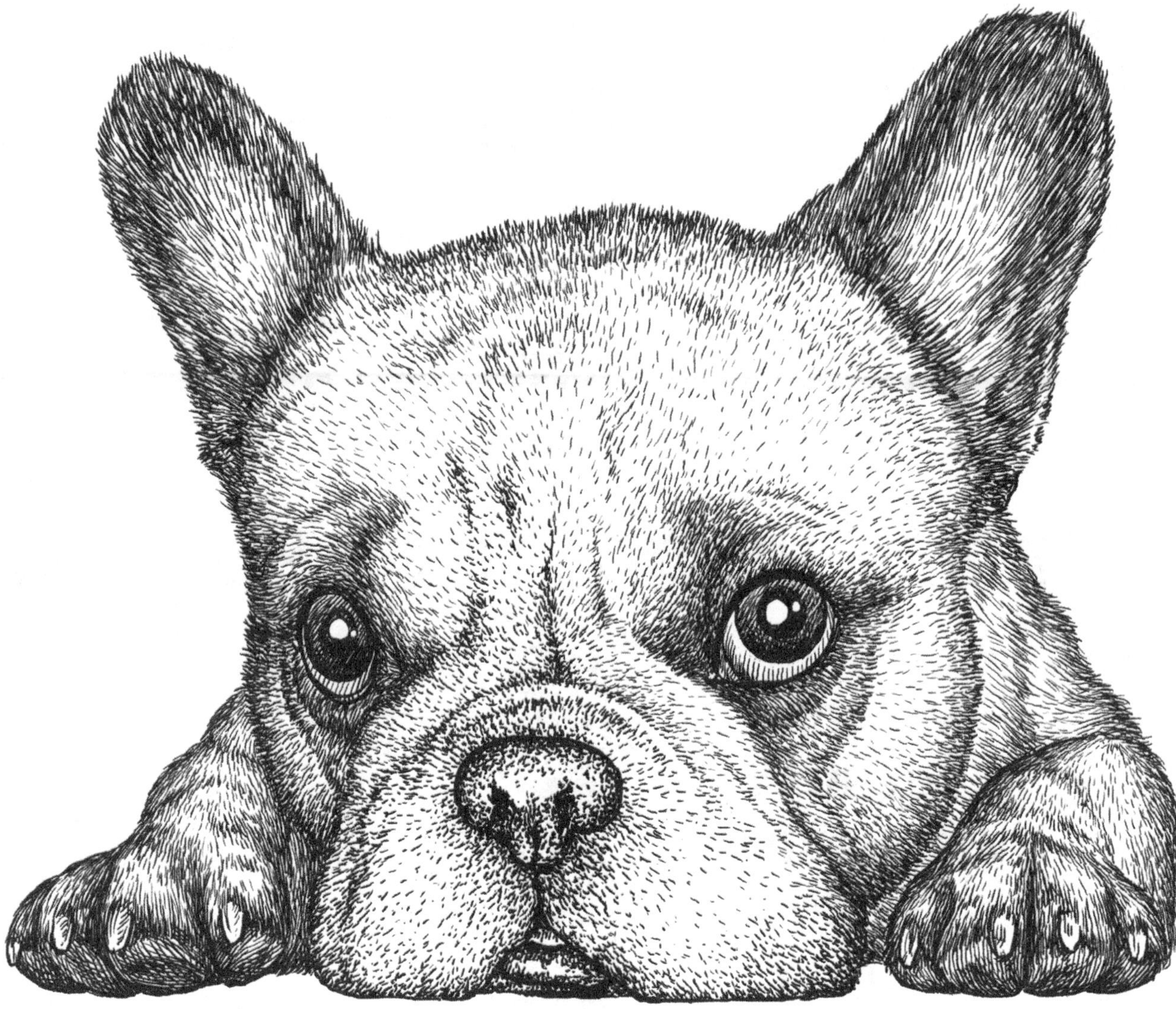

My Thinking Page

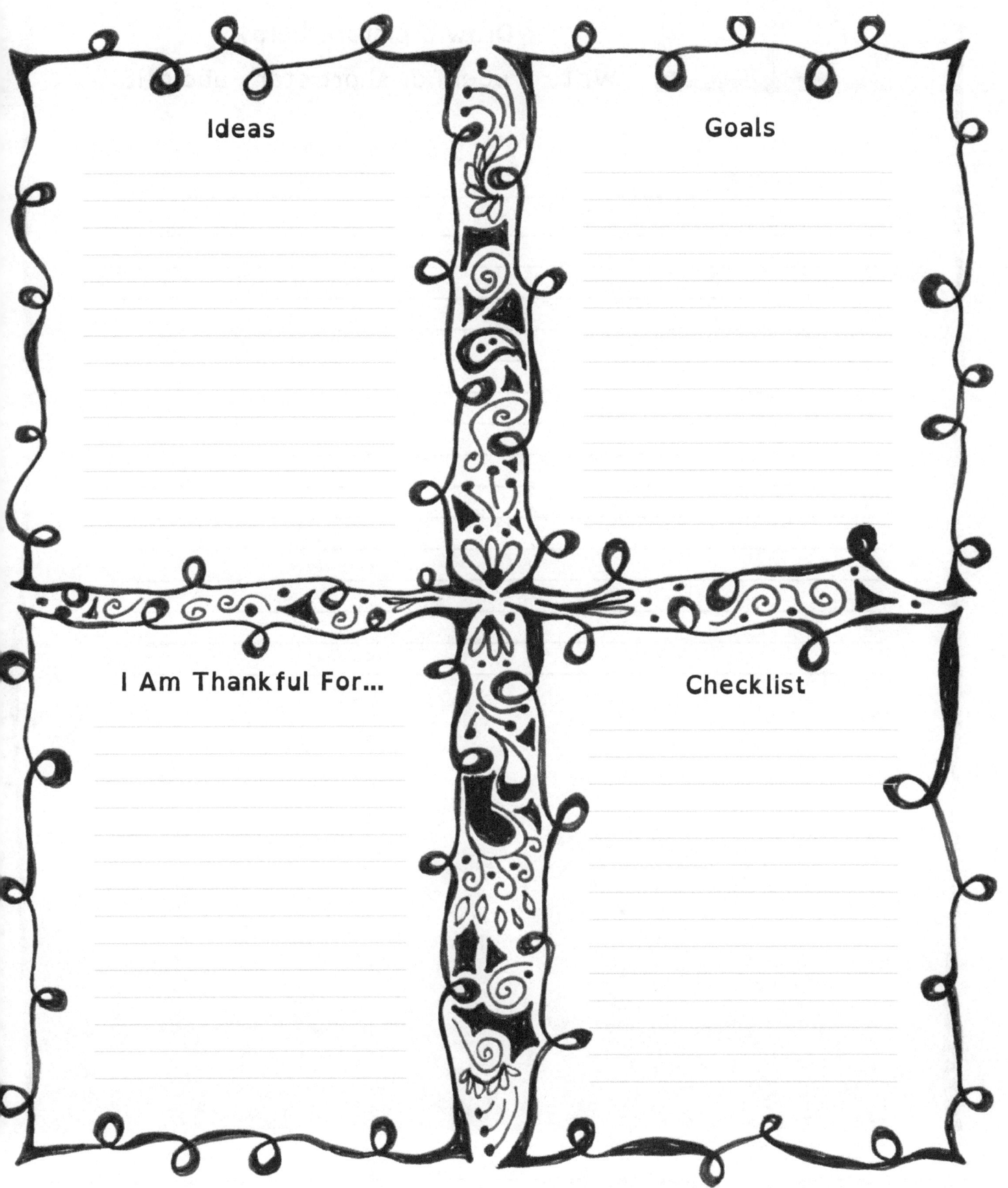

This is where you write down your ideas, goals, and plans - with a thankful heart!

Ideas

Goals

I Am Thankful For...

Checklist

Creative Writing

Draw a picture below.
Write a poem or short story about it.

TITLE: _____

_____
_____
_____
_____
_____
_____
_____
_____
_____
_____
_____
_____
_____
_____

Nature Study

Go outside and make a realistic drawing of something you find in nature.

Reading Time - 1 Hour

Choose Four Books - Read from each book for 15 minutes.
Copy a sentence or picture from each book here:

Airedale Terrier	Whippet	Wire Fox Terrier
Buldog	Norwich Terrier	Bull Terrier

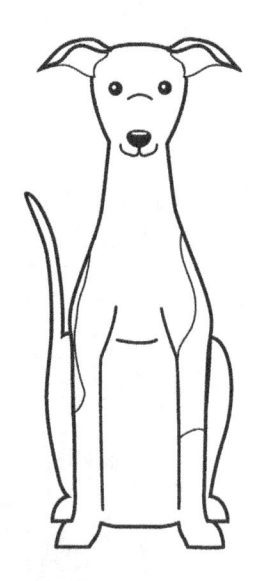

English dogs (part 1)

Bobtail

English Cocker Spaniel

Bedlington Terrier

Smooth Fox Terrier

Beagle

Border Terrier

English dogs (part 2)

Spelling Time

Find 20 Words with 7 letters each.
Look in your books for words.
Write the words here:

Film Study

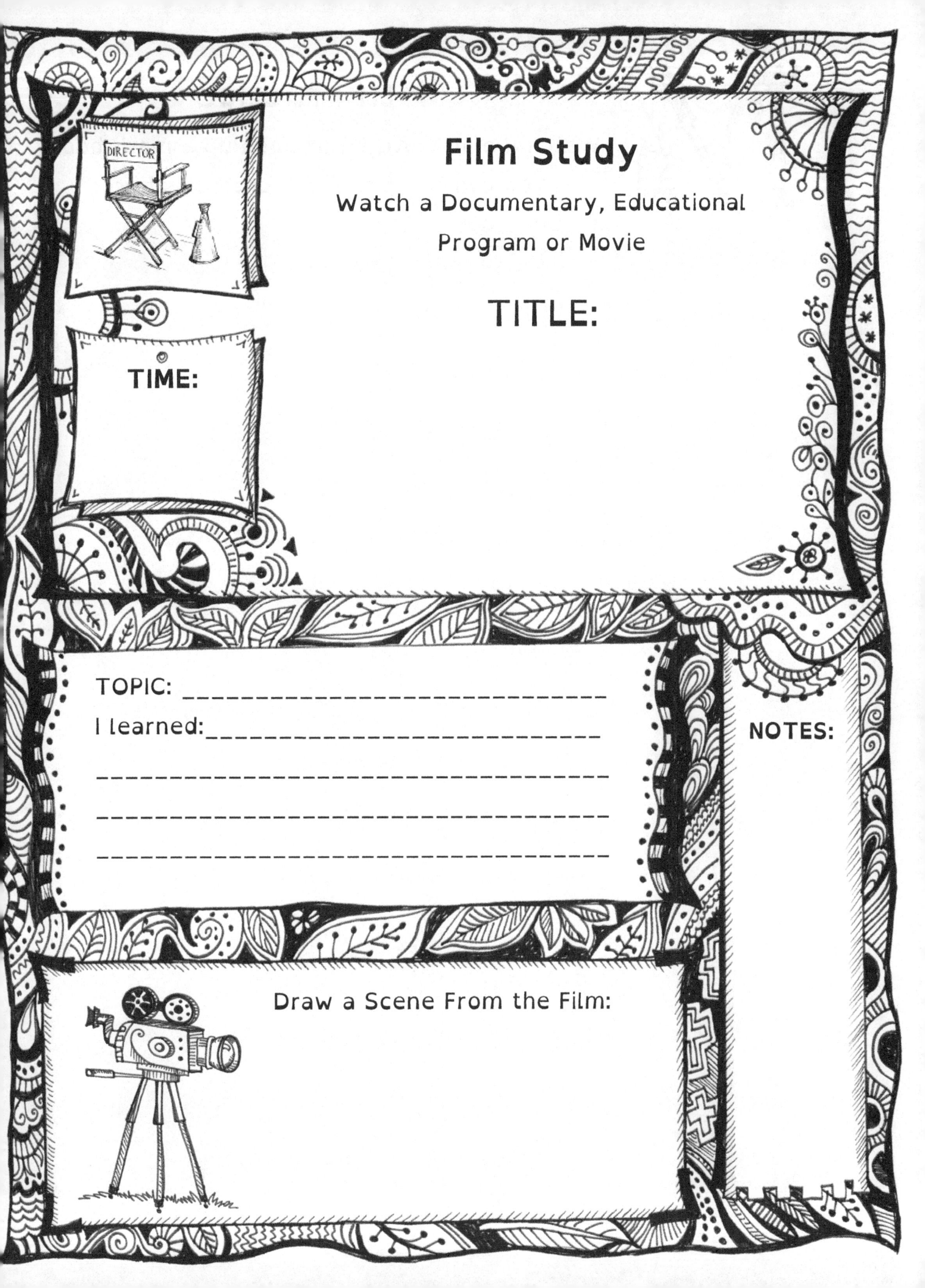

Watch a Documentary, Educational Program or Movie

TITLE:

TIME:

TOPIC: _____
I learned: _____
_____
_____
_____

NOTES:

Draw a Scene From the Film:

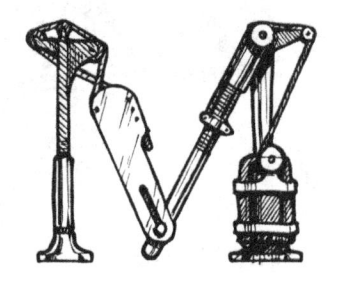

Math Practice

Watch a math tutorial or open up a math book.
You can practice math problems here.

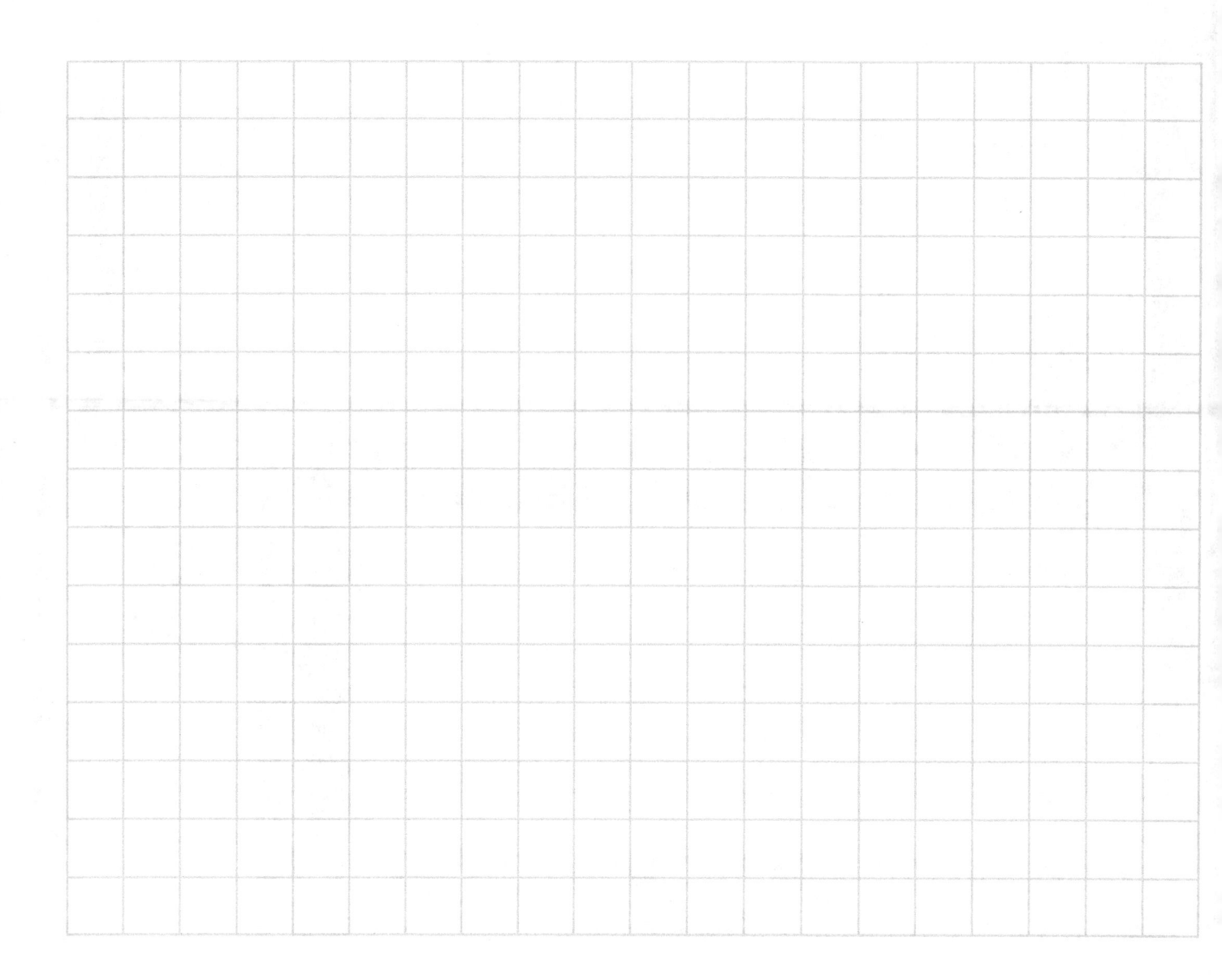

Copywork

Find an interesting paragraph in one of your books and copy it. Be diligent to make your writing look exactly like it does in the book.

TITLE:_____ Page Number:_____

Circle Today's Date

January
February
March
April
May
June
July
August
September
October
November
December

1 2 3 4 5 6
7 8 9 10 11
12 13 14 15
16 17 18 19
20 21 22 23
24 25 26 27
28 29 30 31

MONDAY
TUESDAY
WEDNESDAY
THURSDAY
FRIDAY
SATURDAY
SUNDAY

2015
2016
2017
2018
2019
2020
2021
2022
2023
2024
2025
2026
2027
2028
2029

Write Today's Date: _____

My Thinking Page

This is where you write down your ideas, goals, and plans - with a thankful heart!

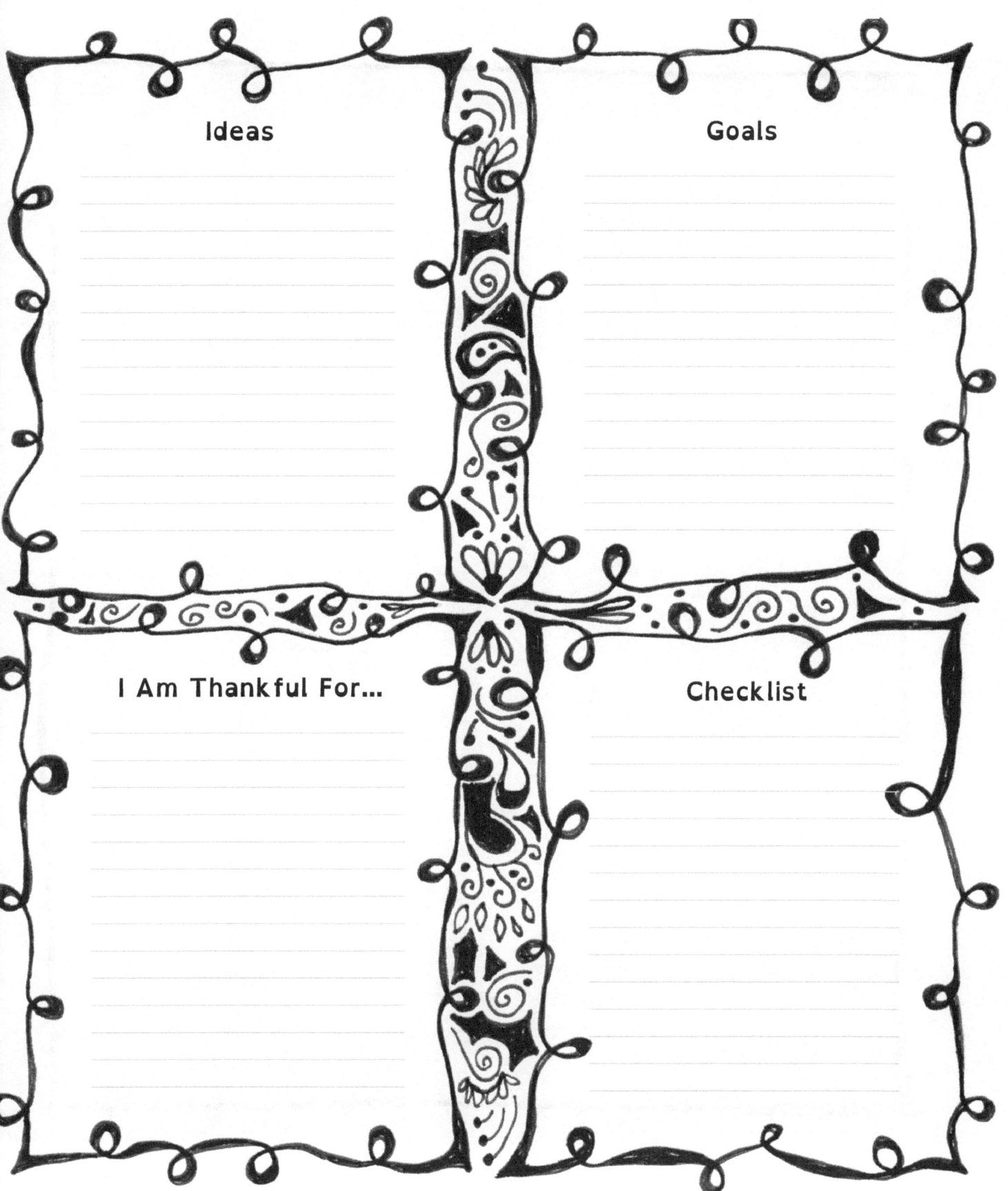

Ideas

Goals

I Am Thankful For...

Checklist

Sketch a Picture

Look through your library books and find something to draw.

Learning a Skill

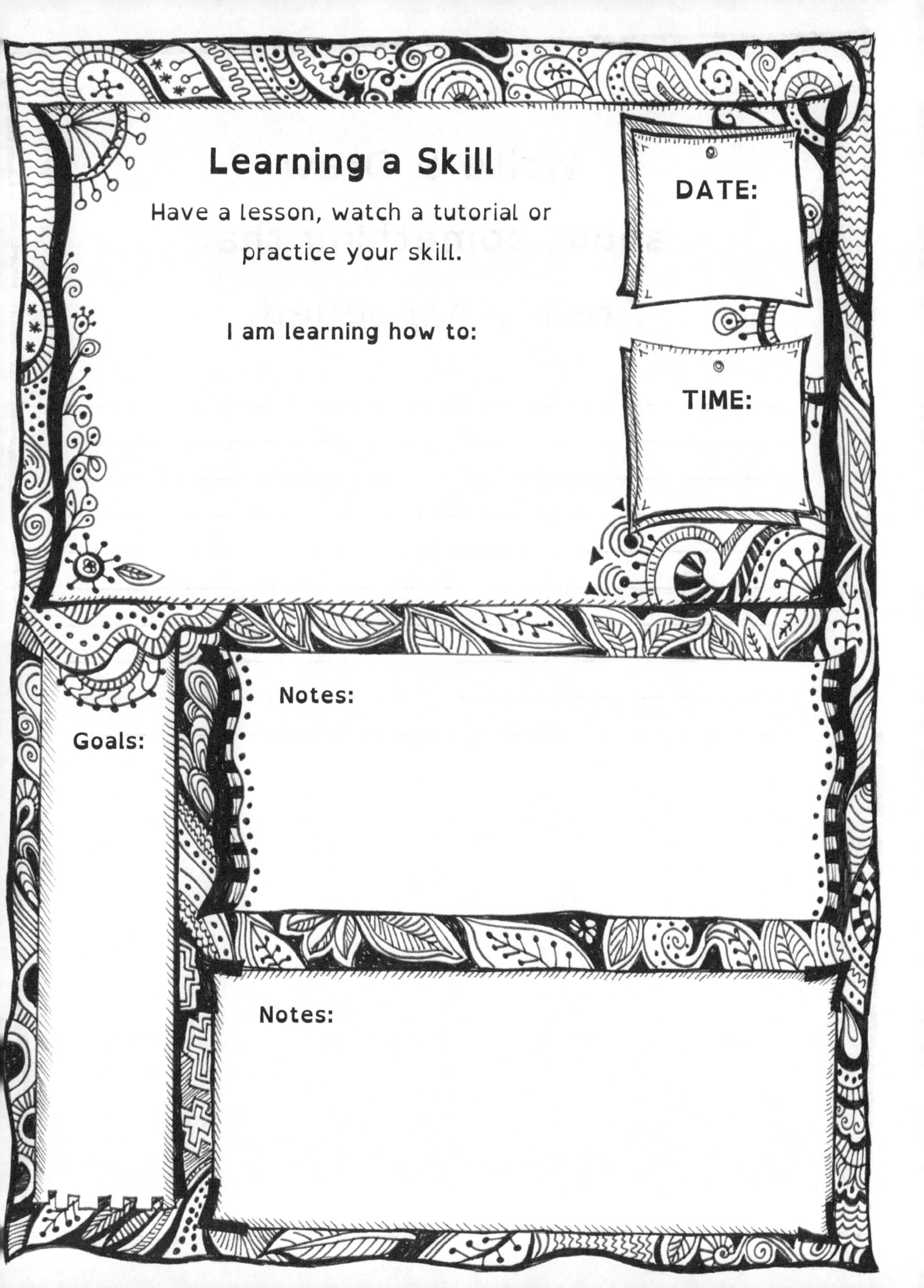

Have a lesson, watch a tutorial or practice your skill.

I am learning how to:

DATE:

TIME:

Goals:

Notes:

Notes:

Write & Draw
about something that really happened.

_____
_____
_____
_____
_____
_____
_____
_____
_____
_____

Circle Today's Date

January
February
March
April
May
June
July
August
September
October
November
December

1 2 3 4 5 6
7 8 9 10 11
12 13 14 15
16 17 18 19
20 21 22 23
24 25 26 27
28 29 30 31

MONDAY
TUESDAY
WEDNESDAY
THURSDAY
FRIDAY
SATURDAY
SUNDAY

2015
2016
2017
2018
2019
2020
2021
2022
2023
2024
2025
2026
2027
2028
2029

Write Today's Date: _____

Nature Study

Go outside and make a realistic drawing of something you find in nature.

Reading Time - 1 Hour

Choose Four Books - Read from each book for 15 minutes.

Copy a sentence or picture from each book here:

Draw a Meal PLAN

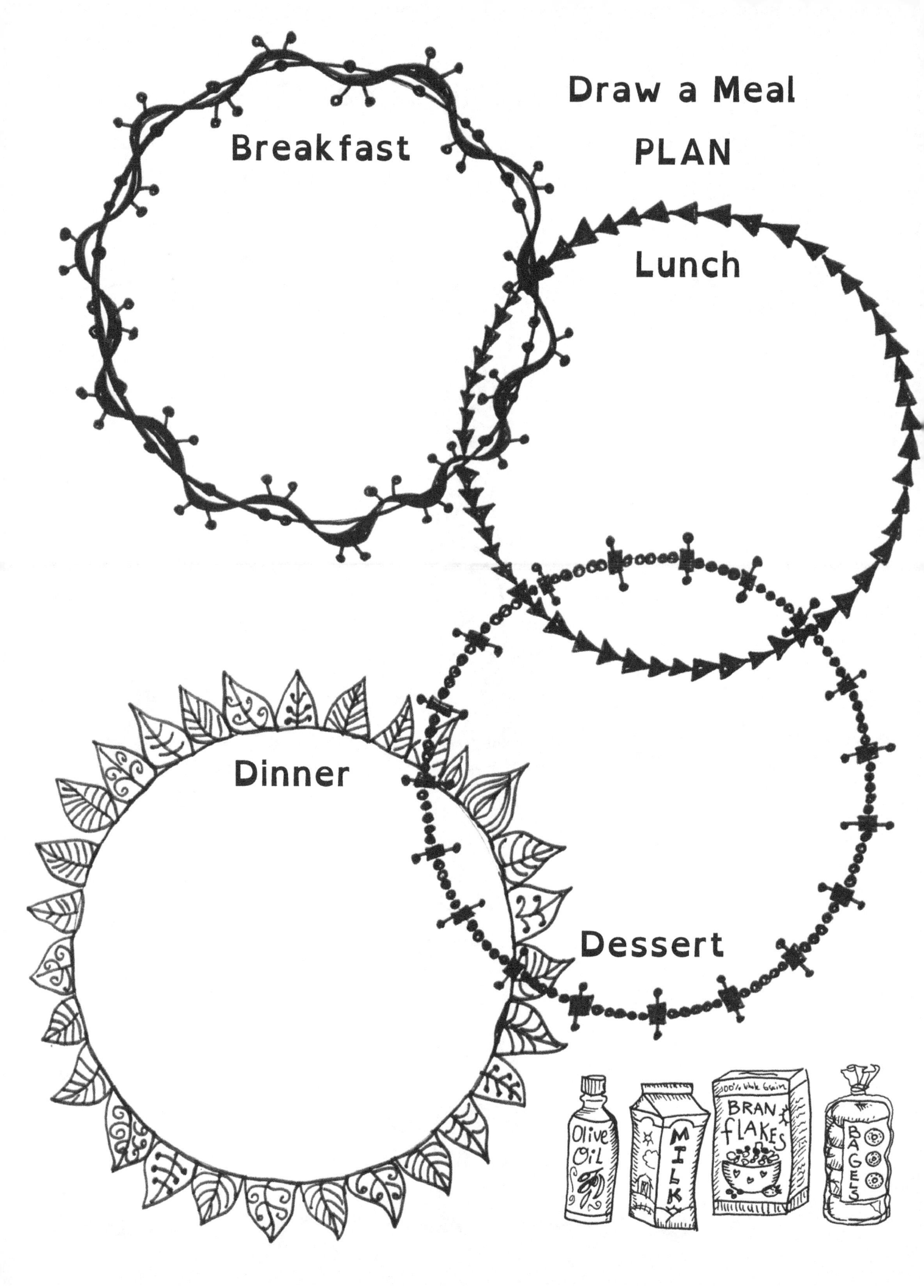

Breakfast

Lunch

Dinner

Dessert

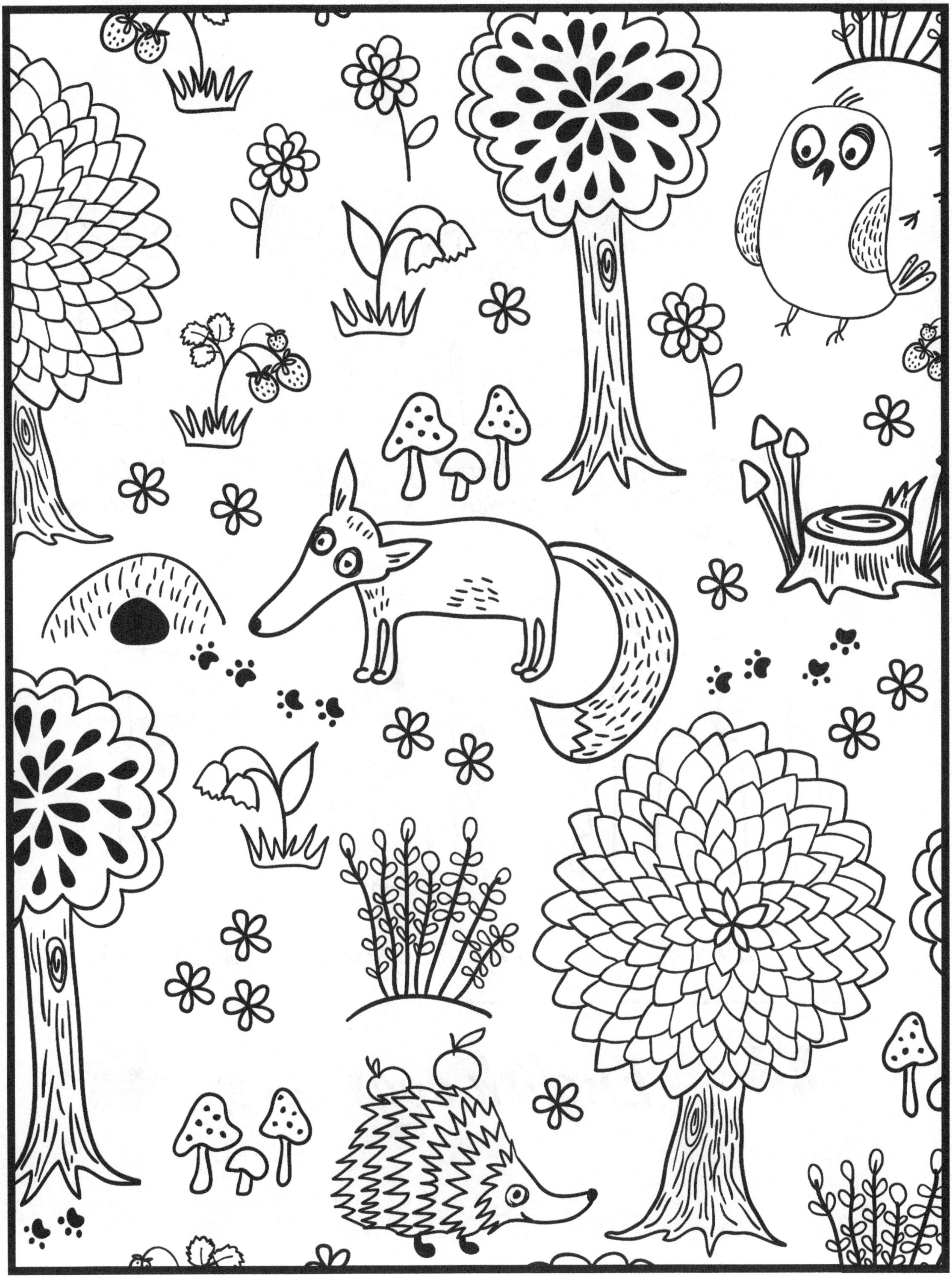

Jack Russel Terrier

English Toy Terrier

Welsh Corgi Cardigan

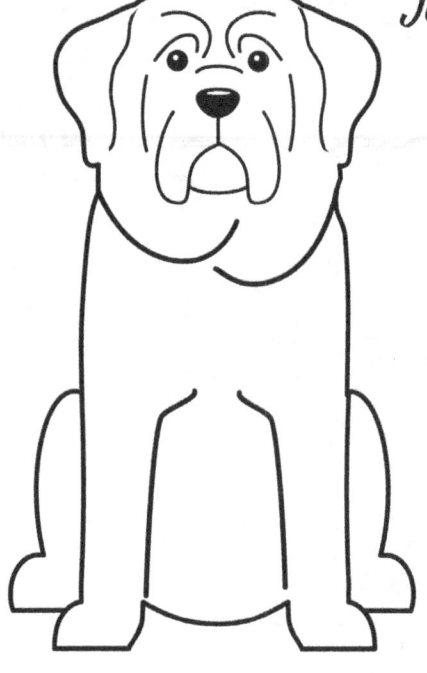

Mastiff1

English Foxhound

Welsh Terrier

English dogs (part 3)

Irish Wolfhound

Irish Red Setter

Irish Water Spaniel

Irish Terrier

Soft-coated Wheaten Terrier

Glen of Imaal terrier

Irish dogs

Circle Today's Date

January
February
March
April
May
June
July
August
September
October
November
December

1 2 3 4 5 6
7 8 9 10 11
12 13 14 15
16 17 18 19
20 21 22 23
24 25 26 27
28 29 30 31

MONDAY
TUESDAY
WEDNESDAY
THURSDAY
FRIDAY
SATURDAY
SUNDAY

2015
2016
2017
2018
2019
2020
2021
2022
2023
2024
2025
2026
2027
2028
2029

Write Today's Date:_____

Spelling Time

Find 20 Words with **8** letters each.
Look in your books for words.
Write the words here:

_____   _____

_____   _____

_____   _____

_____   _____

_____   _____

_____   _____

_____   _____

_____   _____

_____   _____

_____   _____

Film Study

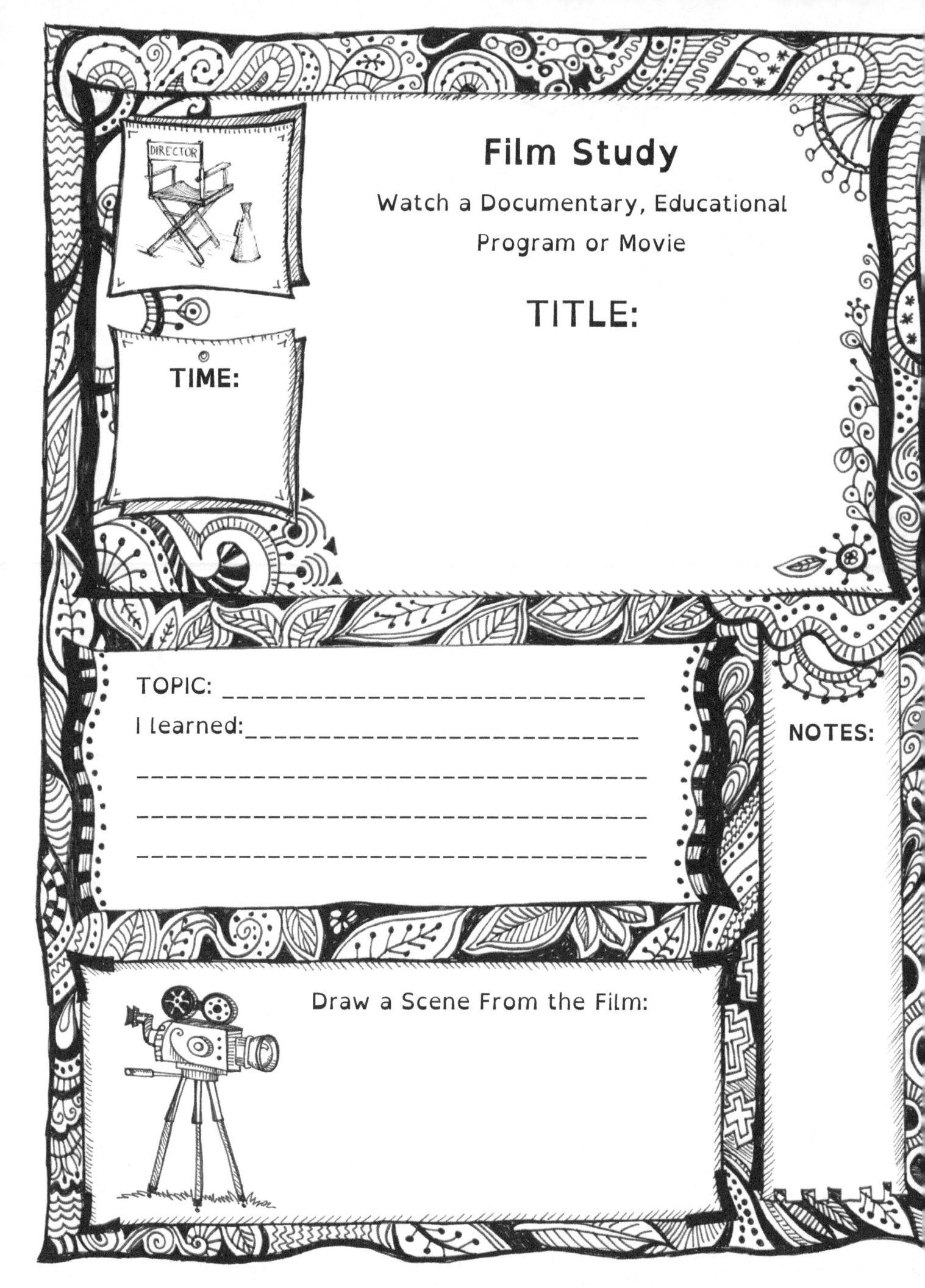

Watch a Documentary, Educational Program or Movie

TITLE:

TIME:

TOPIC: _____

I learned: _____

_____

_____

_____

NOTES:

Draw a Scene From the Film:

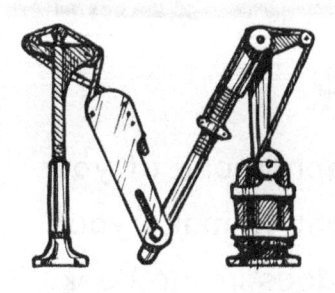

Math Practice

Watch a math tutorial or open up a math book.
You can practice math problems here.

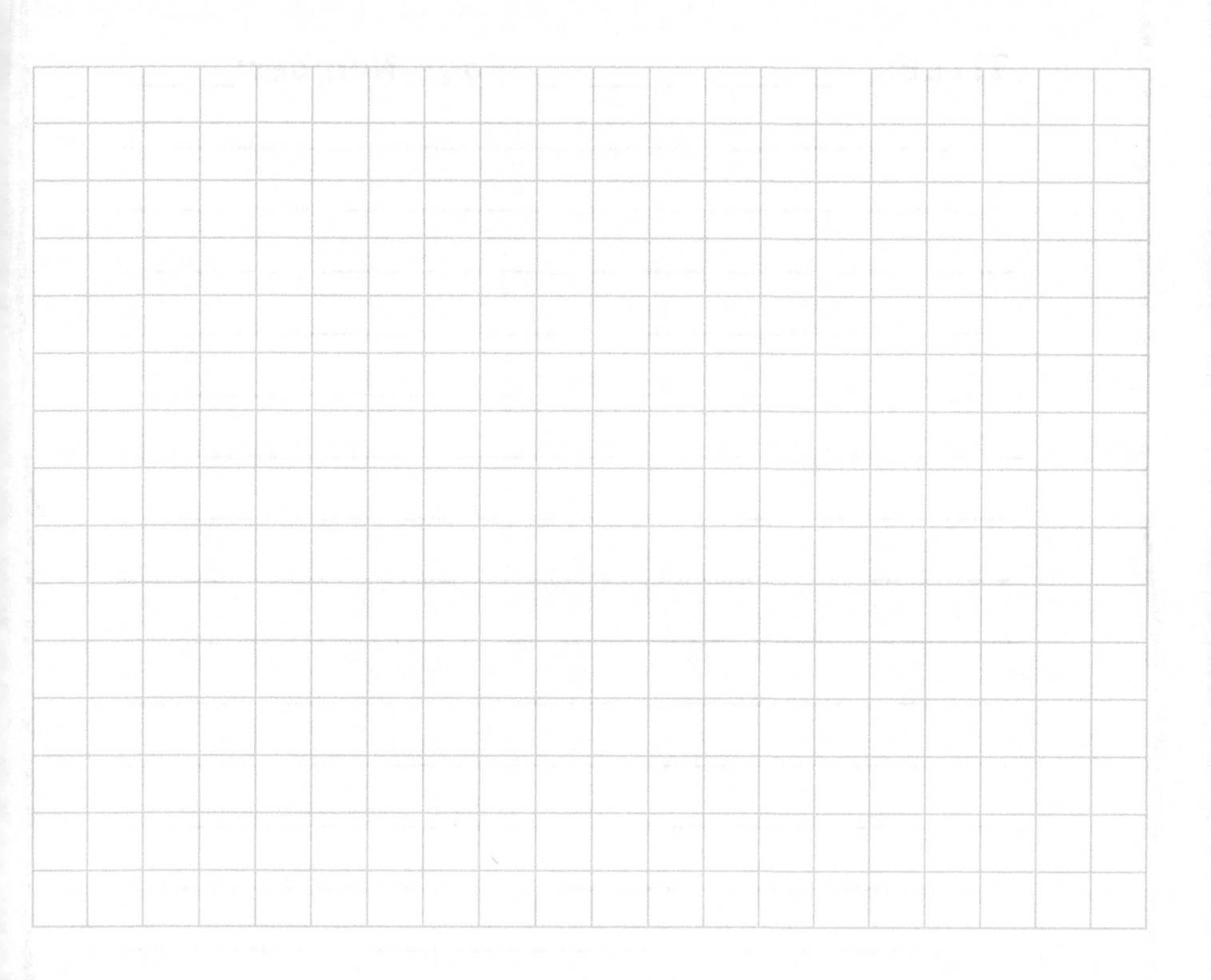

Copywork

Find an interesting paragraph in one of your books and copy it. Be diligent to make your writing look exactly like it does in the book.

TITLE:_____   Page Number:_____

_____
_____
_____
_____
_____
_____
_____
_____
_____
_____
_____
_____
_____
_____

Sketch a Picture

Look through your library books and find something to draw.

Circle Today's Date

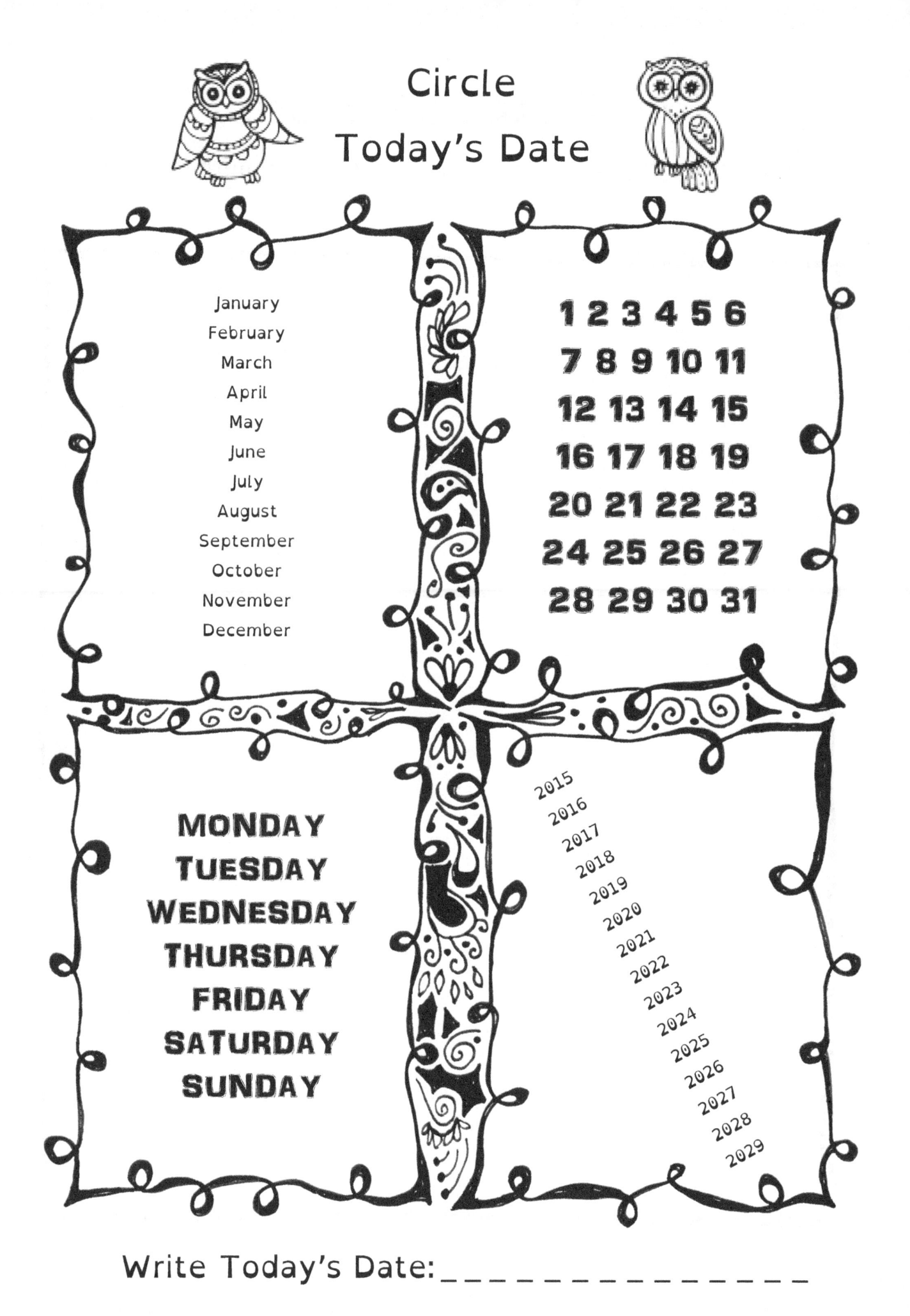

January
February
March
April
May
June
July
August
September
October
November
December

1 2 3 4 5 6
7 8 9 10 11
12 13 14 15
16 17 18 19
20 21 22 23
24 25 26 27
28 29 30 31

MONDAY
TUESDAY
WEDNESDAY
THURSDAY
FRIDAY
SATURDAY
SUNDAY

2015
2016
2017
2018
2019
2020
2021
2022
2023
2024
2025
2026
2027
2028
2029

Write Today's Date: _____

My Thinking Page

This is where you write down your ideas, goals, and plans - with a thankful heart!

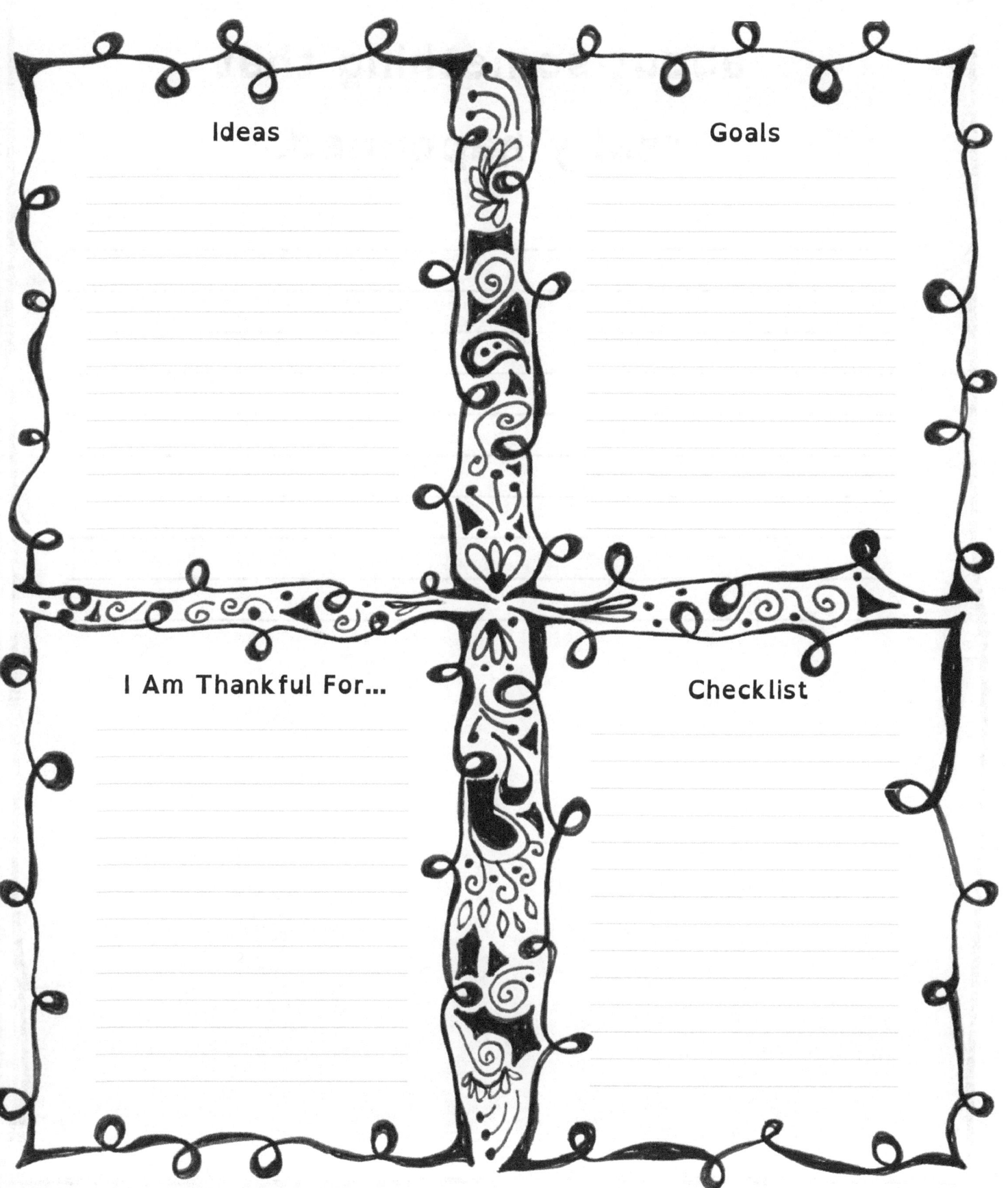

Ideas

Goals

I Am Thankful For...

Checklist

Write & Draw about something that really happened.

_____
_____
_____
_____
_____
_____
_____
_____
_____

Nature Study

Go outside and make a realistic drawing of something you find in nature.

Reading Time - 1 Hour

Choose Four Books - Read from each book for 15 minutes.
Copy a sentence or picture from each book here:

Circle Today's Date

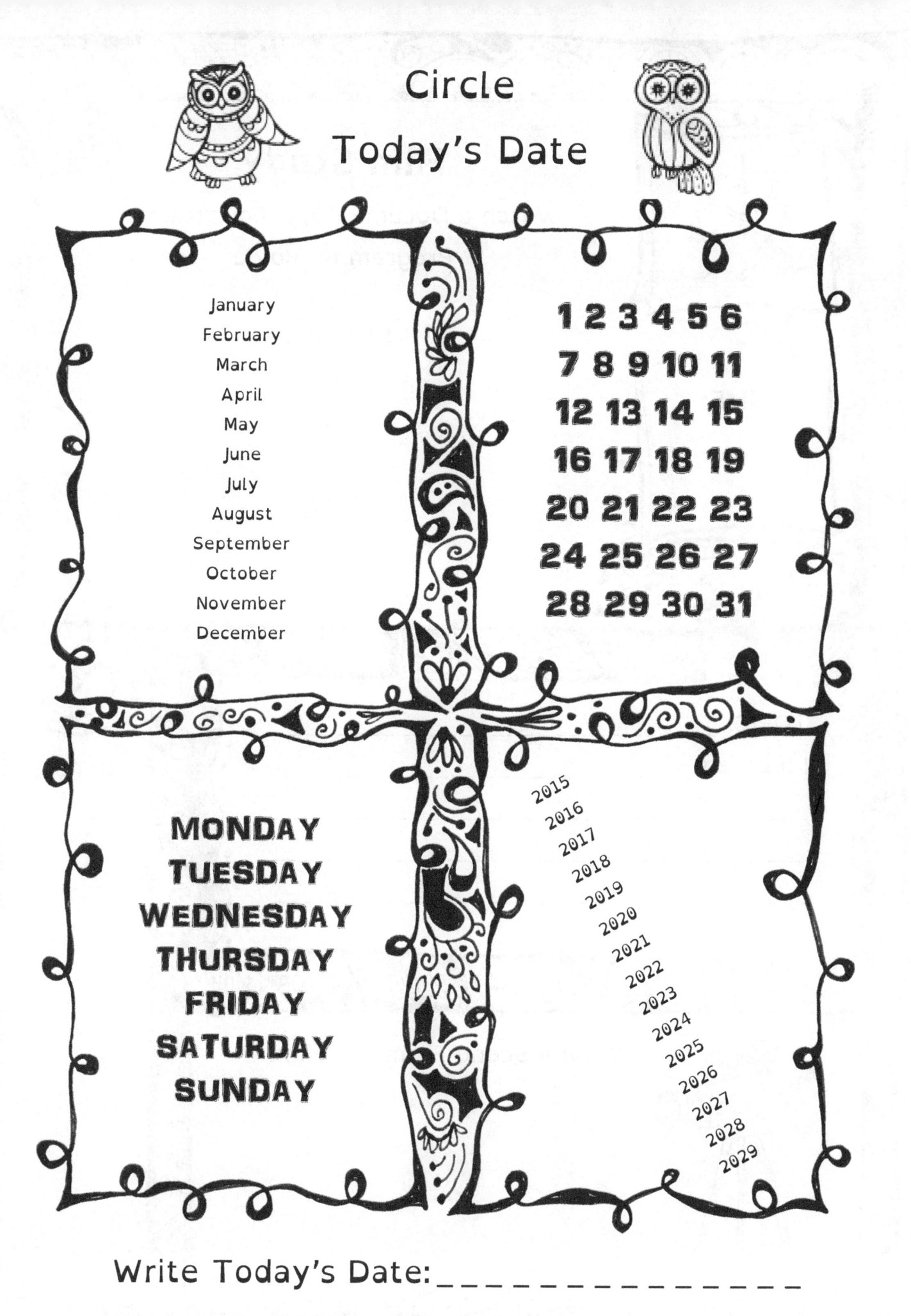

January
February
March
April
May
June
July
August
September
October
November
December

1 2 3 4 5 6
7 8 9 10 11
12 13 14 15
16 17 18 19
20 21 22 23
24 25 26 27
28 29 30 31

MONDAY
TUESDAY
WEDNESDAY
THURSDAY
FRIDAY
SATURDAY
SUNDAY

2015
2016
2017
2018
2019
2020
2021
2022
2023
2024
2025
2026
2027
2028
2029

Write Today's Date: _____

Film Study

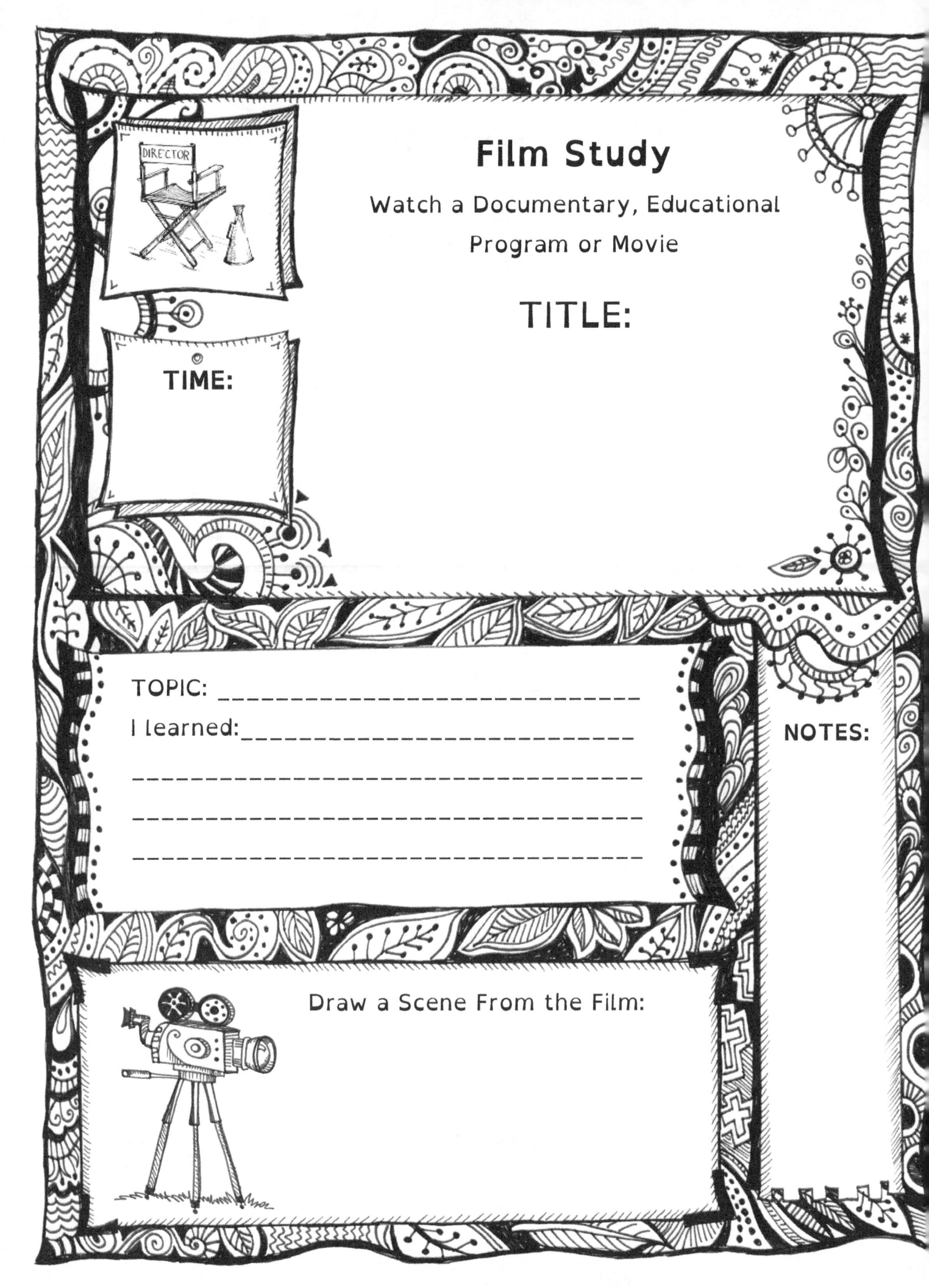

Watch a Documentary, Educational Program or Movie

TITLE:

TIME:

TOPIC: _____
I learned: _____
_____
_____
_____

NOTES:

Draw a Scene From the Film:

Spelling Time

Find 20 Words with 7 letters each.
Look in your books for words.
Write the words here:

_____   _____

_____   _____

_____   _____

_____   _____

_____   _____

_____   _____

_____   _____

_____   _____

_____   _____

_____   _____

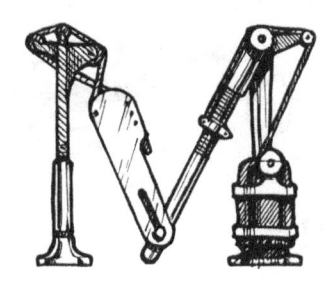

Math Practice

Watch a math tutorial or open up a math book.
You can practice math problems here.

Draw a Meal PLAN

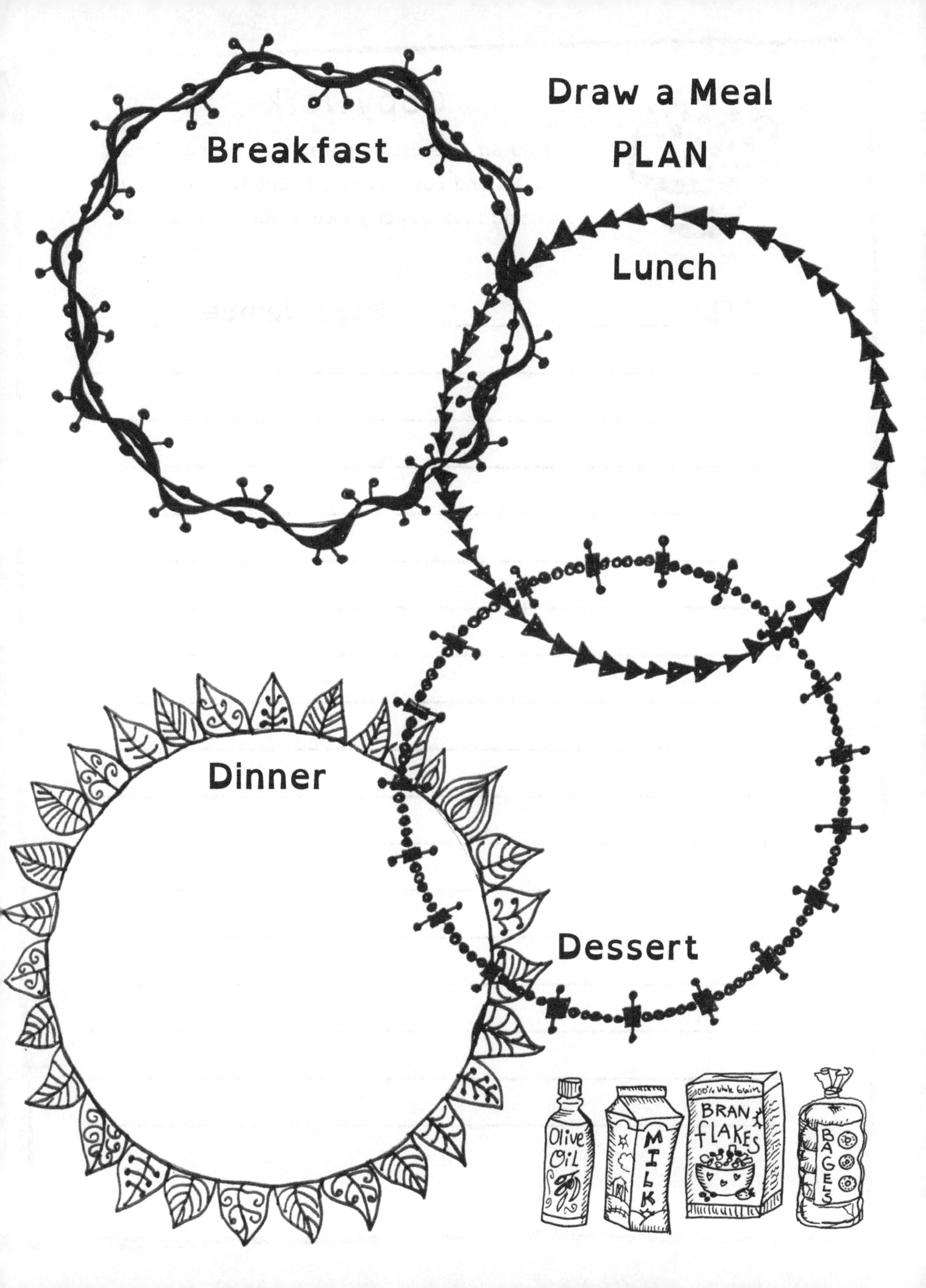

Breakfast

Lunch

Dinner

Dessert

Copywork

Find an interesting paragraph in one of your books and copy it. Be diligent to make your writing look exactly like it does in the book.

TITLE:_____ Page Number:_____

Sketch a Picture

Look through your library books and find something to draw.

Circle Today's Date

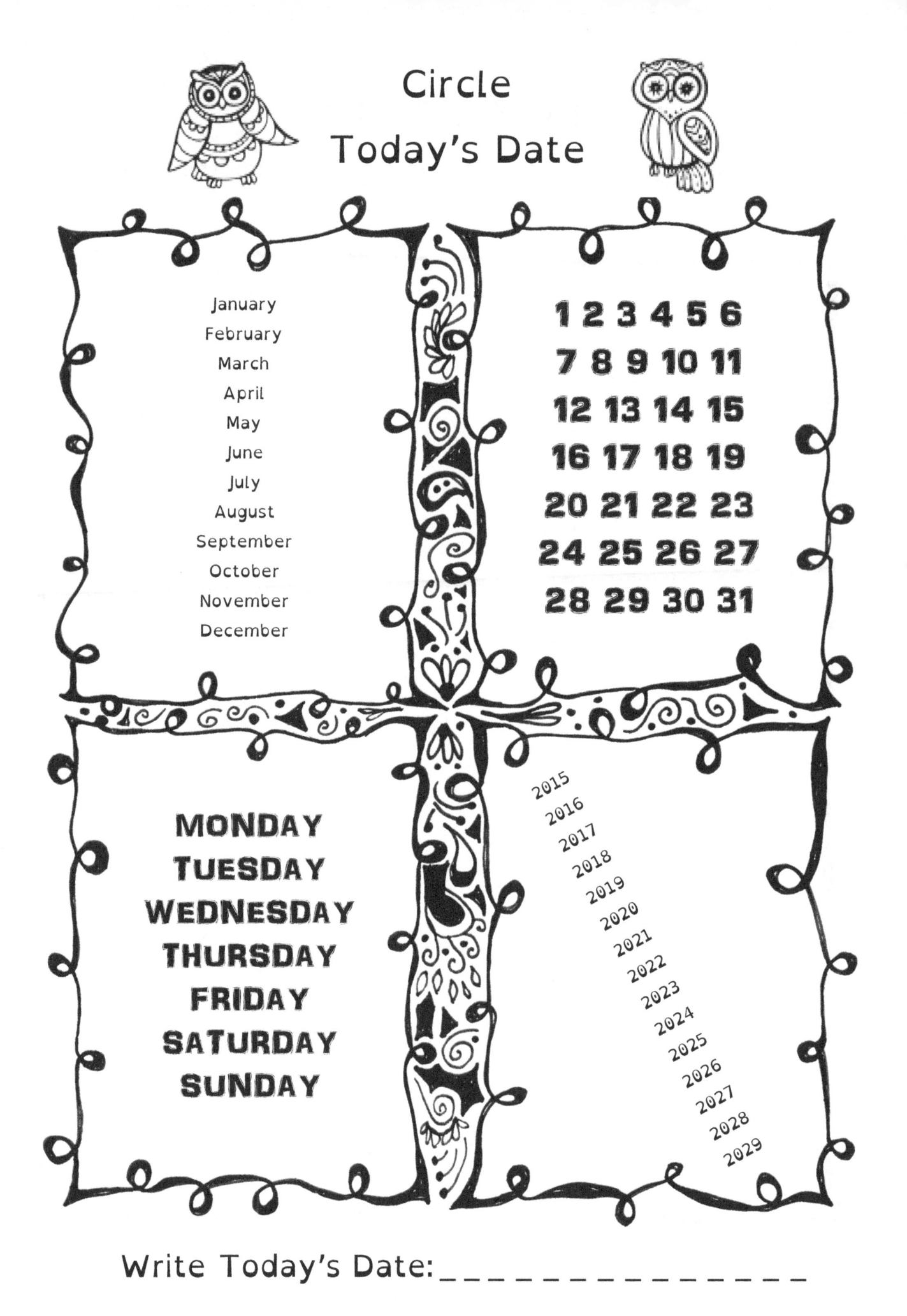

January
February
March
April
May
June
July
August
September
October
November
December

1 2 3 4 5 6
7 8 9 10 11
12 13 14 15
16 17 18 19
20 21 22 23
24 25 26 27
28 29 30 31

MONDAY
TUESDAY
WEDNESDAY
THURSDAY
FRIDAY
SATURDAY
SUNDAY

2015
2016
2017
2018
2019
2020
2021
2022
2023
2024
2025
2026
2027
2028
2029

Write Today's Date: _____

My Thinking Page

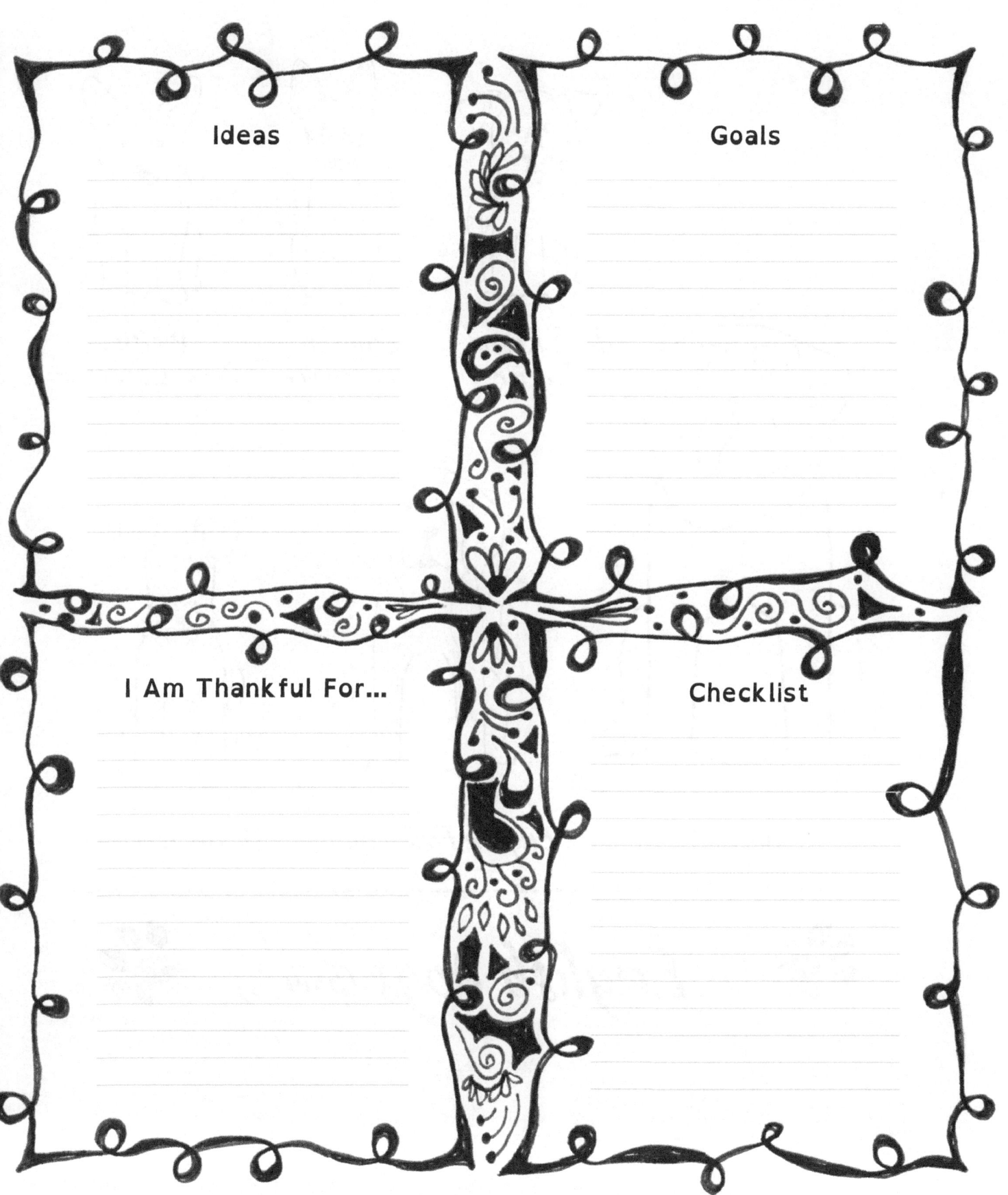

This is where you write down your ideas, goals, and plans - with a thankful heart!

Ideas

Goals

I Am Thankful For...

Checklist

Jack Russel Terrier

English Toy Terrier

Welsh Corgi Cardigan

Mastiff1

English Foxhound

Welsh Terrier

English dogs (part 3)

Irish
Red Setter

Irish Terrier

Glen of Imaal terrier

Irish Wolfhound

Irish Water Spaniel

Soft-coated Wheaten Terrier

Irish dogs

Nature Study

Go outside and make a realistic drawing of something you find in nature.

Draw a Meal PLAN

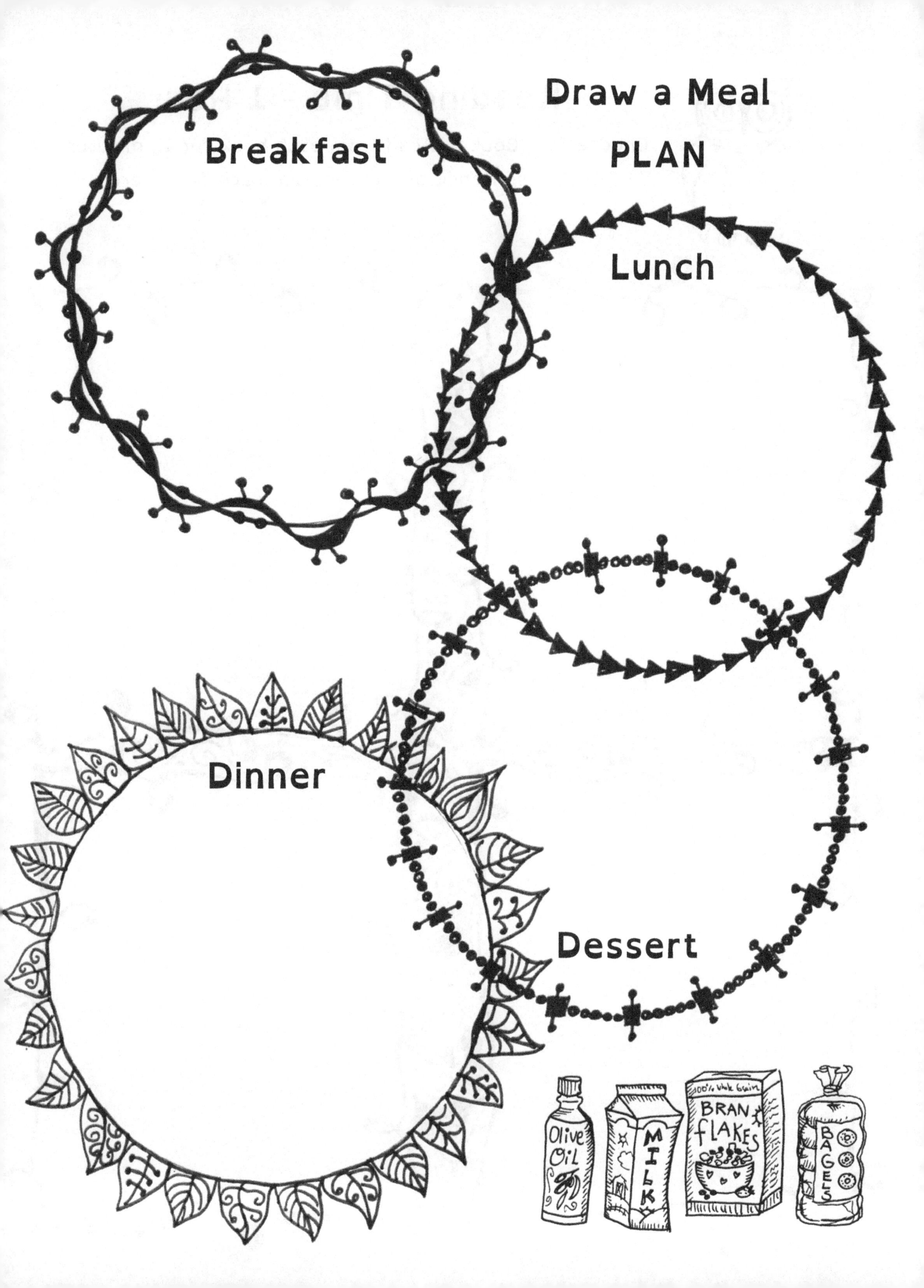

- Breakfast
- Lunch
- Dinner
- Dessert

Reading Time - 1 Hour

Choose Four Books - Read from each book for 15 minutes.
Copy a sentence or picture from each book here:

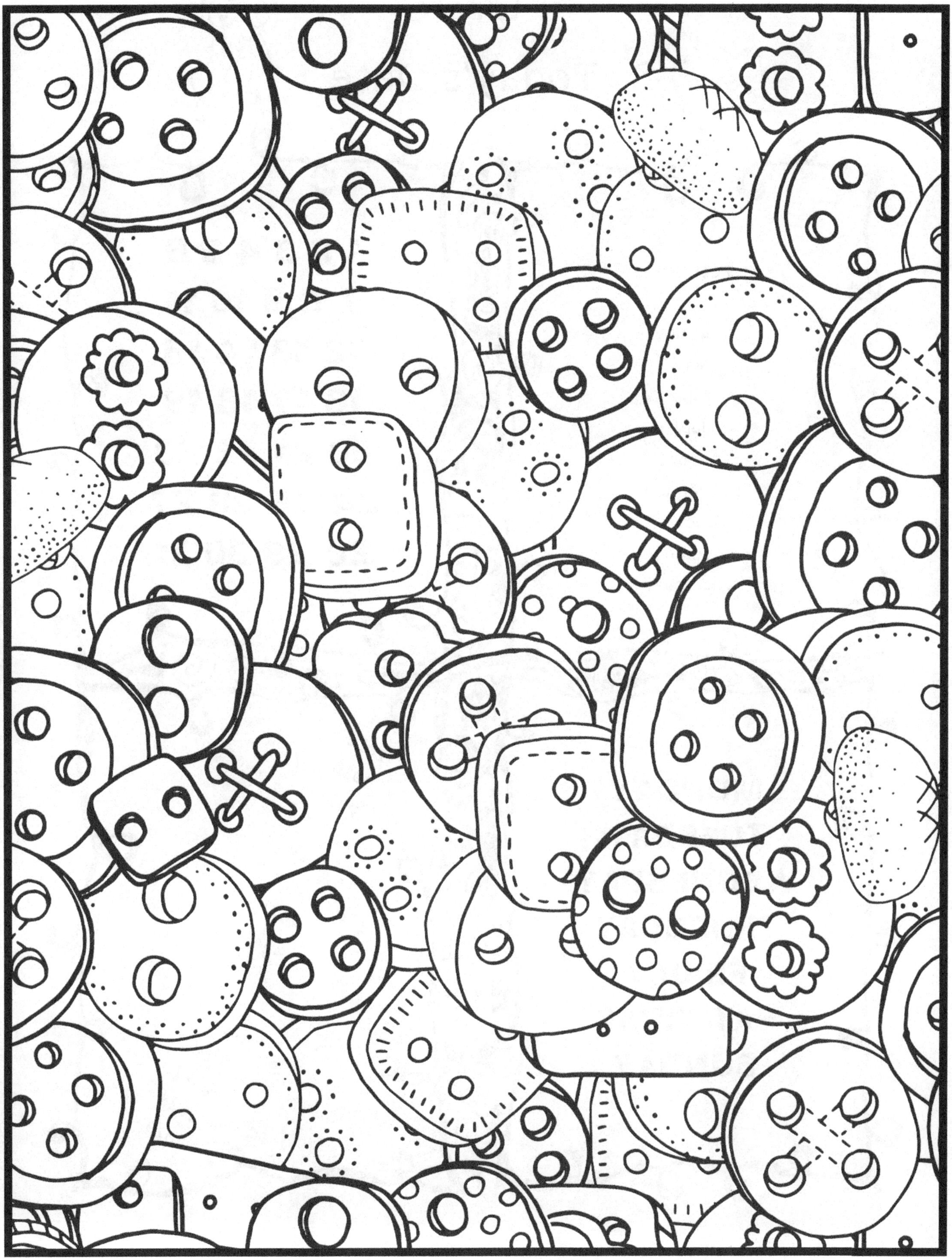

Circle Today's Date

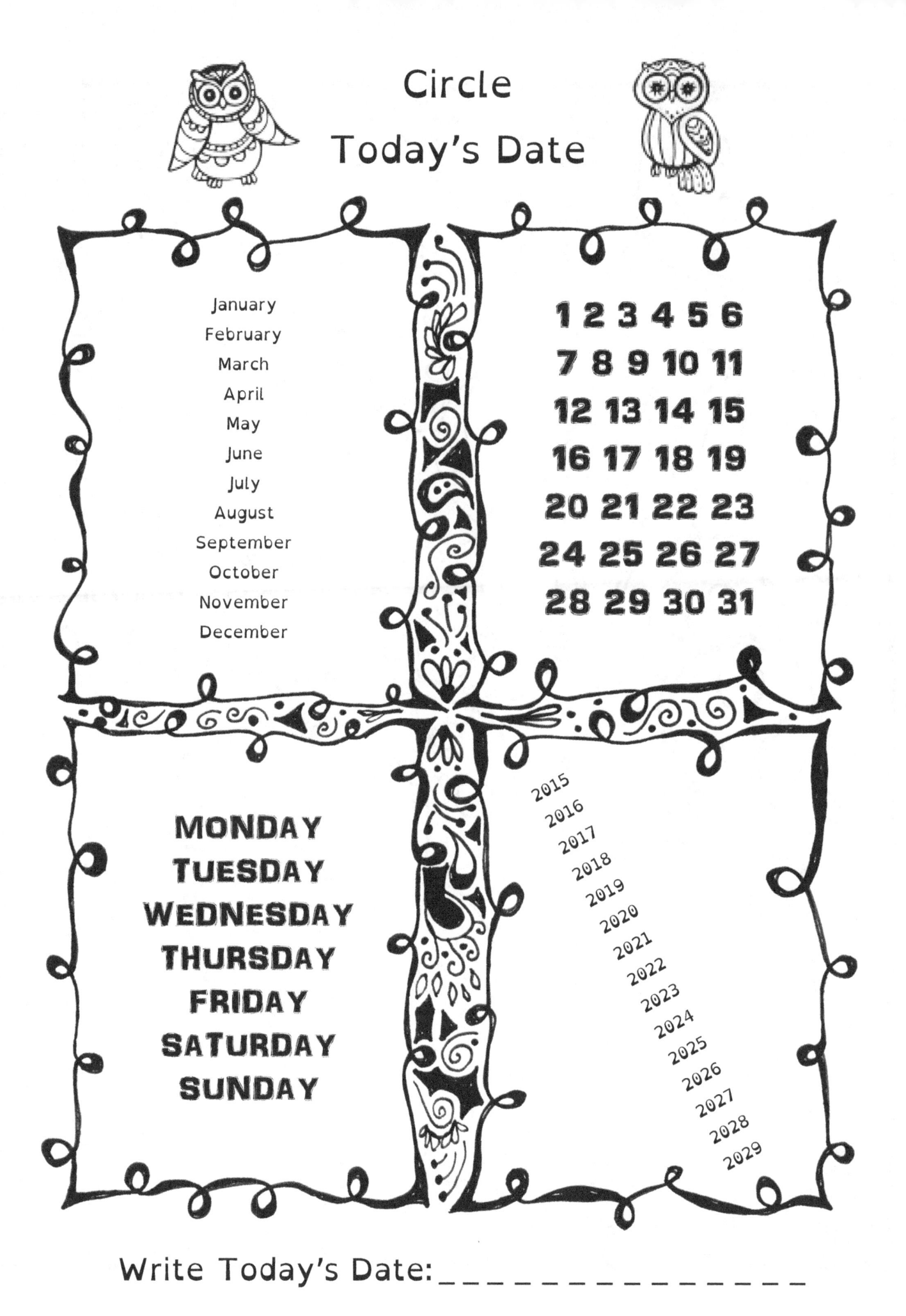

January
February
March
April
May
June
July
August
September
October
November
December

1 2 3 4 5 6
7 8 9 10 11
12 13 14 15
16 17 18 19
20 21 22 23
24 25 26 27
28 29 30 31

MONDAY
TUESDAY
WEDNESDAY
THURSDAY
FRIDAY
SATURDAY
SUNDAY

2015
2016
2017
2018
2019
2020
2021
2022
2023
2024
2025
2026
2027
2028
2029

Write Today's Date: _____

Spelling Time

Find 20 Words with 7 letters each.
Look in your books for words.
Write the words here:

_____   _____

_____   _____

_____   _____

_____   _____

_____   _____

_____   _____

_____   _____

_____   _____

_____   _____

_____   _____

Film Study

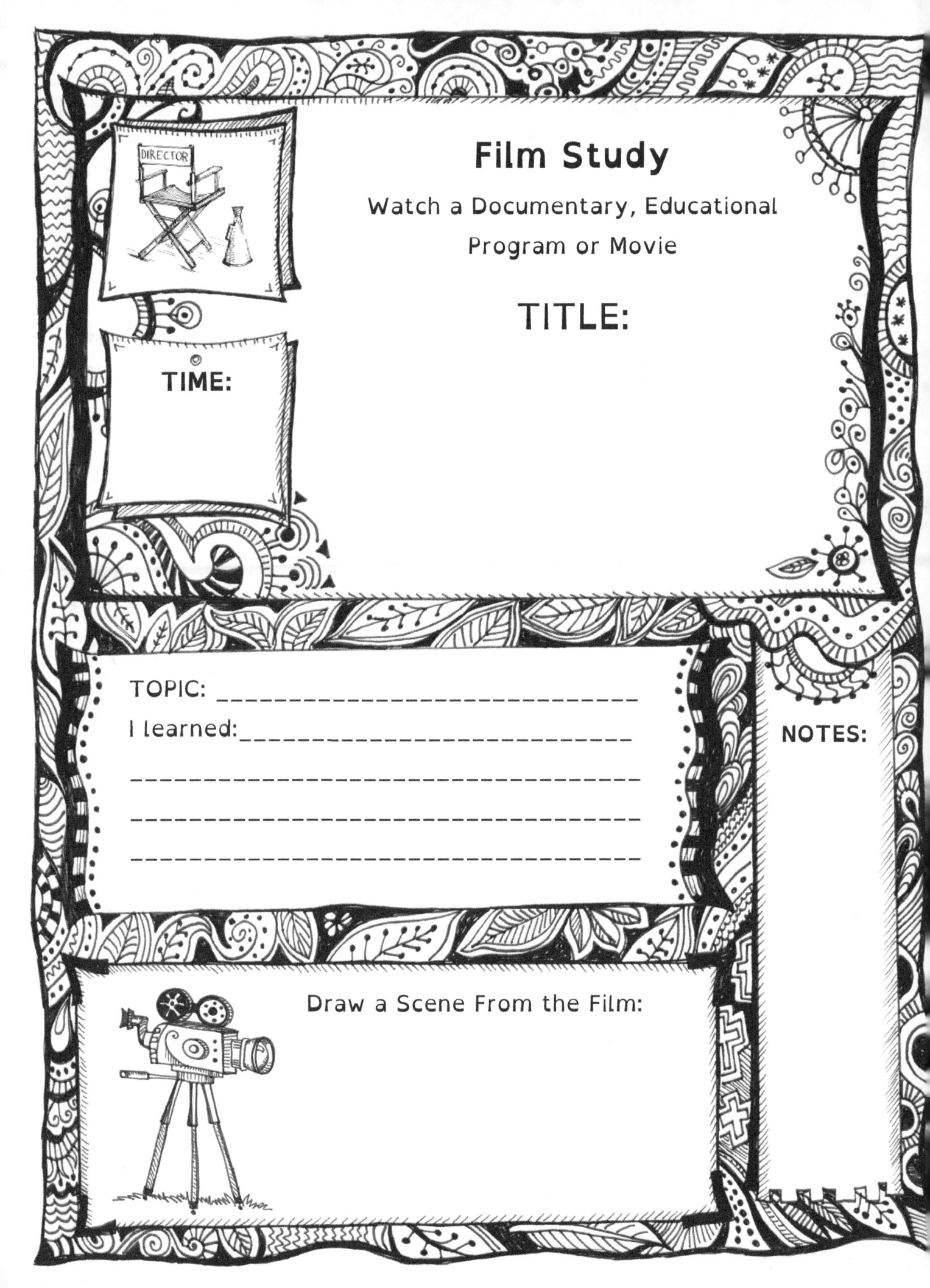

Watch a Documentary, Educational Program or Movie

TITLE:

TIME:

TOPIC: _____
I learned: _____
_____
_____
_____

NOTES:

Draw a Scene From the Film:

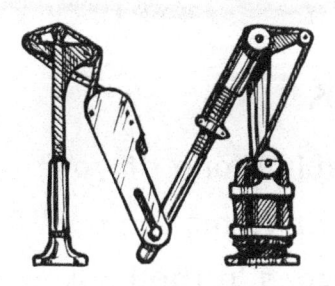

Math Practice

Watch a math tutorial or open up a math book.
You can practice math problems here.

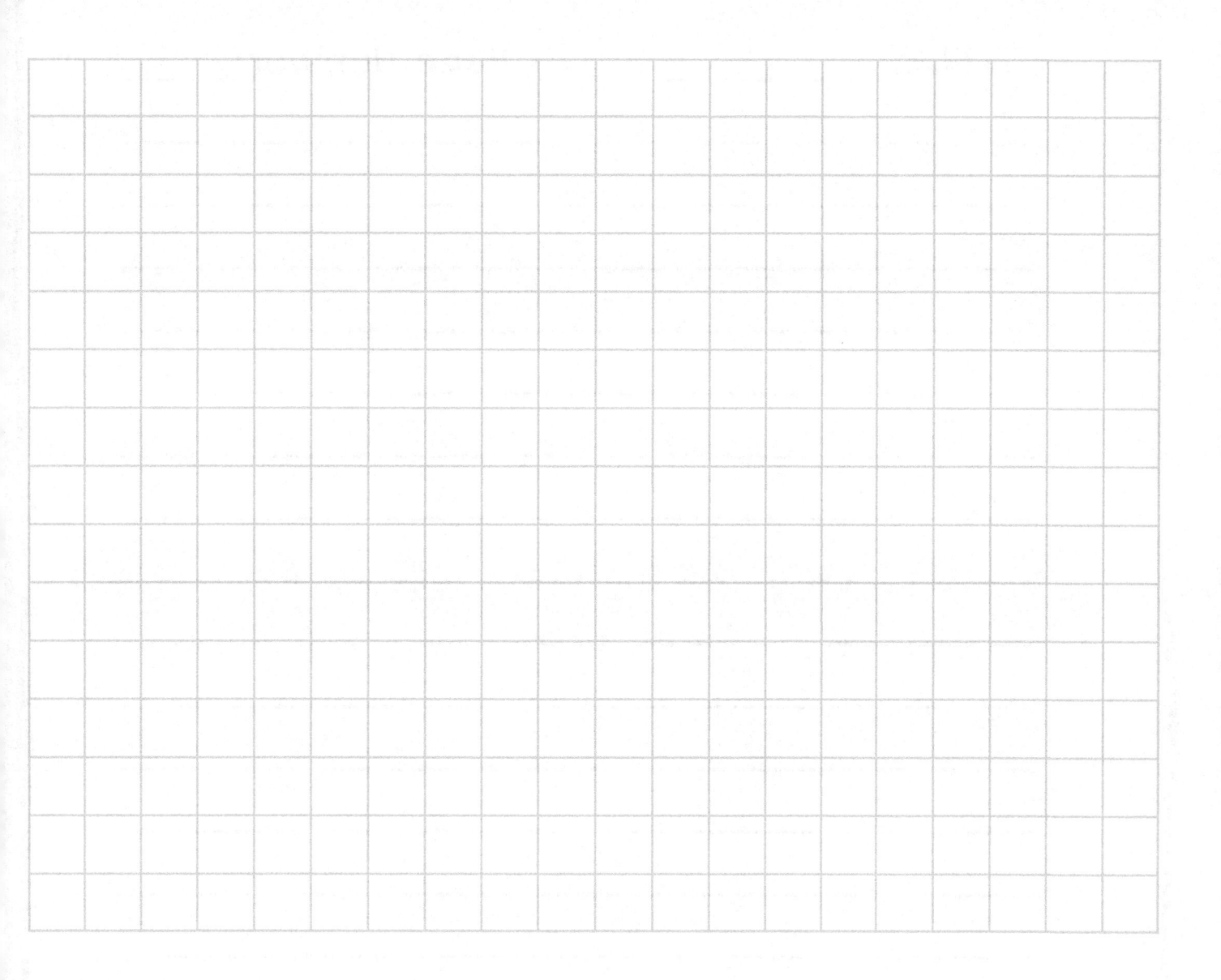

Copywork

Find an interesting paragraph in one of your books and copy it. Be diligent to make your writing look exactly like it does in the book.

TITLE:_____   Page Number:_____

Draw a Meal PLAN

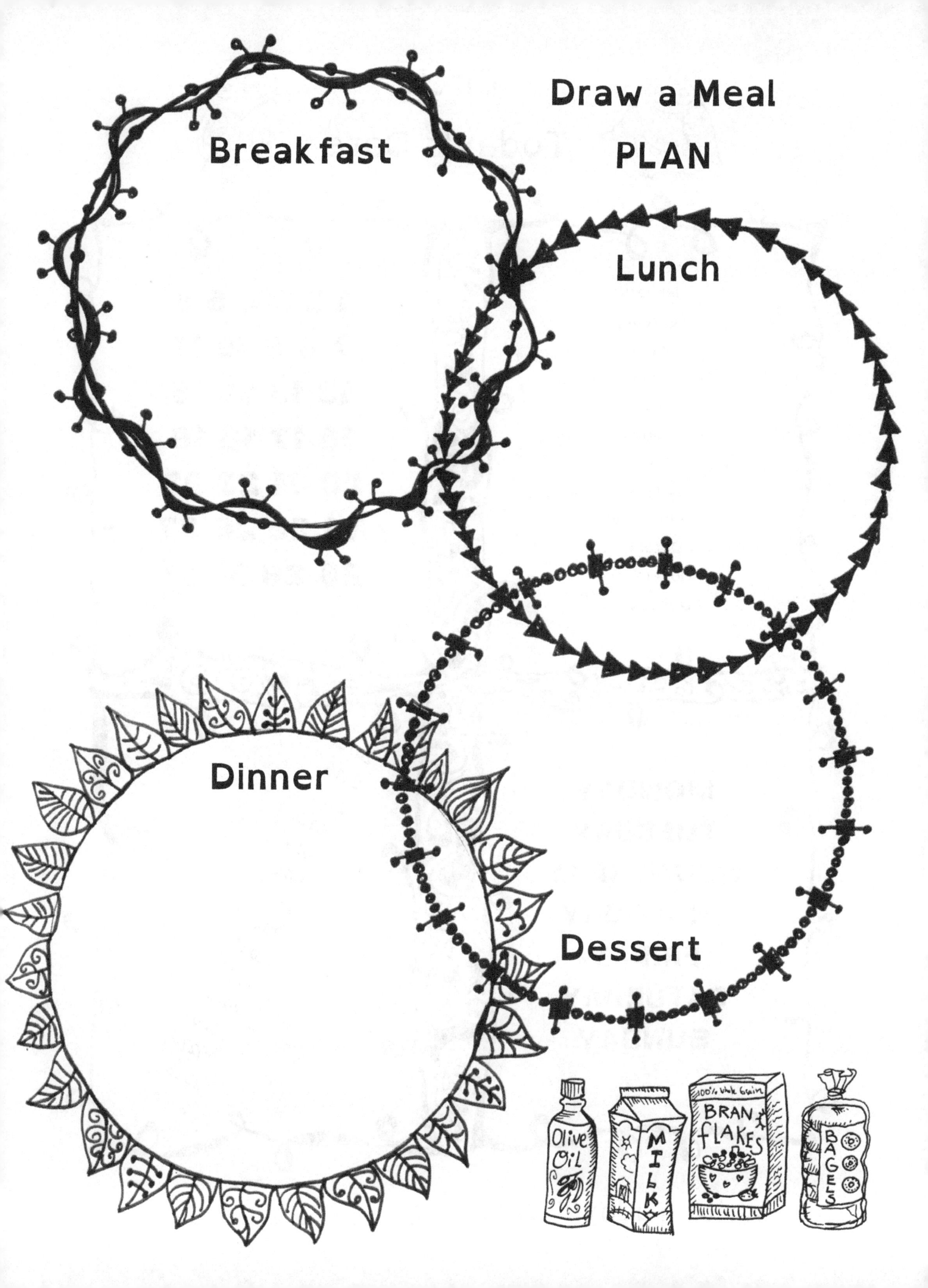

Breakfast

Lunch

Dinner

Dessert

Circle Today's Date

January
February
March
April
May
June
July
August
September
October
November
December

1 2 3 4 5 6
7 8 9 10 11
12 13 14 15
16 17 18 19
20 21 22 23
24 25 26 27
28 29 30 31

MONDAY
TUESDAY
WEDNESDAY
THURSDAY
FRIDAY
SATURDAY
SUNDAY

2015
2016
2017
2018
2019
2020
2021
2022
2023
2024
2025
2026
2027
2028
2029

Write Today's Date: _____

My Thinking Page

This is where you write down your ideas, goals, and plans - with a thankful heart!

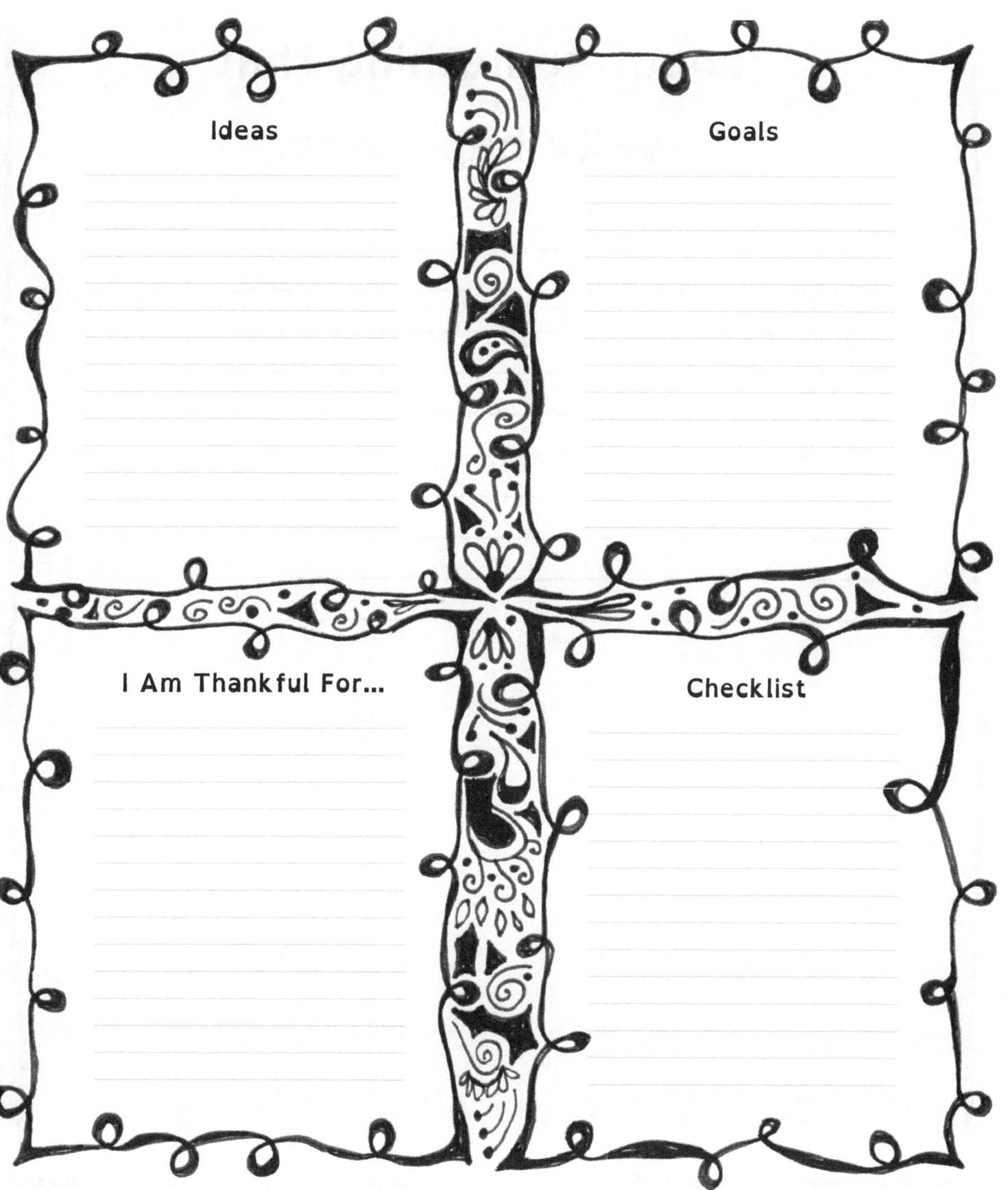

Ideas

Goals

I Am Thankful For...

Checklist

Write & Draw
about something that really happened.

_____
_____
_____
_____
_____
_____
_____
_____
_____

Nature Study

Go outside and make a realistic drawing of something you find in nature.

Reading Time - 1 Hour

Choose Four Books - Read from each book for 15 minutes.
Copy a sentence or picture from each book here:

Circle Today's Date

January
February
March
April
May
June
July
August
September
October
November
December

1 2 3 4 5 6
7 8 9 10 11
12 13 14 15
16 17 18 19
20 21 22 23
24 25 26 27
28 29 30 31

MONDAY
TUESDAY
WEDNESDAY
THURSDAY
FRIDAY
SATURDAY
SUNDAY

2015
2016
2017
2018
2019
2020
2021
2022
2023
2024
2025
2026
2027
2028
2029

Write Today's Date: _____

Chow-chow   Shar Pei   Chongqing Dog

Mops   Chinese crested dog   Shih Tzu   Pekingese

Chinese dogs

Appenzeller Sennenhund

White Swiss Shepherd Dog

Entlebucher Sennenhund

Berner Laufhund

St. Bernard

Berner Sennenhund

Grosser Schweizer Sennenhund

Swiss dogs

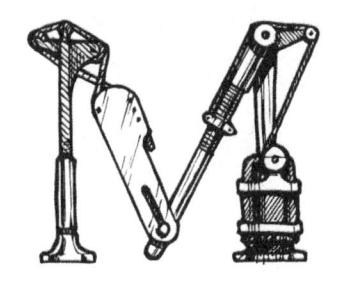

Math Practice

Watch a math tutorial or open up a math book. You can practice math problems here.

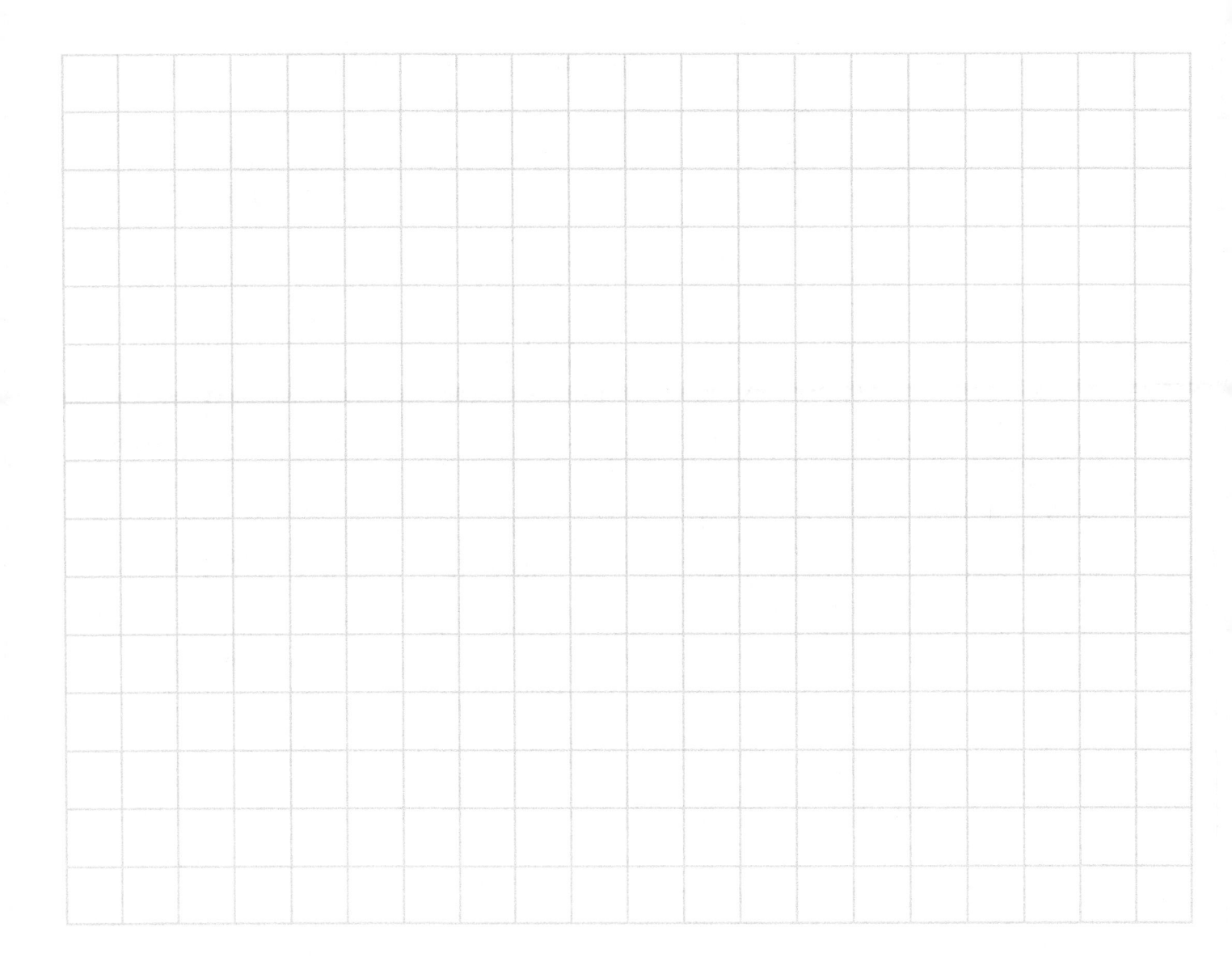

Copywork

Find an interesting paragraph in one of your books and copy it. Be diligent to make your writing look exactly like it does in the book.

TITLE:_____ Page Number:_____

Spelling Time

Find 20 Words with 10 letters each.
Look in your books for words.
Write the words here:

_____   _____

_____   _____

_____   _____

_____   _____

_____   _____

_____   _____

_____   _____

_____   _____

_____   _____

_____   _____

Film Study

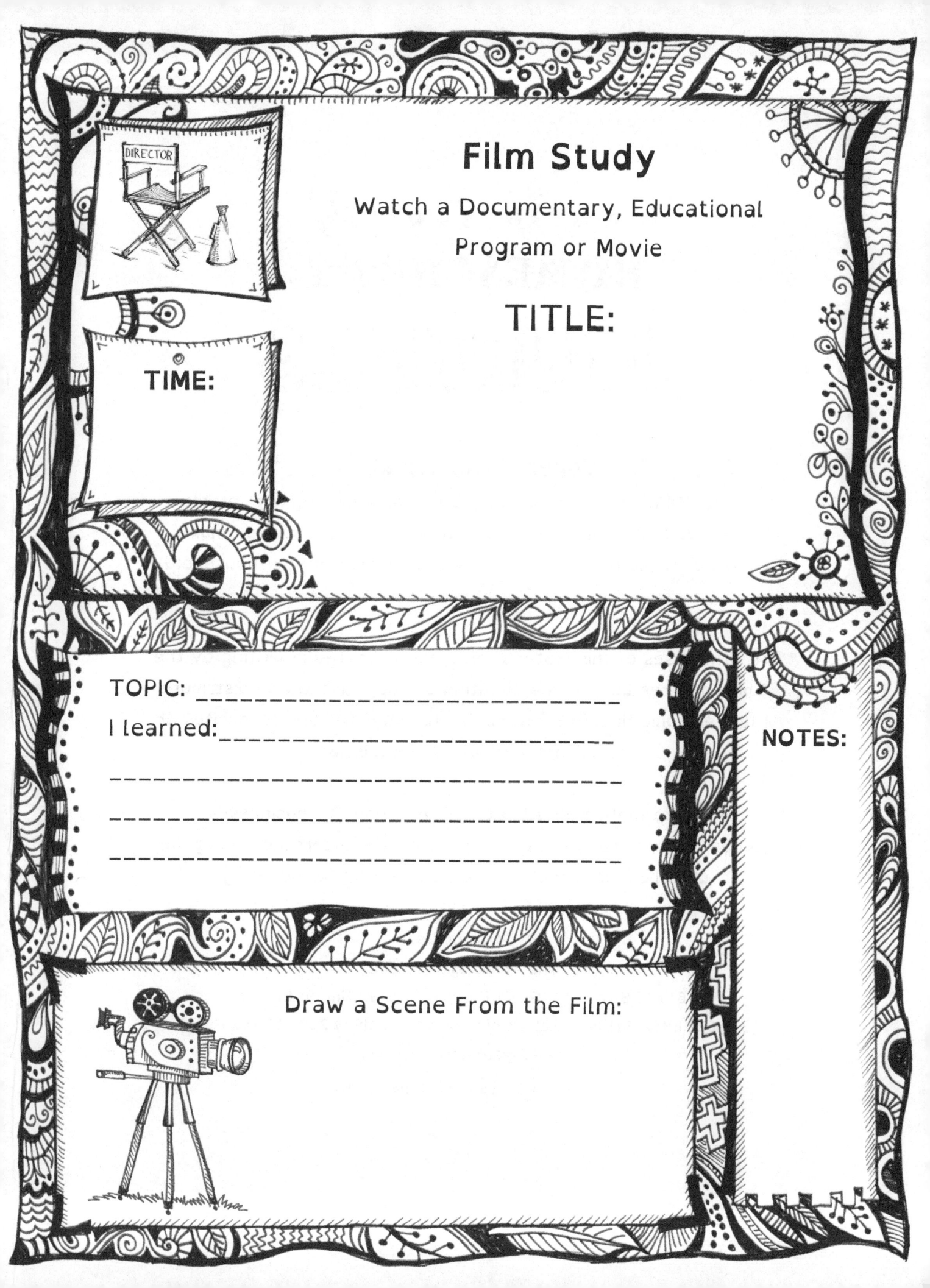

Watch a Documentary, Educational Program or Movie

TITLE:

TIME:

TOPIC: _____

I learned: _____

_____

_____

_____

NOTES:

Draw a Scene From the Film:

Do It Yourself HOMESCHOOL JOURNALS

Copyright Information

Do It YOURSELF Homeschool Journal, and electronic printable downloads are for Home and Family use only. You may make copies of these materials for only the children in your household.

All other uses of this material must be permitted in writing by the Thinking Tree LLC. It is a violation of copyright law to distribute the electronic files or make copies for your friends, associates or students without our permission.

For information on using these materials for businesses, co-ops, summer camps, day camps, daycare, afterschool program, churches, or schools please contact us for licensing.

Contact Us:

The Thinking Tree LLC
617 N. Swope St. Greenfield, IN 46140. United States
317.622.8852 PHONE (Dial +1 outside of the USA) 267.712.7889 FAX
www.DyslexiaGames.com
jbrown@DyslexiaGames.com

Made in United States
Orlando, FL
20 September 2024